THE HISTORY OF
50TH DIVISION 1914–1919

OTHER MILITARY HISTORIES BY THE SAME AUTHOR

BATTALION:
> THE 17TH BN. ROYAL FUSILIERS, 1914–1919.

REGIMENTAL:
> THE WEST YORKSHIRE REGT. IN THE WAR, 1914–1918.
> THE EAST YORKSHIRE REGT. IN THE GREAT WAR, 1914–1919.
> THE DIE-HARDS IN THE GREAT WAR, 1914–1919.
> THE HISTORY OF THE SOMERSET LIGHT INFANTRY, 1914–1919.
> THE HISTORY OF THE KING'S REGIMENT (LIVERPOOL), 1914–1919.
> THE LINCOLNSHIRE REGIMENT, 1914–1918.
> THE GLOUCESTERSHIRE REGIMENT, 1914–1918.
> THE HISTORY OF THE DUKE OF CORNWALL'S LIGHT INFANTRY, 1914–1919.

DIVISIONAL:
> THE HISTORY OF THE 2ND DIVISION, 1914–1918.
> THE 19TH DIVISION, 1914–1918.
> THE HISTORY OF THE 62ND (WEST RIDING) DIVISION, 1914–1919.

50TH DIVISION MEMORIAL, WIELTJE, BELGIUM.
Unveiled by Field-Marshal Lord Plumer on 1st September, 1929.

THE FIFTIETH DIVISION
1914 – 1919

By
EVERARD WYRALL

WITH 13 ILLUSTRATIONS
AND 9 MAPS

PUBLISHED BY
THE NAVAL & MILITARY PRESS

First published in 1939.

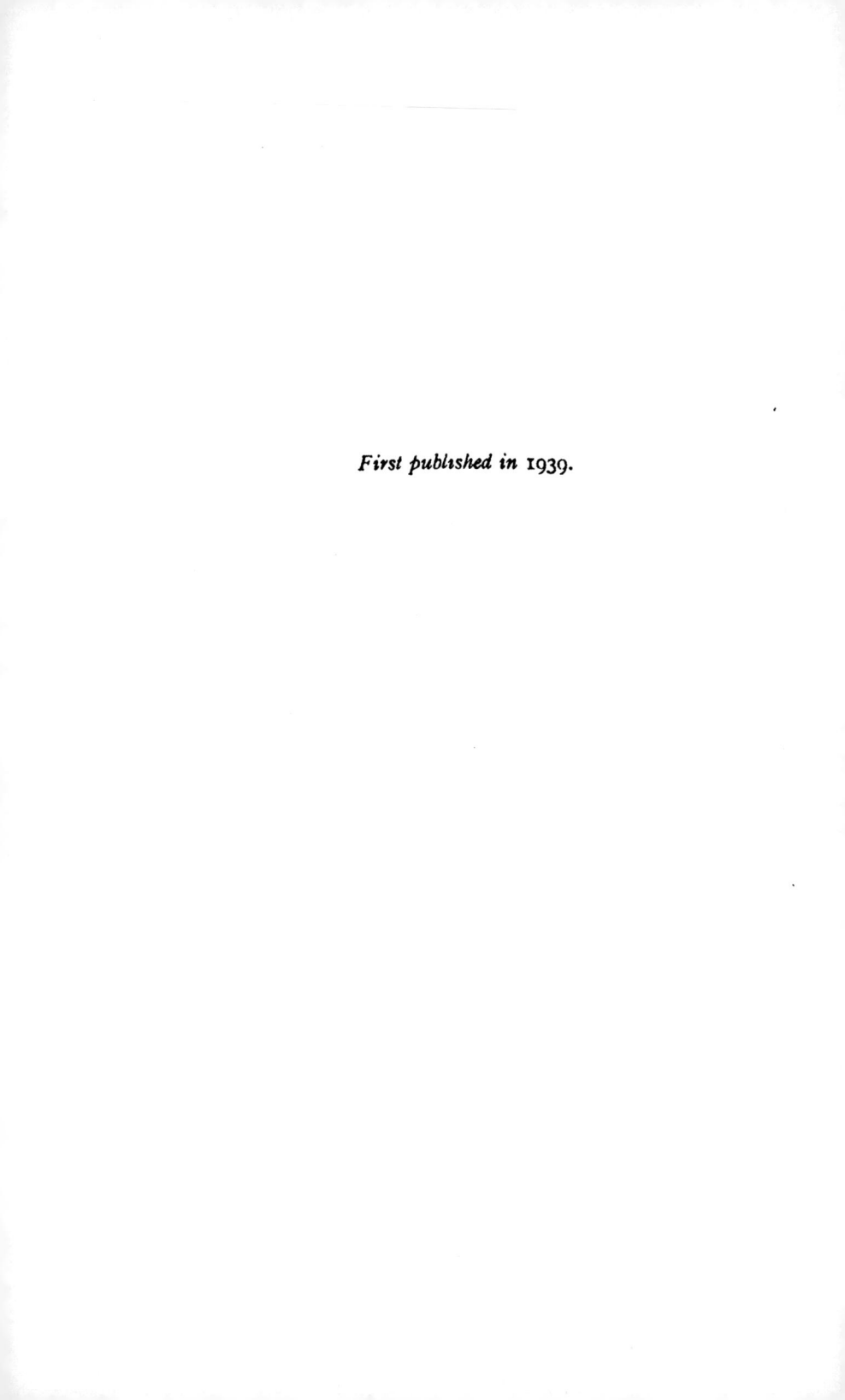

NOTE ON THE AUTHOR

AS a civilian, Everard Wyrall confined his pen chiefly to verse and drama, many of which are as yet unpublished. One of his earliest publications was *The Spike*. In order to see how the State treated "down and outs," he donned rags and went into the casual wards of workhouses, breaking stones and picking oakum.

As a soldier he served in the South African War, 1899–1902; the European War, 1914–1918, and the Afghan War, 1919.

When war was over he began the remarkable series of Regimental and Divisional histories, which cover almost every country where our fighting forces were. In all, twenty-one volumes were written by him, including *The Histories of the 2nd and 19th Divisions*. These occupied him for the rest of his life, and remain his enduring monument.

The History of the 50th Division was fated to be his last book, and his work on it was indeed a soldier's last fight. When he engaged to write it his health was already causing grave anxiety, but his courage, concentration, and conscientiousness never failed him.

It is the simple truth that when the last sentence was written he closed his eyes and died.

Bene actae vitae recordatio jucundissima est.

FOREWORD

THERE is a carved screen near St. Thomas Church, in Newcastle, entitled "The Response," which vividly recalls the magnificent reply of the North when the call came in 1914.

This response was in keeping with the history of the North of England which, for many centuries, had known the necessity of being responsible for its own defence, and was not slow in responding to the greater call.

This feeling was demonstrated by the keenness and strength of the volunteer units, which were the ancestors of the Territorial units whose services are recorded in this history. Some may have had doubts as to whether, when the test of war came, the Territorial Army would prove itself equal to the Regular battalions of the Army, with their old traditions and long-established *esprit de corps* to sustain and strengthen them in desperate situations.

If any had such doubts it was due to ignorance of the family spirit which had animated the old volunteer units, and which had continued on the formation of the Territorial Army. Both were raised locally, the companies often being drawn from one village or one firm, and, knowing each other personally, had also an intense local patriotism. Added to this was a fervent hope that, when the test came, they would live up to the reputation of the Regular units to which they were affiliated.

The first test came a few days after the Divison landed, at the battle of St. Julien, and the Division had few harder battles during the War. During the first two days each Brigade fought in turn over the ground where the 50th Division Memorial now stands, and during this action made that reputation for hard fighting which it maintained throughout the War.

I would wish to stress that what I have said about the Infantry Brigades applies fully to the Royal Artillery, the Royal Engineers, the Royal Army Medical Corps, and the Royal Army Service Corps.

The complete trust the infantry could place in the support of their artillery under all circumstances, the strain saved by the duckboard tracks so quickly laid by the R.E., the devotion of the medical officers, and the never-failing supply of rations, under many difficulties, made success possible when failure at any point might have resulted in disaster.

It seems fitting that the record of those who served with the Division should be preserved, and that those who played an active part in its career during the Great War, as well as those who follow after, should have the opportunity of reading this History.

I commend the following pages to their notice, and to the notice of all who are in any way concerned with the lives of these Northcountrymen, knowing well that in their reading they will find much that will be a source of both interest and pride.

I have been requested to write this foreword, although I was not in command of the Division in the earlier part of the War, and ended my service with it in February, 1918. My only claim to such an honour lies, perhaps, in the fact that I was born in Yorkshire and come from a Durham family with connections in Northumberland, and was thus known by name to many of those with whom I served.

Percival S. Wilkinson.

CONTENTS

CHAPTER		PAGE
	Foreword	vii
I and II.	The Call to Arms	1
III.	The Battles of Ypres, 1915	6
IV.	Trench Warfare: June 1915–August 1915. The Action of Bellewaarde, 16th June Sanctuary Wood, Neuve Eglise, Armentières	71
V.	The Battles of the Somme, 1916	135
VI.	The Winter of 1916–1917	192
VII.	The Battles of Arras, 1917	202
VIII.	The Summer of 1917	228
IX.	The Battles of Ypres, 1917. The Second Battle of Passchendaele: 24th October–10th November	238
X.	The Winter of 1917–1918	250
XI.	The German Offensive on the Somme, March 1918	256
XII.	The German Offensive on the Lys, 1918	308
XIII.	The German Offensives in Champagne, 1918	335
XIV.	The Re-constitution of the 50th Division	350
XV.	The Advance to Victory	354

APPENDICES

A.	Battle Honours	357
B.	50th Division	358
	Divisional Troops	359
C.	Letter of Appreciation	361
D.	Reorganisation of Artillery, 16th May, 1916	362
E.	Reorganisation of Artillery, 16th November, 1916	364
F.	Order of Battle, 15th July, 1918	366

LIST OF ILLUSTRATIONS

Memorial to the 50th Division .. *Frontispiece*

FACING PAGE

Major-General Wilkinson with officers of the 2nd Northumberland Fusiliers 2
5th Northumberland Fusiliers cleaning clothes and equipment. Toutencourt, October 1916 .. 138
Battle of Flers-Courcelette. German prisoners coming in from Morval 192
Battle of Arras, 1917: Infantry moving up in artillery formation 210
Battles of Arras: Broad wire entanglement. Hindenburg Line, near Héninel 224
Battle of Passchendaele: General view of battlefield, October 1917 240
Shelled ground. Passchendaele, February 1918 .. 242
The Passchendaele Salient 248
German Offensive: Stores and hutments burning at Omiecourt, 1918 276
Battle of Estaires: British wounded awaiting evacuation. Bethune, 1918 310
Battle of Hazebrouck: Troops passing over a mined railway bridge, Merville, 1918 332
H.M. King George V inspecting the 149th Brigade, 50th Division 354

LIST OF MAPS

	FACING PAGE
Map of the theatre of war on the Western Front	1
The Battle of Ypres: April–May 1915. Chapter III	6
Hill 60 and Sanctuary Wood sectors, 1915–1916. Chapter IV	71
Operations—September–November 1916: On the Somme. Chapter V	143
Operations—April–May 1917: At Arras. Chapter VII	202
Operations—October–November 1917: Ypres—Passchendaele. Chapter IX	238
Operations—March 1918: The Retreat. Chapter XI	256
Operations—April 1918. Chapter XII	308
Operations—May 1918. Chapter XIII	335

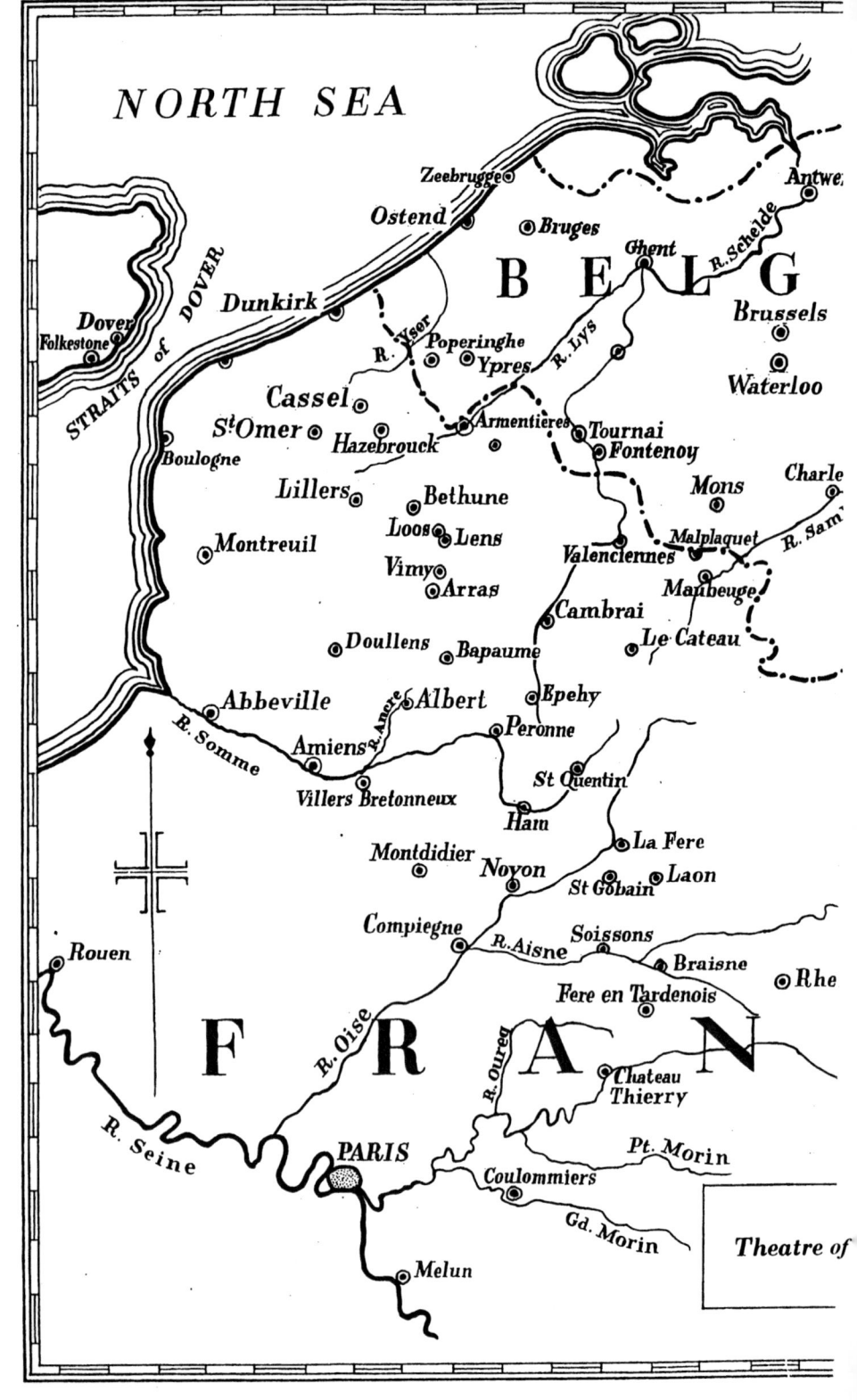

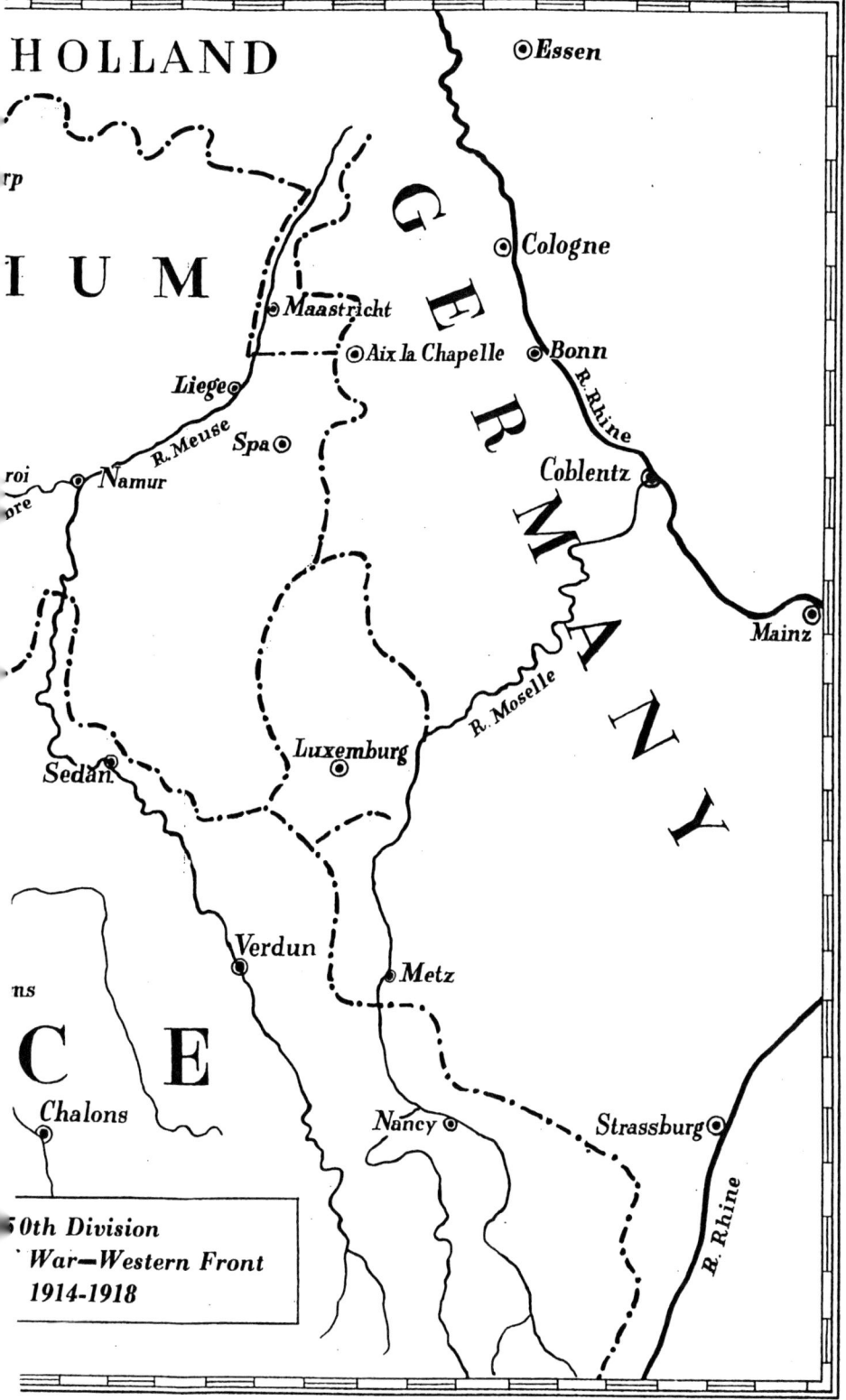

CHAPTERS I AND II

THE CALL TO ARMS

THE hardy nature of the north countryman was never more in evidence than during the Great War. The fine physique of the Territorial and Service battalions of regiments coming from the counties of Northumberland, Durham and Yorkshire was more than once commented upon by famous generals: and fine physique almost invariably means tenacity and courage in the face of extreme danger. Not to say that men of shorter build lacked those qualities, for many miners belonged to the 50th Division and often they were short and stocky, possessing great strength both of mind and body.

The Northumbrian Division (its official designation before, and on, the declaration of War) forming part of the Territorial Army, had its Headquarters on the outbreak of hostilities at Richmond, Yorkshire. The counties of Northumberland, Durham and Yorkshire supplied the three infantry brigades. The Northumberland Infantry Brigade consisted of the 4th, 5th, 6th and 7th Battalions of the Northumberland Fusiliers; the York and Durham Infantry Brigade of the 4th East Yorkshires, 4th and 5th Yorkshires* and the 5th Durham Light Infantry; the Durham Light Infantry Brigade was formed of the 6th, 7th, 8th and 9th Battalions, Durham Light Infantry. All were Territorial battalions in a high state of efficiency.

The four battalions of the Northumberland Fusiliers were commanded as follows: 4th—Lieut.-Colonel A. J. Foster; 5th—Lieut.-Colonel D. R. Macdonald; 6th—Lieut.-Colonel G. R. B. Spain; 7th—Lieut.-Colonel R. Scott. Of the York and Durham Brigade the commands were held by Lieut.-Colonel G. H. Shaw—4th East Yorkshires; Lieut.-Colonel M. H. L. Bell—4th Yorkshires (Green Howards); Lieut.-Colonel Sir M. Sykes—5th Yorkshires (Green Howards): the 5th Durham Light Infantry were commanded by Lieut.-Colonel G. O. Spence. The 6th, 7th, 8th and 9th

---
* The Green Howards.

Battalions of the Durham Light Infantry were under the commands of Lieut.-Colonel H. C. Watson (6th), Lieut.-Colonel E. Vaux (7th), Lieut.-Colonel W. C. Blackett (8th) and Lieut.-Colonel F. R. Simpson (9th).

Major-General B. Burton* commanded the Division; Major L. Hume-Spry was G.S.O.2, Captain A. W. B. Wallace, D.A.A. and Q.M.G. The Northumberland Brigade was commanded by Brig.-General J. F. Riddell with Major F. H. Moore as his Brigade-Major. The York and Durham Brigade was under the command of Brig.-General T. F. Bush: Major R. F. Guy was Brigade-Major. Colonel J. W. Sears commanded the Durham Light Infantry Brigade: Major E. R. Clayton was Brigade-Major.

The Divisional Artillery consisted of three Field Artillery and one Howitzer Brigades. The C.R.A. was Colonel A. H. Hussy.

The 1st Northumbrian Brigade, R.F.A. (Lieut.-Colonel G. Fenwick), was formed of the 1st Northumberland Battery (Major H. S. Bell), 2nd Northumberland Battery (Captain F. E. H. Harrison), 3rd Northumberland Battery (Captain F. G. D. Johnston): the 1st Northumbrian Ammunition Column was commanded by Captain N. L. Parmeter. Headquarters were at Newcastle.

The 2nd Northumbrian Brigade, R.F.A. (Lieut.-Colonel F. B. Moss-Blundell), consisted of the 1st East Riding Battery (Captain W. Murray), 2nd East Riding Battery (Major M. B. Allen), 3rd North Riding Battery (Major A. G. W. Wright), and 2nd Northumbrian Ammunition Column (commander not given): Headquarters at Hull.

Of the 3rd Northumbrian (County of Durham) Brigade, R.F.A. (Lieut.-Colonel J. F. I. H. Doyle), the 1st Durham Battery (Major T. P. Guthe) was quartered at Seaham Harbour, the 2nd Durham Battery (Major F. W. Cluff) at Durham, the 3rd Durham Battery (Major G. T. Pearson) at West Hartlepool: the 3rd Northumbrian (County of Durham) Ammunition Column was also at Seaham Harbour.

The 4th Northumbrian (County of Durham) Howitzer Brigade consisted of two batteries only: 4th Durham

---

* These commands and ranks are as given in the Army List for August, 1914; but many changes took place in the Division before it left England and within a short time of mobilisation.

(Imperial War Museum Photographs, Copyright Reserved)

MAJOR-GENERAL WILKINSON, COMMANDING 50TH DIVISION, with one of his Brigadier-Generals and Officers of the 2nd Northumberland Fusiliers, near Millencourt, October 1916.

Facing page 2

(Howitzer) Battery (Major R. Chapman), quartered at South Shields, and the 5th Durham (Howitzer) Battery (Major T. A. Higginbottom) at Hebburn-on-Tyne: the 4th Northumbrian (County of Durham) Ammunition Column (Captain V. P. J. Grunhut) was at South Shields.

The Division also had one battery of Royal Garrison Artillery ("Heavies") at Middlesbrough, under Captain C. J. Hannah.

The Divisional Royal Engineers were the 1st and 2nd Northumbrian Field Companies (commanded respectively by Major G. C. Pollard and Major J. E. McPherson) and the Northumbrian Divisional Signal Company (Captain W. H. Dodds). The C.R.E. was Lieut.-Colonel F. S. Crawford. The Royal Engineers also had their Headquarters at Newcastle.

Three Field Ambulances formed the Divisional Medical units. The A.D.M.S. was Colonel J. V. W. Rutherford, the D.A.D.M.S., Major T. C. Mackenzie. The 1st Northumbrian Field Ambulance (Newcastle) was commanded by Major F. Hawthorn, the 2nd Northumbrian Field Ambulance (Darlington) by Lieut.-Colonel L. J. Blandford and the 3rd Northumbrian Field Ambulance (Hull) by Lieut.-Colonel W. Ranson.

One company, the Divisional Company (Headquarters), and three companies, each named after the particular infantry brigade to which they were attached, made up the Army Service Corps (Transport and Supply) units of the Division. The four companies were commanded respectively by Major E. W. R. Pinkney, Captain F. G. Ager, Lieut. C. Walker (who, according to the Army List, was in temporary command) and Captain R. C. Hudson. The A.D.S. and T. was commanded temporarily by Major T. Dowling.

These, so far as can be ascertained, were the units and the commands of the Northumbrian (T.F.) Division on the outbreak of war. Several of the commands (as given) were probably only temporary, but of that it is impossible to write with certainty: and, although it is interesting to look back over the years to remind oneself of names and officers familiar before hostilities began, many of those old friends were almost immediately superseded on account of age or ill-health, and the Divisional personnel became quickly changed. Still, from an historical point of view, the Order of Battle of the Division on the 4th of August, 1914, is of value.

For the Territorials, mobilisation orders came at a most awkward time. Many units had just arrived at their annual training camps, or had been there several days, whilst others were actually *en route* by train or march. But on receipt of orders to mobilise there was a hurried packing up and scramble back to Headquarters.

The Northumbrian Division had already spent a week in training in North Wales when, on the 3rd of August, orders were received by all units to return to their respective headquarters. At about 5 p.m. on the 4th the expected telegram, "mobilise," was received. The 5th was spent in overhauling and making good equipment, while horses and carts allotted to the various infantry units had to be collected. On the afternoon of the same date battalions were on their way, or had already arrived at their War Stations. These included coast defences, wireless stations, railway centres and dockyards. It is unnecessary to detail all these places garrisoned by the troops of the Division, but most units having arrived, there began a strenuous existence, working morning, noon and night, digging trenches, erecting barbed-wire entanglements and doing guard duty.

For the Artillery of the Division, mobilisation entailed considerable difficulties. Officers were sent out with parties to bring in horses. Ammunition had to be collected on arrival from Ordnance, sorted out and packed into limbers and wagons. Clothing and equipment had to be inspected and made up to scale. New harness had to be fitted to horses and mules—an unenviable job, the temperament of the mule especially being the violent dislike of any kind of harness! But all went well and eventually, like the infantry of the Division, the gunners were "mobilised" to date.

The remainder of August and September passed in hard work, training, and periodical alarms and excitements. The enemy made raids across the North Sea, shelling Scarborough and several towns on the East Coast, which entailed long hours of "standing to" night and day, though no hostile landings were attempted.

Eventually, early in October, the Northumbrian Division concentrated in and around Newcastle, all units being billeted either in the city or nearby. Then began a series of "sham fights," route marches and other forms of training. By this period the Territorials were asked to volunteer for service overseas, their pre-war obligation being to serve in the United Kingdom only. The large majority agreed at once, and those who were unable to accept overseas obligations were replaced from the reserve battalions.

Christmas came and went, the Division still training hard until at last, early in April, the long-expected warning, followed by definite orders, was received to proceed overseas on the 16th. On that date, in the dead of night, the Northumbrian Division* left England, some units going to Havre, others to Boulogne.†

The Steenvoorde area (west of Ypres) had been allotted the Northumbrian Division in which to concentrate and train. Thither the trains carrying the various units began to arrive, and the Diary of the Administrative Staff records that it was on the 23rd of April that "The Northumbrian Division completed concentration in the vicinity of Steenvoorde."

---

* The "Q" Diary of the Division gives the strength as 572 officers and 16,858 other ranks.

† For "Order of Battle" of the Northumbrian Division on arrival in France, see Appendix F.

CHAPTER III

THE BATTLES OF YPRES, 1915

NO one who was serving with the original Northumbrian Division when it landed in France in April, 1915, and survived the long years of the War, will ever forget the extraordinary happenings which took place during the Division's first month on active service; for a newly-arrived unit to be thrust into the battle front and take part in heavy fighting within a few days (and in some instances within a few hours) of disembarkation from England was no ordinary thing. But such was the lot of these Territorials.

The usual procedure after a division had arrived in France or Flanders was for all units to concentrate in a selected area for the purpose of undergoing additional training before moving forward to within marching distance of the front line. Infantry battalions of the division were then attached to troops holding the trenches for final instruction in trench warfare, while the gunners were usually attached to the artillery of a division holding a front-line sector in order to learn liaison work with the infantry, such matters as ranging on targets, and general routine on active service.

With the arrival of the last unit of his Division at Cassel (2nd Northumberland Field Ambulance) on the 22nd of April, the G.O.C. was no doubt looking forward to a short period of hard training behind the line, when late that night (at 10.40 p.m.) news reached him of a German advance and attack on the front Langemarck–Bixschoote. Ten minutes later he was ordered to have six companies of the York and Durham Brigade fully equipped, ready to move by motor-bus. This order was supplemented by another received at 11.29 p.m. to have all units standing by in billets, ready to turn out immediately, fully equipped.

What had happened?

THE BATTLE OF GRAVENSTAFEL: 22ND–23RD APRIL

The daylight hours of the 22nd of April had been of rare beauty, for spring had already dawned in France and Flanders

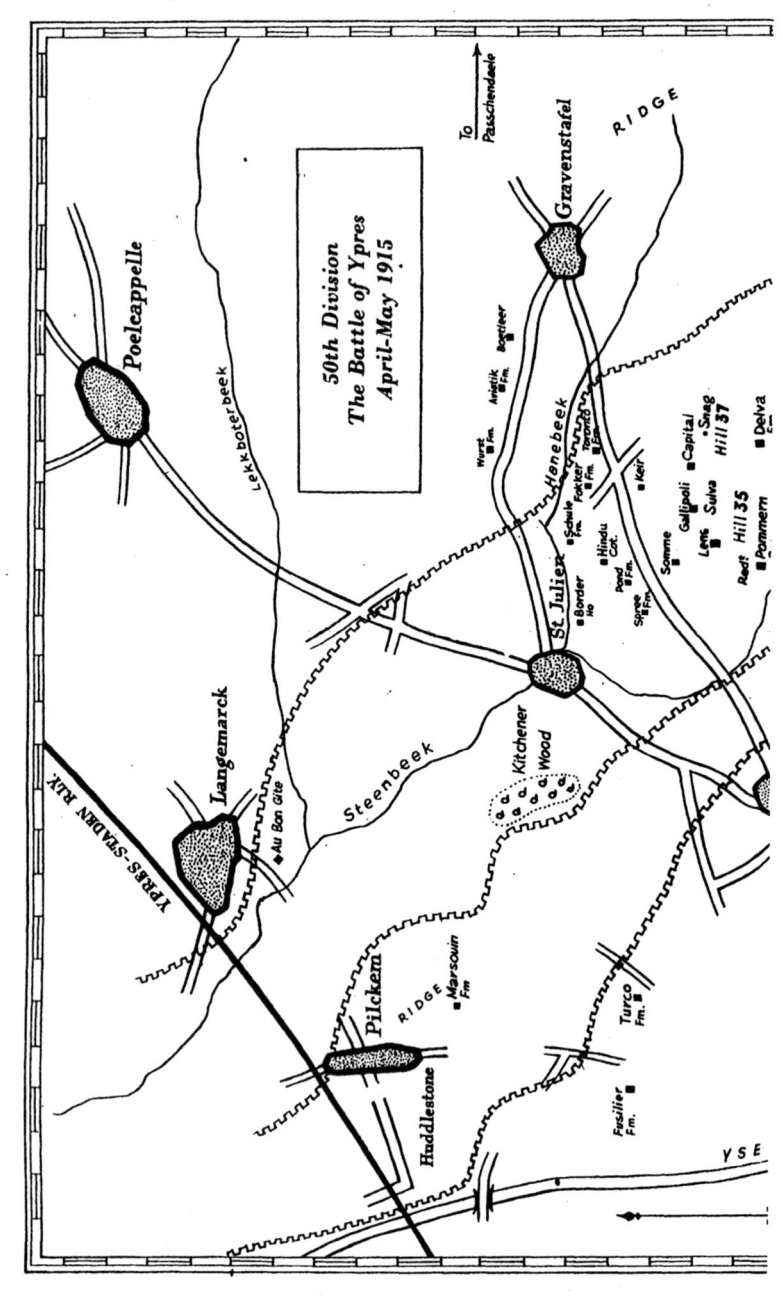

facing p. 6

and, in the Ypres Salient,* though shell-torn, battered and blasted, there still remained trees and shrubs which had begun to bud and bloom with green leaves, reminding one, at times, of springtime in England.

Little that was not usual happened throughout the day; airmen observed considerable movement behind the enemy's line and in the Houthulst Forest area; in the forenoon the big German howitzers had fired 17-in. and 8-in. shells into Ypres, piling a little more destruction on destruction.

Towards 5 o'clock there was a gentle breeze blowing, the skies were clear, and the night had every appearance of falling calm and peaceful, with the possible exception of artillery fire and desultory rifle fire.

But at 5 p.m. the enemy's heavy howitzers suddenly broke out with a fresh and violent bombardment of Ypres and the villages in front of it. Simultaneously there came the characteristically sharp barking of French "75's" firing rapidly. British officers, attracted by the firing and looking in that direction, then observed two curious clouds of a greenish-yellow tint creeping slowly along the ground on either side of Langemarck from the German lines. Presently these two clouds joined up and, carried in a southerly direction by the light breeze, took on the appearance of a light mist enveloping the French positions and screening them from the astonished gaze of those who looked on at this unusual sight. Next, heavy German rifle fire was heard, from which it was evident that the enemy's infantry was advancing.

The deadly mist which had enveloped the French lines was asphyxiating gas.†

---

* The Ypres Salient at this period was held by the following British and French Divisions: From St. Eloi (south of Ypres) to just north-east of Zwarteleen by the 5th Division; from the latter to the south-eastern exits of the Polygon Wood by the 27th Division. The line then curled round the eastern edges of the Polygon Wood following the road to, and just north of Broodseinde, then turning north-west of Berlin Wood; this position was held by the 28th Division. On the left of the 28th Division the Canadian Division held the line from Berlin Wood to south-west of Poelcapelle, the Poelcapelle road being the boundary between the Canadians and the 45th French (Algerian) Division, which, with the 87th French (Territorial) Division, carried the line to Steenstraat. The French line from the Poelcapelle road (including Langemarck) to Steenstraat faced north.

† A remarkable thing concerning the first gas attack at Ypres on the 22nd of April, 1915, is the fact that the Allies had several days earlier received warning that the Germans were about to use it, but refused to believe the information.

What followed baffles adequate description, but Sir John French, in his despatches, written shortly afterwards, describes briefly the results of that first dastardly attack: "The effect of these poisonous gases was so virulent as to render the whole of the line held by the French divisions mentioned above* practically incapable of any action at all. It was at first impossible for anyone to realise what had actually happened. The smoke and fumes hid everything from sight, and hundreds of men were thrown into a comatose or dying condition, and within an hour the whole position had to be abandoned, together with about fifty guns."

Back along the roads leading to Ypres, and to the western bank of the Yser Canal, came crowds of coughing, gasping and suffocating French Territorials and Colonials, staggering along in awful agony, many falling by the wayside, dying there and then in terrible pain. Across country galloped transport and gun teams, all bent upon putting as great a distance as possible between themselves and that ghastly death cloud.

The retirement of the Frenchmen uncovered the left of the Canadian Division, whose flank thus exposed to attack appeared certain to be overwhelmed and cut off from other British troops occupying the Salient to the east.

But with magnificent courage and tenacity the Canadians held their ground and, supported with great promptitude by the reserves of the divisions holding the Salient and by a brigade which had been resting in billets about Vlamertinghe, the enemy was repulsed and some sort of line formed. The formation of this line—imperfect as it was with gaps existing in it—was undoubtedly facilitated by the Germans themselves. They were afraid of their new weapon. With the terrible effects of the gas everywhere evident as they bore down upon and through the French positions, fearing that they too might share the fate of the unfortunate Frenchmen (from their own gas), they hesitated to advance further, for they wore no respirators, neither had they any protection against the poisonous fumes; and as early as 7.30 p.m. they were reported as digging in.

---

* Previously, Sir John French had described the French line from Steenstraat to the east of Langemarck as far as the Poelcapelle road as being held by *one* French division; there were two—45 (A) and 87 (T) Divisions.

This pause in the enemy's advance gave the British valuable time in which to push troops forward to fill dangerous gaps in the line.

Thus the reason the G.O.C., Northumbrian Division, had received, at about 11.30 p.m. that night, orders to have all units of the Division "standing by" in billets ready to turn out immediately, fully equipped.

No moves took place during the night of the 22nd–23rd of April, but at 5.30 a.m. on the latter date Divisional Headquarters received orders from General Headquarters for two infantry brigades to be held in readiness to move. The Northumbrian Infantry Brigade was then ordered to concentrate at Winnezeele, and the York and Durham Infantry Brigade south of Beauvoorde and south of the Steenvoorde and Poperinghe road. Other orders followed, *i.e.*, from General Headquarters at 9.5 a.m. stating that the Northumbrian Division had been placed at the disposal of the Second Army (General Sir H. Plumer), at 10.44 a.m. from the G.O.C., Division, to the Durham Light Infantry Brigade for the concentration of that Brigade at Ryveld, and at 10.45 a.m. from G.O.C., Second Army, placing the York and Durham Infantry Brigade at the disposal of the V Corps and ordering the Brigade to move by motor-bus, via Poperinghe, on Vlamertinghe.*

The York and Durham Infantry Brigade was warned at 12.15 p.m., and almost simultaneously the leading motor-buses moved off. First-Line Transport and Supply Section Train were to follow by the same route.

"Camp A," between Vlamertinghe and Ypres, was the destination of the Brigade, and there during the afternoon the 1/4th East Yorkshires, 4th Green Howards, 5th Green Howards and 1/5th Durham Light Infantry arrived.

At Poperinghe the battalions "de-bussed" and continued on foot. As they tramped along the pavé road, with Vlamertinghe and Ypres ahead, the boom of guns became ever louder. Crowds of refugees were met, hurrying westwards with handcarts, perambulators and almost every kind of vehicle laden with all the worldly possessions left to them, and the troops, for the first time, saw one aspect of the War and what it

---

* The Headquarters Diary of the York and Durham Brigade for April, 1915, is missing, and details, therefore, have to be obtained from battalion diaries.

meant to the unfortunate Belgians, for the latter, before the gas attack, still occupied farms and cottages close behind the line, in the Salient, feeling secure so long as Allied troops were in front of them.

It was somewhere about 4 p.m. when battalions reached Vlamertinghe and, passing through the town, halted in a large field on the eastern side, containing many wooden hutments: this was the famous "Camp A."

Meanwhile Divisional Headquarters at Steenvoorde had, at 11.45 a.m., received orders from Second Army Headquarters for the Northumberland Infantry Brigade with Field Company, R.E., and Supply Section Train, to march from Winnezeele via Watou and occupy the third defence line astride the Poperinghe–Ypres road at Brandhoek.

The Brigade set out just after 1 p.m. in the following order: 5th, 6th, 7th and 4th Battalions Northumberland Fusiliers, 2nd Field Company, R.E., 1st Northumberland Field Ambulance, No. 2 Company, A.S.C. Train.

All battalions reached their destination between 6 and 7 p.m. Their diaries contain few comments on that first approach march. The 4th Northumberland Fusiliers record that the Battalion had marched 14½ miles "very dusty," "no men fell out"; the 6th that it was "St. George's Day" and that on reaching Brandhoek they went into some trenches there "simply for shelter and not for any tactical reason, and there spent the night."

At 12.41 p.m. General Lindsay had received orders to move his Headquarters and the Divisional troops to Poperinghe and neighbourhood, as the Division (less the York and Durham Infantry Brigade) had been placed in Army Reserve. But on sending off a staff officer to arrange billets he returned with the information that there was no room either in the town or the neighbourhood, and Divisional Headquarters and Divisional troops were therefore ordered to remain at Steenvoorde.

At 4 p.m. another order was received from Second Army Headquarters: two battalions of the Durham Light Infantry Brigade were to march at once to Poperinghe, the remaining two battalions to be taken up in buses to Poperinghe and Vlamertinghe respectively. As a result of this order the 6th and 8th Battalions Durham Light Infantry were conveyed in motor-buses to Vlamertinghe, and Brigade Headquarters, with the 7th and 9th Battalions, set out on foot, arriving at their destination after midnight. The 6th Battalion billeted in Poperinghe, while the 8th went on to Vlamertinghe.

At 8 p.m. the Durham Light Infantry Brigade was placed at the disposal of the V Corps.

The final message received on the night of the 23rd of April at Divisional Headquarters at 8.20 p.m. concerned the artillery: not more than one artillery brigade was to be sent to Brandhoek to support the Northumberland Infantry Brigade, the remaining Field Artillery brigades being kept clear of Boeschepe. When the Brigadier-General, Royal Artillery, was informed of this his brigades were already on the road leading to Boeschepe; they, therefore, bivouacked for the night in the neighbouring fields.*

Thus, so far as the Battle of Gravenstafel Ridge (22nd-23rd April) was concerned, the Northumbrian Division had taken no part in the fighting. The Division was, as described above, engaged in moving up towards the battle-front and in carrying out a succession of orders, not always explicit, some of which were by no means easy to execute.

Only one unit of the Division, and that the 1st Northumberland Field Ambulance, was actually near the battle-front. This ambulance had received orders on the 22nd to join the 14th Field Ambulance (of the 5th Division) at the Asylum, Ypres, for work at the Advanced Dressing Station and to learn the methods of collecting wounded from the front by motorambulance at night. The Diary of the A.D.M.S. of the Northumbrian Division is, indeed, the most interesting of the Divisional Diaries on the 22nd and 23rd of April.

On the 22nd the A.D.M.S. went first to the 5th Divisional Rest Station at Reninghelst and then to the Asylum at Ypres. The battered city of the clothworkers was then under heavy shell fire: "The row of the bombardment round about it was so terrific that it was difficult to hear one another speak." The A.D.M.S. then records that, "The improvised methods of conducting the bathing, clean underclothing and other sanitary measures for the benefit of the soldiers at the Rest Station were interesting and instructive."

---

* During the day (23rd April) the 4th Northumbrian (Howitzer) R.F.A. Brigade, the 1st North Riding Heavy Battery, R.G.A., and Ammunition Column and 3rd Northumbrian Field Ambulance arrived by train, the latter moving to Steenvoorde and the artillery units to Caestre.

He returned to Poperinghe via Vlamertinghe: "The din of battle seemed to be increasing and we observed away on our right, as we were returning, a dense cloud of white smoke which Major Martin could not explain." The "dense cloud" was probably the "gas discharge," for it was on the 22nd that the above entries were made in the Diary. Then later, during the evening of the 22nd, the following entry occurs: "Something has happened. Everybody is very excited. The town is crowded with French Colonial troops, Turcos and others, and report says they have fled from their posts, having been attacked by some poisonous gas used by the Germans. The bombardment has lessened considerably, but nobody yet knows exactly what has happened."

The Asylum at Ypres had to be evacuated early on the morning of the 23rd of April, and the 1st Northumbrian Field Ambulance marched back to Reninghelst. But the ambulance had carried out its first job on the battlefield: "He (the O.C., 1st N.F.A.) reported to me," records the A.D.M.S., "that he was out on the Dixmude road with the convoy collecting wounded last night (22nd) and that a large number of cases of gas poisoning came into the Asylum, Ypres, before they left."

So, strange as it may seem, this solitary Field Ambulance saw more of the first of the Battles of Ypres, 1915, than any other unit of the Northumbrian Division. Theirs was the gruesome sight of the tortured dead and of the agonised living in all the throes of that first dreadful and dastardly use of asphyxiating gas.

THE BATTLE OF ST. JULIEN: 24TH APRIL–4TH MAY

At midnight, 23rd of April, the German line ran from between one-half and three-quarters of a mile south-south-west of Poelcapelle, thence in a south-westerly direction west of Keerselare, north of St. Julien along the southern exits of Kitchener's Wood to Oblong Farm; from the latter position it turned north-west to Welch Farm, dropping south-west again from that place to north of Turco Farm, where it took a north-westerly turn to just south of Het Sas; at the latter point the German line crossed the Yser Canal and, embracing Lizerne (captured towards midnight on the 23rd by the enemy), turned thence north-east and recrossed the Canal north-west of Steenstraat.

Throughout the 23rd the only gain made by the enemy had been at the two extremities of the line, *i.e.*, south-west of Poelcapelle and Steenstraat. But the positions of all Allied troops in the Ypres Salient were now precarious, for the enemy, with his preponderance of heavy artillery, was able to enfilade any part of the British front line south, east, and north of Ypres. Even at this date our artillery was woefully weak compared with that of the Germans. Our obsolete heavy howitzers were no match for the big German howitzers, and what guns we had were supplied with only a limited amount of ammunition. The outlook, therefore, was one of great anxiety.

The Canadians, on the right, had put up a splendid fight: the gap in the centre, caused by the retirement of the French, had been filled in places by reinforcements ordered up from whatever British troops were in reserve or in Ypres. Of the French, only a few Zouaves remained at Canadian Farm and a few more on the eastern bank of the Yser Canal south of South Zwhanhof Farm, all other French troops were west of the Canal as far north as west of Lizerne. Belgian troops carried the line northwards, holding it with great gallantry.

Heavy loss during the day of the 23rd was responsible for the issue of orders to the York and Durham Brigade late at night to move to Brielen Bridge to be attached to, and support if required, the 13th Infantry Brigade (5th Division).

The York and Durham Brigade (then in "A" Camp) was turned out shortly after 1 a.m. on the 24th, and all four battalions were soon on the road. Little or nothing is extant among the records which gives any idea of the impression made upon the minds of those who were, for the first time, moving up to positions less than a couple of miles from the enemy, with the flash of guns, the bursting of Very lights and one-hundred-and-one things they had never before encountered in their lives, happening in front of, and to a degree all around, them. Only from one private diary, kept by an officer of the 1/4th East Yorkshires* is it possible to glean anything of that first march to positions well within range of the enemy's shell fire.

It was, of course, pitch dark when the Brigade set out on the march for the Yser Canal.

---

* Capt. B. M. R. Sharp.

"The march to our line," said our diarist, "was a queer one. We knew not where we were going, nor what to do; the men's anticipations were not brightened by seeing a dressing station in a very busy state. We crossed over a pontoon over a small canal—a piece of the Yser Canal but not actually it.[*] The banks were very high and we were on the further one which commanded the other side. It was provided with trenches and dug-outs, and after much scrambling in the dark and moving further down and so forth, we got into our position, holding partly some dug-outs and partly a trench. This was about 2 or 3 o'clock in the morning of the 24th. When day broke we found that there was an old, small factory with a chimney on our right and several farms and cottages still occupied along our front. Ypres was on our right and the French line to our left front. There were some Canadian Scottish in the factory who kindly gave the men some beef and tea."

When dawn broke on the 24th, also, these officers and men of the Northumbrian Division looked on the Ypres Salient, or that portion of it which could be seen from their position, for the first time.

Ypres, the ancient city of the Belgian clothworkers, lay on their right. As yet, though scarred and battered in many places, there was still some semblance to a well-ordered town. For afar off its ruins were hardly apparent. But as one drew closer, passing in at any of the gates over the old moat, the seemingly-whole houses disclosed themselves as mere shells with blackened walls inside as if one looked through the eyeless sockets of a skull discoloured by age.

Due east of their position the Northumbrian troops could see first La Brique and then beyond that place St. Jean, Wieltje and St. Julien—all three of the latter villages lying on the Ypres–Poelcapelle road, which stretched away in a north-easterly direction from the north-eastern exits of Ypres. South of this road there was another, running from the Menin Gate to Broodseinde: Potijze, Verlorenhoek, Frezenberg and Zonnebeke were all on this road. La Brique was on the Ypres–Langemarck road. Some two miles north of the Brigade was Boesinghe, on the western side of the Canal, and just on the southern exits of the village the Pilckem–Lange-

---

[*] Probably one of the many waterways or dykes so frequently met with in Belgium.

marck–Poelcapelle road joined up with the Ypres–Boesinghe road. The Ypres–Roulers railway ran in a north-easterly direction from south of Ypres, while the Ypres–Staden railway ran similarly north-east but north of Pilckem and Langemarck.

These were some of the principal villages and roads in the northern half of the Ypres Salient as it existed on the morning of the 24th of April.

But of equal importance, though they were gradually being reduced to mere heaps of bricks and mortar, were numerous small farms scattered about, and around which some of the fiercest fighting took place. Just south-east of St. Julien was Fortuin—a curious place which no one has ever defined as a village, locality or geographical feature; it existed on maps and that was all. Next, coming west, was Mouse Trap Farm (north of Wieltje) and Oblong Farm (which at this period was in German hands). North-west of Mouse Trap were Hampshire and Canadian Farms; Turco Farm (one of the most notorious farms in the Ypres Salient) was about half a mile west of Canadian Farm; west of Turco was Fusilier Farm, and west of the latter South Zwhanhof Farm, not less than a quarter of a mile from the eastern bank of the Yser Canal. Two more farms—Foch Farm and La Belle Alliance Farm—lay north of La Brique. Behind (south of) Turco Farm was a small ridge known as Hill Top.

Several châteaux were dotted here and there over the Salient, and most of them became famous landmarks before they also sank into the mud, having been reduced to mere heaps of rubble. Potijze Château was one of them.

Most of the roads, villages and farms mentioned above became in time well known to all ranks of the Northumbrian Division.

Two battalions of the York and Durham Brigade were posted on the western bank of the Yser Canal and two on the eastern bank; owing to the loss of the Brigade Headquarters Diary it is not possible to state which were east or west—but the point is not important.

As soon as it was light on the 24th the enemy's guns opened fire, and for the first time the York and Durham Brigade was shelled; some of the enemy's projectiles burst on the canal bank, wounding several men—the first casualties suffered by the Northumbrian Division in the War.

At 4 a.m., after heavily bombarding the apex of the front held by the Canadian Division, the enemy again released dense clouds of gas. The gallant Canadians, using handkerchiefs, towels and any other materials they could lay hands on, dampened with whatever moisture could be obtained in their trenches, put up a splendid resistance and the enemy's gain of ground was small. Nevertheless there was a break in the front line. This occurred at about 6.30 a.m. The Canadians applied for support as there were no reserves, and at 7.40 a.m. two battalions of the York and Durham Brigade from the canal bank were ordered to man the G.H.Q. Line astride the Poelcapelle–Wieltje and Fortuin–Wieltje roads in support of the 2nd and 3rd Canadian Brigades.

The G.H.Q. Line is thus described in the Official History (Military Operations) of the War: "It ran from Zillebeke Lake, where it was one and a half miles behind the front, northwards to a point half a mile east of Wieltje, where it was three miles behind the front, thence it gradually turned north-westwards to join a line covering Boesinghe village and railway bridge. It consisted of well-constructed text-book redoubts, of some thirty yards face, with their flanks turned back, each for a garrison of about fifty men. These redoubts were from four to five hundred yards apart and were eventually joined up by fire trenches. The line was exceedingly well sited from the point of view of a good field of fire, sometimes on a reverse, sometimes on a forward slope, but not overlooked owing to the general flatness of the ground. The real strength of the line lay in its wire—a continuous belt some six yards wide, with openings only at the transverse roads and tracks."

Indeed the G.H.Q. Line was better prepared for defence than the front line. It had been originally constructed by the French as a second line.

The two battalions of the York and Durham Brigade detailed to move up to the G.H.Q. Line were the 1/4th East Yorkshires and 4th Green Howards.

The East Yorkshires record that it was 10 a.m. when they received their orders and they set out shortly afterwards. In order to gain the Wieltje road they had to move down the western bank of the Yser Canal and take the road skirting the northern exits of Ypres. Once on this road the Battalion passed through St. Jean and, striking off to the right, reached a point a few hundred yards north-east of 27th Divisional Headquarters, which were in Potijze Château. Here the East Yorkshires dug in, the time being about 1 p.m.

The 4th Green Howards followed the East Yorkshires, being met by a Canadian brigadier who ordered the Battalion into a section of the G.H.Q. Line near Potijze Château. He sent a guide with the Green Howards, but on arrival at the trenches the latter were found already full of troops and, as the enemy's shell fire was heavy, the Battalion laid down behind the trenches while the C.O. endeavoured to obtain fresh orders.

By this time both Battalions were very tired; their broken rest of the previous night, the nervous tension inseparable from moving up to the battle-front—all tended to a state of exhaustion. From a small wood in front of the East Yorkshires a Canadian battery was in action, and the fumes and smoke from the guns heightened the discomfiture of the Battalion.

At 3 p.m. the East Yorkshires received orders to support an attack by the Canadians from St. Julien.*

The 4th Green Howards state that they were ordered by another Canadian brigadier to attack St. Julien, but this order was cancelled. Headquarters, 27th Division, then ordered the Battalion to dig in close to the Château. Before the Green Howards had properly started digging they received new orders to attack through Fortuin and on to St. Julien; they were to be supported by the 1/4th East Yorkshires.

St. Julien had been lost at about 3 p.m., or rather the Germans occupied it at that hour. And they were already moving southwards out of the village when the attack of the 4th Green Howards and 1/4th East Yorkshires broke upon them.

It may be assumed (no time existing in the Battalion Diary) that the 4th Green Howards, with Lieut.-Colonel M. H. L. Bell in command, moved to the attack between 3 p.m. and 3.30 p.m., for the 1/4th East Yorkshires, under Lieut.-Colonel G. H. Shaw, advanced in support at 3.45 p.m.

Both Battalions were at full strength (the few casualties suffered from shell fire making little difference) and they advanced in full marching order. The sight of these two Territorial battalions advancing, as an officer said, "as if they were doing an attack practice in peace," was inspiring. "It

---

* The Diary of the 1/4th East Yorkshires states that the Battalion was to support the Canadians in an attack "on Fortuin." But Fortuin was in our hands at this period.

was marvellous," continued this officer. "They went on in such a way as if they'd done it all their lives, nothing stopped them."

At the cross-roads just short of Fortuin a few Germans with a machine-gun were encountered; these were very soon put to flight. On through Fortuin the two Battalions went, next encountering the enemy in force advancing south from St. Julien. They forced the enemy to give ground and drove him back into the village. They then found themselves up against a muddy stream, known as the Haanebeek, on the southern exits of St. Julien and, the crossings being swept by heavy rifle and machine-gun fire, the two Battalions were forced to take what cover presented itself.

Casualties during this affair were severe, but the counter-attack was completely successful and, besides preventing the Germans from making any further advance on the 24th, reflected the greatest credit upon the two gallant Battalions.[*]

The Green Howards relate their part in the attack in the following somewhat modest narrative:

"We were ordered to attack through Fortuin and on to St. Julien. The 4th East Yorkshires came with us. We started off, both flanks in the air, with little artillery support. Proceeding under artillery fire to Fortuin, we could find no one in superior command. We heard fighting going on towards St. Julien and saw a few men retiring. We therefore changed front left and joined in. Under heavy rifle and machine-gun fire we took up a position about seven hundred yards south of St. Julien and endeavoured to get orders and information, as things looked pretty bad and there seemed a fair chance of both the 4th East Yorkshires and ourselves being cut off and unable to extricate ourselves. Presently we were joined by the Royal Irish Fusiliers and later by some of the York and Lancasters. They passed down the order to us to hold on till dark and then endeavour to retire. This we did. It was here that we got the name of the 'Yorkshire Gurkhas' from the Royal Irish Fusiliers."

The 1/4th East Yorkshires went forward in artillery formation, in line of platoons, two platoons of "D" Company, led by Lieut.-Colonel Shaw, in front. Just south of the Wieltje-

---

[*] The 50th (Northumbrian) Division Memorial is erected at St. Julien in memory of this gallant attack.

Gravenstafel road the Battalion swung to the north towards St. Julien. The East Yorkshires were met at once by heavy rifle and machine-gun fire, while hostile shrapnel was bursting all along the line over the advancing troops.

"Then came heavy howitzer shells right amongst us, which burst and made neat holes about thirty feet by ten feet and threw up tons of muck when they hit a field. We were in small columns and sections, and more than once sections were blown over by these hellish things. They were systematically spread over our advance, and the men never faltered but went on and on—a splendid sight—they did magnificently, hungry and tired and weary though they were."

In this attack the East Yorkshires lost their gallant Colonel: "As soon as it [the attack] developed we were met by high-explosive shells and 'stinkpots.' Everyone bobbed, then on again. I accompanied the C.O. He and I had reached an infernal area when something happened and he never rose again. He was shot through the head by a sniper. I can't express my feelings. Then a hell of a machine-gun fire swept the place. All I could do was to lie 'doggo' as small as possible. When it was over I went on and found two platoons of 'C' Company which could not advance further. An order came down to stay where we were till dusk. The enemy's fire ceased and we, after some time, collected up and returned to the trenches. Poor Farrell* was shot through the heart close to me, and Theilmann† in the body, and he died on the way back."‡

Besides the three officers mentioned above, the 4th East Yorkshires lost 12 other ranks killed, 66 wounded, 10 wounded and missing, and 7 missing.

The trenches to which the Battalion returned were those at Potijze, the East Yorkshiremen marching in at about 11 p.m.

The 4th Green Howards had also fallen back on Potijze Château "without being rushed," records their Diary. They had lost during the fight Major H. C. Matthews, Capt. and Adjutant G. D. P. Eykyn, Capt. J. V. Nancarrow, Lieut. L. P. I'Anson, Second-Lieut. E. Darwin and 10 other ranks killed, Second-Lieut. H. B. Blackett and 59 other ranks wounded,

---

*Capt. Bede Farrell.

† Major C. E. Theilmann.

‡ From the Diary of Capt. B. M. R. Sharp.

and a number of wounded and missing who, however, turned up later.

Meanwhile the 5th Green Howards and the 1/5th Durham Light Infantry had also moved forward from the Yser Canal. Orders were received at about midday to move to St. Jean in support of the 3rd Canadian Brigade.

Both Battalions in moving forward came under shell and rifle fire, and the Green Howards had one officer (Lieut. E. W. Faber) severely wounded. The 1/5th Durham Light Infantry moved to support trenches near St. Jean, but the Green Howards reinforced Canadian troops just south of Hampshire Farm, and received orders from the C.O. of the 3rd Canadian Infantry Brigade to be "ready to counter-attack when necessary."

The night of the 24th–25th was miserable in the extreme; rain fell constantly, the enemy's shell fire was heavy and the Green Howards had several men wounded and one man killed.

Neither the Northumberland Infantry Brigade nor the Durham Light Infantry Brigade moved from their positions, at Brandhoek and Vlamertinghe respectively, until late in the day.

The former Brigade received orders at 3.45 p.m. to move via Ypres to Potijze (where it was to form a corps reserve) and set out at 6 p.m.

It took the Brigade four hours and a half to reach Potijze, for it was 10.30 p.m. before battalions reached their destinations. The 4th Northumberland Fusiliers state that at one period they halted for an hour in the Market Square, Ypres, shelled all the time: "Someone in front had lost direction in the town!" The 5th Battalion "lay in a field just beyond Ypres for two hours under heavy shell fire," after passing through the ruined town. Their only comment on Ypres was "much dilapidated." The 6th fetched up on the road near Wieltje, where, in farms, the night and early morning of the 25th were spent. The 7th reached Potijze about midnight.

At 1.30 a.m. (25th) the Brigade was placed under the orders of the 10th Infantry Brigade (4th Division) and was ordered to move to Wieltje in support. The Brigade arrived at its destination at about 4.30 a.m.

The Durham Light Infantry Brigade had received a succession of orders, one countermanding the other. During the morning the Brigade received orders that it would come at once under the orders of the Cavalry Corps. These orders were cancelled later, and the Brigade was ordered to move to Potijze where it would come under the orders of General Snow, commanding 27th Division. The 6th Durham Light Infantry after passing through Ypres moved on beyond Potijze, relieving the Shropshire Light Infantry in the G.H.Q. Line; the 7th and 9th Battalions bivouacked in the Château grounds, under shell fire.

To the 8th Durham Light Infantry fell all the excitement of the night of the 24th–25th. The Battalion had first of all been placed under the G.O.C., 85th Brigade (28th Division), and at about 11 p.m. was astride the Verlorenhoek–Frezenberg road, about half-way between those two places. About 11.30 p.m. orders were received to proceed to Headquarters, 3rd Royal Fusiliers, near Gravenstafel, whence guides were to take the Battalion to some trenches which were to have been partly dug by Canadians, but were left unfinished.

The Durhams set out immediately with a guide who was to take them via Zonnebeke. And what a march that was! Consider the condition of both officers and men; they had been "standing to" practically all day, then in the darkness, along roads frequently shelled, they marched from Vlamertinghe, through Ypres, Potijze and Verlorenhoek. All were dead-tired when they reached the latter place; all were wet through, for rain had been falling all the evening, and this was their first experience of battle. And now another two or three miles' march was before them—with what at the end of it? No one could tell, and it was fortunate that no one knew.

The Battalion tool-carts had not arrived, and all the men had were their entrenching tools—of little use. They had with them the unconsumed portions of the day's rations and their iron rations.

Progress was slow. The night was pitch black; the roads, many of them gaping with shell holes, were also frequently obstructed with obstacles of all sorts, such as broken-down wagons, limbers and ambulances. Extra ammunition had been served out to each man and eight pack animals carried a reserve supply.

On arriving at Headquarters, 3rd Royal Fusiliers, the C.O. of that battalion explained to the C.O., 8th Durham Light Infantry, that the position the latter battalion had been ordered to entrench was quite untenable and that it would be impossible to begin work before daylight, especially as only entrenching tools were available. He therefore telephoned to Headquarters, 85th Brigade, and, after explaining the situation, previous orders were cancelled and the Durhams were ordered to relieve the 8th Canadians in the front line north-east of Boetleer Farm, the Headquarters of that battalion being in the Farm. The time was now about 2 a.m., 25th April.

The Durhams set out immediately to relieve the Canadians, who had lost heavily and were much exhausted. It was about 3 a.m. when the trenches were reached and dawn was beginning to break. But no one seemed to have a clear idea of the situation.

Writing in 1925, Lieut.-Colonel G. A. Stevens (who was Captain and Adjutant of the 8th Durham Light Infantry in April, 1915) said:

"The 8th D.L.I. relieved the 8th Canadians about Boetleer Farm. When we relieved the Canadians at early dawn they could not show us on the map where we were, nor could they give us even a diagram of where their trenches were. Things had to be done very hurriedly and we only partly relieved the front line. Two of the 8th D.L.I. companies went up—'A' Company, under Capt. Harvey, and 'D' Company, under Capt. Bradford."

The positions taken over were more clearly described by Major W. H. Coulson who, in April, 1915, was second-in-command of "A" Company, and by Major T. A. Bradford, who was in command of "D" Company. "A" was on the right, "D" on the left.

"My Company," said Major Coulson, "followed 'D.' After proceeding for about one thousand yards from Boetleer Farm, we turned left on some rising ground into a trench held by Canadians, still following 'D' Company. The right of the trench lay in front, *i.e.*, north-west, of some farm buildings. The German trenches at this part lay about eighty yards distant but further off than those towards the north-west."

Major Bradford stated that: " 'D' Company moved off with a Canadian as guide. 'A' Company followed immediately behind. From Boetleer Farm we moved up slightly rising ground then over gradually falling ground, across a ditch, then a short way up rising ground and turned left into a trench held by Canadians. The distance from the Farm to the trench would be at least six hundred yards. 'D' Company moved along this for some two hundred yards, then came to what was a communication trench containing much water, and eventually some two hundred yards further on, reached a trench also held by Canadians, whom the Company relieved. The left flank of this trench was turned to the rear at a right-angle. A portion of the trench, about its centre, was a communication trench. Two platoons were placed on each side of this. This line of trench had originally been French, there being dead buried in and around it; the bodies, which had only been buried in shallow ground, were thrown up by shell fire during the day, and were French Colonial troops. The trench was shallow with a good breastwork but no parados. It contained a number of dug-outs, one occupied by Signals, the rest filled with dead, wounded and gassed Canadians, mostly the latter."

Thus, the positions of the three infantry brigades of the Northumbrian Division throughout the night of the 24th–25th of April and at dawn on the latter date. They were the only units of the Division in the line, for General Lindsey had received orders that, as there were so many commanders in the field who knew all the locality, it was thought unnecessary for him to move from Steenvoorde, and for the present his Headquarters were to remain at that place and the Divisional troops in, and in the neighbourhood of, the town.

The general situation on the night of the 24th–25th of April was distinctly unfavourable to us. The Salient, held so gallantly by the Canadians on the right of the line, "Locality C" (which lay north-west of Boetleer Farm) and St. Julien, had been lost, though up to midnight both that village and Fortuin were clear of the enemy. This fact was, however, unknown to us.

At 4.15 p.m. a message from General Headquarters had been sent to General Plumer: "Every effort must be made at once to restore and hold line about St. Julien or situation of 28th Division will be jeopardised." At 6.30 p.m. General Plumer ordered General Alderson (commanding the Canadian Division) to make the strongest possible counter-attack towards St. Julien with the 10th and York and Durham Brigades and six battalions under the command of Brig.-General Hull. These orders were issued by General Alderson at 8 p.m. on the 24th and were, briefly, as follows: At 3.30 a.m. on the 25th a strong counter-attack was to be made in a general direction towards St. Julien: Fortuin, St. Julien and Kitchener's

Wood were to be the first objectives; the enemy was to be driven as far north as possible; besides the two Brigades already mentioned, two battalions of the 13th Brigade (5th Division), two battalions of the 28th Division, a Canadian brigade and a battalion of the 27th Division were to take part; the Northumberland and Durham Light Infantry Brigades (of the Northumbrian Division), forming the Corps reserve at Potijze, could be called upon to support if necessary.

It will be remembered that of the York and Durham Brigade the 4th East Yorkshires and 4th Green Howards were then (when these orders were issued) in the front line near St. Julien, but returned later to Potijze; the 5th Green Howards and 5th Durham Light Infantry were in reserve near St. Jean.

Four battalions of the 10th Brigade were ordered to attack the line St. Julien–Kitchener's Wood, with one battalion in reserve on the left, while the 5th Green Howards and 5th Durham Light Infantry were to move on the right of the 10th Brigade through Fortuin. It had been impossible to get into touch with other battalions detailed for the attack, but behind the right was the Northumberland Brigade which, in the early hours of the 25th, had arrived near Wieltje. Actually, the attack was made by five battalions, *i.e.*, General Hull's 10th Brigade.

Dawn had broken and the rain had passed away, but it was still misty when the 10th Brigade, passing through the wire of G.H.Q. Line, formed up facing the line St. Julien–Kitchener's Wood.

Both the 5th Green Howards and 5th Durham Light Infantry state that it was 3 a.m. when they received orders, and that the two battalions moved out and arrived at their respective positions at Fortuin by 5 a.m., *i.e.*, 5th Green Howards on the right, 5th Durham Light Infantry on the left.

The mist had covered the 10th Brigade as the battalions passed through the wire, but before they could open out, rifle and machine-gun fire was opened upon them. In faultless order these gallant troops shook out into fighting formation and advanced, but from the houses in St. Julien, from Kitchener's Wood and from Oblong and Juliet Farms, south of the Wood, a murderous machine-gun fire swept their ranks. With superb courage the leading lines reached a position about one hundred yards from the outskirts of St. Julien; they were then forced to lie down under a storm of machine-gun bullets. The lines coming on behind were pinned to the ground and, after several vain efforts to advance, the survivors crawled back to whatever cover the ground afforded. The magnificent but hapless efforts of the 10th Brigade resulted in the enormous casualty list of 73 officers and 2,346 other ranks. There was, however, one compensation for this sacrifice: the position taken up by the units of the 10th Brigade was held until it was voluntarily evacuated on the 4th of May, and they had stopped the German advance from St. Julien.

Meanwhile the 5th Green Howards and the 5th Durham Light Infantry, having reached their allotted positions at Fortuin by 5 a.m., found themselves alone and with their flanks in the air; they therefore fell back to their former positions. This mistake was owing to the fact that zero hour had been altered from 3.30 a.m. to 5.30 a.m., and that information had not reached the two battalions. On discovering their absence on the right of his 10th Brigade, General Hull then ordered two battalions of the Northumberland Brigade, *i.e.*, 4th and 7th Northumberland Fusiliers, to reinforce the right of the 10th Brigade. Instead of thickening the line, however, these two battalions extended it to the right, but still they were not in touch with the 5th Green Howards and 5th Durham Light Infantry, who had returned to their old trenches in front of Fortuin.

The 5th Durham Light Infantry took up a line of trenches east of the St. Jean–St. Julien road, where they apparently remained all day, having several casualties from shell fire, including Lieut. J. C. Brown wounded.

The 5th Green Howards state that their "B" and "C" Companies occupied a line of reserve trenches on the "right of road to left of D.L.I.," but no shelter was available for "A" and "D" Companies who were forced to take refuge in the hedge bottom along the roadside. These two companies, however, at 6 a.m. advanced to support the 1st Royal Irish Fusiliers (10th Brigade) across an open field under heavy shrapnel fire. The leading troops of these two companies had reached their objective when the Royal Irish began to fall back, and the Green Howards were ordered to conform. In this retirement the Battalion lost heavily: 8 other ranks were killed and about 40 wounded, including the Adjutant. Finally "A" and "D" Companies dug themselves in, in the hedge bottom of a field to the left of the road, "D" Company in line with "B" and "C," and with "A" at right-angles on the left of "D." Throughout the day shell and rifle fire continued to worry the Battalion.

At about noon the 5th Durham Light Infantry, who had been ordered to search a farm-house,* requested assistance from the Green Howards, and a party of twenty-five other ranks from "D" Company, under Capt. G. C. Barber and Lieut. H. Brown, was sent out. The party was met by machine-gun fire from the house and Capt. Barber and an N.C.O. were killed instantly. Capt. Purvis then reported small parties of Germans in trenches due north. Orderlies were sent off to Brigade Headquarters stating that the enemy was inclined to press, and asking for orders. No reply was received. During the remainder of the day further casualties were suffered from shell and rifle fire, which died down at nightfall. After darkness the dead were collected and buried and the wounded evacuated to the advanced dressing station. Trenches were improved and preparations made to hold the line during the night.

The 4th and 7th Northumberland Fusiliers, who had been sent up to support the 10th Brigade, had plenty of excitement without much actual fighting.

On receiving orders to support the 10th Brigade, the 4th Battalion moved two companies forward, who pushed on further than was intended and they were forced to take shelter all day, returning to Wieltje when darkness had fallen. They lost during the day one man killed and Capt. D. H. Weir, Lieut. C. M. Joicy, Second-Lieut. W. Robinson and 33 other ranks wounded; 20 men were also reported missing, but most of these reported next day.

The 7th Battalion, with Nos. 1 and 2 Companies forming the firing line, and Nos. 3 and 4 the supports, advanced in lines of platoons. At about one thousand yards from the enemy, at a point just behind a trench occupied by Canadian infantry, the Battalion deployed as it was under heavy rifle fire. At this stage troops were seen retiring on the right of the Battalion. The latter pushed on for another five hundred yards, but now the enemy's machine-gun and rifle fire was extremely heavy and the first line took shelter in a small ditch. Machine-gun fire was observed to be coming from a cottage on the left front,

---

* The 5th Durham Light Infantry make no mention of this incident.

and heavy rifle fire was directed on it. A section on the left was sent off to work round the cottage, when a message was received from an artillery officer* saying that if the machine-guns could be located the guns would shell them. But although the position of the guns was given, and the section recalled, three hours passed and still the artillery had not opened fire.

At about 9 a.m. the 7th Northumberland Fusiliers were informed that the supports had retired, and as there were apparently no troops on either flank the Battalion fell back to positions on the right of the Canadians. Here they remained until nightfall, when they returned to Wieltje and bivouacked for the night.

The 5th Northumberland Fusiliers at 2 a.m. had moved to the cross-roads half a mile south-east of Wieltje, where heavy shell fire compelled them to dig in about four hundred yards south of the village. The remainder of the day was spent in this position, the Battalion suffering some twenty-two casualties.

The 6th Battalion moved at 10 a.m. to trenches north of Wieltje, returning to trenches south of the village at 9.30 p.m.

Of the Durham Light Infantry Brigade, only the 8th Durham Light Infantry were, on the 25th of April, involved in heavy fighting; the 6th, 7th and 9th Battalions had moved to Verlorenhoek. The 9th had one officer killed during the day, *i.e.*, Second-Lieut. A. Little, and Capt. H. E. English missing.†

We left the 8th Durham Light Infantry, at dawn, having just relieved Canadian troops in the neighbourhood of Boetleer Farm, *i.e.*, two companies, "A" and "D" (right and left respectively) in the front line north of the Farm, "B" and "C" Companies lining the hedges east and west respectively of the farm buildings on the southern side of the Gravenstafel road, which ran east and west through the Farm.‡

The positions occupied by "A" and "D" Companies each consisted of two trenches of about one hundred yards in length

---

* No information as to battery.

† From official records.

‡ After carefully examining the records, and considering all things, the original narrative of the operations of the 24th–26th April, 1915, written by Lieut.-Colonel G. A. Stevens (who, in April, 1915, was Adjutant of the 8th Durham Light Infantry), and the disposition map drawn by him, which still form part of the Battalion Diary, have been accepted as the best evidence of the positions held by the Durhams.

connected by a communication trench of from fifty to sixty yards; in their portion of the trench the Canadians had a machine-gun, for not all of the latter had been able to get away before dawn broke.

The trenches were shallow with a breastwork of sand-bags, part of which was loop-holed.

Immediately north of the Farm was a small detachment of Monmouths, and on the left another detachment of the same regiment and some of the Suffolks; on the left of the Suffolks were the 7th and 10th Canadians.

Fields and hedgerows, dead ground, gently undulating ground with the farm buildings standing on the highest portions, briefly describe the terrain of this sector of the line in which the 8th Durhams had their first fight with the enemy.

The German line was about two hundred and fifty yards to the north.

Soon after 3.30 a.m. heavy rifle fire broke out from the west and lasted for about half an hour, when it died down, and for the rest of the morning it was intermittent from this direction.

At about 4 a.m. the German guns began to shell the Farm with high explosive and burst shrapnel over the neighbourhood. At 11 a.m. the enemy's guns increased their fire and for one and a half hours shells fell at the rate of from forty-five to sixty-eight per minute (they were counted)—all nature of shell being used. In the fields south of the Farm, where "B" and "C" Companies had sheltered along the hedges, casualties were considerable. The farm buildings were by this time a mass of ruins, but beneath them was a large cellar which had been made bomb-proof with sand-bags. It was used as a first-aid post and telephone room for communicating with 2nd (Canadian) Brigade Headquarters. But under the heavy bombardment telephonic communication broke down, and all attempts to communicate with 2nd (Canadian) Brigade Headquarters were fruitless.

At 12.30 p.m. the enemy's artillery switched their fire on to the trenches occupied by "A" and "D" Companies, two officers (Lieuts. J. N. O. Rogers and B. H. Richardson)* and three men being mortally wounded in the first salvo. From this time onwards the trenches were continually bombarded till evening, the enemy's trench mortars joining in. Many

---

* Died in German hands, 31st of May, 1915.

dug-outs were blown in, and men who had taken shelter in them were buried.

About 2 p.m. scouts, who had been sent out to the west from "D" Company's trench, reported the Germans massing in dead ground a little north-west of this Company's line. Shortly afterwards the enemy advanced. Rifle fire was opened on him with good effect. Simultaneously the enemy's guns again opened fire on the farm buildings north and south of the road and the fields south of it, the fire being directed by hostile aircraft who were continually hovering over the line. An attack directed by the enemy against the Canadians on the left was easily repulsed.

Meanwhile in the dead ground north-west of "D" Company the enemy continued to mass his troops. The latter could not be seen from the trenches held by the Monmouths and Suffolks, nor from the farm buildings north of the road.

Capt. Bradford ("D" Company) then extended his left, throwing it back in a southerly direction. Lieut. Wilson took this party out into a field of mustard, but lost heavily through hostile machine-gun fire, it being impossible to locate the gun; he, himself, was wounded and many men killed. About four thousand yards north-west of "D" Company three train-loads of Germans were observed detraining and, although several attempts were made to send back information to the C.O., none succeeded, the runners being shot down.

Between 3 and 3.30 p.m. large numbers of Germans were observed about three thousand yards north, in close order, but they were just beginning to extend and advance in a southerly direction. "B" Company (Major Ritson) was then brought up from reserve and placed under cover east of the farm buildings north of the Gravenstafel road, while Capt. Veitch, with a detachment of men was sent off to some high ground about one thousand two hundred yards on the right flank, as no information could be obtained as to what troops there were in that direction or how they were disposed.

Shortly after 3.30 p.m. "B" Company was ordered to reinforce the left company, *i.e.*, "D," and got to a breastwork very near the latter. But shell fire was so violent that they had to evacuate their position and fall back again to the line of the road. Many men were "gassed" by fumes from the bursting shells. They could see little of the situation on the left owing to thick hedge and brushwood.

By 4 p.m. the enemy had extended east and west from his original position north, and had advanced considerably.

"C" Company was then moved up on the right of "B" Company.

The "Narrative" states that one of the difficulties of the day was the fact that the 8th Durham Light Infantry did not know who held command of the sector of the defences they were in or to whom reports had to be sent in. The Battalion was apparently not under the 28th Division: the Canadian staff officers seemed to be responsible only for their own people. Between 4 and 5 p.m., therefore, Capt. J. A. S. Ritson was sent back to ascertain under whose command the Durhams were and explain the situation, pointing out also that there was a big gap between the right of the Battalion and the next troops, that the enemy was in greatly superior numbers, that heavy casualties were being suffered from hostile shell fire in front and flank, and artillery support was necessary.

But the only information Capt. Ritson appears to have gained was that, after dark, an infantry brigade "standing by" would be moved up to reinforce the Durhams; also that a Canadian major had told him he had orders from the Canadian Brigade to tell the Durhams to retire to the south of Gravenstafel. Needless to say the latter order was ignored.

At about 5.40 p.m. a verbal message was received from the O.C. detachment of the Suffolks asking the Durhams if they were retiring.

"An answer was returned," records the Narrative, "that we were *not* retiring, and that he had to hold on; fresh ammunition was sent up to him and arrangements made to send further supplies if required."

Next, at 6.12 p.m., Capt. Harvey ("A" Company) reported that he was being heavily attacked and asked if he should retire; "You *must* hang on at all costs," was the reply sent from Battalion Headquarters. And hang on he did!

About this period the enemy's shell fire increased in intensity, and both "A" and "D" Companies and the companies along the Gravenstafel road suffered heavy losses; there was also a German battery firing shrapnel in rear of the Durhams, *i.e.*, from the eastern apex of the Ypres Salient. This fire was very galling and caused many casualties.

Came 7 o'clock and the situation desperate. Capt. Bradford, of "D" Company, had only about fifty men left and, being heavily shelled and taken in flank by machine-gun and rifle fire, was forced to fall back. He retired through "A" Company's trench. He then tried to find Headquarters, but missed his way and found himself with the 2nd Northumberland Fusiliers of the 28th Division. Soon after Capt. Harvey also withdrew the remnants of "A" Company to the east.

The enemy now came on in considerable strength, but his ranks were torn by rifle and machine-gun fire, and some three hundred yards from the Durhams he was brought to a standstill, having lost heavily.

"The fire discipline," records the Battalion Narrative, "was excellent and well controlled." A little earlier, between 6.30 and 7 p.m., a company of Middlesex and one of Monmouths, both Territorial troops, had arrived. They had come up partly by accident, having been relieved during the night of the 24th–25th. The reliefs had been late and the two companies, unable to get back to their battalion headquarters owing to daylight, had taken cover during the 25th, but in the evening, hearing that the 8th Durhams were engaged, the two companies moved up "to the sound of the guns."

The Middlesex were immediately sent up to prolong the right, whilst the Monmouths were echeloned in rear of the right flank of the Durhams, as a reserve.

As night came down on the battlefield machine-gun and rifle fire gradually ceased; but occasional bursts of shell fire broke the stillness. Every now and then the Germans sent up Very lights (of which the Durhams had none) which threw a weird light over the fields and hedgerows and the ruins of Boetleer Farm.

All this while, *i.e.*, throughout the 25th, the 8th Durham Light Infantry was still without information as to whose command they were under. Between 7.30 and 8 p.m., therefore, Capt. Ritson was again sent back to report the situation and ascertain if possible who the higher command was. Soon after 8 p.m. he reached Headquarters of the 3rd Royal Fusiliers and, after some delay, got through by telephone to 85th Brigade Headquarters. Having explained the situation he was told that a Territorial brigade was due to relieve the 8th Durhams at 9 p.m., and that it was intended to fall back to a line roughly on the line of the Haanebeek, which was to be held.

Time passed and the Territorial brigade did not materialise. The 8th Durhams therefore continued to reorganise and put the new line into a state of defence. Fresh ammunition was served out and water whenever possible. Patrols were pushed out to gain touch with the enemy. The one company of Monmouths was brought up near the field south of the Farm, and two platoons sent forward to the buildings north of the road. Everyone then dug hard so as to be under cover when dawn broke on the 26th. Snipers were busy during the night, but the patrols dealt with some of them.

At about midnight there was a violent action about a mile east of the Durhams, but no information reached the latter of the cause or result. Probably the 1st Hants of the 11th Brigade, who had come up during the night, had had a tussle with the enemy in getting to their positions; the "Territorial brigade," supposed to be moving up to relieve the Durhams, was probably the 11th Brigade (4th Division) formed of regular troops.

At 2.15 a.m. operation orders for the 26th of April were issued; counter-attacks were to be made by the French and British, by the latter against the centre of the German line from south-west of St. Julien to Turco Farm.

But the story turns first to the right of the line, to Boetleer Farm and the Gravenstafel Ridge, where the gallant Durham Territorials, holding an advanced and exposed position, clung to their positions to the very last.

Dawn broke on the 26th with a thick mist covering the ground. But the new line taken up during the night of the 25th–26th had been inspected and found correct. Patrols reported the enemy not only some three hundred and fifty to four hundred yards north, but overlapping the right flank of the Durhams.

Before it was light the company commanders of the Middlesex and Monmouths reported they had received orders to rejoin their battalions. But as reinforcements (the "Territorial brigade") was still expected, the O.C., Middlesex company, was ordered to wait until the reinforcements had arrived, when he could withdraw, while the O.C., Monmouth company, was told that he could withdraw two platoons (which had suffered very heavy casualties from shrapnel fire during the night), but the other two platoons were to remain in the buildings south of the road.

Soon after 4 a.m. the enemy was reported to be advancing. It was then discovered that both the Middlesex and

Monmouth companies had retired. The former was, however, found and brought up again as quickly as possible into the firing line, but no trace could be found of the two platoons of Monmouths supposed to be in the buildings.

The Narrative of the 8th Durhams states that: "The Germans came on dressed in khaki, calling out that they were British and 'Suffolks'." The disappearance of the Monmouths had caused a gap in the left of the line and into this gap the enemy poured, gaining possession of the buildings on both sides of the Gravenstafel road. Machine-gun fire was then opened on the Durhams, taking the line in enfilade. Simultaneously large numbers of Germans advanced against the centre of the line, turning the right flank of the Middlesex.

The situation was now hopeless and the ridge about Boetleer Farm untenable. Indeed this had been recognised earlier, for both flanks of the Durhams before the action started were unsecured and their whole position in advance of the general line.

As the Farm had now fallen, the Durhams and the company of Middlesex fell back. At first the retirement was somewhat confused, as was natural, but this was checked and the line halted about three hundred yards in the rear and reorganised, though under fire. The enemy was in vastly superior force, and as the new line on which the Durhams had halted was commanded by high ground on right and left, a further retirement was ordered. The remnants of this gallant Battalion then fell back by alternate sections, the line being then extended to wide intervals to occupy a larger front. A position was then taken up about the line of the Haanebeek.

In spite of hostile artillery fire the Durhams and Middlesex, being strung out over a wide front, suffered few casualties. On the other hand, by steady fire, they shot down large numbers of the enemy and presently brought him altogether to a standstill. Lieut. Kirkup was then sent back to find out where the promised reinforcements were. They were found south of the Haanebeek and the Durhams were ordered to fall back on them. This retirement was carried out in good order and without pressure from the enemy. At 1 a.m. on the 27th the 8th Durham Light Infantry received orders to withdraw to Verlorenhoek, and at 3 a.m. the Battalion reported at that place. Those who came out of the battle-front numbered only 6 officers (Lieut.-Colonel Turnbull, Capt. and Adjutant Stevens,

Capt. Veitch, Lieuts. Kirkup and Johnson, and Second-Lieut. Whall) and 140 other ranks. They were at once organised into one company and put into dug-outs just west of the village.

The splendid defence of Boetleer Farm and the Gravenstafel Ridge by the 8th Durham Light Infantry and odd troops attached was suitably recognised by General Bulfin, commanding 28th Division. This officer placed on record: "The greatest possible credit is due to the 8th Durham Light Infantry and the small detachments who, in spite of having their flanks turned and being enfiladed, remained in the northern line, beating off all attacks and inflicting heavy loss on the enemy and thereby securing the flank of the 85th Infantry Brigade."

The Battalion had lost 19 officers and 574 men,* but by their hard fighting and heroic sacrifice helped to lay the foundation of the fine reputation held by the Northumbrian Division in France and Flanders throughout the War.

Of the three other battalions of the Durham Light Infantry Brigade during the 26th, the 6th Durham Light Infantry were placed under the orders of Colonel Bridgeford, 2nd Shropshire Light Infantry, and with two companies of the Shropshires moved to a position about half-way between Frezenberg and Zonnebeke, coming under fire at about 11.15 a.m. when they were five hundred yards east of Verlorenhoek. The Durhams were on the right, Shropshires on the left; they faced north-east, the right of the former battalion resting on the Ypres–Roulers railway. In this position they spent the whole of the 26th of April. With the Shropshires they had been sent out to support a mixed detachment of troops who were defending a part of the line on the left of the 8th Durham Light Infantry. Under

---

* In detail: Capts. W. H. Coulson and L. V. B. Johnson, Lieuts. G. E. Blackett, J. L. Wood, W. Marshall, Second-Lieuts. J. N. O. Rogers, B. H. Richardson, J. O. Wilson and 81 other ranks killed; Major J. R. Ritson, Capts. F. G. Harvey, T. A. Bradford, Lieuts. E. A. Leybourne, J. R. Brass, Second-Lieuts. F. M. Weeks, E. H. Motum, T. W. Callinan, Lieut. and Quartermaster W. G. Francis and 153 other ranks wounded; Lieut. J. A. Stenhouse, R.A.M.C. (the Battalion Medical Officer), Second-Lieut. A. W. Nesbitt and 340 other ranks missing; Lieut. J. R. Brass died of wounds on the 27th of April.

The Diary of the Durham Light Infantry Brigade for the 27th of April gives the losses in other ranks as 202 killed, 45 wounded and 325 missing; also Second-Lieut. H. W. Nesbitt wounded and not missing, and Major J. R. Ritson and Capt. J. Turnbull missing.

heavy shell fire the 6th Durham Light Infantry held on all day, suffering many casualties.

The 7th Durham Light Infantry were, at 2 p.m., placed also under the command of Colonel Bridgeford and ordered to advance towards Zevenkote and Gravenstafel. They eventually fetched up north of Zonnebeke, where they supported troops of the 85th Brigade. The 7th also were under heavy shell fire. After dark the Battalion returned to Verlorenhoek. With pardonable pride the Battalion Diary records that: "The advance and retirement were made in good order and all ranks behaved splendidly." For no man can tell how he will behave in the face of an enemy's shot and shell until he receives his baptism of fire.

The 9th Durham Light Infantry appear to have remained all day in the neighbourhood of Verlorenhoek.

Of the York and Durham Brigade on the 26th there is little to record: the 1/4th East Yorkshires and 4th Green Howards were further back in Camp "A." The 5th Durham Light Infantry and the 5th Green Howards spent the day in trenches south-east of St. Julien, shelled heavily and sniped continuously. At night both battalions went into the front line, relieving a London regiment. The 5th Green Howards were on the right and the 5th Durham Light Infantry on the left. The line ran along the northern side of the Wieltje–Gravenstafel road.

For the Northumberland Infantry Brigade, however, the 26th of April was a day of something in the nature of disaster for, though fighting with the utmost gallantry, the three battalions engaged with the enemy (4th, 6th and 7th Northumberland Fusiliers) suffered very heavy losses, while the Brigadier was also killed.

The 4th, 5th, 6th and 7th Northumberland Fusiliers were, during the early morning of the 26th, concentrated at Wieltje and placed under the orders of the 1st Canadian Division, to whom the Northumberland Brigade was to act as a reserve.

At about 10.15 a.m. Brig.-General J. F. Riddell (commanding Northumberland Brigade) received orders from the G.O.C., 10th Infantry Brigade, to verify a report from the 28th Division that the enemy was breaking through the front line near Fortuin; General Riddell was also ordered to counter-attack with whatever force he deemed essential if such action was necessary.

The O.C., 5th Northumberland Fusiliers (Lieut.-Colonel A. H. Coles) was ordered to send out an officer's patrol and then proceed with his Battalion to Fortuin with orders to counter-attack if necessary. The 5th Battalion arrived at its destination at 11.40 a.m. but found no sign of a break through. A message was sent back to Brigade Headquarters to that effect. The Brigade Major then ordered the 5th Northumberland Fusiliers to retire or, if that was inadvisable, dig in. The Battalion had already suffered casualties and was being heavily shelled. A reply was therefore sent back to Brigade Headquarters that the 5th Northumberland Fusiliers would entrench. This they proceeded to do, with the result that they took no part in the operations in which the three other battalions of the Brigade were involved.

At 1.30 p.m. operation orders were received by General Riddell from the 1st Canadian Division. The Northumberland Brigade was to attack St. Julien in co-operation with the Lahore Division and a battalion of the 10th Infantry Brigade (4th Division). The attack was to take place at 2.5 p.m. The artillery was to open fire at 1.20 p.m. when the attacking troops were to advance to positions from which to deliver the attack at 2.5 p.m.

The difficulties confronting the Brigade were considerable: for one thing no officer (regimental or staff) of the Brigade had previously reconnoitred the ground between Wieltje and St. Julien, approximately a distance of one and three-quarter miles. No information was received (nor could it be obtained) of the actual position of the enemy's trenches, or even of our own. It was not then known that the G.H.Q. Line was strongly wired and that there were only certain places through which troops would be able to pass. Finally, no communication was made with the artillery and no artillery officer got in touch with the Brigadier.

Orders only having arrived at 1.30 p.m., the other attacking troops had gone forward to their positions ten minutes earlier (at 1.20 p.m.), the Brigade having only thirty-five minutes in which to prepare for the assault. Nevertheless, considering that any failure to attack on the part of his Brigade might seriously hamper the operations, General Riddell decided to carry out the orders he had received, impossible as they seemed.

By 1.50 p.m. battalions were on the move.

The 4th Northumberland Fusiliers (Lieut.-Colonel A. J. Foster) had been ordered to attack on the right, *i.e.*, with their left on the Wieltje–St. Julien road; the 6th Northumberland Fusiliers (Lieut.-Colonel G. R. B. Spain) on the left, with their right on the Wieltje–St. Julien road; the 7th Northumberland Fusiliers (Lieut.-Colonel G. Scott Jackson) were to support the 4th Battalion.*

It was 2.5 p.m. before the leading battalion reached the G.H.Q. Line. No sooner had they deployed on both sides of the Wieltje–St. Julien road than they came under very heavy shell and rifle fire. The thick wire entanglements in front of the G.H.Q. Line, not having been reconnoitred, caused delay and heavy losses, for the men were bound to bunch together in order to get through the gaps.

However, the wire was presently negotiated and the advance began towards St. Julien. It said much for their pre-war training and stamina that these Territorial troops, subjected to all the nerve-racking experiences of a great battle, advanced steadily and most gallantly in the face of violent machine-gun fire and a murderous rifle fire. Most of this machine-gun fire came from Kitchener's Wood on the left front.

By 2.45 p.m. the 4th and 6th Battalions had reached the front line where they were to find the battalion of the 10th Brigade, which was to connect the Northumberland Brigade with the Lahore Division on the left. By now the 7th Battalion had been absorbed into the line. No troops of the 10th Brigade were seen; indeed their orders had been cancelled earlier and they were not there. But, pushing on with the greatest dash without artillery support, isolated parties of the 6th Battalion reached positions about two hundred and fifty yards in front of the front trench and occupied some small trenches from which the enemy had apparently retired. The 4th and 7th Battalions were unable to get beyond the front line mentioned.

The records state that: "The culminating point in the advance of the 6th Battalion, Northumberland Fusiliers, was reached at about 3.45 p.m. when, unsupported on their left flank and heavily shelled with high-explosive shells, they were compelled to dig themselves in, and remained in possession of the ground

---

* It is worthy of note that the Northumberland Infantry Brigade was the first Territorial brigade (as such) to go into battle during the Great War.

they had gained until dusk, when they returned to the front-line trench."

Just when the 6th Battalion had reached its furthest point in the direction of St. Julien, *i.e.*, at 3.45 p.m., their Brigadier met his death. General Riddell (accompanied by his Brigade Major), for the purpose of getting into closer touch with his battalion commanders, left the support trench in which he had established his headquarters at 3.30 p.m. and proceeded towards Vanheule Farm. At about one hundred and fifty yards south of the Farm he received a bullet through the head and fell dead.

Command of the Northumberland Brigade then devolved upon Colonel Foster of the 4th Battalion, who ordered his own and the 6th and 7th Battalions to dig in as best they could. In this position they remained for the night when, after Colonel Foster had discussed the situation with General Hull (G.O.C., 10th Brigade), the three Northumberland battalions were withdrawn early on the 27th and subsequently sent back to Wieltje.

The Northumberland Brigade in this attack had lost 42 officers and 1,912 other ranks—over two-thirds of its strength.*

"Although the task set to the Brigade had been impossible and its losses devastating, it had not hesitated to obey. Having arrived at a line beyond which no one might pass and live, the men got shelter where they could, but there was no thought of retiring."†

There are in existence further notes (written by officers of the Battalion) on the attack by the 6th Northumberland Fusiliers from which the following extracts are taken, as they are of historical interest to the Regiment:

"Within five minutes of Colonel Spain receiving verbal instructions from Brig.-General Riddell the Battalion deployed into artillery formation, "A" and "B" Companies in the front line and "C" and "D" Companies in the second line at fifty yards' interval and two hundred yards' distance. Directly we left the cover of the village the enemy literally poured shrapnel into our ranks, inflicting heavy casualties. The first rush took us over a shallow hollow of meadow land littered with dead

---

* The 6th Battalion Northumberland Fusiliers lost 7 officers and 112 other ranks killed; 7 officers and 492 other ranks wounded.

† Official History (Military Operations) of the War.

and wounded, for the enemy's fire was intense. Up the rise we began to meet machine-gun bullets, rifle fire and high-explosive shells from all directions, the result of which thinned our ranks considerably.

"We advanced about a mile in this formation and, after clearing some forward trenches, a small wood and a few scattered farm buildings, we were eventually checked within four hundred yards of our objective, although some of our men actually got into the outskirts of the village. As there were no reinforcements available, those that were left held on to their positions until nightfall, when we were withdrawn to the trenches held by the 4th Division."

Referring to the advance again the note adds: "We had not advanced very far beyond the trenches occupied by the 4th Division when we were held up by barbed wire, which had to be cut before we could get forward, and it was at this point where many of our officers and men made the supreme sacrifice, going forward to cut the wire to allow us to pass. All the enemy's machine-guns appeared to be trained on to this wire, for our casualties here were appalling. One of our first officers to fall was Lieut. Mortimer who, together with many of his platoon, was killed by a shell bursting right amongst them. When we got through this wire a prolonged cheer from the Canadian troops in our rear did much to encourage our men and they again went forward, suffering losses that could never be replaced. Lieut. Garton, in spite of heavy machine-gun fire and shells, cut a gap in the wire and turning round, smiling, said, 'Come on, boys! We will get at them now,' but unfortunately he was killed before going much further. Our ranks had been well thinned by now, and even when the 7th Battalion joined us, coming up with great dash, our men were few for they, the 7th, had also suffered great loss.

"This was our first encounter with the enemy, our first taste of actual warfare, and the Battalion acquitted itself in a manner befitting the traditions of the Regiment to which they belonged. Our training stood us in good stead, for the attack was carried out on the same lines as the field days we had had during our sojourn in England, with the exception that we had real warfare conditions to contend with instead of imaginary ones.

"The enemy had everything in their favour, and their gunners and riflemen took every advantage of the target offered them. In spite of this hail of shot and shell, coming as it did from all angles, the line never wavered, and at each forward word those that were able responded manfully to the orders and signals given by their officers and N.C.O.s. The coolness and leadership displayed by our officers was superb and served as a splendid example to the men, inspiring them with confidence and courage."

The first honour came to the Battalion in this action, Corporal H. Smith, of "C" Company, winning the D.C.M. for conspicuous gallantry. Although shot in the shoulder himself, he dressed Lieut. Bowden's wounds and, assisted by Private H. E. Lewis, carried that officer to the nearest dressing station.

As already stated, the three Northumberland Battalions were withdrawn early on the 27th and were subsequently sent back to Wieltje.*

For the Northumbrian Division the 27th of April passed practically without incident. The enemy's shell fire caused further loss, for by now the dangerous salient held by our gallant troops was such that the German artillery could bring destructive fire on it from the south, east and north; indeed it was, as the Official History states, already difficult "for the enemy to avoid hitting something or somebody with every shell."

The Northumberland Infantry Brigade remained all day in bivouacs and dug-outs near Wieltje. At 5 p.m. Colonel G. P. T. Fielding, Coldstream Guards, arrived and assumed command of the Brigade, vice Brig.-General Riddell.

The 1/4th East Yorkshires and 4th Green Howards of the York and Durham Brigade were still in camp west of Ypres; the 5th Green Howards were in the trenches at Horseshoe, taken over from a London regiment, the 5th Durham Light Infantry being on the left.

Of the Durham Light Infantry Brigade, with the exception of the 6th Durham Light Infantry, who still occupied trenches from the level-crossing three thousand yards east-north-east of Verlorenhoek–Hill 37, the 7th, 8th and 9th Durham Light Infantry remained all day in the neighbourhood of that village. The gallant 8th Battalion (5 officers and 148 other ranks) had rejoined the Brigade at daybreak.

---

* The total casualties to date, *i.e.*, to the morning of the 27th (inclusive) as given in the Diary of the "A and Q" Staff of the Division are as follows: officers—26 killed, 45 wounded, 14 missing; other ranks—332 killed, 1,143 wounded, 1,169 missing. The strength of the Division on landing in France was 572 officers and 16,858 other ranks.

During the day the Lahore Division had made further (but fruitless) counter-attacks upon the enemy, but on the right of the line no hostile infantry attack had developed against the 4th and 28th Divisions, though the enemy's shell fire was heavy. His quietude, however, was suspicious and we know now that he was preparing another gas attack.

Again on the 28th there is little to record concerning the Northumbrian Division. On this date all troops under the command of General Plumer were officially designated "Plumer's Force" and when, during the evening, Headquarters of the Northumbrian Division at Steenvoorde received by telegram the constitution of the Force, it was found that the Northumberland Infantry Brigade was attached to the Canadian Division, and the York and Durham and the Durham Light Infantry Brigades to the 28th Division.

The general situation of all British troops in the salient was, at this date, causing Sir John French great anxiety. It had become perfectly obvious that the very vulnerable line now occupied from the Menin Road thence round the Polygon Wood, east of Zonnebeke to Berlin Wood, where the line turned back sharply westwards past Fortuin to the junction between the British and French near Turco Farm, could only be maintained at continued heavy losses. The French, on our left, had cleared the enemy from the western bank of the Canal, but it was becoming increasingly clear to Sir John French that they could not hope to regain the ground lost on the 22nd during the first gas attack. Nor could he (Sir John), in view of larger operations due to take place further south, spare sufficient troops to engage in operations on a large scale in the Salient.

Faced with these difficulties, there was no other course but to withdraw the line to a less exposed position, and with this intention General Plumer was instructed to select new positions and make all necessary arrangements for a withdrawal. The French, of course, protested, but as they were unable to retake their lost positions it was essential to prevent further unnecessary losses in the British Forces.

The new "Ypres Salient," as it was soon to be, is thus described in the Official History (Military Operations) of the War:

"The line on which General Plumer selected to retire retained Hill 60, then ran to a point on the Menin Road in front of Hooge, included Frezenberg Ridge and then continued to Mouse Trap Farm, whence it turned west to the Canal as before. Thus the greater part of it was on the forward slopes of Frezenberg and Mouse Trap Ridges, and therein differed from the switch line begun on the night of the 26th–27th, which was sited behind the crest of Frezenberg Ridge. By withdrawing to the selected line an area would be abandoned about five miles across the base, a mile deep near Hooge, two and a half miles deep near Frezenberg; but once it was decided to leave Gravenstafel Ridge, this line was the first on which a stand could be made."

This new line had to be prepared immediately, and large working parties, drawn from the 28th and Northumbrian Divisions, and all available engineer companies, were employed every night in digging and wiring trenches.

On the morning of the 28th the Northumberland Infantry Brigade received orders from 1st Canadian Headquarters to take over a portion of the G.H.Q. Line east of Wieltje; during the night of the 28th–29th this was done by the 5th Northumberland Fusiliers, the other three battalions remaining where they were. Of the York and Durham Brigade the 1/4th East Yorkshires and 4th Green Howards relieved the 5th Durham Light Infantry and 5th Green Howards respectively in trenches running along the northern side of the St. Jean–Passchendaele road, Green Howards on the right, East Yorkshires on the left.

Capt. B. M. S. Sharp (wounded later during the relief) thus describes a reconnaissance of the trenches to be taken over, which company commanders with N.C.O.s made at dusk, immediately on receipt of orders to go into the line:

"O.C.s companies hied them there with their two N.C.O.s at dusk, through that hell on earth by now strewn with dead animals and bits of everything recognisable in the way of equipment, through St. Jean, now utterly destroyed and slightly more objectionable than even Ypres; church gutted, graveyard shelled and a heap of coffins and battered headstones. The 10th Brigade (4th Division), to which we were attached, had headquarters here—a cottage sand-bagged round—and the shots from a battery of ours just touched the tops of the trees as we passed. We found our 'dump' and by-and-by our trenches occupied by the 5th Durham Light Infantry. Sorry trenches they were, freshly made, very bad, narrow, with scarcely any traverses, nothing at all behind and only 'funk' holes for shelter."

The relief of the 5th Green Howards and 5th Durham Light Infantry was completed at about midnight, but the East Yorkshires had Lieut. S. H. Hellyer and five other ranks killed and eleven other ranks wounded by shell fire. Both the Green Howards and the Durham Light Infantry then marched back to huts near Brielen.

On the 29th the French regained Steenstraat, but the Germans still remained in possession of a narrow strip of ground on the western side of the Canal, from Steenstraat to Het Sas. On the British front the enemy made no attack. Neither did the British attack, as the French were reorganising for attacks which either did not materialise or made little progress.

On this date, at 5.45 p.m., the Northumberland Infantry Brigade received orders that working parties would be required to dig a line south of the Ypres–Zonnebeke road (astride the Menin road). At 6 p.m. the 4th and 6th Northumberland Fusiliers were ordered to find the first relief for these parties.

Some amusement was caused at Brigade Headquarters by the receipt of curious orders. At 7.30 p.m. General Vaughan, commanding a cavalry brigade, had arrived with written orders to take over the dug-outs occupied by the Lahore Division. The dug-outs of the Lahore Division were not to be discovered, and General Vaughan then suggested that a mistake had been made and that he was to take over the dug-outs of the Cavalry Brigade. He received the following astonishing message: "As you are to move permanently the Northumberland Infantry Brigade will *take over the harness of the Cavalry Brigade.*" Further messages elicited the information that "harness" was a clerical error and that "bivouacs" had been meant.

The 5th and 7th Northumberland Fusiliers were then (9.5 p.m.) moved to the neighbourhood of Hell Fire Corner, and the 4th and 6th Battalions informed that they would not be relieved from digging during the night as they were to do a double shift.

Of the York and Durham Brigade on the 29th, the 1/4th East Yorkshires and 4th Green Howards had a most uncomfortable time in moving up to the trenches. Owing to complicated orders it was not until the night of the 30th that the former Battalion (of which two companies had been attached to the 1st Hants and two to the Rifle Brigade) moved into the front line just west of Berlin Wood; the Green Howards (similarly split up) were attached to the 1st Somerset Light Infantry and London Rifle Brigade, and occupied a line west of the other two battalions.

The 6th Durham Light Infantry were relieved from the trenches on the 29th and rejoined the Durham Light Infantry Brigade at Verlorenhoek. On the night of the 29th–30th one company of the 7th Durham Light Infantry was sent off on attachment to the 3rd Middlesex Regiment, who were holding the front line north-east of Zonnebeke. The Brigade furnished 1,400 men the same night as a working party to prepare a defensive line west of Verlorenhoek.

Thus, a week after the first gas attack, the Northumbrian Division was still split up and only the three Infantry Brigades had been drawn into the fight.

There is with the Appendices to the Divisional Diary for April, 1915, an interesting statement giving the "Location of Units," from which it may be gathered that, while the infantry of the Division were having a particularly strenuous time in the front line, the remaining units (with the exception of the Divisional Engineers who were at work on the trenches south-east of Zillebeke) were "kicking their heels" somewhere behind the line; Steenvoorde still sheltered Divisional Headquarters, Headquarters, Signal Company, Yorkshire Hussars, Cyclist Company and the Divisional Train. The Field Ambulances were a mile east of the town; the Divisional Artillery was at Winnezeele, Brandhoek, Le Temple and Riveld, the Ammunition Column being at Terdeghem.

The effect of this enforced absence from the battlefield is reflected in an entry by the A.D.M.S. of the Division in his diary on the 26th of April. Rumours and stories of what was happening in the forward area travelled quickly, and the *esprit de corps* of the Division was so keen that the impatience of the Chief Medical Officer may be understood and forgiven:

"It is herewith recorded," he states, "that the A.D.M.S. and the Divisional Ambulance are deprived by the present arrangements of the honour of doing the work they came out to perform—the succouring of their own sick and wounded. It is a great blow and we feel it intensely."

But if the medical men of the Field Ambulances were kept out of the forward area, the Battalion Medical Officers were doing their jobs splendidly. Four of them had already gone down: Major Mackay, of the 6th Durham Light Infantry, and Capt. D. H. Weir, 4th Northumberland Fusiliers, had been wounded; Lieut. E. Babst, of the 5th Northumberland Fusiliers, had been evacuated to hospital suffering from shock, and Lieut. J. A. Stenhouse, 8th Durham Light Infantry, had been wounded and captured in the last fight of that Battalion at Boetleer Farm. These four officers were replaced from the 1st and 2nd Northumberland Field Ambulances, so that after all the Divisional Medical Officers were not quite left out in the cold.

Mention has been made of the Divisional Engineers: the 2nd Field Company, which was at Brandhoek on the 25th, was warned by the C.R.E., Second Army, and C.R.E., Fifth Corps, that it would be required for work on the 26th. The following night two sections (right half-company) were at work on the new switch line passing through Hooge and joining up with the front-line trenches near Hill 60. On the right the left half-company was at work in the same area.

The 2nd Field Company as a whole was bivouacked one mile east of Vlamertinghe. To get to their work they had to march five miles. Usually sections left bivouacs at 7 p.m. and were at work by 9 p.m. But they had to leave off work at 2 a.m. in order to get clear of Ypres on the return march (another five miles) by dawn.

For several nights this work was continued, always more or less under shell fire; but even in their bivouacs the Sappers were under fire, for on the 29th Capt. Dodds was wounded.

The Signal Company must have been at work in the forward area, for on the 25th two N.C.O.s and one man were killed, and two signallers wounded; on the 29th Lieut. T. L. Bainbridge was killed and five sappers wounded.

On the afternoon of the 1st of May definite orders were issued to General Plumer to begin the withdrawal from the eastern part of the Salient that night. In deference to our Allies, Sir John French had three times postponed these orders, but on the final failure of the French on the 1st of May it was evident that the lost ground could not be recovered.

In view, therefore, of impending operations on the Arras– Neuve Chapelle front the Allied Commanders-in-Chief agreed to act on the defensive about Ypres, the British to withdraw from their exposed positions to the line already described, and the French to maintain their positions on the left of the British.

The withdrawal began on the night of the 1st–2nd of May, beginning at 8 p.m. The first stage did not affect the Northumbrian Division, which on the morning of the 2nd still occupied the following positions: Northumberland Brigade, south of Verlorenhoek; Durham Light Infantry Brigade, Frezenberg; of the York and Durham Brigade, the 1/4th East Yorkshires and 4th Green Howards were still in the front line attached to the 4th Division, while the 5th Green Howards and 5th Durham Light Infantry were near Vlamertinghe.

Dawn on the early morning of the 2nd was comparatively quiet, the enemy practically quiescent. But soon after noon his guns suddenly opened a violent bombardment along the front held by the three brigades of the 4th Division, from Berlin Wood to Turco Farm, and on the right of the French. Without interruption this savage hail of shell fell upon the trenches of our devoted troops until 4 p.m., when gas shells were used until 4.30 p.m. Then from the German trenches issued again deadly clouds of yellowish-green gas, which floated over towards the British line on its ghastly errand of asphyxiation. The line "gassed" was roughly from Fortuin to Turco Farm and the French line east of the Canal.

By this time, however, improvised respirators, made of cotton-wool, handkerchiefs, mufflers and even towels, soaked in soda or whatever moisture was available and held or tied over the mouth, were in use, and although one company of a battalion of the 12th Brigade near Mouse Trap Farm (where the gas was thickest), which had not received warning in time to allow the adjustment of respirators, was temporarily driven from the trenches, the line generally stood firm and the gas attack was a failure.* Every attempt by the Germans to utilise the surprise occasioned by the gas discharge was frustrated, and by 8 p.m. that night all was quiet again.

Yet those battalions of the Northumbrian Division in the line suffered from the enemy's violent bombardment. The 1/4th East Yorkshires had 10 other ranks killed and 13 wounded, the 4th Green Howards 6 officers wounded and 1 "gassed," while in other ranks their losses were 34 killed and 74 wounded of the latter battalion, Major H. L. de Legh is mentioned for

---

* Another gas attack, on the previous day, against Hill 60 was also a failure.

his gallantry in getting fifteen wounded men out of a burning cellar which had been set on fire by the enemy's artillery.

With the exception of the 4th Northumberland Fusiliers, the Northumberland Brigade was still digging and working hard on the line near Bellewaarde; the 4th Battalion, however, was at Wieltje digging second-line trenches in front of the village. Their narrative for the 2nd of May is very brief, but an excellent "tabloid" description of their experiences: "Wet, misty. Balloons. No Taubes. Heavy shelling and gas at 4 p.m. Some of first line through us. Deployed along dug-outs on G.H.Q. Line in case counter-attack necessary. Wet handkerchiefs, cap comforters used. Relieved 11 p.m."

Throughout the night of the 2nd–3rd of May the enemy kept up spasmodic shell fire, but as dawn broke it became more methodical. His trench mortars then joined in. On this occasion the line most heavily shelled was that held by the 11th and 85th Brigades, *i.e.*, the apex of the salient near Berlin Wood, where the 1/4th East Yorkshires were holding the line with the Rifle Brigade and the Hampshire Regiment, with the Buffs and Royal Fusiliers on their right. The East Yorkshires, "under a constant hail of shell and rifle bullets"— to use their own words—lost during the day 1 officer and 22 other ranks killed, and 5 officers and 42 other ranks wounded.

Between 2 and 3 p.m. that afternoon, after concentrating (so it seemed) every gun on Berlin Wood, the enemy again attacked, but all the advantage he gained was a precarious footing in the Wood; but that mattered little as the line at night was to be evacuated by us.

On the night of the 3rd–4th the withdrawal operations were concluded, and when dawn broke on the 4th the enemy shelled the trenches we had occupied in the belief that we still held them. It was not until much later in the morning that he discovered we had retired.

"The new line now established formed a semicircle of three miles' radius round Ypres. The 27th Division held the sector from near Hill 60 to half a mile short of the Roulers railway; the 28th Division across the railway to Mouse Trap Farm; and the 4th Division a short front from Mouse Trap Farm (inclusive) to Turco Farm."*

---

* Official History (Military Operations) of the War.

On the 2nd and 3rd of May brigades and battalions of the Northumbrian Division in the battle area had begun to withdraw, and by the 4th the Division was concentrated in an area about six miles west of Poperinghe, in villages and camps, Divisional Headquarters being still in Steenvoorde.

On the 4th of May also the Commander-in-Chief (Sir John French) inspected and addressed battalions of the three Infantry Brigades, which had been drawn up at various points along the road, Steenvoorde–Droglandt–Hatou–St. Jan Ter Biezen–Poperinghe. Sir John congratulated the brigades on the splendid work they had done and on their fine soldierly qualities.

Thus ended the Battle of St. Julien, which will for all time be memorable in the history of the Northumbrian Division. Tried in the fire, the Territorials had not been found wanting; their pre-war training, their courage, their tenacity and endurance, had all been put to the crucial test and they had emerged, praised and honoured by the Regular Army, by whose side they had fought the common enemy.*

THE BATTLE OF FREZENBERG RIDGE: 8th–13th MAY

On the morning of the 8th of May the British front line in the Ypres Salient, *i.e.*, northerly from the Ypres–Comines railway, just west of Hill 60, ran along the eastern edges of Armagh and Sanctuary Woods, crossed the Menin road about a quarter of a mile west of Clapham Junction, thence east of Bellewaarde Lake, north to Frezenberg. From the latter village the line turned in a north-westerly direction to Mouse Trap Farm and beyond to Canadian and Turco Farms, where it joined the right of the French line. The British line was held by the 27th, 28th and 4th Divisions, in that order from right to left. The Northumbrian Division was still out of the line west of Poperinghe.

Against the three British divisions mentioned above, the enemy had massed the greater part of three corps, for our withdrawal had encouraged him to make another attempt to

---

* Nowhere with the Divisional records is there a statement as to the collective casualties of the Northumbrian Division from the 26th of April to the 4th of May inclusive, but from the Diary of the "A and Q" Staff approximately they were: officers—killed 27, wounded 81, missing 14; other ranks—killed 445, wounded 1,915, missing 1,264. Total casualties—officers 122, other ranks 3,624.

overrun the Ypres Salient. The positions abandoned by us on the Zonnebeke and Gravenstafel Ridges gave the enemy splendid observation over our line which, particularly in the centre about Frezenberg and the ridge on which the village stood, was very exposed.

Following on a disturbed night, the German artillery at 5.30 a.m. on the 8th of May opened a violent bombardment of the whole line, concentrating especially on the exposed forward slopes of Frezenberg Ridge. By 9 a.m. the bombardment had become terrific, and soon parapets were flattened out and the trenches in many parts of the line obliterated. Even so, when at 8.30 a.m. the German infantry advanced, there arose from amidst the battered defences and ruined trenches a line of shaken, but still defiant and determined khaki troops who, with the courage of lions, drove off the attackers. Another attempt, made a little later, shared the same fate, though practically all of that gallant band of defenders were killed, wounded or buried.

In spite of the fine defence put up, Frezenberg, Verlorenhoek and the ground south and north-west of those two villages had to be abandoned, and when night fell on the 8th our line still ran along the eastern edge of the wood east of Bellewaarde Lake, but bent back just west of Verlorenhoek, running north-west to the Wieltje–St. Julien road, west of which no attacks had taken place.

On the 9th, 10th and 11th of May the enemy shifted the area of his attacks to the Menin road in endeavours to break through, but his gains were negligible and there never was any danger of the front being broken. The 12th was uneventful so far as attacks were concerned. On the 13th, however, another heavy attack was launched by the Germans, on this occasion between Hooge and the Ypres–St. Julien road; they gained a little ground in the neighbourhood of Hooge and the Bellewaarde Lake and between Bellewaarde and Mouse Trap Farm, but that was all. Casualties were very heavy on both sides.

During the six days, *i.e.*, 8th to 13th of May inclusive, the Northumbrian Division, though still not entering into the line as a division, was, nevertheless, called upon to furnish troops as reinforcements and for working parties, and for the first time since arrival in France certain units of the Divisional Artillery went into action; indeed the story of the battle (so far as the Northumbrian Division was concerned) begins with the gunners.

As early as the 5th of May (at 3.45 p.m.) Divisional Headquarters received a wire from Plumer's Force stating that with the permission of G.H.Q. two batteries of 5-in. howitzers and one heavy battery would be placed at the disposal of the Fifth Corps. At 7 p.m. another message arrived to say that an officer from each howitzer battery was to report immediately to 28th Division, and one officer of the heavy battery would report to 4th Division for orders. On receipt of these orders batteries were instructed to be held in readiness to move at short notice, and representative officers from the howitzer and heavy batteries were sent up to the 28th and 4th Divisions respectively.

The 4th Northumbrian (Howitzer) Brigade received orders to march at 12.30 a.m. on the 6th to a point one thousand yards west of Vlamertinghe. The two batteries (4th and 5th Durham) with the Brigade Ammunition Column set out at 1 a.m., and reached their destination by 6.30 a.m. The Brigade Commander and the Battery Commanders then spent the morning making a reconnaissance for gun positions to be occupied that night. At 8 p.m. the batteries advanced and went into action, the 4th Battery just north of the Menin road and three thousand yards east of Ypres, the 5th Battery three hundred yards south of La Brique and one thousand yards north-east of Ypres. The wagon lines were eight hundred yards east of Vlamertinghe, on the Poperinghe–Ypres road, while Brigade Headquarters, with the Brigade Ammunition Column, moved to Brandhoek. Batteries were now under the 28th Division.

Both Batteries were now well within range of fire, being only some two miles from the enemy's front line.

On the 7th the 4th (Durham) Battery fired twenty rounds, and the 5th (Durham) Battery sixteen rounds; these were probably registration rounds, for when, on the 8th, the attack on Frezenberg began the 4th Battery fired three hundred and ninety-two rounds; the number of rounds fired by the 5th Battery is not given.

The following narrative, taken from Brigade Headquarters Diary, being of historical interest as it was the first battle in which the Brigade was engaged, is given in full:

"About 5 a.m. the enemy commenced a serious attack which developed until, about 9 a.m., when the 4th Battery was obliged to start gun fire. By 10.30 a.m. they were reduced to eleven rounds. Ammunition was replenished under heavy fire about 12.30 p.m. The teams were hidden in an avenue of trees four hundred yards in rear of the Battery, while single wagons were driven up to the guns. Between 1 p.m. and 2 p.m. Farrier-Sergeant Robertson returned to the Wagon Lines and had orders to bring that wagon and four gun limbers out full. Between 4 and 5 p.m. he was again on the position and emptied the wagon and gun limbers. He then returned with the five wagons and gun limbers hidden in the avenue; he had orders to return with five wagon-loads of ammunition, but on arrival at the Wagon Lines that order was cancelled, and Farrier-Sergeant Robertson was ordered to take out the wagon teams only, as the Battery was to be withdrawn.

"About 9 a.m. the 5th Battery was heavily engaged, and by about 10.30 a.m. orders were sent to the Wagon Lines for ammunition. About 1.30 p.m. four wagons arrived close to the position, but could not go right up to the guns, as they would, in so doing, mask the fire of the 103rd Battery, R.F.A. The teams had, owing to shell fire, to be withdrawn two hundred yards further down the road under cover of some buildings, and ammunition was carried up by hand. The teams got back to the Wagon Lines without casualty."

The 4th Battery on the 8th had 1 man killed and 1 N.C.O. and 1 man wounded; the 5th Battery also had 1 man killed, 8 N.C.O.s and men wounded, and Lieut. A. Coulson and 2 men missing.

By 4 a.m. on the 9th all guns, carriages, horses and personnel of both Batteries (less wounded) had arrived at the Wagon Lines. During the day reconnaissances were made for fresh gun positions, and at night the 4th Battery came again into action two hundred yards north-west of Lock No. 12 on the Ypres Canal (immediately north of Ypres), and the 5th Battery four hundred yards south-west of Ypres Lunatic Asylum. Neither of these places could be described as a "healthy spot." Neither Battery fired during the 10th or 11th of May, but the 4th was heavily shelled for four hours, though only one man was wounded. The 5th, during the day, was placed at the disposal of the 27th Division and, having reconnoitred a position alongside the Ypres–Roulers railway, just north of the Menin road, two thousand eight hundred yards from the centre of Ypres, one section (under Capt. Anderson) occupied that position at night. In coming into action, 1 man and 5 horses were wounded. On the 12th only the 5th Battery fired eight rounds.

Both Batteries were still in action on the 13th of May, but the 4th did not fire. The 5th, however, tells the following story: "About 7 a.m. the 4th D.G.s [Dragoon Guards], who were occupying trenches 1,600 yards in front of the 5th Battery forward section, were heavily shelled and put out of their trenches. Lieut. W. Golding, who was in these trenches as F.O.O. [Forward Observing Officer] joined in a bayonet charge (himself killing three Germans with his revolver) and then, on our cavalry being driven back, he raced across the open under very heavy fire and switched the fire of the Section on to the advancing enemy. The Section fired 202 rounds between 8 a.m. and 9.30 a.m. and materially assisted in stopping the enemy. Orders were then sent to the Wagon Lines for three wagon-loads of ammunition. This message was taken by Gunner Graham on a bicycle under very hot shell fire. Ammunition arrived about 12.30 p.m. Remainder of the day was quiet, but the teams were shelled on approaching and leaving the position; they had wonderful escape from machine-gun fire as they were returning."

Three men of the 5th Battery were wounded during the day.

The Heavy Battery (1st Northumbrian R.G.A.), having been placed under the orders of the 13th Brigade (4th Division), moved on the 6th to positions just east of the Vlamertinghe–Elverdinghe road and came into action. On the 8th the Battery engaged targets just north of St. Julien. The Battery records are very brief and of a technical nature. Apparently, however, their old 4·7-in. guns did fair shooting.

In the meantime Divisional Headquarters at Steenvoorde were kept continually on the *qui vive,* for on the 6th of May Plumer's Force and Second Army Headquarters had wired saying that the Northumbrian Division would be under the orders of G.H.Q. from 6 a.m. on the 7th, in general reserve and held in readiness to move at two hours' notice. Though orders to move were momentarily expected on the 8th (after news of the enemy's attack had been received) none arrived, and it was very early on the 9th of May before the Division was again warned to be ready to move at short notice, the Durham Light Infantry Brigade being placed at one hour's notice. Between 8 a.m. and 9 a.m. the Division (less Artillery) was ordered to move by bus to Brandhoek during the evening and early hours of the 10th of May. The Artillery was to close up west of Poperinghe.

At 2.30 p.m. the Durham Light Infantry Brigade set out for Watou for the woods north of Brandhoek, the men's packs being carried on lorries. Motor-buses carried the York and Durham Brigade to Brandhoek, where all units bivouacked north of the main road west of that place, from 4 p.m. onwards. At 7.30 a.m. on the 10th the Northumberland Infantry Brigade "bussed" to Brandhoek and bivouacked in the woods north of the village. On the 11th the Field Company, R.E., also moved to Brandhoek.

At 11.35 a.m. on the 11th orders arrived directing one Brigade of the Division to relieve the 1st Cavalry Division in the G.H.Q. Second Line during the night of the 11th–12th. The Durham Light Infantry Brigade was detailed for this duty, while the York and Durham Brigade was ordered to move to huts one mile west of Ypres, and the Northumberland Brigade to hold all units in readiness to move at two hours' notice. Certain working parties were also ordered.

The Durham Light Infantry Brigade set out at 7.50 p.m., three battalions, *i.e.*, the 7th, 6th and 9th Durham Light Infantry, in that order from right to left, moving up to the G.H.Q. Line astride and just north of the Menin road, while the 8th Durham Light Infantry were placed in huts near Brielen, in reserve.

The 7th Battalion furnished seven hundred men that night for digging purposes, and a long dig they had too: for five and a half hours they were at work on the Zillebeke Switch. Neither the Northumberland Brigade nor the York and Durham Brigade appear to have moved during the 11th of May. On the 12th of May the situation in the front line was "quiet," but several items of importance happened in connection with the Northumbrian Division. By 11 a.m. the whole of Divisional Headquarters were concentrated in Poperinghe. Just before noon V Corps Headquarters wired to say that certain moves and reliefs would take place during the night of the 12th–13th, also the York and Durham Brigade was placed at the disposal of the 27th Division.

The next item worthy of record is that arrangements were made for one officer and two N.C.O.s from each brigade and of the Cyclist Company to be trained as bomb-throwers by the 4th Division. This was the first time the Division had anything to do with bombs. Hand grenades at this period were still somewhat primitive and their numbers few, for less than four thousand per month were being received in France and Flanders during the early part of 1915.*

The third incident of importance was the receipt during the day of notification from Second Army Headquarters that the designation of the Division had been changed. The Northumbrian Division was henceforth to be known as the 50th (Northumbrian) Division; the designation of the three infantry brigades was also altered, the Northumberland Brigade becoming the 149th Brigade, the York and Durham Brigade the 150th and the Durham Light Infantry Brigade the 151st; and as such they are henceforth referred to.

The night of the 12th–13th also was comparatively quiet, for which there was much thankfulness, seeing that reliefs were taking place and large working parties were busy on the defences.

Of the 151st Brigade, the 7th Durham Light Infantry again furnished seven hundred men for work on the trenches north of Zillebeke village, while the 6th and 8th Battalions supplied parties of six hundred men for work north of Ypres.

The 149th Brigade, at midday, had been ordered to detail two working parties, each of three hundred men, for work during the night of the 12th–13th. The 5th Border Regiment furnished these parties, *i.e.*, one hundred and fifty from each company, who moved at dusk to just west of Ypres, where they filled sand-bags and formed barbed-wire entanglements. The Battalion Diary records that they came under shell fire for the first time, but suffered no casualties. Early on the 13th the parties returned to Brandhoek.

Of the 150th Brigade,† the 1/4th East Yorkshires, who on the 11th had moved to Château des Trois Tours, remained in that place; the 4th Green Howards were north of Vlamertinghe; of the 5th Green Howards, "C" Company was sent up for attachment to the 1st Leinster Regiment in Sanctuary Wood, the three other companies remaining in an open field near Brielen; the 5th Durham Light Infantry (less Battalion Headquarters) also moved up through Ypres to trenches in

---

* Hand grenades are described more fully in Chapter IV, which deals with trench warfare.

† The Diary of the 150th Brigade Headquarters is also missing for May, 1915.

Sanctuary and Hooge Woods. They were very much split up, companies being attached to various regiments, *i.e.*, Royal Scots, 5th Hussars and 16th Lancers.

Ypres had now become a dreadful place through which to pass at night. Its appearance is thus described by one of the 5th Green Howards:

"Ypres presented an awe-inspiring sight. One long street we passed through going towards the Cloth Hall was on fire on both sides of the road. The middle of the road was strewn and piled with debris from falling walls, whilst the darkness of the city was changed to vivid illumination from flames of burning buildings. We passed through then to the east of Ypres, and dug trenches."

It must be pointed out that although the line is described as "quiet," shell fire was almost always going on. The Germans, with their big howitzers, were able to pour (and did pour) an almost continuous fire upon the doomed city. Their great howitzer shells crashed into the place, piling destruction upon destruction with the idea not only of reducing Ypres to ruins, but in order to cause casualties among troops moving up to or from the front line, and transport units who "carried on" chiefly at night.

"C" Company of the 5th Green Howards, on reaching Sanctuary Wood, took over some huts. They were only about two hundred yards from the firing line, "constantly under shell fire and bullets whistling continuously through the wood."

At 3.30 a.m. on the 13th there was a terrific roar as the German guns opened fire on the trenches and back areas, the heaviest bombardment falling on the line (held by the 27th Division and cavalry) between Hooge and the Ypres–St. Julien road. High explosive and shrapnel lashed the trenches in the area with extraordinary violence; heavy shells fell on the trenches and communications. It was the heaviest bombardment put down by the enemy since the gas attack on the 22nd of April. From north, from south, from the east, hostile guns swept the Salient with a storm of shell.

The British artillery could do little to protect the infantry in the front line; most of the "Heavies," *i.e.*, 4·7-in., 60-pounders, were old-pattern guns, many worn out, having reached the limit of the number of rounds allotted to their "lives." Some of the field howitzers, *i.e.*, 5-in., were also old guns. And to add to the British artillerymen's difficulties, the shortage of ammunition was acute. With every disadvantage, however, the gallant troops in the front line met the savage hail of shell poured upon them with a magnificent courage and tenacity. Only when their trenches had been battered and practically flattened, leaving them no cover, did they retire, but even then they later counter-attacked the enemy. The bombardment continued—intense all the while—until 1 p.m., and after that hour, throughout the remainder of the day, it became intermittent.

With the exception of a portion of the Divisional Artillery (whose operations on the 13th have already been described) no unit of the 50th Division was involved directly with the enemy. The 2nd Northumbrian Brigade, R.F.A., just before 5 p.m. was ordered to move forward at the disposal of the C.R.A., 28th Division, attached to the Cavalry Force, but gun positions were not occupied until about 11 p.m. In pitch darkness batteries had had to move up, but with the exception of some vehicles getting into ditches and shell holes in advancing across country, there were no mishaps. Batteries went into action south of Potijze, between the Menin and the Ypres-Potijze roads, where they covered the zone between the Ypres–Westroosebecke road and the Ypres–Roulers railway.

Although shelled most of the day, "C" Company of the 5th Green Howards, in Sanctuary Wood, made no move. Of the other battalions of the 150th Brigade, the 1/4th East Yorkshires marched first to some trenches near Shrapnel Corner (just south of Ypres), thence at 10 p.m. to Wittepoort Farm, where they took over trenches from the 3rd Cavalry Division; the 4th Green Howards made no move until the early hours of the 14th; the 5th Durham Light Infantry, still split up among various units, record that "companies moved about in turn from firing line to support and reserve trenches."

The 6th, 7th and 9th Durham Light Infantry (151st Brigade) made no move during the day; their labours began after darkness had fallen, for eight hundred of the 6th Battalion dug trenches for the 3rd Cavalry Division south-west of Verlorenhoek, six hundred of the 7th were similarly engaged to the north of Zillebeke village, and four hundred of the 9th were at work improving the line south of Wieltje, held by the 1st Cavalry Division. The 8th Durham Light Infantry were moved up from west of Ypres during the day, and occupied trenches about Potijze.

Ordered at 7.30 a.m. to hold itself in readiness to move off at short notice, the 149th Brigade moved forward at 10 a.m., arrived at noon, about one thousand seven hundred yards west of Ypres, and bivouacked (in pouring rain) south of the Ypres road. At 5 p.m. the 4th and 5th Northumberland Fusiliers and 5th Border Regiment moved into trenches north of the road, the 6th and 7th remaining in bivouacs. These two Battalions were, at 10.30 p.m., placed under the orders of the 10th Brigade, and at midnight moved off, the 6th Battalion eventually fetching up on the eastern bank of the Yser Canal near Ecluse No. 5, where, wet through and very tired, they occupied dug-outs in the Canal bank. The 7th reinforced the 1st Royal Irish Fusiliers near Wieltje and occupied reserve trenches near the village.

So far as the 50th Division was concerned, the Battle of Frezenberg Ridge was a period of moving and marching about, much shell fire and great discomfort, but no actual fighting with the enemy.

THE BATTLE OF BELLEWAARDE: 24TH–25TH MAY

From the 14th to the 23rd of May the situation in the Ypres Salient remained unchanged. Artillery fire was desultory, for which the British gunners, having to conserve their ammunition, were thankful. It was thought that the Battles of Ypres, 1915, were over. But another serious attack, including the heaviest gas attack yet experienced, was launched by the enemy on the morning of the 24th.

The intervening period, *i.e.*, between the 14th and 23rd, had been spent in relieving tired and exhausted units, and doing all that was possible to strengthen the trenches and communications against further attacks.

The infantry of the 50th Division was split up to reinforce other divisions in the front line; split up to such an extent that it is almost impossible to follow accurately the doings of each battalion. As an instance, the 5th Northumberland Fusiliers were divided between four other battalions—a company to each. Even the Divisional Cavalry, "A" Squadron, Yorkshire Hussars, and the 50th Divisional Cyclist Company were placed at the disposal of the Cavalry Corps for work. And changes were so frequent that often units were uncertain as to whose command they were under.

There is, therefore, little of outstanding importance to record of those nine days, but it may be said that probably no division of the Territorial or New Armies had such a gruelling or violent introduction to actual warfare as the 50th Division. When the Battle of Frezenberg Ridge ended on the 13th of May the Division had been less than a month in France, had taken part in very heavy fighting without any previous experience, had acquitted itself splendidly, and had won golden opinions from the Commander-in-Chief and seasoned warriors of the Old Army.*

On the night of the 23rd of May the three infantry brigades of the Division were split up as follows: 149th Brigade with the 4th Division, whose sector ran from west of Verlorenhoek in a north-westerly direction to near Turco Farm, the right flank of the French; the 150th Brigade was with the Cavalry Corps (from the south-eastern corner of Armagh Wood to west of Bellewaarde Lake); the 151st Brigade was attached to the 28th Division, which held the line from the left of the Cavalry Corps, just west of Bellewaarde, to the right of the 4th Division.†

Headquarters of the 50th Division were at Poperinghe.

The night was without incident, but at 2.45 a.m. on the 24th red lights from the German lines soared up into the sky. The lights were immediately followed by a heavy outburst of artillery, machine-gun and rifle fire from the enemy's trenches. Dawn had broken, and as the crash of gun fire tore the morning air great clouds of gas were seen to emerge from the German line and float slowly on towards the British trenches. The discharge took place from opposite our line near Hooge, thence northwards nearly to Turco Farm. It was so violent that, even through the roar of guns, the hissing from the gas cylinders could be heard from across No Man's Land where the British and German trenches ran close together, *i.e.*, especially astride the Menin road. The effect of the gas was felt later some twenty miles behind the front line, so that what it must have been in the latter can best be imagined. The gas clouds soared

---

* For the text of a letter of appreciation from Major-General E. S. Bulfin (G.O.C., 28th Division) to Major-General Sir W. Lindsay, see Appendix C.

† This does not mean that all battalions were in the line; several were, but others were back in the second line and in reserve west of Ypres when the battle opened on the 24th of May. They moved forward during the early morning on that date, or later in the day.

as high as forty feet and were so dense as to blot out houses and farms.

But the wind being favourable, many officers in the front line were on the alert and, as a surprise attack, the gas failed. Nevertheless, owing to the proximity of the opposing lines in certain places, the troops had little time in which to adjust their primitive respirators before the fumes overcame them.

The enemy's infantry assaulted immediately but, met by a withering fire from machine-guns and rifles, experienced a heavy and costly repulse. Only in one part of the line, *i.e.*, at Mouse Trap Farm, held by two platoons of the Royal Dublin Fusiliers, did he succeed in over-running our position. At this point the opposing trenches were only thirty yards apart, and the Germans were in the "Farm" (now only a rubble heaps of bricks and mud) ere the garrison had an opportunity of putting up a defence. South of Mouse Trap Farm, however, the struggle continued for many hours. With dogged courage and a tenacity which surprised and thrilled even those who expected them to make a stand, those units of the Old Army, reinforced by partially-trained reinforcements, upheld the great traditions of the past, and "Ypres '15" was fought with the glorious spirit of "Ypres '14."

Until between 7 a.m. and 7.30 a.m. that intense and violent bombardment continued, gas shell being mixed with high explosive, making the eyes water but, fortunately, little more.

The Official History states that: "All telephonic communication was now cut, observation was nearly out of the question, as the enemy had the advantage of the higher ground and the front line was shrouded in a black pall of smoke and dust formed by the continuous shelling with heavy howitzers."

Scattered up and down the line, one company here, one platoon there, seldom a whole battalion in one place, attached to regular battalions, several battalions of the 50th Division fought, or were engaged in the immediate neighbourhood of the front line on that day of hard trial; and again they upheld the fine reputation gained by their Division.

To begin with the right, *i.e.*, the Cavalry Corps. Of the 150th Brigade, the 4th Green Howards were with the 9th Lancers astride the Menin road at Hooge.* Their story is a

---

* They left Vlamertinghe on the night of the 23rd and were split up among the 9th Lancers squadrons.

very gallant one: "At about 2.30 a.m. on Whit Monday came the great gas attack. From trench to trench we fought and, thank Heaven, stuck to our trenches, but at great cost."* Capts. Leather, Bowes-Wilson and Charlton and Lieut. McLaren are mentioned as doing specially good work, and the Diary states:

"Company-Sergeant-Major Myers again distinguished himself. Company-Sergeant-Major Bainbridge was splendid. Privates Perry and Ekins also deserve mention. One man got into the machine-gun emplacement of one of the Hussar regiments, where he found only the officer, working the gun with him. He stayed until he (the man) was killed. During the day Major H. G. Scott drove round and round in the commandeered ambulance car picking up wounded and gassed men who were straggling back to dressing stations. At night the remainder of the garrison of our trenches were relieved and straggled back." There, for the moment, we must leave the remnants of the Battalion.

The 5th Green Howards were in reserve, but at 11 p.m. were sent forward to the G.H.Q. Line.

The 1/5th Durham Light Infantry, who for several days before the attack began had been attached to the Hussars and Lancers of the 2nd Cavalry Brigade, were on the north-eastern side of Sanctuary Wood near the 4th Green Howards, but not in the front line. Their Diary records that some companies were gassed and that there were many casualties, but the number is not given.

The 1/4th East Yorkshires were very much split up. The Battalion had been placed under the orders of the 1st Cavalry Brigade at noon on the 23rd, and at night moved up to the front line on the eastern edges of Sanctuary Wood. "D" Company was attached to the 5th Dragoon Guards (right), "B" Company to the Queen's Bays (centre) and "A" Company to the 11th Hussars (left), while "C" was held in reserve further back in the wood.

At 3 p.m. the C.O. (Lieut.-Colonel H. R. Beddoes) received a report that the 4th Green Howards, 9th Lancers and 1/5th Durham Light Infantry had been gassed, and that the enemy had broken through the line held by the Lancers near Hooge. At once No. 11 Platoon of "C" Company was sent to the north

---

* Their casualties were 5 officers and 198 other ranks.

of Zouave Wood and took up a position in support of the 9th Lancers. At 10 a.m. the remainder of "C" Company was sent forward to support the left of the 11th Hussars, but two hours later were withdrawn. At 1 p.m. "A" Company (hitherto attached to the 11th Hussars) was also sent to support the 9th Lancers in the left sector of the trench, part of which had been captured by the enemy. But the trench was found already blocked with men, and the Company was withdrawn some two hundred yards in rear. At about 3 p.m. "C" and "A" Companies dug a new trench connecting the support trench with the fire trench.

There is little more of importance to record of the 1/4th East Yorkshires during the 24th. Their casualties were 3 other ranks killed and 21 wounded.

The story turns now to the line held by the 85th Brigade (28th Division) between Bellewaarde Lake and the Ypres–Verlorenhoek road. Here the trenches were in a deplorable condition. The rain and rough weather of the past few days had turned them into mud channels, knee-deep in water. From the Lake northwards to the Verlorenhoek road the line was held by "A" and "B" Companies of the 7th Durham Light Infantry, 3rd Royal Fusiliers (both these battalions being south of the Ypres–Roulers railway), two companies of the 8th Middlesex, "C" and "D" Companies of the 9th Durham Light Infantry and the 2nd East Surreys (these three battalions holding the line between the railway and the Verlorenhoek road).

The 151st Brigade had been placed under the orders of Brig.-General C. E. Pereira (commanding 85th Brigade) on the 21st of May, the 7th Durham Light Infantry sending two companies forward to the positions named above and two to the 3rd Middlesex north of the railway, but these returned to hutments near Brielen on the 23rd. The 9th Durham Light Infantry moved to the G.H.Q. Line, and on the 23rd sent two companies into the front line as stated.

The 8th Durham Light Infantry* moved up at 7 p.m. on the 23rd to the G.H.Q. Line, but it was 7 a.m. on the 24th before the 6th Durham Light Infantry also proceeded to the G.H.Q. Line.

On the front held by the 85th Brigade the enemy's attack on the 24th fell with particular violence. The right of that sector

---

* Strength: 14 officers, 261 other ranks.

between the railway and the Verlorenhoek road was the first to fall to the enemy. For, two hours after the gas clouds had rolled over the line, and the enemy's guns had practically eliminated the line, the two companies of Middlesex and a company of the Surreys on their left were overwhelmed, though only after a magnificent defence. But yet, north of them, the remainder of the East Surreys, with the two companies of the 9th Durham Light Infantry, stuck to their positions all day with splendid tenacity and courage, and beat off all attempts to turn them out of their battered position. The C.O. of the 9th (Lieut.-Colonel A. Henderson) and four more of his officers with over fifty other ranks were casualties, but they held on.

Frustrated in his efforts to break down the indomitable defence of the northern part of the sector, the enemy turned his attention to exploiting the gap he had made in the southern portion, attacking from front and flank the 3rd Royal Fusiliers and the two companies of the 7th Durham Light Infantry. The Fusiliers sent up half a company to cover the left flank, but in vain; the deadly gas had done its work only too well, and with all the officers killed, wounded or gassed, as well as those of the two companies of the 7th Durham Light Infantry, the two battalions were forced from their trenches. First a company, then a company and a half of the 2nd Buffs were sent forward from Brigade Reserve, but few reached the hard-pressed Fusiliers and Durhams, and with the third remaining company of Buffs the survivors rallied in the third-line trenches behind the remains of Railway Wood, where they held on all day. The record of the 7th Durhams states that "The Royal Fusiliers, with whom were our 'A' and 'B' Companies, were compelled to retire to a second line. From accounts received from officers (in the evening) the men of 'A' and 'B' Companies behaved in the most valiant manner."

In the meantime the 8th Durham Light Infantry had been drawn into the front line. The Battalion (now consisting of two companies only, *viz.*, Nos. 1 and 2), on reaching Potijze on the night of the 23rd, was ordered: No. 1 Company (Capt. J. A. Ritson) to dug-outs on the northern side of the Château grounds, No. 2 Company (Capt. T. A. Bradford) into the G.H.Q. Line and the northern end of the Wood. After the gas attack began on the 24th the fumes hung about the Wood for nearly half an hour, and caused many casualties.

At 11.45 a.m. orders were received for No. 1 Company to move also into the G.H.Q. Line south of the Verlorenhoek Line. At 12.10 p.m. orders came to hand for the Battalion to move immediately to the level-crossing on the Ypres–Roulers railway at Railway Wood to support the 3rd Royal Fusiliers.

The advance began at 12.30 p.m., No. 2 Company leading; guides from the Royal Fusiliers led the two companies. The direction first was south from the Château, behind a hedge, but evidently the Durhams were "spotted" by the enemy, for his guns opened fire. The advance was then made down the G.H.Q. Line as far as the station. But progress was slow, as the line was full of troops. To have gone over the open would have led to heavy casualties; as it was many men were killed and wounded by shell fire in the G.H.Q. Line. On arrival at the station thick wire entanglements were found placed across the line, but these were quickly cut by Capt. Bradford, who volunteered to do it. Companies then crossed in parties of from four to six men and took cover under the embankment. At 1.20 p.m. an advance began up the northern side of the railway for five hundred yards and then continued up the southern side. The Durhams now came under rifle fire and casualties were incurred. On arrival at the level-crossing the O.C., 3rd Royal Fusiliers, explained the situation.

The enemy was from six hundred to seven hundred yards north of the railway line. The trench held by the remnant of Fusiliers was about two hundred and fifty to three hundred yards up the railway, and extended from near the latter to the ruins of some houses two hundred yards north. The trench held from twenty to thirty Fusiliers—gallant fellows who had held on with magnificent courage, but now were almost spent. Two attempts by the Buffs to reinforce and support them had been beaten back with heavy loss. From the ruined houses to the north the continuation of the trench was held by the 2nd East Surreys, though the latter were only in small numbers. The enemy had already gained a footing in Railway Wood and were partly behind the trench on the northern side of the railway. The Royal Fusiliers held the trench north of the railway and the western edge of Railway Wood.

Colonel Turnbull (O.C., 8th Durhams) was then asked to reinforce the line held by the remnants of Fusiliers between the railway and the ruined houses. Capt. J. A. S. Ritson and

Lieut. Johnson were immediately ordered to make the attempt.

Major E. H. Veitch, in his history of the 8th Durham Light Infantry, thus narrates the advance of the Durhams: "From the level-crossing the road running north towards Verlorenhoek was slightly sunken, and along this the men, having removed their packs, were extended. About fifty yards east of the road were two lengths of unoccupied trench, then for two hundred yards an open field, without a vestige of cover, had to be crossed. This was strewn with the bodies of those who had fallen in previous efforts to reach the front line. The orders issued to Capt. Ritson were first to make for the unoccupied trenches fifty yards in front and then to wait until a favourable opportunity offered itself to get on.

"Upon the signal being given, Capt. J. A. S. Ritson and Lieut. Johnson at once led their men towards these trenches; no fire was opened on them, so the Adjutant signalled them to continue the advance over the remaining two hundred yards. The men obeyed the order splendidly, got out of the trenches together and went forward at a rapid pace in full view of the Germans in a trench captured by them, and in which they were engaged in reversing the parapet. This was actually a support trench of the British front line between it and the level-crossing, but to the right. These (the Germans) were apparently quite taken by surprise, for about half the distance was covered before fire was opened. This, when it did come, was heavy, both in artillery and rifle, but at first bore too far to the right and by the time the line of advance was formed the first line had been reached without loss. It was a very fine feat well carried out. The spirit of the men going forward was splendid, and it was entirely due to their eagerness that the attempt was successful. Later on reinforcements were sent up by way of a drain and a partly-dug communication trench leading towards the ruined houses, and the gap between the Royal Fusiliers and East Surreys was then closed."

Late that night the 8th Durham Light Infantry were relieved and moved back to the G.H.Q. Line, where at about 3.30 a.m. the Battalion arrived—or all who were left, for so reduced in strength was the Battalion that it was organised into a single company.*

---

* Their losses were, so far as can be ascertained, 4 officers and 103 other ranks.

The 6th Durham Light Infantry reached the G.H.Q. Line just north of the Potijze–Verlorenhoek road and apparently remained there throughout the 24th.*

We now come to Mouse Trap Farm† which had been lost during the enemy's first assault, and the line on both flanks of it.

From the Verlorenhoek road to near Turco Farm the 4th Division held the line with the 10th Brigade on the right and the 12th on the left, the 11th (when the battle opened) being in reserve two miles north-west of Vlamertinghe.

For several days the 149th Brigade had been under the orders of the 4th Division, and during the attack on the 24th the five battalions forming the Brigade held the following positions: the 4th Northumberland Fusiliers were at 10 a.m. moved up to the Divisional second line, but later sent half a company to the 2nd Essex and one company to the 2nd Royal Dublin Fusiliers, those two battalions holding front-line trenches; the 5th Northumberland Fusiliers were very much distributed, one company each being attached to the 5th South Lancs., 1st King's Own, 2nd Essex and 2nd Royal Irish. The 6th and 7th Northumberland Fusiliers were, until 5 a.m. on the 24th, in reserve west of Vlamertinghe, then marched first to Reigersburg Camp and later crossed to the eastern bank of the Canal, the 6th Battalion taking up positions near La Brique, and the 7th astride the St. Jean–Wieltje road. The 5th Border Regiment (like the 5th Northumberland Fusiliers) was split up, one company each attached to the Royal Irish Fusiliers, Seaforth Highlanders, Royal Warwickshire Regiment and Argyll and Sutherland Highlanders.

The front line of the 4th Division was held (from right to left) by the following units. Immediately north of the Verlorenhoek the 1st Royal Irish Fusiliers with "A" Company, 5th Border Regiment; 7th Argyll and Sutherland Highlanders and "D" Company, 5th Border Regiment; 2nd Royal Dublin Fusiliers; 2nd Royal Irish and "D" Company, 5th Northumberland Fusiliers; 1st King's Own and "B" Company, 5th Northumberland Fusiliers; 2nd Essex and "C"

---

* The Battalion Diary is missing for April and May.

† It is necessary to point out that at this period Mouse Trap Farm is still designated in the diaries of units as Shell Trap Farm. The latter name was considered by G.H.Q. to be ill-omened and was altered to Mouse Trap Farm.

Company, 5th Northumberland Fusiliers. When the 4th Northumberland Fusiliers arrived in the Divisional second line (south-west of Wieltje) they had on their left the 2nd Seaforth Highlanders, to whom were attached "C" Company, 5th Border Regiment. The Royal Warwicks. came next with "B" Company, 5th Border Regiment, and the 5th South Lancs., one company 2nd Lancashire Fusiliers, and "A" Company, 5th Northumberland Fusiliers, held the left of this second line.

Mouse Trap Farm was very nearly the centre of the 4th Divisional front line. Blasted and crumbled by weeks of heavy shell fire, "Farm" had become a misnomer and it merely consisted of a pile of broken bricks and rubbish which the Dublin Fusiliers had turned into a defensive position, though of a weak nature. Only a few yards (not more than thirty) separated the "Farm" from the enemy's front line, so that when the hissing noise of gas coming through the dense clouds of poisonous fumes reached the Irishmen their line was almost immediately enveloped by the deadly vapours.

Again it is preferable to quote rather than paraphrase the story as told by the 5th Northumberland Fusiliers: "At 2.30 a.m. the Germans commenced an attack with asphyxiating gas, the wind being favourable for its use against our trenches. This gas was accompanied by heavy shrapnel and high-explosive shell fire, with the result that portions of the trenches were practically demolished. The Essex,* who were on the left of the line held by the 12th Brigade, endeavoured to disperse the gas by rapid fire, but with little effect, although no doubt it saved many men from becoming asphyxiated had they lain low in the trenches.† Directly the bombardment started, the company of the Essex which had been in support advanced to the front line, losing several men during the advance, and two companies of the South Lancs., who had been held in reserve on the Canal bank, were ordered to move up into the second line. The King's Own,‡ who succeeded in holding their line, although suffering heavily from the gas and shell fire, unfortunately, however, suffered severely from the gas fumes, large

---

* And "C" Company, 5th Northumberland Fusiliers.

† When we first used gas at Loos the Germans lighted fires on their parapets for the purpose of dispersing the fumes.

‡ And "B" Company, 5th Northumberland Fusiliers.

numbers of men being overcome before they could take steps to combat them. Under cover of the gas the Germans delivered an infantry attack against the Dublin Fusiliers and Royal Irish,* on the right of the King's Own. The Dublins were forced to retire, with the result that the trenches occupied by the Royal Irish were enfiladed, large numbers of men being killed and wounded. The Irish were now compelled to vacate their trenches, leaving many men behind suffering from gas poisoning, these men being either killed or taken prisoner by the Germans who swarmed into the trenches. From the trenches abandoned by the Royal Irish the enemy delivered their attack against the King's Own who, however, repulsed it, not without losing several officers."

The narrative then records that "C.S.M. Allan and 2107 Private J. Scott showed conspicuous bravery whilst defending a barricade in the King's Own trenches, C.S.M. Allan gallantly defending the barricade with a revolver when he was mortally wounded in the back with a hand grenade."

The enemy, though not in great force, attacked the Essex, but were easily driven back.

Until 5 p.m. the German guns shelled the line. At 8 p.m. a counter-attack by the Lancashire Fusiliers and Warwicks. failed. As this attack was unsuccessful the King's Own and Essex received orders to retire, and during the night of the 24th–25th the Divisional second line, behind and parallel with the road from Wieltje to near Turco Farm, was re-organised as the new front line. At this point the movements of the four companies of the 5th Northumberland Fusiliers become obscure. Both the Essex and Royal Irish moved back to, and in front of, Irish Farm, and it is presumed that "C" and "D" Companies of the 5th Northumberland Fusiliers were with them.

The Battalion's losses throughout the 24th of May were heavy: "A" Company (with the 5th South Lancs.) had 3 other ranks killed, 18 wounded and 12 missing; "B" Company (with the King's Own) lost 2 officers and 5 other ranks killed, 31 wounded, 8 "gassed" and 13 missing; "C" Company (attached Essex Regiment) had 5 other ranks killed, 15 wounded and 13 missing; "D" Company's casualties were heaviest—2 officers and 5 other ranks killed, 5 officers and 11

---

* And "D" Company, 5th Northumberland Fusiliers.

other ranks wounded and 123 other ranks missing.* The Machine-Gun Section, attached to the Royal Irish, had 2 men wounded and 9 missing; the Section also lost its guns.

Of the 5th Border Regiment there is practically nothing in the records. Their own diary contains only the following brief reference to the day's happenings: "Enemy attacked with poisonous gas. Attack repulsed, but we suffered heavy losses on account of gas. Difficulty was experienced in accounting for casualties owing to Battalion being split up."

"D" Company, with the 7th Argyll and Sutherland Highlanders, was on the immediate right of the gap made in the line by the loss of Mouse Trap Farm. The Highlanders' sector was maintained throughout the day, though the line bent back almost at right angles. On the right of the Highlanders the 1st Royal Irish Fusiliers, with "A" Company of the Border Regiment, held their line, though heavily gassed.

The Battalion, which Lieut.-Colonel T. A. Milburn commanded, showed plenty of pluck and courage, and it is recorded that "most of its men were miners and showed great unconcern as regards gas; their example is reputed to have done much to fortify the confidence of the other troops."†

When the 5th Border Regiment was relieved on the 28th and marched back to Hospital Farm near Vlamertinghe, "roll call" gave the casualties between the 16th and the 28th of May as 1 officer and 18 other ranks killed, 3 officers and 113 other ranks wounded, 90 other ranks "gassed" and 48 other ranks missing, all of which were eventually accounted for—a total of 4 officers and 269 other ranks.

The 4th Northumberland Fusiliers reached the 4th Divisional second line at about 10 a.m., but, finding it already full of troops, moved to the support line at View Farm. "C" and "D" Companies were then put into a trench at Hill Top Farm. A little later "C" Company was ordered up to Mouse Trap Farm, but the O.C., Warwicks., stopped the Company as the Farm at this period was held by the enemy. Next the Battalion was ordered to support a counter-attack which, however, did not materialise. Gas shells were still falling heavily, and half of "B" and half of "C" Companies were moved out of their

---

* Some of these "missing" other ranks rejoined, having become attached to other units, while a number of "gassed" had been picked up and evacuated to hospital unbeknown to the C.O.

† Official History (Military Operations).

trenches along the road west. At dusk "B" Company was ordered to a trench running east of the St. Jean–Wieltje road and south of Wieltje, "A" and half of "C" Company west of the road, "D" in support west of the road, though half of this company was sent up to the South Lancs.,* who had asked for a company to fill a gap at Turco Farm.

A message to the Dublin Fusiliers, ordering a counter-attack, did not reach that unit, for it was captured by the enemy; the attack was, therefore, cancelled.

Nothing of outstanding importance happened to the 4th Northumberland Fusiliers during the 25th of May.

The 6th Northumberland Fusiliers remained on the eastern bank of the Canal, in reserve, until 2 a.m. on the 25th; they were then split up among the battalions of the 12th Brigade, two companies with the Machine-Gun Section moving up to the 4th Divisional second line and the other two to dug-outs east of La Brique.

Working parties were again furnished during the night of the 25th–26th, and an officer of the Battalion records that the men hated working parties as much as they hated the Germans.

The 7th Northumberland Fusiliers moved up at 2.15 p.m. on the 24th to the G.H.Q. Line astride the St. Jean–Wieltje road. In moving through St. Jean they came under shell fire and lost about twenty men. At night they took over support trenches in which they remained until the night of the 26th of May.

The Battle of Bellewaarde ends officially on the night of the 25th of May, and for some weeks there was comparative quietude in the Salient, *i.e.*, so far as attacks on or by the enemy were concerned; indeed the German Higher Command had ordered all offensive operations in the Salient to cease for the time being in view of larger operations taking place further south.

Exhaustion also, not only of troops but of ammunition, was another forceful reason why offensive operations were stopped; with the British the ammunition question had reached a desperate stage.

The 50th Division emerged from the Battles of Ypres, 1915, sadly depleted in numbers. The total British losses from the

---

* The Diary says "*East* Lancashires," but obviously South Lancashires were meant.

22nd of April to the 31st of May, 1915 (in the Battles of Ypres and the attack on Hill 60) amounted to no less than 2,150 officers and 57,125 other ranks. Owing to the large number of all ranks given in the diaries as "missing," who were subsequently accounted for, it is impossible to give an accurate figure of the casualties sustained by the 50th Division.

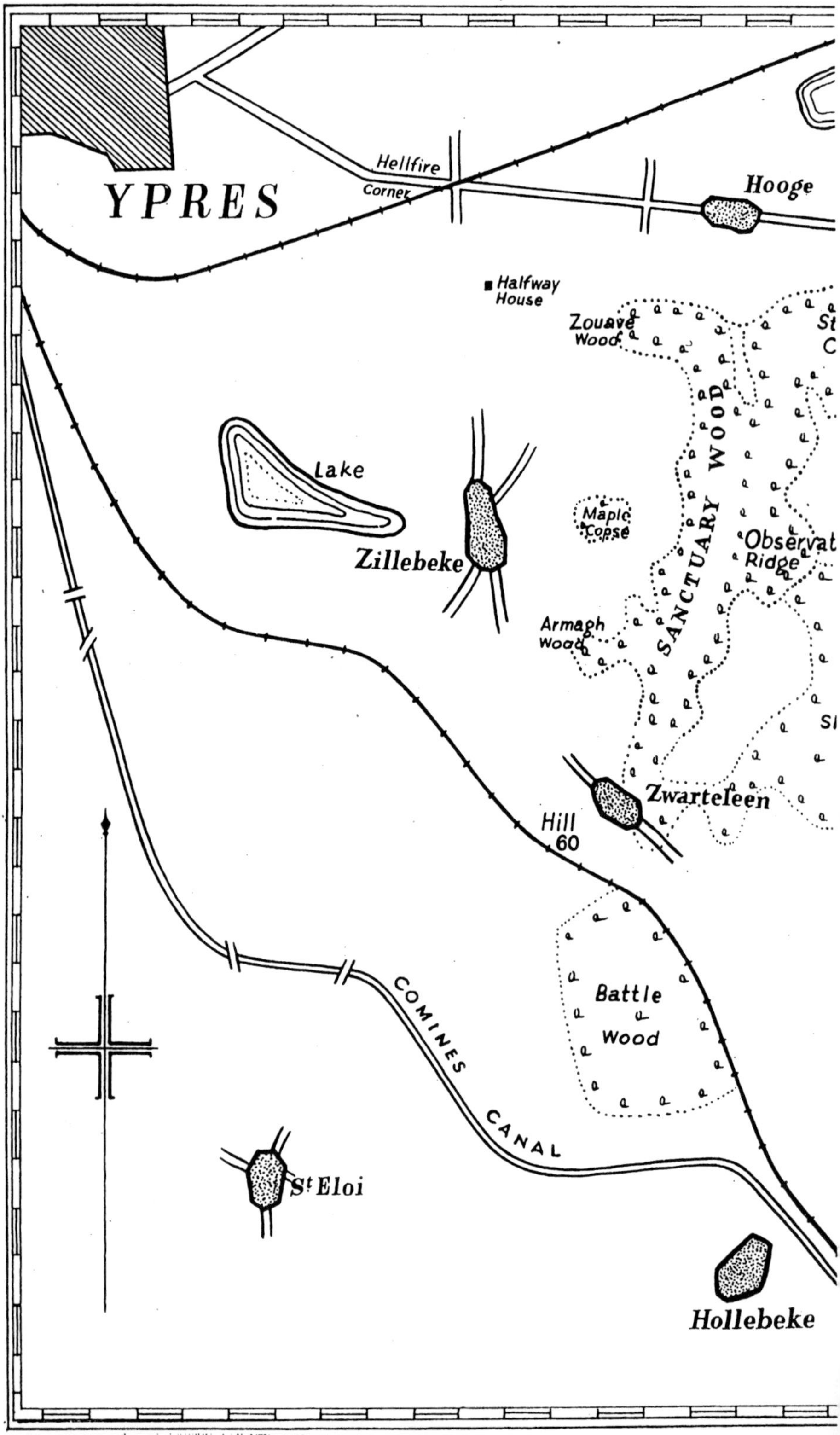

YPRES
Hellfire Corner
Hooge
Halfway House
Zouave Wood
SANCTUARY WOOD
Lake
Maple Copse
Zillebeke
Armagh Wood
Zwarteleen
Hill 60
Battle Wood
COMINES CANAL
St Eloi
Hollebeke

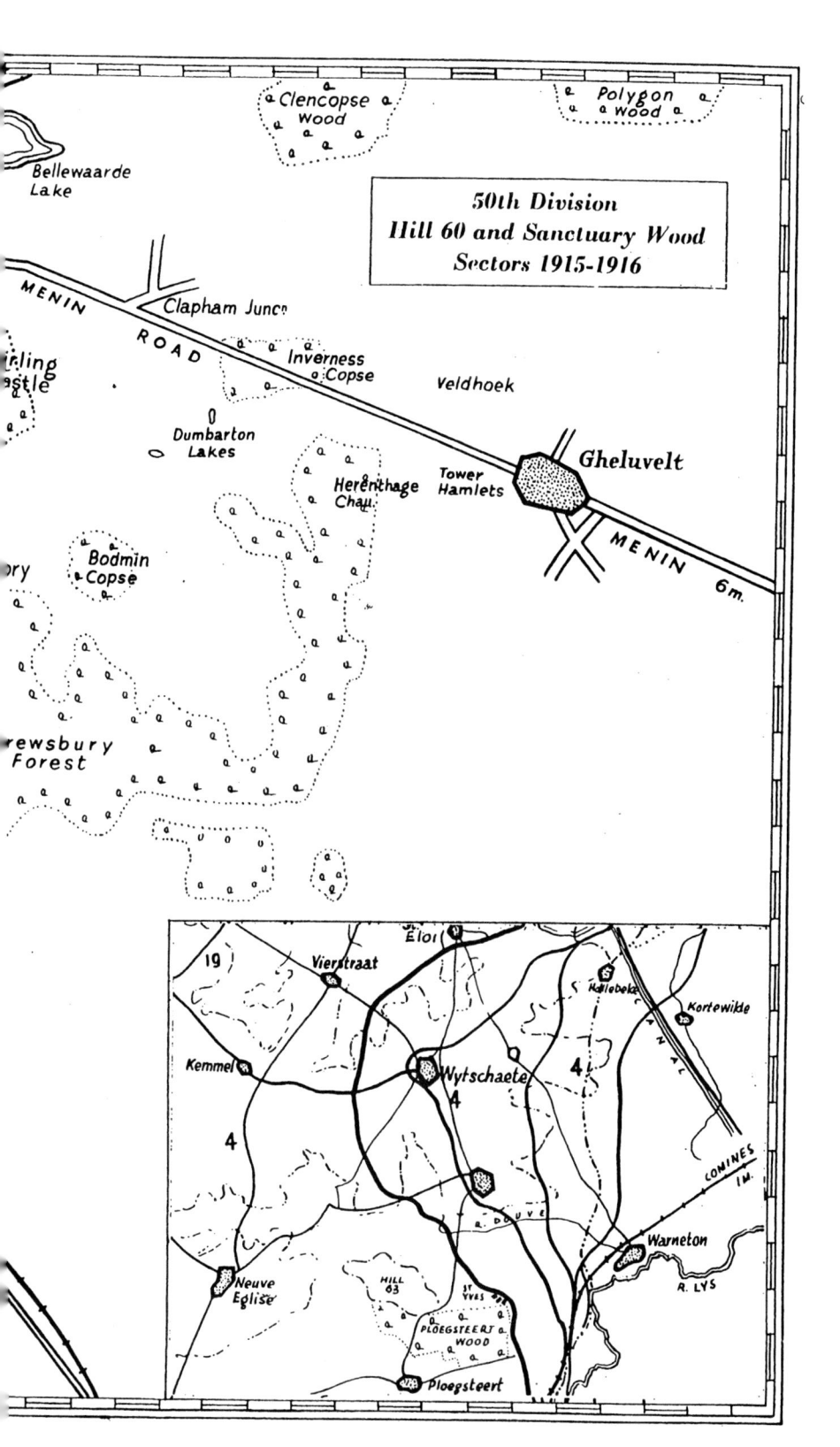

**50th Division
Hill 60 and Sanctuary Wood
Sectors 1915-1916**

CHAPTER IV

TRENCH WARFARE: JUNE, 1915–AUGUST, 1915
THE ACTION OF BELLEWAARDE, 16TH JUNE
SANCTUARY WOOD, NEUVE EGLISE, ARMENTIERES

STRANGE as the statement may seem, the 50th Division, having been engaged for a month or more in heavy fighting at close quarters with the enemy, had now to learn the business of holding the line; in other words the Division was to take over a sector of the line "on its own" and gradually become practised in trench warfare as opposed to offensive operations. For the two were different, with a difference which increased year by year as the making of war grew more technical and highly skilled. A strange and awful spectacle indeed for coming generations: all the science, all the inventive genius of mankind bent upon one object— that of killing mankind!

News that the Division was to take over a part of the front line was received in a wire from V Corps Headquarters on the 1st of June. The Division was first to be reassembled: the 150th and 151st Brigades were to come again under the command of the G.O.C., 50th Division, from 6 a.m. on the 2nd of June, and the 149th Brigade from 6 a.m. on the 5th of June. The artillery of the Division was to be brought into action in support of that portion of the line taken over, for hitherto only a few batteries had been used.

Divisional Headquarters were at this period in the Arbre Woods and Abeele area.

The 50th Division was to relieve the 3rd Division, and the latter suggested that four officers and eight N.C.O.s from two battalions should be sent to spend twenty-four hours in the trenches in order to become acquainted with the locality and trench methods; the 151st Brigade was then ordered to send representatives from two battalions at 8 p.m. on the 3rd of June. This was the Division's first acquaintance with that system of reconnoitring trenches previous to taking over, which afterwards was carried out almost mechanically; at present, however, it was a new experience.

On the 1st of June also the Yorkshire Hussars, Divisional Cyclist Company and the 1st Northumberland Field Company, R.E., returned to the command of the Division, which was gradually becoming once more a solid unit. Probably no division on the Western Front ever went through such a process of disintegration as fell to the lot of the 50th Division on first landing in France.

In his private diary for the 27th of May, 1915, Lieut.-Colonel A. H. Coles, commanding 5th Northumberland Fusiliers, thus aptly expressed the situation: "It is a curious state of affairs. My Battalion is in the trenches split up among four battalions, and I have nothing to say to them. The 149th Brigade is all up in the trenches, and General Fielding (G.O.C., Brigade) has nothing to say to them. The 50th Division has been engaged almost the whole time they have been out here, and General Lindsay has never had them under his command yet."

Divisional Operation Orders were issued on the 5th of June: the 150th Brigade was to relieve the 9th Brigade of the 3rd Division on the night of the 6th–7th of June; the 3rd Northumbrian Brigade, R.F.A., was to take over gun positions from a Field Artillery brigade of the 3rd Division on the nights of the 5th–6th and 6th–7th of June.

SANCTUARY WOOD

The sector to be taken over (expressed in official language in the diaries as from "right of V Corps in I.30 C.8.8. to I.24.d.9.9.") lay on both sides of the Observatory Ridge–Zillibeke road, the right flank at the southern edge of Armagh Wood and the northern at the south-eastern edge of Sanctuary Wood. Opposite this sector the German trenches ran along the western edge of Shrewsbury Forest. As we held the latter in April, the enemy had had little time in which to dig fresh trenches; similarly our line in Sanctuary and Armagh Woods was very far from complete.

West of the front line were Zillebeke village and Lake, and some one thousand two hundred yards north-west of the latter lay the Lille Gate into Ypres. The area between was dotted with woods, farms and houses, the land cut up by fields and ditches, all of which were soon to become familiar to almost every officer and man of the 50th Division.

The reassembling of the Division was no easy task, for battalions and units were very much scattered, being still attached to other divisions in the Salient.

Of the three infantry brigades, the 149th was ordered to concentrate in "Square A.24," which, interpreted, meant just west of Hôpital Fme. (north of the Vlamertinghe road). The 5th and 6th Northumberland Fusiliers, who had been attached to the 4th Division, arrived very early on the 2nd of June and went into bivouacs; the 4th and 7th Battalions marched in during the early hours of the 3rd. The 1/4th East Yorkshires, 1/4th Green Howards, 5th Durham Light Infantry and 5th Green Howards (the 150th Brigade) arrived in bivouacs just north of Vlamertinghe on the 3rd and 4th of June.

The 151st Brigade moved to an area immediately south of Poperinghe, the 6th and 9th Durham Light Infantry rejoining the Brigade on the 2nd of June.

Thus the infantry of the Division was reassembled west of Ypres.

Of the Divisional Artillery the C.R.A. gives few particulars, but from the Brigade and Battery Diaries the following has been adduced: the 1st Northumbrian Brigade, R.F.A., did not go into the line until the 28th of May, when the 1st, 2nd and 3rd Northumberland Batteries went into action just north of Ypres.

"We had at last got our poor old cannon pointing at the Bosche. The zone covered by the Brigade extended from the Roulers railway northwards to the Verlorenhoek road and we 'observed' from the remains of a cottage about a quarter of a mile from the front trenches. To get to this O.P., which was no healthy resort when you did arrive, you had to run across the open for about three hundred yards."*

The Brigade received orders to move back to billets on the Poperinghe–Abeele road on the 6th of June. The only "casualties" suffered during this, the first, tour in the line of the 1st Northumbrian Brigade, was the destruction of a wagon belonging to the 2nd Battery and (so Lieut.-Colonel Ommanney records) the grazing of the skin of Battery-Sergeant-Major Renton's nose. Major Johnston, commanding the 3rd Battery, had an exciting experience: "In his zeal to

---
* From *The War History of the 1st Northumbrian Brigade, R.F.A. (T.F.)*, by Lieut.-Colonel Ommanney.

find an O.P. close enough to the Battery, he donned an old suit of overalls and climbed a neighbouring chimney. On descending, all nice and sooty and presenting a thoroughly disreputable appearance, he was greeted by a posse of infuriated infantrymen who, at the point of their bayonets, demanded his life as a spy and were only dissuaded from marching him off there and then by the intervention of some of his own officers."

The 2nd Northumbrian Brigade, R.F.A., moved off to fresh billets (from St. Jans ter Biezen), south-east of Wippenhoek, on the 4th of June.

The relief of the 3rd Northumbrian Brigade, R.F.A., began on the night of the 31st of May, and all batteries had been withdrawn to the Abeele area by the 4th of June. The Brigade was, however (as already stated), due to relieve a brigade of the 3rd Divisional Artillery in the line on the nights of the 5th–6th and 6th–7th of June.

The 4th Northumbrian (Howitzer) Brigade, R.F.A., having been in action for nearly a month in various positions in the Salient, the 4th Battery on the 4th of June occupied a position on the bank of the moat round Ypres, near Ecole d'Equitation. On the 29th of May the G.O.C., 50th Division, was asked to convey the following message from the C.R.A., 27th Divisional Artillery (to which the 4th Battery had been attached): "The G.O.C. is asked to convey to all ranks of your Battery his keen appreciation of the work done by them during the recent fighting, work which was carried out under very trying and arduous conditions."

A pleasant tribute to the Territorial gunners, who were keen soldiers.

The 5th Battery, on once more coming under the command of the G.O.C., 50th Division, on the 5th of June, moved back by mistake to the wagon lines, but on the same date returned to the front-line area, coming into action four hundred yards north-west of the Zillebeke Lake.

The 1st/1st North Riding (Heavy) Battery, R.G.A., appears to have remained throughout May and June in the same gun positions taken up west of the Yser Canal in the angle formed by the Brielen, Vlamertinghe and Elverdinghe roads on the 6th of the former month.

The Divisional troops, *i.e.*, Field Ambulances, Royal Engineers, the Train, Veterinary Corps, etc., were all in the Divisional area.

The 5th Durham Light Infantry and the 5th Green Howards of the 150th Brigade were detailed to take over front-line trenches from the 9th Brigade (3rd Division) on the 6th, the 1/4th East Yorkshires to support the Durhams, and the 4th Green Howards their 5th Battalion.*

Trenches 1–6 had been allotted the Durhams, and 7–12 to the Green Howards. There is only one description extant of that first relief, for not one of the four battalion diaries describes what was always an eventful happening in the life of any unit in France and Flanders, *i.e.*, the first "taking-over" of front-line trenches. The one narrative, as contained in *The Fifth Battalion, the Durham Light Infantry*, 1914–1918, is given in full:

"We left the field we were bivouacked in on Sunday evening at 6.30 and set off along a cross-country track through the fields. After about four miles of this we got to a village to the south of Ypres (Kruisstraat), halted there, sent our horses back and waited for the arrival of guides from the Liverpool Scottish, whom we were relieving. Our guides met us about 8.45 p.m. Just as it was getting dusk the companies set off at intervals, each with a couple of guides at the head. We went along well-defined roads across the fields, crossed the main road between Ypres and Lille, then on again, leaving Ypres on our left. The bridle path soon resolved itself into a very second-rate footpath and we had to move in single file. We next passed the ruined village of Zillebeke, and could just make out the remaining fragments of its church. Near here we had to halt for some time, as we had caught up with the company in front and, to avoid confusion, it was desirable to let them get ahead again. After a while we went on again and had to go quickly across an open space near Maple Copse, which was notorious as being the meeting-place of half the stray bullets in the district. We got across without mishap, though some of the bullets were unpleasantly near. We then went into a wood [Armagh Wood], then into a communication trench and up into the fire trenches. The usual procedure was gone through, and the Scottish departed and left us in possession of the trench. It lay along the ridge of a small hill [Mount Sorrel] and so was well drained. It was also pleasantly deep so that one had not to walk about half doubled up. I believe

---

* The Diary of 150th Brigade Headquarters for June, 1915, is also missing.

the trench was originally dug by the French, as there are a lot of their graves around here. The odour suggests that they were not buried very deep!

"We had three days in this trench and had a very quiet and uneventful time. We, *i.e.*, the company, lost only one man: he was shot through the head, poor chap, when exposing himself rather recklessly in trying to spot a German sniper."

The 5th Green Howards relieved the 1st Northumberland Fusiliers and had two other ranks wounded during the relief.

Meanwhile the 3rd Northumbrian Brigade, R.F.A., had relieved the 42nd Brigade, R.F.A., of the 3rd Division and had come into action on the 5th and 6th, the 1st Battery west of Zillebeke Lake and just south of Shrapnel Corner (on the Ypres–Lille road), the 2nd Battery south of Kruisstraat, and the 3rd Battery east of the latter village and just east also of the Ypres–Comines Canal.

Ten months of the War had passed and still (so far as we were concerned) trench warfare was in its infancy. The enemy, better prepared for static warfare, was well provided with trench mortars, hand and rifle grenades, and rifles with telescopic sights for sniping. Behind his front line he had howitzers of all calibres with a plentiful supply of ammunition.

Our trench weapons were woefully inadequate. The trench mortars we were using were either hastily-improvised weapons or centuries old. Some were of iron, others of brass; all (at first) more dangerous to the firers than to the enemy. Hand grenades were similarly primitive and of the several improvised patterns the "jam-pot," "Battye bomb" and "hairbrush" were most generally favoured.

The Official History gives the following recipe for making the "jam-pot" bomb. "Take a jam-pot, fill it with shredded gun-cotton and ten penny nails, mixed according to taste. Insert a No. 8 detonator and short length of Bickford's fuze. Clamp up the lid. Light with a match, pipe, cigar or cigarette and throw for all you are worth."

The "Battye bomb" consisted of a cast-iron cylinder about four inches in length and two inches in diameter, filled with an explosive, generally ammonal, and closed by a wooden plug through a central hole in which detonator and fuze were inserted.

The "hairbrush" was made by making fast a slab of gun-cotton to a flat piece of wood of hairbrush shape. It was ignited in the same way as the "jam-pot" grenade.

Of bomb-throwers there were various—the catapult being much in use, though everyone "took cover" when this apparatus was going to perform, for its action was decidedly erratic, to say the least of it!

Neither trench mortars nor hand grenades were popular, for the enemy had a nasty habit of retaliating with his *minnenwerfer* and very soon put an end to our activities with our own poor little weapons. That was, of course, until we had had time to manufacture more effective mortars and grenades on a larger scale; then it was the enemy who very soon gave in, for our retaliation was invariably heavier than his; it often took the form of "giving him" three or four rounds for every *one* he fired.

At this period the Maxim and Vickers machine-guns were more widely used than the Lewis gun, of which there were not many in France and Flanders, though orders for their manufacture had been given.

Schools of Instruction were springing up everywhere behind the front line, and on the 5th of June the Divisional Diary mentions for the first time the Machine-Gun School, to which two officers and fourteen other ranks were despatched to undergo a course.

Instruction in using trench mortars was usually given by "experts," who travelled from one sector of the line to another, and whose coming was generally hailed with scowls, and, not infrequently, unkind remarks from the officers.

The introduction of "log bombs," kept by Brigade Headquarters and later by every company commander in the line, first came into use in the 50th Division in June.

At 3 a.m. on the 7th of June a wire was despatched to V Corps Headquarters stating that the G.O.C., 50th Division, had assumed command of that part of the line previously held by the 9th Brigade. Thus, for the first time since arriving in France, the Division held a portion of the front line under the command of its own General Officer Commanding.

The sector taken over by the Durhams and Green Howards (Trenches 1–12) has already been partly described by the former battalion. Each battalion found its own supports. The 4th East Yorkshires and 4th Green Howards, the Brigade Reserve, took over dug-outs in Sanctuary Wood. But "dug-outs" at that period were similarly poor in construction and effectiveness in keeping out shell fire. Indeed it was not until the Somme Battles of 1916 and we had captured German dug-outs that we really knew how to build them, for the enemy's constructions were little less than underground fortresses. So, at present, "dug-outs" were mostly "funk-holes," scooped out in the ground, the entrance covered with a waterproof sheet or a chance tarpaulin if it could be obtained from the stony-hearted Ordnance Department.

Fine weather, misty in the early mornings but clearing later when the sun blazed down on the trenches, made life bearable in the front line. The enemy was quiet, *i.e.*, he was not inclined to be aggressive, being evidently as tired as were the troops of the 50th Division, after the recent fighting. But the careful "Higher Command" had devised a programme of work from which there was no escape; in the front line or out of it the words "working parties" grated upon the ears of all who heard them or, worse still, read them in "Orders." The brigade in the front line was to improve wire-entanglements, existing communication trenches and dig fresh ones; construct a lateral traversed communication trench, improve strong points and construct others; work on the support trenches to the front line and construct machine-gun emplacements. As little work could be done during the day for fear of attracting the enemy's shell fire, it is obvious that what with keeping an eye upon a vigilant enemy during the day and working hard at night, life in the front line was a strenuous business.

Maple Copse was also the scene of much hard labour, but the troops for this work were supplied by the brigade "next for the trenches" which, when the order was issued, was the 151st. The latter had moved to an area three thousand yards south-west of Vlamertinghe on the morning of the 4th of June, the 7th Durham Light Infantry taking over dug-outs west of Kruisstraat on the 6th of June, one company being sent to Maple Copse to begin the work of placing it in a state of defence for rifles and machine-guns.

In this work the infantry were assisted by sections of the 2nd Northumbrian Field Company, R.E. The 7th Durham Light Infantry were periodically relieved by other battalions of the 151st Brigade.

The 149th Brigade from the neighbourhood of Hôpital Fme. moved on the 5th of June to an area south-west of Poperinghe, near Busseboom. The Headquarters Diary gives a good description of the life of the Brigade while training during the early days of June. One item is especially interesting, *i.e.*, that relating to asphyxiating gas. After the first use of gas by the Germans at Ypres in April the Allies had decided to adopt a similar weapon, and on the 8th of June the 149th Brigade Diary has the following entry: "Instructions received from 50th Division for one officer per battalion and one man per company to proceed to Brandhoek at 11.15 p.m. to-morrow for *experiments with gas.*" And on the following day the results are given: "Officers and men experimented on with gas. The men were tried first with respirators and then with smoke helmets on. The effect of the gas was hardly noticed with the smoke helmet, but could be distinctly felt when wearing a respirator only."*

On the 10th of June the 149th Brigade received orders to relieve the 7th Brigade (3rd Division) in the trenches, and arrangements were made to take over the line on the nights of the 10th–11th and 11th–12th.

This sector was on the left of the 150th Brigade, and included the greater part of Sanctuary Wood and the ruins of Hooge, on the Menin road.

The sub-sectors of these trenches were numbered, from right to left, B1, 2, 3, 4, 7, 8, 9, 13, 14, 15, 16. The 5th Northumberland Fusiliers were to take over B1 and B2, the 6th Northumberland Fusiliers B3 and B4, the 4th Northumberland Fusiliers B7 and B8. The 5th Border Regiment was to hold Trench B9 and Hooge (which included 13, 14, 15 and 16), the 7th Northumberland Fusiliers were to be in reserve with two companies in Zouave Wood and two in Sanctuary Wood.

The whole Brigade was to go into the line, as it was only half the strength of the 7th Brigade whose trenches were to be taken over.

The 5th and 6th Northumberland Fusiliers were to "take over" on the night of the 10–11th of June; both battalions were to move by bus to the western entrance to Ypres, where guides from the 7th Brigade would meet them.

The 5th Battalion thus describe their first "taking over": "At 4.30 p.m. we suddenly received orders that we were to go into the trenches that night in the neighbourhood of Hooge. Colonel Coles and the company commanders had to proceed

---

* Asphyxiating gas was discharged for the first time on to the enemy's trenches on the 25th of September, 1915, in the Battle of Loos.

at once by bus to reconnoitre the trenches we were going to take over while it was light. The remainder of the Battalion paraded and left in motor-buses about 7 p.m. We disembarked just south of Ypres on the main road and marched into the town, where we were met by guides from the 4th South Lancashire Regiment, whom we were relieving. We left the town by the St. Eloi (Lille)* Gate, crossed the railway (the Ypres–Roulers railway and went across country to Sanctuary Wood. Our guides led us all right, but it came on to rain, was pitch dark, and what with the numbers of troops on the road and transport we had numerous halts to let the rear catch up, and it was very late by the time we got to Maple Copse; there, after some difficulty and a long wait, we found the company officers who took their companies straight off through the Wood to the various trenches; it was a nasty job going up through the Wood; there were a lot of bullets coming over striking the trees ricocheting in all directions; one man was killed and several wounded. We took over the trenches at last.... 'A' and 'B' Companies were in the front line, and 'C' and 'D' in support trenches about two hundred yards behind in the Wood. We found the trenches pretty fair on the whole, though rather swampy in parts. 'B' Company (left) were within one hundred and fifty yards of the enemy trenches, while on the right, opposite 'A' Company, the German trench was out of view, over the ridge some five hundred yards away."

The 6th Northumberland Fusiliers record that: "The Battalion 'embussed' at 7 p.m. and went as far as Ypres in buses. The relief was completed about 3 a.m. after a very dark, wet night."

Everyone was anxious for dawn on the 11th.

"It is surprising," said an officer of the 6th Northumberland Fusiliers, "how one longs for dawn when occupying trenches for the first time. Everything seems so strange, and the artificial light supplied by star shells does not last long enough for one to get a good idea of the position you hold. There is a certain feeling of uneasiness until the first streak of dawn enables you to take a cautionary peep over the bags and see for the first time the dark outline of the enemy's position. A general survey of your own position is also one's first thought

---

* The Brigade Operation Order says "Menin Gate."

for, knowing exactly where you are inspires confidence in no small degree.

"The trenches were quite deep with a firing step in each bay; the parados and traverses required building up, lateral communications were exceedingly bad and dug-outs or shelters of any description were conspicuous by their absence. A peep 'over the top' revealed a great scarcity of wire in front of our position, and from B4 trench only ten yards separated our sap head from that of the enemy, and from some parts of B3 the enemy's trenches were invisible, so queerly did the line run."

The 6th describe the 11th of June as "a quiet day on the whole," but it is evident from the Battalion Diary that the Battalion intended getting "top dog" over the enemy, for on a few rifle grenades being fired by the latter "double the number were fired back at them." This form of retaliation the Germans detested, but it was almost always effective and put an end for the time being to their activities.

On the night of the 11th–12th the 4th and 7th Northumberland Fusiliers and 5th Border Regiment moved up into the line.

The Diary of the 4th Battalion, though very brief, is nevertheless descriptive: "Marched 6 p.m. Guides at Kruisstraat at 8.45 p.m. Crossed Canal (Ypres–Comines Canal) 9.15 p.m. Delayed by battalion in front and forms of transport. Two wagons overturned in the road. Very muddy. Bad marching. Sanctuary Wood at midnight. One of relieved guides lost his way, and one company and the Machine-Gun Company did not get on that night. . . . Other ranks, three wounded."

From the diary of an N.C.O. of the same battalion it is once more evident that the grim brutalities of war could not crush from the minds of some men their love of Nature. For this N.C.O. records: "We left at 5.30 p.m. I had a rest until the Battalion congregated. Saw the Marsh and Palmate Spotted Orchis, Water Forget-me-not, Water-bird-straw. On our march up we passed a plot of red and white Samfon."

Strange how some men found it possible to observe and admire humble flowers, growing nervously within a few hundred yards of death and destruction and all the horrors of a bloody war.

"It was an awful distance," continues this N.C.O. when he had ceased to write of Nature, "and the trenches were in a pitch-dark wood. We were lost once or twice, and what with slipping about and falling down, and the pace that was set, everybody was 'fed up.' It was turned 2 a.m. when we manned the trench."*

The 4th Battalion was on the immediate left of the 6th.

The 5th Border Regiment, on the left of the 4th Northumberland Fusiliers, merely state that "A" Company and a portion of "B" Company took over B9 trench, and the remainder of the Battalion the Hooge defences.

The 7th Northumberland Fusiliers relieved the H.A.C., two companies going into Zouave Wood and two into Sanctuary Wood.

The relief of the 7th Brigade was completed by 4.30 a.m. on the 12th of June, at which hour Brig.-General Fielding assumed command of the 149th Brigade sub-sector.

At last the 50th Division held a *whole* sector, with two brigades in the front line and one in reserve.†

Sniping and sapping were very active, but it was early yet for those constant nightly patrols which later were so prominent a feature of trench warfare; and raids had hardly been thought about.

German snipers were deadly and a real pest; the careless exposure of a head was immediately followed by a sharp report and the dull thud of a bullet on sand-bag or flesh and bone. Many officers and men were lost in this way before we were on anything like equal terms with the enemy. We had no rifles fitted with telescopic sights to begin with, or rather they were not "an issue"; on the other hand, the Germans were well armed with them, and in the hands of expert riflemen they were deadly.

The chief activities, therefore, of that early period in the front line were sniping and sapping, the occasional use of rifle and hand grenades and desultory shell fire, for in places the opposing trenches were too close together to permit either side to shell their opponents' line. Of work on, and in the neighbourhood of, the front-line trenches there was a great deal.

On the 12th of June also the 7th Durham Light Infantry of the 151st Brigade relieved the 4th Green Howards in the

---

* Lance-Corporal R. H. Temple, late 4th Battalion, Northumberland Fusiliers.

† The first sector held has been dealt with fully as the occasion was always of historical interest to a division.

front line, the latter leaving Sanctuary Wood at 12.30 a.m. on the 13th and reaching the neighbourhood of Vlamertinghe two hours later.

The 151st Brigade at this period had undergone reorganisation. As a result of the heavy casualties sustained in the fighting in April and May, the 6th and 8th Durham Light Infantry were formed into one composite unit, *i.e.*, the 6th/8th Durham Light Infantry, on the 8th of June. The amalgamation is thus referred to in the diaries of both battalions:

"June 8th. Tuesday. The 6th Durham Light Infantry and the 8th Durham Light Infantry were this day amalgamated into a composite battalion. Lieut.-Colonel J. Turnbull, V.D., was appointed C.O., Capt. C. A. Stevens (Royal Fusiliers), Adjutant, Lieut. Hope, Quartermaster."

The Battalion was organised into four companies: "A" Company (8th Durham men) under Capt. T. A. Bradford; "B," "C" and "D" Companies (6th Durham men) under Lieut. Gill, Lieut. Heslop and Capt. Livesay respectively. The transports were reduced to the establishment of a single battalion under Lieut. L. A. Ramsay of the 8th Battalion. All supernumerary staff were sent to the Base Camp at Harfleur.

To bring the Brigade up to four-battalion strength the 1/5th (T.F. Battalion) the Loyal North Lancashire Regiment was transferred from the 6th Division and joined the Brigade south-west of Vlamertinghe on the 11th of June, under the command of Lieut.-Colonel G. Hesketh.

THE ACTION OF BELLEWAARDE: 16TH JUNE

About midday on the 13th of June Divisional Headquarters (which had for some days been established at Busseboom) received information that the 3rd Division was to make an attack on the Bellewaarde Ridge. On the 14th V Corps Operation Orders for the attack arrived; the assault was to take place at 4.15 a.m. on the 16th, the 50th and 6th Divisions, on the right and left respectively, co-operating by rifle and machine-gun fire.

The 149th Brigade was to seize any opportunity of taking the offensive and improving its position about Hooge.

From opposite our line at Hooge to the Ypres–Roulers railway, at the north-eastern corner of Railway Wood, the

German line formed a salient which included the Bellewaarde Ridge and Lake, both included in the objectives of the attack to take place on the 16th. The capture of the Ridge was important, as it would deprive the enemy of observation.

Opposite Hooge there was a point in the German trenches marked on the operations map and designated in Operation Orders as "Y.21." This point the 149th Brigade was to assist the 3rd Division in attacking.

The Hooge defences were held by the 7th Northumberland Fusiliers, two companies of that battalion having relieved the 5th Border Regiment on the night of the 14th–15th of June. Capt. F. Buckley of the former battalion, writing on the 17th of June (just after the attack on Bellewaarde) in describing the line said:

"It was hardly a line at all, but a perfect maze. A division of ours was to make an attack yesterday, and I was honoured by being placed in command of this section of trenches with my own company and half another company and four officers. My instructions were to defend this place at all costs and not to retreat at any price even if everyone was wiped out. I was given this pleasant piece of news at 5.30 p.m. (on the 14th), shown a rough sketch and told to go off and look round the trenches myself before taking the company in. The way to the trenches was through a long communication trench which ran zig-zagging up a hill for half a mile or more. A lot of it was up to the knees in water and mud. Arrived at the company officer's dug-out, the captain in charge took me round. You cannot imagine what it was like. Tunnels and burrows running in all directions. Ruined houses, detached from the trenches, had to be defended. Places which you had to run across like a scalded cat, and others which you had to wriggle across on your stomach. Dead men lying everywhere, some that had been there for weeks. German trenches never more than thirty yards away, and in some places only fifteen. You had to talk in whispers for fear they would hear what you said. Many of the houses were at the point of collapse, and all were riddled with bullet and shell holes. . . . I floundered about in the dark round the trenches for an hour or so trying to get the hang of the thing."

Capt. Buckley then went back to fetch his company up: "We got into the trench somehow or other and the other people got out.* . . . The fun started about 6 a.m. (15th) when the Germans began shelling and sniping us. They also threw bombs out of a trench mortar at us. These are beastly things and make as much noise as a gas works blowing up. That day we had two killed and seventeen wounded. Lieut. A. J. Trinder was shot dead by a shrapnel bullet as he sat smoking in the bottom of the trench."

The writer thus describes how the enemy was heard mining down to and under the trench—not a pleasing sound!

"All this time the Germans were busy digging a mine towards our trench, evidently with the object of blowing up Bull Farm, a ruin in our lines. We, of course, watched the progress of this work rather intently. During the afternoon one of our men lying in the trench heard the Germans talking beneath him. This was verified by the Royal Engineers. I then took the men from the trench in front of the farm and from each side for a distance, and had machine-guns trained on the farm from the rear. Then, of course, we had to sit and wait for the explosion—a nice tonic for the nerves!"

The artillery bombardment of the enemy's trenches began at 2.50 a.m. on the 16th. The guns of the 50th Division lent assistance, but the 15-pounders (the "poor old cannon" referred to previously) fired for ten minutes only, as ammunition was very short.

The 9th Infantry Brigade advanced to the attack at 4.15 a.m., and the 149th and 150th Brigades co-operated with bursts of fire at intervals on the German trenches.

This is what the 7th Northumberland Fusiliers said of the attack: "The bombardment started and gave the Germans a real bad time. Very soon on our left up went a white flag on a long pole. I reported over the telephone and asked for instructions. The reply was 'turn a machine-gun on to them.' Well! the white flag being no use, a lot of Germans left their trench, holding up their hands. They were soon knocked back into their trench again. Then a lot of them ran out and fled across country, and some Liverpool Scottish (1/10th King's Regiment of the 9th Brigade, 3rd Division) on our left jumped out and chased them with the bayonet. Altogether the Bosche had an uncomfortable morning. Our people

---

* The 5th Border Regiment had had a number of casualties, Major A. F. Broadley-Smith being killed during this tour in the line.

captured three lines of trenches and took between two hundred and three hundred prisoners. But the trenches in front of us were not taken; being so close to us our artillery could not shell them properly."

Eventually the 3rd Division had to fall back to the old German front line, which was consolidated and held.

At one period the 5th Border Regiment was ordered to assault "Y.21," that part of the German line in front of the 149th Brigade which had not been captured. But a reconnaissance showed that the wire was uncut and that an attack would be sheer madness, resulting almost certainly in further heavy losses. The attack was, therefore, abandoned.

During this small operation the garrison of the Hooge defences had a poor time of it, and the 7th Northumberland Fusiliers lost rather heavily.*

NEUVE EGLISE—LINDENHOEK—KEMMEL

On the 17th of June news reached Divisional Headquarters of another change: V Corps Headquarters wired that the 3rd Division would relieve the 149th Brigade at Hooge on the 18th–19th. Later, a secret message was received stating that the 50th Division, as a whole, was to be temporarily transferred to the II Corps, and the 46th Division to the V Corps. The 50th was to take over the line held by the 48th Division, opposite Messines and Wytschaete.

The 150th Brigade moved to Dranoutre and went into the line during the night of the 21st–22nd of June. The 149th Brigade marched to Ravelsburg on the 21st, and the 150th Brigade followed to the same place on the morning of the 24th. The artillery of the Division began to move to the new area on the 20th of June. By the 24th the Division had taken over the new sector, all three infantry brigades being in the front line, i.e., 149th, 150th and 151st, in that order from right to left. Each brigade had two battalions in the front line.

Peace had, for the time being, come to the 50th Division, for the Neuve Eglise sector (by which it was known to all members of the Division) was very quiet. Both infantry and artillery settled down to what, in reality, was a well-earned rest.

An infantry officer of the Division said: "We have got to a quiet place at last. A real quiet place. Also we have left the

* The 50th Division lost on the 16th of June about ninety all ranks.

Ypres Salient which, of course, is acknowledged to be the most beastly part of the whole line. We have settled down in some wooden huts with furniture, home-made, but furniture nevertheless. There is a laundry where they wash clothes for nothing, and baths. I understand we do a week in the trenches which are very quiet ones, and a week out, so it is going to be an improvement on what we have had. The weather is terribly hot, and the men had a very rough time marching here. We are near Neuve Eglise, close to the French border."

The Divisional Artillery, which went into action east and west of the road from Neuve Eglise, through Lindenhoek to Vierstraat, similarly looked forward to a quiet time. About Neuve Eglise and Lindenhoek there was good observation over the enemy's trenches, the latter village having Mont Kemmel in rear.

"We spent a very comfortable and peaceful time here," said one of the gunners. "Mont Kemmel gave us a magnificent view over the whole country. We were able to watch the Bosche moving about, and whenever we had the ammunition, which unfortunately was not often, we used to tickle him up to some purpose. We saved up our weekly allowance of ammunition as much as we could; it amounted to three rounds per gun per day, so that by Saturday we had no less than eighty-four rounds to play with, unless there had been some Bosche absolutely 'asking for it' during the week, or 'Higher Authority' had ordered us to take an active part in the War. The last day of the week was, therefore, a great one and we all used to assemble in the O.P.s in Bloke Row and fire series for wagers."*

It should be understood that whenever the word "quiet" is used to denote the situation, it is used in the comparative sense. For in those days all men lived by comparison. Therefore although there may have been no attack on, or by, the enemy in progress, the artillery of both sides was seldom silent; snipers were busy, watching like hungry wolves for the thoughtless exposure of heads or bodies; trench-mortar bombs and grenades exploded in the trenches; mining and sapping were

---

* Survivors of the 3rd Battery (1st Northumbrian Brigade, R.F.A.) will remember the windmill standing on the top of Kemmel, the owners of which had been given permission to use the mill until it was discovered that on the nights an infantry relief was in progress it started working, thus communicating news to the enemy. The owners of the mill were subsequently arrested as spies.

going on; mines were "blown"; working and wiring parties were out each night on their dangerous work in front of the line—in short, *that* was what "quietude" meant.

It was often a deadly quietude too, for the Battalion Diary of the 5th Northumberland Fusiliers records that on the 24th: "We lost a brave and valuable officer early in the morning in Capt. W. G. Graham, who was sniped through the head while looking over the parapet," and another diary, that of the 9th Durham Light Infantry of the 23rd of June, states: "Second-Lieut. A. J. Haughton killed during the night whilst out examining wire in front. A great loss to the Battalion as he was a most reliable and energetic officer."

The trenches in the new sector varied considerably. The River Douve ran just south of the 149th Brigade sub-sector, and the centre of the Divisional line was in low-lying ground. In place of deep trenches, therefore, the defences were mostly sand-bag breastworks built up on damp ground.

The 6th Northumberland Fusiliers describe their part of the line thus: "Our trenches were of the breastwork type, and with small forts in the rear made quite a formidable garrison. There were a few dug-outs in the parados in the front-line trench, but they were in a sad state of repair, and it looked as if our spell here meant work with a capital 'W.' Even some of the traverses were only two sand-bag thick and the parapet hardly bullet-proof."*

Apparently the enemy was rather annoyed to find that the new-comers to this sector of the line were not likely to let him lead a complacent life, for the 149th Brigade Headquarters Diary records the following amusing incident: "Enemy do not like our activity at night judging from following remarks shouted across to D.3: 'Go away you b—— Northumbrians; why don't you let us sleep.' On other occasions notice-boards were put up on the enemy's parapets, one having the words: 'What do you b—— Northumbrians want here?' and the other (evidently by a sportsman): 'Buck up, Newcastle United!'"

For a month only the Neuve Eglise sector was held, and then the 50th Division moved to Armentières. Before that event,

---

* The 6th Northumberland Fusiliers on the 27th June record the award of the Military Cross to Second-Lieut. W. Anderson and the D.C.M. to Lance-Corporal H. G. Smith for gallant services in the field.

however, the Division had a new commander, Major-General Sir W. F. L. Lindsay handing over command to Major-General the Earl of Cavan on the 29th of June. The 149th Brigade also had a new Brigadier in Brig.-General H. F. H. Clifford, who succeeded Brig.-General G. Fielding, the latter having vacated command on the same day as General Lindsay.*

ARMENTIERES

The move to the Armentières sector was occasioned by the formation of a new Army, *i.e.*, the Third, and the 50th Division was ordered to take over the right of the new II Corps line.

The relief of the 50th Division began on the night of the 14th–15th of July and continued on the two following nights, the G.O.C., Division, assuming command of the new sector at midnight, 17th–18th July.

The Division seems to have settled down in the Armentières sector by the end of July, and on the 31st of that month there is a sketch map of the Divisional area which practically shows the location of all units.

In *The 5th Battalion, The Durham Light Infantry* the sector is described thus: "The line held by our Division ran from the Armentières–Lille road on the right, through the ruins of the hamlet of L'Epinette to a point near Houplines.† The trenches were mainly breastworks and, as trenches went, were very comfortable, as one could walk about behind them with impunity, and to get into them one simply walked through a gap in the built-up parados. When resting, the men occupied recesses in the parapet, and the officers had wooden or sand-bag huts which were comfortable but useless as a protection against shell fire. In one trench there was a piano actually in the front-line, and the men had many good sing-songs. . . . The communication trenches were mostly wide and good. Some were not so good; who will ever forget 'Plank Avenue'—a

---

* On the 4th of July Brig.-General J. S. M. Shea arrived and assumed command of the 151st Brigade vice Brig.-General H. Martin. On the 6th the 2/1st Northumberland Field Company, R.E., joined the 50th Division, but was transferred to the 28th Division on the 10th of July; the 7th Field Company, R.E., joined the 50th Division on the 17th of June.

† Pont Ballot was roughly the left of the Divisional front.

double row of planks laid suspended over a ditch for several hundred yards and perilously slippery in wet weather, as many an unhappy member of a ration party discovered to his cost? . . . Some will remember the moat round the ruins of the farm, 'Grand Porte Egal,' and the perch which they frequently fished for and occasionally caught. Others will remember the huge chimney at the same farm, inside which, on the top rung of a long ladder, they used to stand observing the enemy's lines. Others will remember living in the 'Mushroom,' an advanced trench which was said to be mined. . . . The trenches were two or three hundred yards apart and a good deal of patrolling was done."

At the end of July, 1915, Divisional Headquarters were in Armentières; the 151st Brigade held the right sub-sector of the front line with the 6/8th Durham Light Infantry on the right, 7th Durham Light Infantry on the left and 5th Loyal North Lancs. (less one company near Fme. du Biez) and 9th Durham Light Infantry in billets in Armentières; the 150th Brigade held the left sub-sector with the 4th Green Howards, 5th Durham Light Infantry and 5th Green Howards (from right to left) in the front line and the 4th East Yorkshires in the Lunatic Asylum in Armentières; the 149th Brigade was in Divisional Reserve, two battalions being billeted in Armentières and three in Pont de Nieppe; "A" squadron Yorkshires and 50th Divisional Cyclist Company were also in Armentières. Of the Divisional Artillery, the 4th Durham (Howitzer) Battery was just south of Chapelle D'Armentières, the 5th Durham (Howitzer) Battery on the eastern outskirts of Armentières; the three batteries of the 1st Northumbrian Brigade, R.F.A., were in action as follows: 1st and 2nd just west of Chapelle D'Armentières, 3rd just north of the Lunatic Asylum; of the 2nd Northumbrian Brigade, R.F.A., the 1st and 2nd East Riding Batteries were west of Fme. de la Buterne, and the 3rd North Riding Battery just east of the Lunatic Asylum and railway; the 3rd Northumbrian Brigade, R.F.A., was in reserve, and the 1st, 2nd and 3rd Durham Batteries in Pont de Nieppe, and Brigade Headquarters in Armentières. The "Heavy" Battery, R.G.A., was still, apparently, west of the Yser Canal, supporting troops in the Ypres Salient. Of the three Field Ambulances, the 1st Northumbrian was at St. Jans Capel, the 2nd and 3rd Northumbrian in Armentières, where the A.D.M.S. also had his Headquarters;

the 50th Sanitary Section was also in the town. The C.R.E.*
had his Headquarters in Armentières, where also the 1st and
2nd Northumbrian Field Company, R.E., and the 7th Field
Company, R.E., were billeted. The Divisional Train,
D.A.D.O.S., the Mobile Veterinary Section were also located
in the town.

From time to time there were small units serving with the
Division who kept no diaries. There is, for instance, mention
of the 31st Trench Howitzer Battery which did good work,
also of a Mountain Battery.

At this period each infantry brigade served sixteen days in a
front-line sector, but early in August the time was reduced to
twelve days.

August began quietly with a continuance of fair, warm,
weather, but thunderstorms and deluges of rain were not
infrequent.

The enemy was quiescent and was inclined to adopt an
attitude of "live and let live." But that was not war, and it
was necessary to remind him very frequently of the fact. As
an instance: opposite Trench 70 (just south of Fme. Pt. Porte
Egal) the enemy had placed several iron shields in position
which obviously covered something important in his line. On
the night of the 3rd of August therefore arrangements were
made by the Brigadier of the 149th Brigade (which had taken
over the line of the 151st Brigade) to bring up one gun from
No. 2 Mountain Battery into Trench 70 for the purpose of
destroying the iron shields and the adjacent parapet, on the
night of the 4th. At 8 p.m. on the latter date the mountain
gun fired lyddite and shrapnel while the infantry in the trenches
opened simultaneous fire with rifles and machine-guns. After
ten minutes, during which considerable damage had been done
to the German trenches, fire was stopped.

Meanwhile the enemy (after the third round from the
mountain gun) had replied with a field gun and a maxim,
adding thereto subsequently the fire from trench mortars and
rifle grenades. This again drew retaliation with rifle grenades
and bombs from the 149th Brigade. The latter used on this
occasion a "new experimental trench mortar from the Second
Army workshops which worked with rapidity and accuracy."

---

* Lieut.-Colonel C. W. Singer assumed command of the Divisional R.E. as
C.R.E. on the night of the 16th of July.

In spite of all this commotion no casualties were sustained by the 149th Brigade: "This is doubtless due," records the Divisional Diary, "to the ample accommodation in the Steel Shelter Trenches."

On the afternoon of the 4th of August Major-General P. S. Wilkinson arrived on appointment to command the 50th Division vice Major-General the Earl of Cavan, who left on the 5th to assume command of the Guards Division, then in the process of formation.*

On the 7th the 151st Brigade provided four N.C.O.s and twenty privates to be trained at the Trench Howitzer School, Berthen, and drafted to the trench-howitzer batteries attached to the Division when their training was complete.

On the 11th of August, to the unbounded satisfaction of all ranks, the 6th and 8th Durham Light Infantry were again reorganised under separate commands. The temporary amalgamation had done much to cement the friendship existing between the two battalions. The Composite Battalion had ceased to exist from the 7th, but the new C.O. of the 6th (Lieut.-Colonel Borritt) did not arrive until the 11th.

The Division remained in the Armentières sector until the 12th of November and then moved to the Merris area, but certain items in the intervening period, *i.e.*, between August and November, should be recorded.

In France and Flanders the second half of the year 1915 was a period of great reorganisation and introduction of new methods of making war. Not only were New Army troops arriving in large numbers, which necessitated considerable training programmes, but it is possible to see from the records of all units how warfare was gradually becoming more and more scientific. Rifles with telescopic sights, Lewis guns, hand and rifle grenades in larger quantities, trench mortars, improved gas masks, were issued to the infantry in the front line, while at the end of October and in November the "poor old cannon" of the Division were at last, to the great satisfaction of the artillery, replaced by new 18-pounders and 4·5-in. howitzers. Truly heroic efforts had previously been made by the Divisional gunners to cope with the enemy's shell fire by

---

* On the 6th Lieut.-Colonel G. R. B. Spain, 6th Northumberland Fusiliers, assumed temporary command of the 149th Brigade, Brig.-General Clifford having been placed on the sick list.

means of their obsolete and limited-range 15-pounders. With new guns and a more generous allowance of ammunition the artillery were able to retaliate on the enemy with marked effect and decreased casualties amongst the front-line troops of the Division.

"It is to be doubted," said Capt. C. H. Ommanney, "if any of us were really sorry to see the last of the poor old decrepit things [the 15-pounders]. They eventually found their way to the coasts of Norfolk and Suffolk, where they eked out the remainder of their days in pathetic silence, waiting for a foe that never came. . . . With the departure of our old 'pip-squeaks' the Brigade [1st Northumbrian, also the Divisional Artillery generally] entered upon a new phase of its existence and a new chapter in its history."

It has already been pointed out that all men lived by comparison in those days and, compared with later periods of trench warfare, the time spent by the 50th Division in the Armentières sector, from August to November, 1915, was peaceful indeed. Still, unforgettable things happened even in that quiet period.

Take, for instance, the records of the 4th Northumberland Fusiliers, 149th Brigade. With that inimitable humour which formed so great a part of the British soldier's temperament, especially in war, the names of various enemy projectiles had been adopted by the Territorials. "Whizz-bangs" represented a particularly nasty type of shell, while "sausages" and "footballs" also adequately described the shape of other objectionable contraptions which the ingenious Bosche had invented for our annoyance. The firing of our trench howitzers produced "a large variety of *stuff* sent back at us."

On the 24th of September (the day before the Battle of Loos) the guns of the Third Army, on the right of the Second Army, were heard heavily bombarding the enemy all day. The Second Army had been ordered to co-operate on the 25th by making "demonstrations" and pretended attacks. The 50th Division, in addition to artillery, rifle and machine-gun fire, was to burn a lot of straw and phosphorous bombs out in front of the trenches in order to deceive the enemy into thinking that a gas attack was imminent. For this purpose the 4th Northumberland Fusiliers, with other units, had to carry straw up to the trenches during the daylight hours of the 24th, there being a thick mist at the time. But suddenly the mist lifted and disclosed to the eagle-eyed enemy parties of heavily-laden men moving from the support trenches up to the front line. Whereupon the German guns opened fire, with the result that twenty-two men were wounded, of whom seven belonged to the 4th Battalion. The work was then abandoned until nightfall.

The next morning (the straw, phosphorous bombs, etc., having in the meantime been put out in No Man's Land) the battalion on the right of the 4th Northumberland Fusiliers fired their "collection" too early, and soon the whole front of the Division became enveloped in smoke.

Result—complete silence from the enemy's trenches. A heavy mist also arose which put an end to observation. Altogether the events of the 25th of September "panned out" very differently from what was intended. Very heavy bombardments southwards are recorded on the 9th, 10th and 11th of October; the Germans were counter-attacking at Loos. Again, on the 13th of October (on which day the First Army at Loos was making a big attack on the Hohenzollern Redoubt) the Division co-operated with "demonstrations." "To-day," records the 4th Northumberland Fusiliers' Diary, "has been a 'joy-day.' At 2 p.m. the artillery fired for an hour and a half, four thousand rounds, and eight hundred rounds of high explosive at a selected sector of the enemy's wire and trenches. At the same time hundreds of phosphorous bombs were thrown over our parapet and made a tremendous cloud. All this was done to try and keep as many of the enemy here as possible while the First Army attacked in the south."

The Battalion (being then near Strazeele) began the formation of a Grenadier Company on the 29th of October, having been relieved on the 27th. Nothing of interest occurred until the 16th of November, when it is worth noting that a practice attack took place on trenches, "the same as German trenches in front of our Trench 80, in front of Armentières, taken by aeroplane photos."

Practice attacks over "model trenches" were later a very marked feature of training when out of the line; in November, 1915, they were somewhat of a novelty.

Some official diaries reveal the life of a unit on active service in a very interesting manner. The Diary of the 5th Northumberland Fusiliers contrives to give the reader a good idea of the existence lived by that battalion, without going into exhaustive and wearisome details.

On the 9th of August "there was a tremendous bombardment up north" (probably at Ypres). The 6th Division was engaged in recapturing Hooge (well known to the 50th Division) which had been lost in July. Next, on the 12th, "the men were in high spirits," for the Bosche, having treated the trenches to a "perfectly good" bombardment with "whizz-bangs," 4·2-in. shell and trench-mortar bombs—at least two hundred and fifty in all—had only succeeded in wounding one man slightly.

Flies were a great pest. The country was littered with refuse and old tins, which attracted them. Spraying the trenches with creosol, plus absolute cleanliness, was the only remedy.

On the 24th of August Second-Lieut. W. Winkworth was shot whilst on patrol. He was pluckily brought in by Sergeant Coppick and stretcher-bearers, but died on the 26th. "He was a very keen and promising officer and will be greatly missed," stated the C.O. of the 5th Northumberland Fusiliers in his diary.

"The Jesmond Jesters" gave a show at the Ecole Professionelle on the night of the 4th of September which "served as a refreshing contrast to life in the trenches and war in general. It is hoped to continue these concerts every Wednesday and Saturday throughout the winter if the War lasts long enough and the Bosches permit." The War *did* last long enough to permit the formation of, and performance by, many a famous concert party.

With October came wet and disagreeable weather. The trenches turned to mud channels—a forecast of the coming winter.

The records of the 6th Northumberland Fusiliers mostly describe the amount of work done in the trenches, and indulge in "small talk" of no particular interest historically. Two entries, however, are not without interest. The first is a statement that the daily expenditure of small arms ammunition in August was approximately eight rounds per rifle, taking the strength of the Battalion as the trench strength, *i.e.*, 13 officers and 307 other ranks.

The second entry is one to stir the imagination of those interested in espionage. The entry is dated the 28th of August, 1915: "The following was observed this morning; at 5.10 a.m. pigeons observed flying from behind our lines to the German lines; 5.40 a.m. three pigeons flew from German lines towards

Armentières; 7 a.m. two pigeons came from direction of Armentières and flew over German lines."

The new "tubular pattern smoke helmets" were issued in September and the "respirators" were withdrawn.

On the 29th of September a wire was received from Corps Headquarters emphasising the importance of obtaining a prisoner for identification purposes. The 6th Northumberland Fusiliers then concocted the following scheme: an excellent dummy figure in khaki was made. This was carried out and placed on the road near the enemy's lines. The figure was provided with a rifle and bandolier and, lying on its face on the road, looked just like a dead British soldier shot while patrolling. To complete the scheme two Very lights were fired from the ditch close by, the idea being to draw fire and then give a cry and a groan to induce the enemy to believe they had really shot the patrol. Watch was kept on the "corpse" from a ditch near by from 2.30 a.m. that morning and all next day and night until 1 a.m. the following morning, but without success.

This scheme having failed, another inducement was offered to Fritz to leave his trenches in the form of the latest daily paper placed in a cleft stick outside his wire. But still he refused to walk into the trap.

A certain number of steel helmets for experimental purposes were issued during September.

Little of more than ordinary interest is contained in the records of the 7th Northumberland Fusiliers.

The 5th Border Regiment were apparently great patrollers of No Man's Land, for their diaries contain almost daily entries concerning patrols carried out during the previous night. Successful patrolling was carried out on the night of the 27th of September by Capt. R. R. Blair and ten N.C.O.s and men, who discovered a German patrol and practically annihilated it, bringing back the body of one man, thus securing an identification. Valuable information was also obtained by Lance-Sergeant Tiffin and three men who went out again the same night and brought in several articles, including a German post-card.

The life led by the 149th Brigade during August, September, October and early November, as described in the foregoing pages, was very closely followed by the 150th and 151st Brigades. Every battalion went into the front line, served several days in varying degrees of comfort and discomfort, suffered casualties (small at this period compared with the daily total later), then handed over the line to other troops and went back into Armentières or the neighbourhood for a short rest. The word "rest," however, was somewhat of a snare and a delusion, for frequent "working parties" gave very little leisure and made one feel that the front-line trenches were far more preferable.

It is, therefore, only so far as "family matters" were concerned that one battalion diary differed from another. For instance, the arrival of a new C.O., such as happened to the 1/4th East Yorkshires when Lieut.-Colonel C. J. Deverell assumed command of the Battalion on the 21st of July, handing over a few months later (on the 10th of November) to Lieut.-Colonel W. T. Wilkinson.

"Our recollections of the Armentières trenches," said Major A. L. Raimes, "are mostly pleasant ones," but that was in summer. "As winter approached and the rains came they became extremely unpleasant. It was very difficult to drain them, and in most places they were at least knee-deep in water. To make things worse, the sand-bagged breastworks, which had looked so nice in the dry weather, began to give way and it was almost impossible, work as we would, to keep pace with the destruction."

Occasionally the diary of the 5th Durham Light Infantry takes a humorous turn. On the 21st of September it is recorded that: "The Division tries to brighten up our spare hours by succumbing to fashion's call and starting a cinematograph performance at the Ecole Professionelle, Armentières"; which was really a very worthy effort on the Division's part. On the 26th it is stated, "This being a Sunday we quite expected a noisy day, but the only signs of movement were in the village of Perenchies opposite where the Germans, living no doubt up to their reputation as 'Kulturists' were to be seen chasing some fair damsels about."

The Diary of 151st Brigade Headquarters contains only "casualties" and moves of battalions. The 6th and 8th Durham Light Infantry had resumed separate formations (11th August) only three days when Major Borritt, who had arrived to command the former battalion, left to command the 5th King's Shropshire Light Infantry.

The 6th Durhams on the 4th of October have the following pertinent remark in their diary: "Instructions have been received that every man in the Battalion should be taught to throw bombs and to fire them. *The many different patterns now in use in the Army render this a very difficult matter."*

On the same date also a store of brandy, *eau de vie*, and absinthe, was discovered by some men in a large cellar in Houplines village and carried off to billets. "There was a certain amount of trouble," records the Diary, "which was soon checked by the Battalion and Company-Sergeant-Majors."

"In trenches as above," varied by "In billets as above," are the almost daily records of the 7th Durham Light Infantry. Only occasionally is it possible to obtain any idea of what happened to the Battalion when in the line, and then from such entries as, "Our patrols acted with great energy and obtained some very useful information. . . . Hostile patrols are still conspicuous by their absence."

The lighter side of this period of trench warfare is touched upon by Major E. H. Veitch in his history of the 8th Durham Light Infantry. Writing of the new gas helmets issued in September he tells the following anecdote: "There was a story current about this time concerning a well-known general who, on his way to visit the trenches, discovered after he had gone some distance that he had omitted to bring his helmet, and one of his staff thereupon borrowed a satchel from a man for the use of the General. Whilst passing along a trench the General found a man minus his helmet and, after trying to impress upon the culprit the seriousness of the omission, said: 'You see, even I always carry one,' and putting his hand into the borrowed satchel drew out a pair of old and dirty socks."

Another incident related was the bagging of some champagne, evidently left behind by civilians in a distillery in Houplines, for which place the 8th Durhams had to find a guard.

"Whilst 'C' Company were finding this guard it became known by means of the Company Secret Service that there was still some champagne left in the building. Lieut. 'Jimmy' Schofield, always ready for anything, thereupon made up his mind that this must be rescued at all costs. He therefore paraded three of the officers' servants in full marching order, but with their packs stuffed with paper, etc., and marched them down to the distillery. There he filled the packs with the bottles of the last case of champagne and whatever he could lay his hands upon, and marched them back to Company Headquarters which, needless to say, lived in style for the next few days. Fortunately none of the Brigade Brass Hats, or other obstructionists, were about, their attention at the moment being fully occupied in enquiring into the dastardly conduct of certain officers who had caused their servants to remove a number of chairs from a deserted house into their mess in order that they might all be able to sit down at the same time."

The diaries of the 8th Durham Light Infantry make interesting reading, for they were well written and describe the life of the Battalion much more fully than the brief records kept by other units. On the 20th of September there is a specially interesting entry:

"The *morale* of the men in the trenches is excellent. There is a thorough spirit of quiet confidence, and all the men are conscious of being individually and collectively superior to the Germans. A few examples are given for record: On two or three occasions on going into the trenches the German snipers have been 'top dog' and have caused trouble. All ranks immediately lay themselves out to change this and are not satisfied until they have demonstrated their superiority. Careful watch is kept by observers, special snipers are put on and, if necessary, when the actual post of a hostile sniper cannot be marked down but only the general location, our field guns are asked to co-operate, which is nearly always effective. In every case we have left the trenches of late with a very distinct superiority of fire on our side. Again, men think nothing of firing over the parapet in daytime, there is no snap-shooting about it; they pick a target, it may be a loop-hole or a periscope, or a machine-gun emplacement, or a point where work is going on (it is quite the exception to see a German and when he does show himself he generally pays the penalty), they then take the most careful aim before firing and as often as not get a comrade to observe for them on their own initiative. After firing, men do not at once take cover but watch intently to see if there is any result from their shot. During the usual daily bombardments of our trenches officers and N.C.O.s have to be very quick to make the men get under cover; they will go on with their work until the last possible moment. It is not an uncommon sight to see a man go after the nose-cap of a German shell for a souvenir whilst the firing is going on. No opportunity is lost of bombing the enemy (when there are sufficient supplies of ammunition) on every occasion possible, and this is looked on with great delight by the men, who poke their heads over the parapet to watch results, and remarks are heard after good shots such as 'share that amongst you' and 'that's a bonnie y'en.' The catapult is the favourite bombing instrument, and the bombers always make it a point of honour to have the last shot, no matter what the German retaliation may be."

Only two incidents need be recorded from the diaries of the 9th Durham Light Infantry.*

On the 5th of October the 9th Battalion had received orders to train all men in bomb-throwing. Companies were, therefore, lectured and practised first of all in throwing "bully"-beef tins. In the afternoon "Lieut. Callandar was lecturing to 'D' Company on the G.S.II bomb when he exploded the bomb he had in his hand, killing himself and Private Renforth. Lieut. Boys-Stones and Second-Lieut. Edgar were slightly wounded and about seventeen N.C.O.s and men of one platoon wounded." The detonator had not, apparently, been first removed from the bomb.

This incident illustrates the dangerous nature of bombing when first introduced, for accidents were not infrequent.

The other concerned the wounding of an N.C.O. who had previously done good work in sniping and patrolling for the Battalion. On the 7th of November Lance-Corporal Carr was out in front of the wire. Fog covered the ground, but lifted suddenly and he was shot. At once Lieut. Palmer and Private Bell ran out and brought the wounded man in.

The tour of the 50th Division in the Armentières sector came to an end on the 12th of November when General Wilkinson handed over command to the G.O.C., 21st Division, at 11 a.m. The Division was then concentrated in the Merris–La Crèche area for training.

Divisional Headquarters during this period were at Merris; the 149th Brigade was in the Strazeele area, the 150th Brigade, Outtersteene, and the 151st Brigade, La Crèche.

THE SALIENT AGAIN

On the 7th of December General Wilkinson was informed by II Corps Headquarters that his Division was to rejoin the

---

* The Battalion Diary records that on the 20th of November Sergeant-Major Crouch, who had served seven years with the 9th Durham Light Infantry, left, as he had been given a commission as second-lieutenant in the 1st Durham Light Infantry.

V Corps and relieve the 9th Division in the front line, the relief to be completed by the 22nd of December. The move to the V Corps area was to take place between the 13th and 21st of that month.

One battalion from each of the three infantry brigades moved to the new area by train on the 17th of December, *i.e.*, 5th Northumberland Fusiliers to Canada Huts, 4th East Yorkshires and the 6th Durham Light Infantry to Dickebusch Huts, and one company of the 7th Durham Light Infantry to Canada Huts.

Certain changes had again taken place in the Division. While in the Armentières sector Army Headquarters had decided on the formation of Pioneer Battalions, each division to have one battalion, and on the 16th of December the 7th Durham Light Infantry of the 151st Brigade were formed into Divisional Pioneers. This necessitated the transfer of the 5th Border Regiment from the 149th Brigade to make the 151st up to four-battalion strength. The 5th Loyal North Lancs., who had joined the 50th Division on the 11th of June, were transferred on the 20th of December to the 55th Division.

The three battalions which moved to Canada and Dickebusch Huts on the 17th of December formed Divisional Reserve to the 9th Division, then holding the front line south-east of Ypres. On the 19th of December these battalions relieved three battalions of the 9th Division (one in each brigade of the latter division) in the front-line trenches.

This move was anything but propitious, for on this date the enemy again discharged gas on our line about Wieltje and as far back as Dickebusch Huts men had to wear their gas masks.

The sector of the line allotted to the 50th Division ran from just south-west of Hill 60 to a little short of the Menin road—a great change from the Neuve Eglise and Armentières areas.

"Gone were the peaceful days of Kemmel and Armentières," said Capt. Ommanney in his story of the 1st Northumbrian Brigade, R.F.A., while Colonel Shiel records, "from this time on we met real and bloody war." And what was true of the gunners was true also of the infantry and all units of the Division—days and nights of fighting and noise and discomforts innumerable.

The discomforts began with the arrival of the three battalions at Canada and Dickebusch Huts. The former were thus described by the 6th Northumberland Fusiliers (who followed the 5th Battalion a few hours later): "These huts were in good condition, but the approaches were just the reverse, for they were duck-boards supported on piles, and if by some misfortune you stepped off these duck-boards you sank knee-deep in liquid mud." The 5th Durham Light Infantry, at Dickebusch Huts, record much the same thing: "The huts were passable, but they were like islands in a sea of mud, into which it was very easy for a luckless wayfarer to fall."

On the 18th the 6th Durham Light Infantry, the 1/4th East Yorkshires and the 5th Northumberland Fusiliers moved forward still closer to the front line, *i.e.*, the former battalion to Canal Dug-outs, Maple Copse, Sanctuary Wood and Redoubts 2, 3 and 4; the East Yorkshires to Railway Dug-outs, and the Northumberland Fusiliers to Bedford House and Blawepoort Farm.

The 19th began badly, all battalions recording that early that morning they were awakened by violent gun fire: "We were woken up at 5 a.m.," record the 5th Northumberland Fusiliers, "by hearing rapid rifle fire and guns firing. Soon it was taken up all round, and it was evident that there was something on, as the fire became very heavy. Shortly after we got a message telling us to 'stand to' and that the Germans were making a gas attack. Soon we were able to smell the gas, which was apparently coming over from the north side of the Salient where the attack seemed to be taking place, as the guns on our side soon quietened down. The gas was not strong at Bedford House, and we did not put on our helmets, though our eyes were affected, probably by gas shells, and we had to put on our eye-protectors."

"In the meantime the intense gun fire by both sides was being kept up, the Germans shelling everywhere indiscriminately, all round Bedford House and the roads, so that there seemed to be shells dropping everywhere one looked. About noon we got orders to 'stand down,' which was a relief, and we heard that the gas attack had been made on the 6th and 49th Divisions, who were holding the line in the neighbourhood of Potijze and Wieltje, and that no infantry attack had followed the gas.

"The Germans kept up the bombardment all day, still shelling all the roads indiscriminately, and we thought towards evening that unless things quietened down a bit we should not be able to carry out the relief. However, the company officers and the C.O. went up to look at the trenches we were taking over and we got orders to 'carry on.'

"The 6th Battalion (Northumberland Fusiliers) relieved us in Brigade Reserve and we got up to the trenches without any casualties, which was very lucky considering the amount of shell fire there was through the night.

"We relieved the 8th Gordons in trenches 36 to 38. . . . The relief was completed by 8 p.m."

All three brigades of the 50th Division were to go into the front line, the 149th on the right, 150th in the centre, and the 151st on the left. The right sub-sector was immediately west of the famous Hill 60, and the centre, Mount Sorrel—both the scenes of subsequent heavy fighting.

The relief of the infantry of the 9th Division was completed on the night of the 20th–21st of December, and by the following morning battalions holding the front line (from right to left) were 5th and 6th Northumberland Fusiliers (149th Brigade), 4th East Yorkshires and 4th Green Howards (150th Brigade) and 6th and 8th Durham Light Infantry (151st Brigade).

Divisional Headquarters were established at Hooggraaf, south of Poperinghe.

The Divisional Artillery went into action north, south and west of the Zillebeke Lake, *i.e.*, the 1st Northumbrian Brigade, R.F.A., had batteries in the neighbourhood of Hell Fire Corner (east of Ypres), French Farm, and north of Lankhof Fme.; the 2nd Northumbrian Brigade, south-east of Trois-Rois, south of Kruisstraat and by the side of the Ypres–Comines Canal, north of the Doll's House; the 3rd Northumbrian Brigade occupied positions between Trois-Rois and Woodcote House, near Blawepoort Fme. and near French Farm; of the 4th (Howitzer) Brigade, R.F.A., one battery was near the School, east of Ypres, and the other in the neighbourhood of French Farm.[*]

All these battery positions are expressed in co-ordinates in the official documents, but no description of the horrible surroundings in which the gunners found themselves, nor of the vile conditions under which they lived, are contained in the records. From the private writings of Colonel Shiel and

---

[*] These positions are as near as possible to the co-ordinates given in an appendix with the G.S. Diary of the Division.

Capt. Ommanney, however, the existence of the gunners of the 1st Northumbrian Brigade is graphically described:

"The positions were as follows: 1st Battery in a ruined château at Hell Fire Corner, between the Menin road on the north and the Roulers railway on the south. The guns were in what remained of a rose pergola, firing south-eastwards over the trenches at Mount Sorrel, across Halleblaast Farm and Zillebeke. There was an O.P. on the chimney at the Tuileries near Zillebeke, and another in a mined dug-out at Rudkin House on Observatory Ridge, behind Armagh Wood; but the best place for observing the zone was from a point in the trenches on the left of Mount Sorrel. As a matter of fact the chimney at Zillebeke was knocked down by the Bosche the very first day we were there, and Rudkin House was smashed to pieces a few days later."

Of this position Colonel Shiel says: "For honest filth and disgusting conditions it would be hard to beat. . . . There was an excellent academy picture of an aeroplane fight above, *i.e.*, 1916 or 1917, and I was interested to see that our particular position was shown by the artist as a cloud of dust and bursting shells, which we found very true to life.

"The 2nd Battery was in a hedge near Blawepoort Farm, not a very nice position, with very little protection or comfort for anyone. Observation was from the trenches for the most part, but Rudkin House was also used. The 3rd Battery was in a very exposed position in front of Bedford House near the Lille road. The position was strong enough to resist direct hits from quite heavy guns, but was so open to observation from the neighbourhood of Wytschaete that it became practically untenable.

"The zone normally covered by the Brigade extended from the northern flank of Hill 60 up to and including Mount Sorrel."

All that the above two officers said of their Brigade regarding conditions was shared by the other brigades: the area between scarred and battered Ypres and the German trenches east of the city was shell-torn and blasted; roads almost obliterated had been replaced by duck-board trenches which spanned mud pools and led across water-logged and broken craters, the troubled earth knowing no peace from the storm of screaming and bursting shells which continually fell upon it.

The ridge along which the opposing front line ran was marked at its southern end by the bald and blasted hummocks of Hill 60 and The Bluff, whence it circled round a low-lying, menacing upland, scrubby as an unshaven chin, with the ragged stumps of Sanctuary, Armagh and Green Howard Woods to the Menin road and the heap of bricks and rubble that had once been Hooge.

Within this semicircle, scanned by the watchful eye of the Hun, lay a country of tangled weeds and crops run wild; of ruined farms and broken country houses, sodden, stinking, pestilential. Movement in daylight by parties of more than two or three was impossible, and the very trees looked hopeless and desolate.

Day by day, what had once been fair countryside was dying a slow and agonising death; not a humble flower grew in the hedgerow, or crouched beneath some kindly wall, but was torn from its setting and tossed to the winds, as if to demonstrate man's contempt for Nature.

Looking east from the ramparts of Ypres one saw a smoking country, as if numerous cauldrons were sending wreaths of smoke heavenwards, so frequent were shell bursts. The city, itself, was the abode of Death. No one lingered in the streets, silent and deserted in the daylight hours save for the awful roar of bursting shells. As if they were plague spots, such places as the Menin and Lille Gates were shunned and avoided, for the German gunners had marked them down, and "gate" had long been a misnomer. Even at this period Ypres was horrible, ghastly.

More closely defined, but only as far as can be gathered from various sources (there being no maps of any description with the divisional, brigade or battalion diaries), the front line held by the 149th Brigade ran from about five hundred yards south of Verbrandenmolen, thence in a north-easterly direction to the Ypres–Comines railway on the northern side of which was Hill 60, the crest of the latter being held by the enemy. From the Hill the line bent back slightly, forming a small re-entrant, to the Zillebeke–Zwarteleen road, thence from the latter took an easterly turn, the left boundary of the Brigade area being north of Zwarteleen village: the 150th Brigade then continued the line which curved north-eastwards to Observatory Ridge road and the southern slope of Hill 62. From (and including the latter) the 151st Brigade line ran almost northerly, up through Sanctuary Wood until within five hundred yards of the Menin road and due west of Stirling Castle, the latter being held by the enemy. The distance between the opposing lines of trenches varied; opposite Stirling Castle, for instance, they were only about twenty yards apart, on Hill 60 there was a distance of some few feet only, while in other sections of the line some two to three hundred yards separated British and Germans.

In rear of the 149th Brigade line were The Dump, the ruins of Verbrandenmolen village and Larch Wood; the Verbranden road; Ypres–Comines railway and Zillebeke–Zwarteleen road ran from north-west to south-east through the sub-sector. Behind the front line of the 150th Brigade were Armagh House and Wood, Fosse Wood, Knoll Farm, Battersea Farm and Rudkin House. Observatory Ridge was apparently the dividing line between the centre and left sub-sectors of the Divisional front. The 151st Brigade line was more "wooded" as it followed the eastern outskirts of Sanctuary Wood; west of the Wood lay Maple Copse and Lodge, Valley Cottages, Dormy House and Yeomanry Post. Zillebeke Lake, with the village at the eastern end, occupied roughly the centre of the Divisional area. Other places of note (not already mentioned) were Shrapnel Corner (a very "unhealthy" spot), about seven hundred yards south of the Lille Gate, Ypres, Transport Farm, the Moated Grange (north of Zillebeke Lake), Halfway, Bedford and Gordon Houses.

To get to the centre sector of the line the usual route was via Shrapnel Corner and Transport Farm, thence along the railway line to Zillebeke station, past the outskirts of Zillebeke village and along the road to Observatory Ridge. From the latter point duck-board tracks led to short communication trenches into the front line.

The 8th Durhams, who followed the 6th into the line, on the march up went via Kruisstraat then, following the road which skirted the northern end of Zillebeke Lake, passed Yeomanry Post and through Maple Copse to the front line.

The storm of shell fire which swept the Salient during the enemy's gas attack on the 19th of December was continued throughout the 20th, at the close of which the first three battalions in the line had already suffered between 30 and 40 casualties. The 5th Northumberland Fusiliers had lost 1 officer and 12 other ranks wounded, the 1/4th East Yorkshires 3 other ranks wounded. The 6th Durhams, on the left, lost 6 men killed and 12 wounded during the night of the

19th–20th. Their C.O., Lieut.-Colonel J. W. Jeffreys, was wounded in both legs, the same shell also wounding Major Simmons and a Royal Engineers officer, besides killing 3 men. While the C.O. was being evacuated from the front line no less than forty "whizz-bangs" burst in the area.

Gone indeed were the comparatively quiet days at Neuve Chapelle and Armentières!

Little more than a week now remained before the close of 1915—a year long to be remembered by those who survived the War as a period of great preparation as well as of great privation; a year which saw a tremendous advance in the invention of war material and appliances and in the making of war.

Colonel Shiel and Capt. Ommanney have already given some idea of what conditions were like behind the front line, but only an isolated phrase here and there in the diaries of the infantry battalions refers to the condition of the forward trenches. The 4th Northumberland Fusiliers on Christmas Eve state that "the trenches are perfectly appalling and the mud indescribable."

Mud! mud! mud! Ankle-deep, knee-deep and sometimes waist-deep, in which men carried on an agonising existence during the whole tour in the front line, then emerging like half-drowned rats, smothered in mud from head to foot, aching and shivering!

"Trench foot" had made its appearance, but rubbing the feet with whale oil and the frequent changing of socks helped greatly in reducing the agonies of that horrible complaint.

Came Christmas Day and, whether in the front line or in reserve, or billeted some distance behind the lines, all units did their best to be "cheery."

The 6th Northumberland Fusiliers record that this Christmas Day was cold, showery and muddy, "but everyone seemed very cheery for all that. Plum puddings from home gladdened the sight and appetites of all ranks"; the officers had "a turkey brought away captive from Strazeele."

But, generally, there is little of outstanding importance to record of the remainder of 1915, at the close of which one battalion wrote in its diary:

"Well! so ends, perhaps, the most memorable year in history —most of us, I think, hope that in this case history won't repeat itself!"

A vain hope, alas! For the sun which dawned behind leaden skies on the 1st of January, 1916, was to look down later during that year on an orgy of bloodshed such as had never before been witnessed in all the battles of the world.

And here, for a moment, it is necessary to digress from the history of the 50th Division to give the reader some idea of the military situation in France and Flanders when the New Year dawned.

Sir John French had handed over command of the British Armies to Sir Douglas Haig on the 19th of December, 1915. By that date the "Little Army" of four infantry divisions plus one infantry brigade, a cavalry division and a cavalry brigade, which had withstood the first onslaughts of the enemy at Mons on the 23rd of August, 1914, had expanded already to three Armies consisting of forty infantry and cavalry divisions, besides which there were three Canadian divisions and a host of Army Corps troops attached to the fourteen corps then in existence; a vast increase indeed. Territorial and New Army division had been pouring into France and Flanders during 1915 and had won golden opinions for their military spirit and fighting qualities. The year 1916 was to see those qualities tested still further.

New Year's Day, 1916, was celebrated by every gun in the 50th Division firing for five minutes on the German trenches. The enemy took this provocation all very meekly and did not reply.

The year began with all three brigades in the front line, 149th on the right, 150th in the centre, and 151st on the left, though before the close of January the first-named brigade had handed over a section of its right to the 3rd Division, retaining only a small portion of trench line on the southern side of the railway cutting held by half a company. The 150th Brigade was withdrawn into Divisional Reserve on the 1st of February, Corps Headquarters having ordered the G.O.C., 50th Division, to hold the line with two brigades only.

Two other items of general interest happened in the Division during January. The trench-mortar units were definitely formed into "light" and "medium" batteries, the former (4-in. and 4-pounders) being manned entirely by infantry personnel, and the latter (1½-in. and 2-in.) by artillery personnel; one battery of each was allotted to each infantry brigade. The second was the formation of Brigade Machine-Gun Companies.

Previously each battalion had a machine-gun section, but under the new organisation these four sections were formed into one company as a Brigade Machine-Gun Company. Lewis guns had begun to arrive in larger quantities and several were issued to each battalion.

"The old order changeth," and gradually the 50th Division (and indeed every division in France and Flanders) was being completely reorganised.

To describe the life of every battalion in the front line early in 1916 would mean a good deal of repetition, for one sector was very much like another so far as the general trend of trench warfare was concerned. An excellent idea of the sort of thing which happened at all hours of the day and night is given in the Headquarters Diary of the 149th Brigade on the 17th of January:

"11 a.m. Reports from the trenches: about 6.30 p.m. yesterday evening a dozen bombs were thrown over by our men from a West thrower in Trench 40, and one of our machine-guns opened fire at the same time. The enemy seemed to think it was a bombing attack and started throwing bombs vigorously into No Man's Land. This was kept up for about ten minutes. When they had quietened down we started again with the West throwers, but the enemy realised what was happening and replied with rifle grenades and 'sausages.' We then again had our innings with the West throwers, rifle grenades, 18-pounders and howitzers, which again brought into action the enemy's 'whizz-bangs,' causing two small breaches in 47 S."

This activity was practised in order to keep up the offensive spirit in both officers and men, for life in the trenches was apt to become stagnant. The line had to be held between the fighting of great battles and actions. For this reason patrol work and raids were invaluable in keeping all ranks braced up to the highest pitch. It was good also to induce our front-line troops to obtain and retain the mastery over their opponents across No Man's Land. One finds in the records, for instance, a statement that on such-and-such-a-date the Bosche threw twelve bombs across into our trenches; he was given twenty-four in reply which successfully cooled his ardour. In some divisions it was a recognised thing that the enemy was paid doubly for what he gave. And yet it was astonishing how frequently little damage was done by a storm of shells. One gun of the Divisional Artillery had been marked down by the enemy, who put over one hundred heavy howitzer shells without doing any damage!

The most prominent features of the German line were Hill 60 and The Snout in the right sub-sector, and the Birdcage in the left sub-sector. These three places occasioned a lot of shelling, bombing and trench-mortaring; they were the object of almost nightly patrolling.

The dispositions of the Divisional Pioneers and the Royal Engineers Companies at this period were as follows: the Field Companies at Bedford House, Manor Farm and Zillebeke; the Pioneers (7th Durham Light Infantry) at Canada Huts, Bedford House, Ypres and the Canal Dug-outs.

The 7th Durhams since their formation into Divisional Pioneers had done good work, and the records speak of their untiring energies on behalf of their comrades in the line. It took the Battalion a little time to fall into its new work, but once the training period was over all ranks "set to" and did their job well.

The Divisional Royal Engineers (1st and 2nd Northumbrian Field Companies and 7th Field Company) worthily upheld the great reputation which the "Sappers" generally, from the beginning of the War, had made for themselves.

The enemy's heavy and constant shell fire was responsible for temporary breaches in the signal lines at all hours of the day and night. Yet, they were repaired almost immediately. Wading about in seas of mud, laying cables in ground which was nothing more or less than a morass, the Sappers carried on with their unenviable tasks uncomplainingly, and won the golden opinion of all for whom they laboured.

The two units, Royal Engineers and Pioneers, were thrown much together by the partial similarity of their work, chiefly in digging field works which were almost always supervised by the Sappers, whose training was superior.

The medical diaries of the 50th Division furnish interesting reading to those who would know something of the care of sick and wounded during the War. The diaries of the A.D.M.S. of the Division (Colonel H. S. Thurston) are full of detail, brief at times but nevertheless very readable. His three field amulances were, at this period, situated as follows: 1st Northumbrian Field Ambulance on the Poperinghe–Reninghelst road, about half-way between the two places; 2nd

Northumbrian Field Ambulance at Wippenhoek; 3rd Northumbrian Field Ambulance, near the 1st Northumbrian Field Ambulance. These were the headquarters of the three ambulances. The Advanced Dressing Stations were in Armagh Wood, just south of the Observatory Ridge road, in Maple Copse and in Railway Dug-outs, south-west of Zillebeke Lake. Regimental Aid Posts were just east of Verbrandenmolen (2); in Armagh Wood, Sanctuary Wood (2), Maple Copse, Blawepoort Farm, and just south-west of Railway Dug-outs.

It is very evident from Colonel Thurston's records that the Division was fortunate in its doctors. "Trench foot," that most distressing complaint, was so well kept under by preventative measures that during January, 1916, there were only eight cases in the whole of the Division. "Scabies" was, however, the source of much trouble and accounted for a large proportion of the sickness. It was apparently largely brought into the Division by drafts, for on the 25th of January the A.D.M.S. wrote in his diary: "The men, on the whole, are of good physique, but many turn up in a dirty condition suffering from lousiness and scabies. In one draft of one hundred and fifty men twenty-three were found with scabies.

Of "lousiness" he records: "It has been proved that practically every man in the front line suffers from some degree of lousiness, and that the extent depends a good deal on the personal element. Disinfection, even for thirty or forty minutes, does not in every case destroy the lice, and though their destruction would be helped by subsequent washing in water to which creosol has been added, the washerwomen strongly object to creosol as it affects their hands."

"Lousiness" was part of the War—everybody suffered from it, from G.O.C. to private, and the only thing was to make light (as many constantly did) of a disgusting condition from which there seemed to be no escape.

In the midst of all the filth and mud and abominable conditions prevailing in the forward areas it was surprising that the health of the Division remained "generally very good"—surely a great tribute to the A.D.M.S. and his energetic medical officers.

In tending the wounded the devotion of the doctors was remarkable. Here, for instance, is the story of what happened on the 2nd of March.

"The trenches on 'The Bluff' were captured early this morning by the Division on our right. The 50th Division made a demonstration and drew heavy fire. The enemy placed a barrage of high explosive and shrapnel behind the railway cutting lasting, intermittently, for several hours. During this time considerable difficulty was experienced in evacuating the wounded; the Regimental Aid Post near the cutting was partially destroyed, and was unapproachable on account of heavy shell fire. Lieut. Bluett, 3rd Northumbrian Field Ambulance, acting Medical Officer to the 8th Durham Light Infantry, showed conspicuous gallantry and presence of mind in removing the wounded to a sap under cover, thereby undoubtedly saving many lives. The stretcher-bearers of all Field Ambulances did excellent work in attending to and evacuating wounded under heavy shell fire and difficult conditions, particularly those of the 3rd Northumbrian Field Ambulance, whose duty it was to evacuate the wounded from the railway cutting. These men, though having several casualties, made their way to the cutting and all the wounded were cleared by 10 a.m. No. 1523, Corporal Cheery, No. 1606, Lance-Corporal Filer, and No. 1541, Private Scott, of this unit, have been recommended for the D.C.M., and Lieut. R. P. Bluett for the Military Cross for conspicuous gallantry and devotion to duty."[*]

It is good to read the above in praise of the stretcher-bearers, whose splendid devotion to duty and unselfish work on behalf of their stricken comrades so often passed unnoticed. No troops were ever more worthy of commendation than those who worked day and night in picking up and carrying to safety wounded officers and men.

The non-combatant troops of a division were seldom in what was called the "limelight," but their work, their staunchness, deserved very much more praise than was given them. For instance, at no time of the day, and seldom at night, was it "safe" to traverse the rear communications, but the Army Service Corps in delivering rations and supplies "carried on" amidst shell fire and, at times, under extraordinary difficulties, in order that the troops in the front line might not go short of food. The supply arrangements were one of the marvels of the War.

---

[*] Extract from the diary of the A.D.M.S., 50th Division.

The Refilling Point at this period was apparently Wippenhoek, and there the O.C., Divisional Train (Lieut.-Colonel E. W. R. Pinkney), gathered his companies.* A German aeroplane bombed the Refilling Point on the 18th of February but whether there were casualties, or the extent of damage done, is not recorded.

On the 8th of February the General Staff Diary of the Division gives the following list of General Staff Officers at Headquarters: Major-General P. S. Wilkinson, commanding 50th Division; G.S.O. I, Brevet Lieut.-Colonel A. G. Stuart; G.S.O. II, Major H. W. B. Thorp; G.S.O. III, Capt. W. Anderson.

In his first despatch, dated the 19th of May, 1916, Sir Douglas Haig gave a very excellent description of trench warfare during the winter of 1915–1916, and although somewhat lengthy it is so informative and interesting as to merit repetition, for it gives (more than the official diaries give) a complete insight into trench life generally and, so far as the 50th Division was concerned, the kind of existence followed by units in the front line during their tour in the Sanctuary Wood–Hill 60 sectors:

"The maintenance and repair of our defences alone, especially in winter, entails constant heavy work. Bad weather and the enemy combine to flood and destroy trenches, dug-outs and communications; all such damage must be repaired promptly, under fire, and almost entirely by night.

"Artillery and snipers are practically never silent, patrols are out in front of the lines every night, and heavy bombardments by the artillery of one or both sides take place daily in various parts of the line. Below ground there is continual mining and counter-mining, which by the ever-present threat of sudden explosion and the uncertainty as to when and where it will take place, causes perhaps a more constant strain than any other form of warfare. In the air there is seldom a day, however bad the weather, when aircraft are not busy, reconnoitring, photographing and observing fire. All this is taking place constantly at any hour of the day or night and in any part of the line. In short, although there has been no great incident of historic

---

* The four companies, *i.e.*, Northumbrian Divisional Company (Headquarters), Northumberland Brigade Company, York and Durham Brigade Company and the Durham Light Infantry Brigade Company, had been numbered respectively 467, 468, 469 and 470 Companies, Army Service Corps.

importance on the British front during the period under review, a steady and continuous fight has gone on, day and night, above ground and beneath it. . . .

"One form of minor activity deserves special mention, namely, the raids or 'cutting-out parties,' which are made at least twice or three times a week against the enemy's line. They consist of a brief attack with some special object on a sector of the opposing trenches, usually carried out by a small body of men. The character of these operations—the preparation of a road through our own and the enemy's wire—the crossing of the open ground unseen—the penetration of the enemy's trenches —the hand-to-hand fighting—in the darkness and the uncertainty as to the strength of the opposing force—gives scope to the gallantry, dash and quickness of decision of the troops engaged, and much skill and daring are frequently displayed in these operations."

From the 19th of December there had been over sixty local actions, amongst which were "The operations at The Bluff, the Hohenzollern Redoubt and at St. Eloi; the mining operations and crater fighting in the Loos Salient and on the Vimy Ridge, and the hostile gas attacks north of Ypres in December and opposite Hulluch and Messines in April."

Between the 18th and 19th of February the enemy's activity increased in the Ypres Salient. A series of small infantry attacks, preceded generally by intense bombardments and the explosion of mines, were made by him. These attacks may have been solely for the purpose of securing local points of vantage, but they may also have been made with the idea of drawing attention from the French line about Verdun, upon which the enemy had made plans to launch a great attack on the 21st of February. In these small attacks the 50th Division were concerned more or less.

The Bluff was just outside, and on the right of, the Divisional area and was held by the 17th Division. This place was a narrow ridge some thirty to forty feet high, covered with trees, on the northern bank of the Ypres–Comines Canal. It was probably formed when the Canal was dug—a heap of earth thrown up by the excavators. At this period, however, it was a distinct feature at the southern bend of the Ypres Salient, and ran outwards through the British lines almost into the German area; our trenches ran over the eastern end of this ridge, known as The Bluff.

On the 12th of February the 149th Brigade had taken over the left sub-sector of the Divisional front line, the 150th Brigade remaining on the right. Twice that day the Germans had left their trenches and had attacked our line north of the Menin road, but had been shot back again.

Just before 3.30 p.m. on the 14th the enemy opened a heavy bombardment of the Hooge trenches, held by the 24th Division immediately on the left of the 50th Division. At 3.30 p.m. he began to shell Trenches 37, 38 and 39 (opposite Hill 60 and astride the railway) and the area in rear held by the 150th Brigade. The 4th Green Howards were holding the line on the right, and the 4th East Yorkshires on the left, the 5th Green Howards being in close support and the 5th Durham Light Infantry in Brigade Reserve. Of the 149th Brigade, the 7th Northumberland Fusiliers were on the right and the 4th Battalion on the left; the 6th were in close support, and the 5th in Brigade Reserve.

The 149th, however, seemed to have escaped the very heavy bombardment to which units on their right and left were subjected: "The whole of the day the trenches immediately to our right and left came in for a very heavy and, at times, intense bombardment, and it was apparent that the enemy intended to put in an attack at some point or other." All the approaches up from Kruisstraat were shelled with "whizz-bangs" and high explosive, and the Brigade Office at Zillebeke Dug-outs was blown in and a good deal of material destroyed.

The enemy's bombardment continued until 5 p.m. Meanwhile the 151st Brigade had been warned to move at half an hour's notice. At 5.25 p.m. V Corps heavy artillery opened fire and put down "intense retaliation." Twenty-five minutes later there was a roar—the enemy had blown two mines short of Trenches 49 and A.1. Our line, however, suffered no damage, and patrols immediately went out and reconnoitred the craters which were found clear of the enemy. One crater was no less than sixty feet in diameter and about fifteen feet deep. At 6 p.m. there was another roar and another mine was exploded at the eastern end of 41, where there was a bombing sap manned by the 4th Green Howards. The sap was completely destroyed, thirteen of the Green Howards being killed and four wounded. But still the enemy made no attempt to advance. Several small parties of the enemy came out in front of 50, but were shot down.

Meanwhile the heavy bombardment of Trenches 37, 38 and 39 continued, and at 7.36 p.m. General Wilkinson received a message from the 51st Brigade (17th Division), on his right, that the Germans had advanced and taken Trenches 33 and 34, the garrisons being driven back to their support line. A counter-attack by the 51st Brigade on the 15th was unsuccessful. The 16th is reported as fairly quiet by the 150th Brigade Headquarters, whose diary also records that "The 4th Yorkshires (Green Howards), in spite of their losses (1 officer killed, 2 wounded, 20 other ranks killed, and 51 wounded) from the bombardments and explosion of mines, were cheerful and unshaken."

The remainder of February was passed in normal trench warfare, though secret preparations were being made to recapture The Bluff.

Seventeen days elapsed and then, on the 2nd of March, the 17th and 3rd Divisions, after several days' preliminary bombardment of the enemy's trenches and more than one simulated attack to deceive him, recaptured The Bluff.

The 50th Division assisted with "demonstrations," *i.e.*, artillery bombardments, bombing and trench-mortaring. In fact the 151st Brigade, holding the right of the Divisional front, appeared to have "let off" everything they had, producing a great deal of "jumpiness" in the German lines, the enemy evidently expecting an attack also by the 50th Division.

In March also trench warfare was very strenuous. Mining activity was considerable, the peculiar nature of the ground lending itself to deep digging.

Changes along the Divisional front took place; the 24th Division relieved the 149th Brigade in the left sub-sector of the Divisional front, and only one brigade (with two battalions and half a machine-gun company attached) held the line. Towards the end of the month, however (on the 23rd), the Division took over from the 3rd Division (which had relieved the 17th), from the Ypres–Comines Canal at The Bluff to Trench 34, the 50th Divisional front being held once more by two brigades and extending from The Bluff to Trench A.3.

The trench-mortar batteries were again reorganised during March. Stokes guns had been issued and three light trench-mortar batteries were formed, each armed with 3-in. Stokes light trench mortars; they were manned by the infantry. The medium trench-mortar batteries, of which there were three, were numbered X.50, Y.50 and Z.50, and manned by the artillery. The new medium mortar was a 2-in. gun.

A West spring gun for throwing grenades was also in use at this period.

On the night of the 7th–8th of March snow fell to a depth of four inches, and the whole countryside was white the next morning.

There is an entry in the Divisional General Staff Diary on the 18th of March which does not make very pleasant reading, but it should be recorded: "Germans held complete command of the air over 50th Divisional front and observed our dispositions at their pleasure." Our air service was, early in 1916, still in process of development. The enemy's Fokker 'plane had made its appearance during the autumn of 1915, and up to May, 1916, held command of the air; by the 1st of July, however, when the Somme Battles began, we had recovered command by the introduction of new machines and newer methods of aerial fighting and manœuvre. But such was the reason German aeroplanes, in March, 1916, flew at will over the 50th Divisional area.

On the 27th of March the 3rd Division blew six mines under the German salient at St. Eloi, and the right of the 151st Brigade, especially near The Bluff and Lankhof, came in for a good deal of hostile artillery fire. The Brigade Diary records that "A mountain of flame [was] seen and what were reported as the largest craters yet found on the Western Front were made. The mines were deep and big, and one huge crater was one hundred and twenty-five yards in diameter. On the 29th of March two battalions of Canadians arrived to relieve two of the 149th Brigade. For on the 15th of March V Corps Headquarters had notified General Wilkinson, in a secret communication, that portions of the V Corps and the Canadian Corps were to change places in the line between the 25th of March and the 6th of April, the 50th Division relieving the 2nd Canadian Division.

On the 28th of March the 150th Brigade, then in Divisional Reserve, marched from Ouderdom to No. 2 Canadian Rest Area between Méteren and Bailleul. The relief of the 149th Brigade by the 3rd Canadian Brigade was completed at 11.45 p.m. on the 30th of March. The 151st Brigade was due to be relieved by the 1st Canadian Brigade on the 2nd of April. But before the Brigade got away it suffered a heavy gruelling from the enemy's artillery. With four aeroplanes observing and registering targets the German guns fairly plastered the whole area and the whole of Brigade Headquarters dug-outs at Zillebeke were blown in. Capt. J. G. Harter (Brigade-Major 151st Brigade) was severely wounded and died the next morning; ten of the servants, clerks and signallers attached to Headquarters were also wounded, some dying later. The relief was carried out with great difficulty owing to artillery activity and dense fog, and was not completed until 2.20 a.m. on the 3rd.

During the afternoon of the 3rd of April 50th Divisional Headquarters moved from Hooggraaf to Westoutre, and General Wilkinson assumed command of the new sector at 3 p.m.

WYTSCHAETE

The Wytschaete sector ran from the neighbourhood of Spanbroekmolen (in the German lines) thence northwards in an irregular line, crossing Vandamme Hill to the Vierstraat–Wytschaete road, just north of Byron Farm; thence the line bent in a north-easterly direction to just south of the eastern extremity of Bois Confluent.

All three infantry brigades were in the line, 150th on the right, whose sub-sector ended west of Petit Bois; 149th in the centre from the left of the 150th to just north of Byron Farm and the 151st on the left to Bois Confluent. E.1 to H.1a were the trenches on the right, H.3 to L.5 in the centre and M.1 to O.4 on the left.

Wytschaete lay in the centre, behind the German lines, and the Ridge gave the enemy observation over a good deal of the Divisional area. To a certain extent, however, the advantage thus held by the enemy was nullified by the Kemmel Hills (of which Mont des Cats was the highest feature) being just behind the Divisional forward area, and from which good observation over the enemy's trenches and back areas was obtainable. The 50th Divisional gunners were thus able to detect the enemy's gun positions. As a consequence, his artillery fire was not nearly as severe as it might have been had he not been afraid of giving away the positions of his guns. From behind Wytschaete, however, the enemy concentrated a good deal of his fire on the Ypres Salient.

To counter the disadvantage of not being able to use his artillery as freely as he wished on the Divisional gun positions the enemy had installed large numbers of trench mortars in, and just in rear of, his front line, with which he proceeded to give the infantry of the 50th Division a "rough time." His artillery also shelled the front-line trenches pretty heavily.

There had, however, been heavy fighting round about the St. Eloi craters, St. Eloi being on the immediate left of the Divisional sector, and that may have accounted for the unusual activity shown by the enemy when the 50th Division took over the line, for the Canadians had said that the Wytschaete sector was quiet and peaceful.

"When we were relieved by the Canadians," (in the Ypres sector), said the 6th Northumberland Fusiliers, "they told us that the trenches they had left were a 'bed of roses' in comparison with those they were taking over."

But this quietude existed only for the first two or three days after the Division had taken over the line, for on the 9th of April the expected usual rude awakening came.

"To the rear and left of their line [the Germans'] was a small wood known as Petit Bois, in which trench-mortar batteries and guns of all sizes were housed, which we later got to know to our cost, for between noon and 1.30 p.m. on the 9th of April we were heavily shelled with 5·9-in., 4·2-in. and 'whizz-bangs,' and suffered a number of casualties. This was indeed a surprise for, judging by the state of the trenches, they had not been subjected to treatment of this kind; the sand-bags looked old and had evidently stood some time, for grass and a few flowers were sprouting here and there. It took no trained eye to weigh up whether the place had been recently repaired or treated to a dose of Fritz's "hate." At 6 p.m. that night he shelled us more heavily still, but again we were very fortunate and only a few casualties occurred. This convinced us that the 'bed of roses' *might* have existed, but was *now* a 'bed of thorns.'"

On the 10th the Bosche was again active: "We were served up with another lot of 'whizz-bangs' and 'crumps.'"

"The next day—April 11th—was a disastrous one, for they shelled us for an hour and a half in the morning and again in the afternoon for a longer period, and our casualties were appallingly heavy—over thirty wounded and four killed, amongst the latter being Second-Lieut. H. L. Benson, one of our own having been promoted from the ranks.

"He joined the Battalion the day war broke out and, step by step, had risen to the rank of Company-Sergeant-Major of "A" Company and eventually was commissioned on the field, coming back to his old Battalion as an officer. His death was keenly felt, for 'Laurie,' as he was affectionately referred to, was loved and respected by all who knew him, and his loss cast a gloom over the whole Battalion, for his popularity was immense. Capt. R. W. Nicholson and Second-Lieut. E. L. Bell were also wounded that day, this being the third time that Capt. Nicholson had been wounded."*

This activity continued for some days, and the losses among some battalions in the front line were considerable.

"All kinds of stuff came our way," said the 6th Northumberland Fusiliers, "but in spite of this they could not kill that spirit of cheerfulness that many of our boys were blessed with, for in the midst of one of their 'strafs' one fellow was heard to say in a real Tyneside tongue "Ah wish they would hoy their b—— guns at us and be done wid.' "

And Capt. Buckley, in his *War History of the 7th Northumberland Fusiliers*, said on the 14th of April: "We have by this time come to the conclusion that this part of the line is not so nice as we had anticipated. Moreover, it is getting worse and worse daily."

The Northumberlands (as already explained) held the centre sub-sector of the Divisional front line. One of the reasons, probably, that the enemy's activity was on the increase was his efforts to keep the British Armies busy and prevent them sending troops to assist the French in the defence of Verdun, against which the enemy had launched a tremendous attack in February, but had not succeeded in reaching his objectives—of which more later.

On the 150th Brigade front also the enemy's shell fire was unusually active from the 8th of April, and daily the trenches were breached in places, while the communication trenches were badly damaged. The 5th Durham Light Infantry were in the trenches from the 7th to the 15th and their experiences were thus described:

" 'A' Company and two platoons of 'D' held Trenches G.1 and G.2. 'B' Company and the other two platoons of 'D' were

---

* Diary, 6th Northumberland Fusiliers.

in G.3 and H.1a, while 'C' formed the garrison of four support points. Battalion Headquarters were at 'the Doctor's house'—a small, partly-damaged villa near Kemmel. Major Ensor was in command during the Colonel's absence on leave. The tour was an unpleasant one. G.1 was an awkward salient.* At one point it was within forty yards of the German line, and had not only been much knocked about by trench mortars, but part of it had been destroyed by mines on more than one occasion. It was known as the 'Glory Hole' and was at the junction of two roads—'Suicide Road' and 'V.C. Road.' 'B' Company, holding the left sector, had a very bad time as, two or three times every day, the enemy subjected them to shell fire. The enemy also repeatedly put down heavy barrages as well behind our left brigade front, no doubt in connection with the fighting that was going on at St. Eloi, a mile and a half to the north of us. The trench-mortaring generally took place just before dusk, when it was too dark to see the shell and just too light to see the burning fuse. At that hour it was a strange sight to see every man and officer in the trench listening intently for the unmistakable 'pop' of the mortar and looking heavenwards in a vain attempt to see the bomb coming. When the first one dropped the strain was at an end, as the others usually fell near it, and all we had to do was to avoid that part of the trench till the 'strafe' was over. The nights were peaceful except on one occasion when the front line was shelled at midnight for some twenty minutes. . . . The casualties during this tour included two company commanders—Major A. L. Raimes and Capt. W. Marley—and the Adjutant—Capt. V. F. Gloag—all wounded, and Company-Sergeant-Major N. Green, who was very badly wounded and died in hospital. Capt. Gloag was never able to return to the Battalion. . . . Sergeant-Major Green was also a serious loss to us, as he was a very capable and promising soldier."†

The 8th Durham Light Infantry, who went into the line M.1–N.2a on the evening of the 8th of April, reported a "quiet night," but from the 9th onwards until the evening of the 14th the Battalion had to put up with the enemy's shell fire.

---

* It was just opposite "Peckham"—a strong point in the German line, and on the Kemmel–Wytschaete road.

† Major A. L. Raimes.

"The M. and N. trenches ran north and south along the slopes below Wytschaete, its ruined hospital being a very prominent feature on the right, whilst immediately in front lay the Grand Bois and Bois Quarante. Behind the trenches the ground sloped gradually away to Dickebusch and its lake, Hallebast Corner, Mille Kruis and the village of La Clytte."*

The reserve positions were known as the Vierstraat Defences and ran along a line midway between Ridge Wood and Bois Carre. Ridge Wood was seldom shelled, and its ample trees afforded cover from observation. Battalion Headquarters were situated there.

The 6th Durham Light Infantry, who went into the front line the same evening as the 8th Battalion, took over trenches, the condition of which (from their description) did not reflect much credit on the previous tenants:

"The trenches," records the Battalion Diary, "were in bad condition, communications being few or in rather bad condition, supports either derelict or lacking, parapets in front line either too low or not bullet-proof, parados practically non-existent, dug-outs few and poorly protected." And when the enemy's artillery and trench mortars got to work they created fresh havoc.

"Enemy artillery still busy," records the Diary of the Durhams on the 11th. "Their trench mortars, 'rum-jars,' fish-tailed bombs, creosol tins and *minnenwerfer* are more nuisance than their artillery."

It is obvious from all battalion diaries that the activity at St. Eloi was responsible for the heavy shell fire on the 50th Divisional area, for the 9th Durhams on the 15th state that the "enemy infantry in trenches opposite very quiet," and although trench-mortar and 60-lb. bombs were distributed among them they failed to bring any activity on their part: "No targets for our snipers." The enemy was a little more lively on the 16th and sent over a number of rifle grenades in the early hours of the morning. One of these grenades killed Capt. M. H. Bettison, who had returned from leave only the previous evening.

On the 19th the Battalion records an interesting item: "This being the anniversary of our arrival in France, our casualties for the year have been heavy and are as follows: —Officers:

---

* "The 8th Battalion, The Durham Light Infantry."

killed, 7; died of wounds, 1; wounded, 16; sick, 26. Other ranks: killed, 98; died of wounds, 31; wounded, 560; sick, 575. Total: 50 officers and 1,264 other ranks."

With the exception of one or two references, the diaries kept by the many units of the Division contain no reference to the anniversary of the landing of the 50th Division in France. Yet, for comparison's sake, it might have been done, for how changed was the Division since April, 1915. From the command of the Division downwards, brigades, battalions and other units had lost many of their original officers and men. Reorganisation had been busy and would be still more so in the time to come. The Division as a whole had become a seasoned war unit, had served its apprenticeship as it were, and had so far come through with honours. One of the Brigadiers (Brig.-General J. Shea, a very popular officer) had, as recently as the 4th of April, 1916, said to a battalion whom he had addressed and congratulated on its behaviour during the time it had been in the Ypres Salient: "He would give them the highest compliment which any soldier could receive —'Men! you are good soldiers.' " And what was true of this one battalion was true also of all units of the 50th Division, for they had been proved and had not been found wanting.

The Diary of the 5th Northumberland Fusiliers gives an interesting note concerning the civilian population in the Divisional area: "The civilian inhabitants are living very close up to the line, and few farms behind Battalion Headquarters have been seriously damaged. Ploughing the land is still being carried on by the local farmers *in front of our 18-pounder battery positions.*"

This Battalion also records: "We had hoped that this would be a peaceful part of the line—but are disappointed!"

The 4th Northumberland Fusiliers were more fortunate than any other battalion who went into the front line, for they had only a dozen casualties between the 3rd and the 8th, of whom only two were killed and the remainder wounded.

This tour of the 50th Division in the Wytschaete sector was of short duration, for on the 25th of April General Wilkinson handed over command to the G.O.C., 3rd Division, whose troops had taken over the three sub-sectors of the front line and area in rear. Headquarters of the 50th Division then moved back to Flêtre, west-north-west of Bailleul, into Corps

Reserve. By the end of April all units of the Division were in the Corps Rest Area.

At the end of April the enemy made a gas attack, and all units received orders to "stand to," but, as the attack was parried, the Division was not called upon.

May dawned fine and hot and the "rest" period began auspiciously for all ranks; nor were their anticipations dissipated. There were alarms of course, and rumours floating around almost every day, but the month passed quietly in training and recreation.

Certain changes and innovations took place in the Division. A Divisional Scouts School, under Capt. W. Anderson, G.S.O. III, was established on the 3rd of May for training scouts, observers and snipers, and proved of considerable value later. On the 5th a demonstration in the use of the new Fullerphone was given to signal officers of the Royal Artillery and infantry brigades.

"A" Squadron of the Yorkshire Hussars left the Division on the 9th on transfer to the XVII Corps Cavalry Regiment.

On the 11th the Divisional Artillery of the Division was reorganised and the brigades were renumbered; the 1st, 2nd, 3rd and 4th Northumbrian Brigades, R.F.A., became respectively the 250th, 251st, 252nd and 253rd Northumbrian Brigade, R.F.A.*

The Artillery also had a new C.R.A.: Brig.-General W. A. Robinson was evacuated sick on the 21st of May and did not rejoin the Division. He was succeeded by Lieut.-Colonel A. U. Stockley (appointed Brig.-General on the 20th of June, 1916).

Corps orders to hand on the 13th of May stated that between the 23rd and 30th of May the 50th Division would relieve the 3rd Division in the same trenches handed over to the latter at the end of April, *i.e.*, at Wytschaete.

On the 17th Brig.-General J. S. M. Shea, who had been appointed to command the 30th Division, said farewell to his Brigade (151st)—his "Tigers," as he called them. A stern disciplinarian, he was nevertheless well liked by all ranks. The same day Brig.-General P. F. Westmoreland assumed command of the 151st Brigade.

---

* For full details of the reorganisation of the 50th Divisional Artillery on the 16th of May, 1916, see Appendix D.

The 149th Brigade was the first to return to the front line, taking over the centre sub-sector from the 9th Brigade (3rd Division) on the 24th of May. On the night of the 27th–28th the 150th Brigade took over the right sub-sector, and the 151st Brigade the left; at 12.15 a.m. on the 28th General Wilkinson once more assumed command of the Wytschaete sector, *i.e.*, from Trench E.1 to Trench O.4.

The ten weeks which followed the second tour in that part of the line were typical of trench warfare in all its aspects, for it was during June and July that troops of the 50th Division raided the enemy's trenches—the first raids recorded since the arrival of the Division in France.

June began noisily; the enemy north of the 50th Division shelled and attacked the Canadians north of Hill 60, Mount Sorrel, Armagh and Sanctuary Woods and Hooge; the Salient itself was like a seething furnace, the smoke from bursting shells drifting over the whole area.

On the 4th of June Lieut.-Colonel A. G. Stuart, G.S.O. I of the Division, was killed by a stray bullet when inspecting trenches. He was succeeded on the 12th by Lieut.-Colonel D. Forster, R.E., who, however, was wounded on the 17th while reconnoitring the same ground near Vierstraat. Ten days later Lieut.-Colonel H. Karslake, R.A., arrived and assumed duty as G.S.O. I.

Along the front of the 50th Division the struggle for fire supremacy began almost immediately the sector was taken over, but gradually the Division mastered the German gunnery. In the front line the enemy's trench mortars were the chief source of annoyance and loss, but they also were frequently silenced after firing a few rounds; these few rounds, however, often caused the death of brave and gallant officers and men, besides damaging the defences. There was one huge trench howitzer used by the enemy which seemed to elude the vigilance of the Divisional gunners, who tried to put it out of action but failed to do so. It seldom fired more than three or four rounds, but the projectile hurled by it into our trenches created havoc. The Divisional Artillery at once retaliated as soon as it opened fire, which no doubt caused the Germans to seek cover, but a direct hit was never scored on this particular mortar.

In each sub-sector two battalions held the front line: one battalion was in Brigade Reserve and the other in Divisional Reserve; tours in the line lasted seven days.

It is evident from the diaries of all three infantry brigades that, owing to energetic and nightly patrolling, complete ascendancy had been obtained in No Man's Land, German patrols being hardly ever encountered. But the Bosche, driven out of that dread space between the opposing lines, devoted himself diligently to mining, though his efforts in this direction were only partially successful. On one occasion he "blew a mine" which destroyed part of his own front line, and his troops in that sector seemed absolutely dazed and paralysed when, as was usual, the Divisional Artillery and our front-line troops opened very heavy fire on the crater formed by the explosion.

Our mining efforts were constant and met with varied success.

On the 150th Brigade front the most tragic incident during June was a gas attack on the night of the 16th–17th. The 1/4th East Yorkshires at this period held the right sub-sector of the Brigade line, and the 4th Green Howards the left.

At about midnight the enemy suddenly opened very heavy rifle and machine-gun fire along the whole of the Brigade front. The back of the front-line trenches was also bombarded by trench mortars, while a barrage from 77-mm. guns was placed behind the support line.

Then from the parapets of the German trenches on the southern front of Spanbroekmolen two huge clouds of gas emerged and floated over Trenches E.1, E.2 and E.3, held by the East Yorkshires. The latter related this incident in the following terms:

"Enemy released gas opposite E. Trenches. The wind at this time was north and rather variable. It blew the gas across the "New Cutt" trench, E.3, E.1 and E.b trenches. The gas cloud was very thick and lasted about twenty minutes. Few casualties were caused at first, but the after-effects proved fatal in eleven cases. Second-Lieut. W. F. Carlton was killed in Trench F.4; Second-Lieut. G. Gresham* was severely wounded, Second-Lieut. Sutton slightly wounded, Second-Lieuts. W. R. R. Brown and Marshal were affected by shock and gas and left the trenches. The total casualties were: officers, killed 1, wounded 3; other ranks, killed 10, wounded 74, missing 1."

---

* Died of wounds 18th of June, 1916.

The enemy's trench-mortar and rifle fire were responsible for most of the "killed."

The 4th Green Howards do not appear to have suffered much from the gas, but the shell fire caused casualties and (what is interesting) the Battalion Diary mentions a barrage of gas shells:

"Immediately after the relief (an inter-company relief had just taken place) the Bosche commenced a heavy bombardment of Trenches G.1 and G.2 and S.P.10, and *a gas barrage from shells* fired by trench mortars about fifty yards behind G.1, G.2 and G.3, right and left. Gas was emitted by the enemy immediately on our right. Casualties: Major B. H. Charlton, Capt. C. Sproxton and Second-Lieut. A. D. Scott wounded; other ranks, killed 1, wounded 16."

No infantry attack followed the projection of gas, but the General Staff Diary of the Division estimated the casualties as 140 all told.

The report of the A.D.M.S. of the Division also has considerable interest:

" . . . The enemy when letting off the gas tried to cover the hissing of the cylinders by rapid machine-gun fire . . . the symptoms appear to have been more severe than in recent gas attacks. The gas used was chlorine and probably phosgene also. The causes of the men being gassed may be summed up as follows: (*a*) Parties in dug-outs and working behind the line not receiving the alarm soon enough; (*b*) some difficulty was experienced by the machine-gunners in adjusting their Tower respirators soon enough; (*c*) men removing their smoke helmets before ordered to do so. The signallers were able to carry on their duties in their dug-outs by blankets dropped over the entrance and sprayed."

Although the General Staff Diary of the Division first mentioned raids on the 26th of June and report others in the words, "Raid ineffective," they were the forerunners of many a successful descent upon the Bosche trenches and should therefore be recorded.

As early as the 4th of June the 4th Green Howards mention a raid carried out by the 24th Division, on the right of the 50th, and as the month passed it was rumoured that similar attempts on the German lines were to be made by the latter.

On the night of the 19th–20th of June the 73rd Brigade of the 24th Division took over the line held by the 4th East

Yorkshires, and on the following night the sector held by the 4th Green Howards, the G.O.C., 150th Brigade, then handing over command and moving back to the Kemmel defences. The night of the 25th-26th, however, saw one company from each of the above two battalions back again in the right and left sub-sectors of their old front line, having temporarily relieved troops of the 73rd Brigade in order to raid the enemy.

No original orders for the raid are with the Divisional Diaries, and only the following brief account exists (apart from similar brief accounts in the diaries of the two battalions concerned) in Brigade Headquarters Diary:

"At 1.30 a.m. on the night of the 26th-27th two raiding parties as under—4th East Yorkshires: Lieut. Slack and twenty-five other ranks; 4th Yorkshires: Lieut. Laing and twenty-seven other ranks—attempted to raid the German trenches opposite E.1 and G.2. The German wire had previously been cut by the fire of our artillery and the 2-in. trench mortars. At 1.30 a.m. Lieut. Slack and his party were close up to the German wire. At that moment our barrage began and certain shells fell amongst the raiding party, with the result that Lieut. Slack and one man went forward; the rest of the party lost touch with their leader, some being blown off their feet by the shell explosions, and after a time returned to their own lines. Lieut. Slack went on as far as the enemy's second line, shooting two Germans in a mine shaft on the way, and returned safely to his own lines about 1.55 a.m. Casualties: two other ranks wounded.

"At 1.30 a.m. Lieut. Laing and his party were passing through the German wire about N.30 a.7.9½* when our artillery commenced their barrage. For some unknown reason our shells fell on the German front-line parapets and parados, establishing a barrage through which the raiding party were unable to move. After waiting some minutes, having had one casualty from our own shells, and as the barrage still continued, Lieut. Laing withdrew his party to their own trenches. Casualties in raiding party: one sergeant killed, four other ranks wounded."

The following night the two companies of East Yorkshires and Green Howards were relieved from the front line and returned to Battalion Headquarters. But to these gallant

---

* In front of Peckham, the section of the German trench raided.

fellows belonged the honour of making the first raid by the 50th Division.

The Divisional front was now held by the 149th Brigade on the right and the 151st Brigade on the left.

The 24th Division carried out two small raids on the night of the 28th–29th of June, but it was the 9th of July before the 50th Division again raided the enemy, the 150th Brigade carrying out the operations.

The 150th Brigade had taken over the front held by the 149th Brigade, *i.e.*, J.3 to L.5 inclusive, on the night of the 2nd of July, the 151st Brigade holding the left sub-sector trenches, M.1 to O.4.

The 5th Green Howards (of the former brigade), who carried out the raid, took over the right sub-sector in front of which was a large crater just opposite the north-western corner of Petit Bois.

Fortunately there exists a full narrative of the raid—the first real narrative, by the way, of operations with the Divisional Diaries, for it was about this period that the C.O.s of all units were ordered to send in full reports, with sketches and maps (if possible) of any operations in which their units took part.

First, the objects of the raid: these were three, "(i) to obtain identifications by contact, (ii) to kill Germans, (iii) to discover if Crater 'E' had a mine shaft."

The raiding party was divided into seven groups (A, B, C, C-Dash, D, E, F), each of three or four men and an N.C.O. Three of the groups (A, B and E) were commanded by officers. The first four groups were to enter the crater, and of the three remaining, one was to stay at the point of entry to take over captures, one to cut wire to provide an alternative exit, and one to remain half-way across No Man's Land as a covering party. The strength of the whole raiding party was three officers, eight N.C.O.s and twenty-five men.

Capt. H. Brown (O.C., raid) commanded "A" party, Second-Lieut. H. P. Bagge, "B" party, and Second-Lieut. E. R. Saltonstall, "E" party.

As may be supposed, the beginning of raids in the 50th Division* caused a great deal of interest and excitement.

---

* The first recorded raid by British troops was made on the night of the 3rd–4th of February, 1915, by the 1st Royal Worcestershire Regiment of the 8th Division.

Volunteers were usually called for, and there was never any lack of these, for the spirit of adventure never lagged amongst our troops in France and Flanders. But even at this period (the summer of 1916) they were still in their infancy and very different from the highly-organised "shows," practised beforehand over models of the enemy's trenches to be raided, of 1917 and 1918. It is interesting, therefore, to see how the early raiding parties of the 50th Division were dressed, armed and equipped.

All marks of identification, such as cap badges, shoulder titles, letters, etc., were removed. Steel helmets were not worn, being too conspicuous and liable to drop off; as a good deal of crawling also had to be done they were not suitable. In place, S.P. caps were worn reversed. The faces and hands of the raiders were blackened. In order to deaden all sound when walking on duck-boards in the enemy's trenches, rubber bars were fixed to the bottoms of boots. Watches, electric torches, rope-ladders and twenty-foot lengths of rope were carried.

All officers, sergeants and corporals were armed with revolvers, the men with a bayonet and a knobkerry tucked into the waist-belt. Some men carried six grenades, others twenty-four, the total carried being about three hundred. Only a small proportion of men carried rifles (cut down) and fixed bayonets, the latter also being blackened. Each man of "A," "B," "C" and "C-Dash" parties had a small wire-cutter in case he lost his way and encountered wire.

It may be assumed that clothed and equipped as above the raiders did not present a very attractive appearance; indeed they may well have been taken for buccaneers of the old type.

The crater, which was the objective of the raid, was one of considerable proportions. Its near lip, *i.e.*, the edge nearest the Divisional front line, had dug-outs tunnelled beneath the surface, the entrance to each having overhead cover. Inside the crater there was a sand-bagged wall, about three feet high, running round the sides, which were also encircled by a duckboard track. Right across the centre there was a high sand-bagged wall, protecting a duck-boarded walk. On each side of the crater was a communication trench leading back to the enemy's front line, while in the latter was a fire trench so constructed as to cover the front edge of the crater. Altogether it was a difficult place to attack, especially as there was to be no preliminary bombardment, though the guns were ready to fire if called upon.

The point on the left of the crater, where the communication trench joined up with the latter, was termed "A" on the sketch provided with orders to the raiders.

At 1 a.m. on the 10th of July the seven parties collected in the front-line trench and made ready to "go over." The scene can be well imagined; the black night, the trench crowded with weird-looking troops with blackened faces, of "cut-throat" appearance; final orders given in low tones, for the Bosche was comparatively near; everything and everyone as still as possible. A hand-grip between the raiders and their pals and then "over the top."

At 1.15 a.m. the parties, in alphabetical order as already given, crawled out, two deep and made for Point A. Their progress was watched breathlessly by those left behind until they were swallowed up in the darkness.

The Bosche trenches were reached in complete silence and without alarming the enemy. "A" and "B" parties then assembled at Point A, on top of the enemy's parapet, the broken nature of which gave a certain amount of cover.

The Battalion story of the raid states: "What transpired after this can only be shown by the following narratives, given by members of different parties."

Capt. Brown's story, being the most exciting, besides practically telling all there was to tell of the raid, stated:

"Sergeant Daggett and I were now lying in close touch with Fire Bay No. 1.* We waited until a Very light was put up and then saw that this bay was untenanted, though a rifle with fixed bayonet was leaning against the parapet. A party of about ten or fifteen men now passed beneath us, moving from our left to right. As soon as they were past I rose and was just preparing to get into the trench when a sentry entered the post followed by another man. One of these, picking up the rifle and looking straight into my face, said, 'Ach!' at the same moment firing at me from the hip, just as I pulled the trigger of my automatic pistol within an inch of his head. He went over; the discharge of his rifle singed my right eye-brow, but the bullet passed over my head. I jumped into the trench and Sergeant Daggett shot the other man in the bay. Bombs now

---

* Fire Bay No. 1 was only a few yards from Point A.

began to fly from the crater, and 'A' and 'B' parties replied with showers of Mills grenades. I was met by two Bosches from the right, who came at me with fixed bayonets. I was able to shoot them before they had time to get within striking distance. I now sheltered for a minute or two under a piece of overhead cover, as bombs were falling too close to be pleasant. I saw numbers of the enemy in fire bays all round the crater; a few were throwing bombs in my direction, but for the most part they were hurling them over their parapet from their respective fire bays. I saw some running away and others falling as our bombs exploded among them. I then moved to the next fire bay on my right and found two men, one of whom was firing and the other throwing bombs. I shot them at close quarters from behind. Then, remembering that my objective was the C.T. [communication trench] X,* I proceeded there. I met a Bosche officer or N.C.O. hurrying up and shot him in the chest. As I was stooping to get his effects a man ran into me from the crater. I covered him and made him put up his hands. He cried 'Kamerad, Kamerad!' I signed to him to get over the parapet (here some eight or ten feet high), but he refused and screamed. As he was obstinate I shot him. Immediately afterwards another man approached. My magazine, which had only contained seven cartridges, was now empty, but I covered this man and, after some trouble, managed to induce him to get over the parapet. About twenty yards off I found our main party still outside the crater. As it was ten minutes after the time arranged for return, I gave the order for all to return to our trenches."

The prisoner taken by Capt. Brown, however, proved obstreperous, for Second-Lieut. E. R. Saltonstall (in charge of "E" party, detailed to take charge of prisoners) said: "On the way back we came across the party with the Bosche prisoner. He was causing considerable trouble, shouting and struggling to get away. As he could not be got in peaceably I had to apply a little persuasion with the butt end of my revolver on his head. This partially dazed him and he gave little further trouble."

Others of the raiders who got into the crater, under Second-Lieut. Bagge ("B" party), bombed round to Point C† and

---

* The communication trench on the left of the crater.
† South of Point A.

killed several Germans before the time to return. Second-Lieut. Saltonstall and Sergeant Francis, whose group was to cut the wire at B, had a lively bombing contest over the parapet.

The raiding party returned in safety, though Capt. Brown, Second-Lieut. Bagge and four other ranks were slightly wounded (all remaining at duty) and seven other ranks more seriously wounded. One "other rank" of the enemy was captured and at least fifteen killed which, states the C.O. of the 5th Green Howards (Lieut.-Colonel J. Mortimer), was a conservative estimate.

The success of this operation brought the 5th Green Howards congratulations from the Army, Corps and Divisional Commanders, and they were well deserved, for the raid was excellently planned and carried out.

The same night (9th–10th July) the 6th Durham Light Infantry of the 151st Brigade also sent over a small party to raid the crater opposite N.4. The raiders, under Second-Lieut. Annett, had not proceeded very far when they came upon one of the enemy near the wire in front of the Durhams' trenches. He was captured, being one of a hostile patrol. As the remainder of the party had evidently given the alarm, Lieut. Annett withdrew his men. The Durhams also received congratulations from Army, Corps and Divisional Commanders.

The next raid took place on the night of the 13th of July, when the 8th Durhams tried to enter the enemy's trenches at Hollandscheseur, but without success.

On the 15th the 149th Brigade relieved the 151st in the left sub-sector. The 149th had a new Brigade-Major on the 19th of July, Capt. W. Anderson, who had been G.S.O. III on the Divisional Staff, taking over the former duties from Major P. S. Rowan, who left on appointment as G.S.O. II to another division. Capt. Anderson was replaced on the Divisional Staff by Capt. N. R. Crockett, who assumed the duty of G.S.O. III on the 20th of July.

Major R. F. Guy, Brigade-Major of the 150th Brigade, left on the 15th of July to take up appointment as G.S.O. II, 11th Division, and was succeeded on the 18th by Capt. Boys.

On the 20th also the 151st Brigade relieved the 17th Brigade (24th Division) on the right of the 50th Division: thus the latter had all three brigades in the line once more.

One small (and unsuccessful) bombing raid by eight or nine of the enemy on a listening post held by the 7th

Northumberland Fusiliers in front of Trench 161 is mentioned on the 23rd of July, otherwise the enemy appears to have taken the Divisional raids "sitting down."

On the 15th of July the 5th Northumberland Fusiliers were ordered to raid the enemy on the 25th, but the Brigade moved to another sub-sector before that date and the operation was therefore cancelled.

No more raids took place before the 50th Division was withdrawn from the Wytschaete sector early in August. But they had served their purpose; identifications had been obtained and that was most important, for south, in the Somme area, the great battle which had opened on the 1st of July was proceeding with great intensity, and G.H.Q. had to be kept well informed of any changes in disposition of the enemy's troops.

In many of the Divisional Diaries early in July the operations on the Somme are mentioned as having begun; they were in everyone's mind. Rumours of the progress of the great battle reached all sectors not in the Somme area, and conjecture was rife as to how long it would be before a move was made south to join in the operations.

On the 1st of August the Second Army Commander and Corps Commander both called on General Wilkinson and informed him that the 50th Division was to be relieved by the 19th Division and, on relief, would proceed south, on or about the 10th of August.

The relief by the 19th Division was completed on the night of the 9th–10th and the following day entrainment began at Bailleul and Godewaersvelde for Doullens and Fienvillers Candas.

By the 17th of August the Division had arrived in the Montigny area, Headquarters being at Montigny Château, 149th Brigade at Hénencourt Wood, 150th Brigade at Millencourt and 151st Brigade at Baizieux Wood. The 7th Durham Light Infantry (Pioneers) were also at Baizieux, while the Divisional Artillery was scattered north and south of Montigny.

The Division now formed part of the III Corps, Fourth Army, and was in III Corps Reserve. Training began almost immediately.

CHAPTER V
THE BATTLES OF THE SOMME, 1916

FROM the 1st of July, 1916, thence onwards throughout the remainder of that momentous year, all roads led to (and from) the Somme. Fifty-four infantry and two cavalry divisions were engaged in that titanic struggle with the enemy who, before the winter for the time being put an end to the prodigious shedding of blood, had flung into the field of battle four-fifths of his divisions along the Western Front.*

The Battles of the Somme, 1916, created (and will continue to create) much discussion. There are some (who should know better) who aver that the operations were a failure; that the great struggle was a "blood bath," resulting only in the deaths of thousands of brave and gallant men; that, strategically, the Allied plans were wrong; that we achieved nothing. They have not hesitated to say that the enemy was victorious. A little knowledge is a dangerous thing, and in tactics and strategy worse than none at all, for it leads to the drawing of wrong conclusions and deductions.

The great battle which opened on the 1st of July, 1916, had been discussed by Generals Joffre and Haig at the close of 1915. As neither the French nor the British were deemed strong enough to undertake, unaided, an offensive on a large scale, a combined attack was decided upon. The area selected was north and south of the Somme river. Whatever the intention of the Allies when these plans were made, they had subsequently to be modified and, from the point of view of the British Army, the success or failure of the operations can only rightfully be assessed on the three objectives of the offensive launched on the 1st of July, *viz.*:

"To relieve the pressure on Verdun.

"To assist our Allies in other theatres of the War by stopping any further transfer of German troops from the Western Front.

---

* Reference to *Die Schlachten und Gefechte*, etc. (an official list of battles compiled by the German Great General Staff, giving formations, etc.), reveals the enormous number of troops used by the enemy on the Somme from (and including) July, 1916, to the end of that year.

"To wear down the strength of the forces opposed to us."*

In the original plans the French were to undertake the principal attack south of the Somme, the British making a subsidiary attack north of the river. The French had already begun to mass troops for the offensive when, in February, 1916, the Germans launched their great attack against Verdun. Gradually the French troops, massed for the attack south of the Somme, were drawn eastwards to stem the tide of the German advance, the result being that the whole role of the British Army was changed; it was agreed that the latter should make the principal attack and the French, south and astride the Somme, should act in a subsidiary manner.

In May the Austrians had attacked the Italians, and by the end of that month had reached Arsiero and Asiago.

The pressure at Verdun and in Italy was very great when, in June, the Russians attacked the Austrians and caused the Germans to transfer troops from the Western to the Eastern Front. But at Verdun the situation was serious, and it was agreed between Generals Joffre and Haig that the combined offensive should not take place later than the end of June.

A tremendous bombardment by one thousand five hundred odd guns of all calibres was opened on the 24th of June on the enemy's trenches, rear defences and communications. Gas was discharged and numbers of raids were made; the assault took place at 7.30 a.m. on the 1st of July, having been postponed from the 29th of June owing to climatic conditions.

It was not, however, until the third phase of the operations—the exploitation of success—which opened on the 15th of September, that the 50th Division entered into the struggle, although the artillery of the Division had already been in action some days under the C.R.A. of another division.

The Divisional Artillery had not properly settled down in their new quarters north and south of Montigny on the 17th of August, when they received orders to move into the line and relieve the gunners of the 34th Division, who had had a very "hectic" time since the 1st of July.

The gunners of the 50th Division were looking forward to a few days' rest in a peaceful area. But alas! it was always so with "the guns." They were always the last to leave the line

---

* The three objectives of the Somme Battles, 1916, as given by General Haig in his despatches.

and the first to go back again. Often, long after their division had been withdrawn from a battle they were left in to lend assistance to an incoming unit.

The gunners of the 50th Division had been warned what the Somme was like by gunners of the 19th Division, who had relieved them on the nights of the 8th and 9th of August. Colonel Shiel describes them as "pale and dusty individuals . . . who said they came from the Somme, where it was hell on earth and where we were to go to as quickly as possible."

Hell on earth! Yes! it had become that even as early as August, for at that period there was a saying that a subaltern's life was worth about a week's purchase.

So, on the 19th, the 251st and 252nd Brigades of the Divisional Artillery took the road eastwards, moving via Baizieux, Hénencourt and Millencourt, leaving the 250th and 253rd Brigades to carry on with the training programme.*

On the 18th–19th the 251st and 252nd Brigades relieved the 34th Divisional Artillery, who were covering the 15th Divisional front, at Contalmaison. The 250th Brigade went into the line on the 24th–25th of August, relieving the 70th Brigade, R.F.A.

A gunner quarter-master-sergeant† thus describes the approach march of his battery, and first sight of the Somme battlefields:

"During training period we passed through all the small villages immediately behind Albert, whose falling Virgin on the spire we could see in the distance. Our amazement increased as we got nearer the great dumps of ammunition and a string of lorries and wagons filling up. Water tanks, R.E. dumps, everything on a big scale, and troops everywhere. We could hear the roar of gunfire and the usual quaint remarks of our north-country lads. In the pitman's lingo they chaffed each other and said: 'There's a war on here. Aa hope we've got a good cavil,' etc.

"Arriving in Albert we saw the destruction of the Cathedral as we passed by, and also a few civilian shop-keepers still holding on to their shell-marked houses. Getting out of the town the battle front met our gaze.

---

* The four artillery brigades of the 50th Division were commanded at this period as follows: 250th, Lieut.-Colonel H. S. Bell; 251st, Lieut.-Colonel F. B. Moss-Blundell; 252nd, Lieut.-Colonel F. L. Pickersgill; 253rd, Lieut.-Colonel H. E. Hanson. The C.R.A. was Brig.-General A. U. Stockley.

† Quarter-Master-Sergeant W. Donnington.

"Never since arriving in France had we seen such scenes. Sausage balloons, both ours and the Germans, in hundreds as far as you could see. Hundreds of our planes, which seemed to have it all their own way, and we witnessed numerous combats. Troops and camps dotted the expanse of the bare hills and valleys. All this we saw as we finally fixed our wagon lines at Bécourt.

"The guns, under Major Chapman, went straight into action in what remained of the village of Contalmaison. The gunners immediately began to fix the guns, and at daybreak next morning we were at it for all we were worth."

At 1 p.m. on the 7th of September Divisional Operation Orders were issued, which stated that the Division was to move forward and take over the right sub-sector of the 15th Division, who held a portion of the front line north and north-east of Bazentin-le-Petit. The 50th Division would then have the 47th Division on the right (in the High Wood sector) and the 15th Division on the left (south-west of Martinpuich).

The line allotted to the 50th Division was an extraordinary tangle of trenches, roads and tracks. The right of the line was Sutherland Alley, a north and south communication trench which joined Clarke Trench at the Bazentin-le-Petit–High Wood road. From the junction of the two trenches the line ran westwards, *i.e.*, Clarke Trench and Swansea Trench to a point which can only be described as in Operation Orders, *i.e.*, "S.2b.6.i," since no other description is given, nor is the trench in which the point is given, named. This was, apparently, the main front line, for out in front, and running almost parallel with it, was another trench (Eye Trench) connected with the former by five communication trenches, that on the right being Bethel, that on the left Pioneer Alley. East of Eye Trench was High Wood, of which the enemy still held about half, his trenches running through the centre. Due west of Eye Trench were Bottom road and Bottom Trench, both held by the Germans. Hook Trench was the enemy's front line and ran the whole length opposite Eye Trench.

Thus the line to be taken over by the 50th Division would not only be open to fire from the front, but also from both flanks; a more than uncomfortable situation.

The 149th Brigade (Brig.-General H. F. H. Clifford) was to take over the right sub-sector and the 150th (Brig.-General

5TH NORTHUMBERLAND FUSILIERS CLEANING CLOTHES AND EQUIPMENT after their return from the attack on Le Sars; Toutencourt, October 1916.

(Imperial War Museum Photographs, Copyright Reserved)

B. G. Price) the left; the 151st Brigade to be at Bécourt in Divisional Reserve.

The relief was to be completed by noon on the 10th of September. Subsequently there was a slight alteration in the Divisional front, the 149th Brigade being ordered to hand over a small section of Clarke's Trench to the 47th Division and extend its left to Jutland Avenue, which the 150th Brigade took over from the 15th Division, as far west as the junction of Pioneer Alley with Macfarlane Alley.

Of the 149th Brigade the 5th Northumberland Fusiliers were ordered to take over the front line, the 1/4th East Yorkshires on the left moving into the line attached to the 150th Brigade.

The 5th Northumberland Fusiliers (Lieut.-Colonel C. Turner) set out for Hénencourt at 1.30 p.m. on the 8th, and marched via Albert to the Quadrangle, but finding that place occupied moved back to dug-outs round Lozenge Wood in the old German second line. On the 9th the Battalion moved up to the front line and by midnight had taken over Clarke's Trench, Bethel Sap, Brecon Trench, Argyll, Chester and Mill Streets.

On the 9th the 1/4th East Yorkshires (Lieut.-Colonel W. T. Wilkinson) similarly marched via Albert and Bécourt to Shelter Wood. At 2 a.m. (10th) they moved to the north-western corner of Mametz Wood, where they met guides from the Seaforths and Gordons whom the East Yorkshires were relieving. By 7.30 a.m. the relief was complete.

From the diaries of these units it is impossible to gather anything of the state of the line or their first impressions when moving up and during the relief.

Even at this period (two and a half months from the first day of the offensive) no words can adequately describe the Somme. For sheer tragedy, wholesale destruction, the first vision of that ghastly battlefield almost blotted out from one's mind memories of the Ypres Salient.

The two battalions of the 50th Division just mentioned crossed the old British front line of the 1st of July just east of Bécourt; they then had to traverse between two hundred and fifty and three hundred yards of what had once been No Man's Land before passing over the old Bosche front line. So battered and blasted by our gun fire was the latter that it was hardly distinguishable; only the second and succeeding lines were in anything like their original form, though dug-outs had been wrecked and timber and other débris thrown about in all directions. Lozenge and Shelter Woods were two of a cluster north of Fricourt and Fricourt Wood. The Quadrangle was about five hundred yards south-west of Mametz Wood, the latter presenting a truly terrible appearance. Bitter fighting had taken place for the possession of the Wood and Contalmaison village west of it. Swept by an awful holocaust of shell fire, first by the British guns and then by the German artillery on the Wood passing into our hands, it had become a place of evil repute—worse even to live in; for beneath and among the broken and lacerated trees men had their habitation in tents or had burrowed into the ground—anywhere as shelter from the enemy's guns, which still kept the place under furious bombardments.

From the Quadrangle the "way up" led through a valley between Contalmaison and Mametz Wood, thence on to the road which ran east and west, dividing the two Bazentins (le-Petit and le-Grand) and villages and woods. But "Wood" was a misnomer, for only gaunt skeletons of what had been trees remained to show what they had passed through. The route now led across a shell-torn country, pock-marked and broken with countless craters and holes gaping from the battered earth. Tangles of barbed wire, tossed and flung about in endless confusion, were everywhere.

Bazentin-le-Petit stood on high ground, beyond which in a small valley were the trenches to be taken over. There was no mistaking them, for they were covered by wreaths of evil black smoke from bursting shells, punctured every second or so by sharp stabs of flame as explosion succeeded explosion and fountains of earth and débris shot up into the sky.

Such was the introduction the infantry of the 50th Division had to front-line trenches on the Somme.

The general situation immediately preceding the third phase of the offensive is thus summarised in Sir Douglas Haig's official despatches: "Practically the whole of the forward crest of the main ridge, on a front of some nine thousand yards from Delville Wood to the road above Mouquet Farm was now in our hands, and with it the advantage of observation over the slopes beyond. East of Delville Wood, for a further three thousand yards to Leuze Wood, we were firmly established on the main ridge, while further east, across the Combles Valley the French were advancing victoriously on our right. But, though the centre of our line was well placed, on our right flanks there was still difficult ground to be won."

About the centre of the line, however, High Wood had proved a difficult problem, and by the 12th of September only half of it was in our hands, for immediately in rear of the Wood, extending on the right along the high ground north-east of Delville Wood and Ginchy and on the left south of Martinpuich, was the powerful German Switch Line, that portion in front of the 50th Division consisting of three lines of trenches, *i.e.* (1) Hook Trench, (2) Martin Trench, the Bow and the Starfish Line, and (3) continuation of the Starfish Line and Prue Trench, all running east and south-east from Martinpuich.*

To continue the story of the relief of the right of the 15th Division. Of the 149th Brigade the 6th (Lieut.-Colonel G. R. B. Spain) and 4th (Lieut.-Colonel B. D. Gibson) Northumberland Fusiliers on the 9th followed the 5th Battalion, the 6th to the Quadrangle and the 4th to Bécourt; the 149th Machine-Gun Company (Major G. E. Wilkinson) and 149th Trench-Mortar Battery moved to Mametz Wood where, early on the morning of the 10th Brigade Headquarters were also established. During this day the 7th Northumberland Fusiliers (Lieut.-Colonel G. Scott Jackson) moved up to the Quadrangle, and two companies of the 5th Green Howards (Major C. H. Pierce) were sent up to support the 1/4th East Yorkshires.

On the 10th also the remaining units of the 150th Brigade followed the 1/4th East Yorkshires into the line, the 4th and 5th Green Howards moving up to Shelter Wood and the old German line (between Mametz and Bazentin-le-Petit Woods) respectively. At 10.30 that night the 5th Green Howards relieved one company of the East Yorkshires in the front line.

During the 10th the enemy's guns were active and the frontline and support trenches came in for fairly heavy, but intermittent, shell fire.

Calamity fell on the 149th Brigade early on the 11th. At 7.25 a.m. Brig.-General Clifford set out with his Staff-Captain

---

* This Switch Line had been begun by the Germans as early as the 2nd and 3rd of July, after the opening of the offensive; they had weeks in which to complete its defences.

(Capt. D. Hill) to reconnoitre the assembly trenches, and was shot dead by a sniper. An N.C.O. of his brigade (Lance-Corporal R. H. Temple, 4th Northumberland Fusiliers) fully expressed the opinion of all ranks when he wrote in his private diary: "It is a very great blow to the Brigade as he was a splendid soldier, a fine gentleman, and very brave. The last little act performed by him was when we marched away from Hénencourt Wood. He saluted each platoon of the Battalion and we all thought it was very kind of him. He was practically the first in the Brigade to give his life in the 'Great Push.' "

Lieut.-Colonel Turner, 5th Northumberland Fusiliers, then assumed temporary command of the Brigade. That night (11th) large working parties were at work digging assembly and "jumping-off" trenches, for orders had been received at Divisional Headquarters that on the 15th the Fourth Army, in conjunction with the French and Reserve Armies (right and left respectively) would renew the attack.

The general scheme of this great battle is thus described by Sir Douglas Haig:

"The general plan of the combined Allied attack . . . on the 15th of September was to pivot on the high ground south of the Ancre and north of the Albert–Bapaume road, while the Fourth Army devoted its whole effort to the rearmost of the enemy's original system of defence between Morval and Le Sars. Should our success in this direction warrant it, I made arrangements to enable me to extend the left of the attack to embrace the villages of Martinpuich and Courcelette. As soon as our advance at this point had reached the Morval line, the time would have arrived to bring forward my left across the Thiepval Ridge. Meanwhile, on my right, our Allies* arranged to continue the line of advance, in close co-operation with me from the Somme to the slopes above Combles, but directing their main effort northwards against the villages of Rancourt and Frégicourt, so as to complete the isolation of Combles and open the way for the attack upon Sailly-Saillisel."

---

* It is interesting, and of importance, to note that by this time the British operations on the Somme had compelled the enemy to relax his pressure at Verdun. The French forces on the Somme were, therefore, considerably increased, though the British Armies south of the Ancre still constituted the main striking force of the offensive.

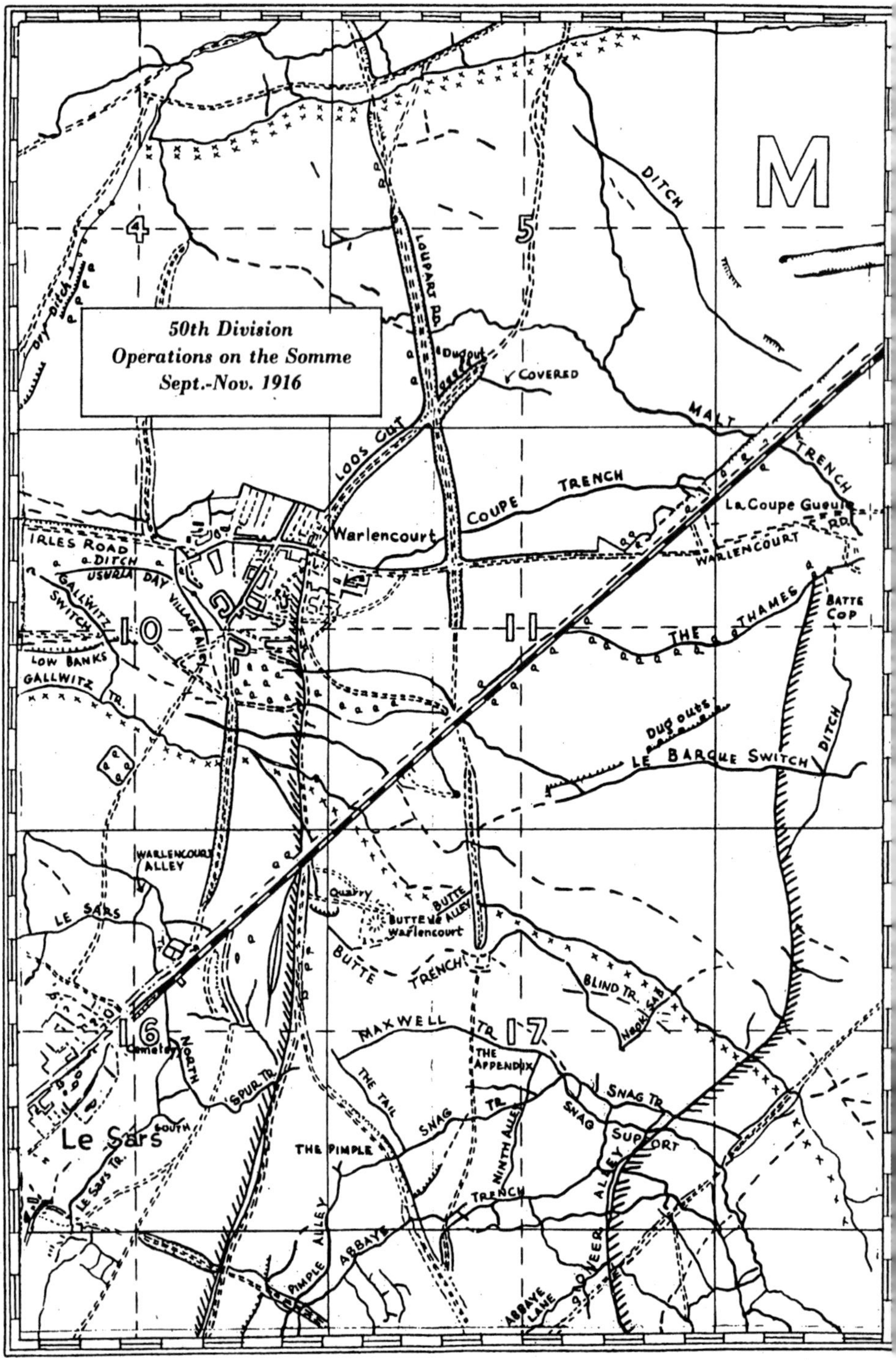

50th Division
Operations on the Somme
Sept.-Nov. 1916

facing p. 143

THE BATTLE OF FLERS-COURCELETTE: 15TH–22ND SEPTEMBER, 1916

Sir Douglas Haig's plan, as already given, in so far as it referred to the attack between High Wood and Martinpuich, was to be carried out by the 50th Division in the following manner: the Division was to attack with the 47th Division on the right and the 15th Division on the left; the assault, to be made in three bounds (first objective) Hook Trench from north-west of High Wood to just south-east of Martinpuich; (second objective) Martin Trench, The Bow and a portion of the Starfish Line; (third objective) Prue Trench and the left of the Starfish Line; these three objectives, respectively, were the Brown, Green and Blue Lines.

The Division was to attack with the 149th Brigade on the right and the 150th Brigade on the left; the 151st Brigade was to be in reserve and at zero move to O.G.1, O.G.2, Mametz Wood and Quadrangle Trench.

One company of Pioneers (7th Durham Light Infantry) was to be attached to each assaulting infantry brigade; they were to be used for making communication trenches between the successive lines.

The 7th Field Company, R.E. (J. A. McQueen), with two platoons of Pioneers, were to repair the road running northwards from Bazentin-le-Petit Cemetery towards Martinpuich; the 1st and 2nd Northumberland Field Companies, R.E. (commanded by E. C. Burnup) to be in reserve about Railway Copse.

The Divisional Artillery were to bombard the enemy's defences during the two or three days prior to the attack, the assault being also assisted by light and medium trench-mortar batteries. "Z" Day was the 15th of September and zero hour 6.20 a.m.

On the 14th, however, it was deemed necessary to issue further orders in closer detail concerning the co-operation between the 50th and the 47th and 15th Divisions, on either flank; for it will be remembered that the front line of the 50th Division was in advance of the lines held by the 47th and 15th Divisions, the flanks of the 50th being open to enfilade fire.

These orders had been the subject of much thought by General Wilkinson, G.O.C., 50th Division. He was faced by a difficult problem, very clearly given in the Divisional Narrative of Operations:

"The front allotted to the 50th Division was about 1,100 yards in extent, increasing to 1,800 yards at the final objective. On the right flank the enemy held High Wood,* and on the left flank Martinpuich. The 47th Division, on the right, had to start about 300 yards in rear of the right flank of the 50th Division, which was thus exposed to the enemy in High Wood. On the left the 15th Division had to start some 250 yards behind the left flank of the 50th, leaving that flank entirely exposed to fire from trenches south of Martinpuich and from Martinpuich itself.

"Both flanks of the 50th Division were, therefore, in a most dangerous position, and the Major-General commanding had to decide whether to delay his attack until the flank divisions came up level, or whether to take the risk of the losses and start at zero *so as to help the other two divisions get forward, by threatening to envelop the enemy in High Wood and Martinpuich.*

"The latter course was decided on."†

It has already been stated that the assault was to be carried out by the 149th Brigade on the right and the 150th Brigade on the left.

Orders were issued from 149th Brigade Headquarters to the 4th and 7th Northumberland Fusiliers to form the right and left attacking battalions of the Brigade; the 6th Northumberland Fusiliers were to be in support and the 5th in Brigade Reserve. The attack was to be delivered from two lines of assembly trenches connecting Bethel Sap and Jutland Avenue and to the north of Clarke's Trench.

The 150th Brigade was to attack with three battalions in the front line and one battalion in reserve, i.e., 1/4th East Yorkshires on the right, 4th Green Howards in the centre, 5th Green Howards on the left, the 5th Durham Light Infantry to be in reserve in front of Bazentin-le-Petit (presumably in Cardiff Trench). The assembly positions for the attacking troops were Eye and Swansea Trenches.

---

* A trench map with the diaries of the 50th Division shows the enemy holding over two-thirds of High Wood and the 47th Division the lower portion, the front line of the latter being Queen's Trench.

† Neither the Histories of the 15th or 47th Divisions make any reference to the assistance given to them by the 50th Division, though it must have been apparent.

Of the 7th Durham Light Infantry (Pioneers) "B" Company was attached to the 149th Brigade and "D" Company to the 150th Brigade.

The 7th Durhams, since their transition from fighting infantry to Pioneers, had become very efficient in their new duties. Their work, at all times arduous and often hazardous, had been reported on as first class, and at the time that these operations took place the Battalion was regarded by their commander with that affection which all divisions gave to their Pioneers.

The artillery arrangements are of particular interest. Not only was Flers-Courcelette the first big "set" battle in which the 50th Division was engaged, but it was the first time the gunners fired a "creeping barrage"; the first time also the infantry of the Division had attacked under such a barrage.

The earliest mention of the "creeping barrage" is on the 12th of September, *i.e.*, in XV Corps Artillery Operation Orders,* but there is evidence that such a barrage (though not termed "creeping") was in use on the 1st of July, the first day of the Somme Battles. For the infantry of the 30th Division, who attacked from Maricourt, got close up to the barrage and as soon as it "lifted" from the enemy's front line were into his trenches before he had time to come up out of his deep dug-outs and bring machine-gun and rifle fire to bear on our troops.

The difference between the "creeping" barrage and the barrage which "lifted" from one line to another was that the former caught, in moving back slowly, shell-holes and dug-out posts to which the enemy had retired as soon as the barrage opened. It will be obvious that a screen of fire, moving back over *the whole area* between the enemy's first and second lines of defence, would fall upon hostile troops sheltered between the two lines; whereas a barrage which lifted from the front line on to the second line direct would miss the intervening shell-holes and dug-out posts.

Moreover, the "creeping" barrage enabled our infantry to climb out of the trenches into No Man's Land and lie up close under the barrage so that, when it began to creep back to the enemy's second and rear lines, the troops were "into" the enemy's trenches before he had time to man his defences.

---

* See *The Coming of the Creeping Barrage*, by Major A. F. Becke, late R.F.A.

Flers-Courcelette *was*, therefore, the first battle in which the "creeping barrage" was known as such, but it *had* been used before.

For the battle the 50th Divisional Artillery, with the 276th Brigade, R.F.A., attached, was mainly disposed in the Caterpillar Valley and the valley west of Bazentin-le-Grand Wood. In these positions they formed the centre group of the Divisional Artillery of the III Corps. The batteries of the 250th Brigade, R.F.A., were, however, split up and attached to the 251st, 252nd and 253rd Field Artillery Brigades of the 50th Divisional Artillery.

From the gunners' point of view the front held by the 50th Division had been divided into four equal sectors, each being covered by one sub-group of the Divisional Artillery, *i.e.*, 252nd Brigade covering the right sector, then in the following order: 251st, 253rd and 276th. An artillery officer was sent to each infantry brigade as liaison officer and to some of the battalions.

The "creeping" (18-pounder) barrage to be put down by the 50th Divisional Artillery was to fall at one hundred and fifty yards from the Divisional front line. "This advanced fifty yards a minute till a line two hundred yards from the first objective was reached. It dwelt there for an hour and then again lifted at the same rate till a similar line was reached beyond the second objective, and a similar procedure was adopted with the final objective."*

The artillery (as already shown) had been almost a month in the forward area before the infantry took over the front line, and the gunners had already gained experience of the Somme battlefields.

"Accustomed as we were to the more or less surreptitious methods of the Salient and trench warfare, it was an extraordinary sight to see the country covered with troops of all sorts moving about in large and small bodies; guns of all descriptions and sizes blazing away in the open with no other cover than a piece of camouflage netting; and streams of motor transport and wagons packing the roads up to, and beyond, the gun positions. The whole scene was one of intense activity and movement, and this impressed one far more than the devastation and ruin that spread itself as far as the eye could

---

* Narrative of Operations, 50th Division Headquarters.

reach. The churned-up ground over which one walked told the tale of the terrific shell fire to which the whole area had been subjected. But the chief impression that remained was one of intense effort and complete confidence, an effort that was being pushed steadily forward after months of careful preparation. The contrast between the sights we now saw for the first time and the almost deserted country we had left was extraordinary."

Major Ommanney was indeed right when he wrote the above description of the Somme battlefield as he and his brother officers and men saw it. The place was like a huge camp. How the Bosche shells failed to take toll of man or animal or war material whenever they fired into our lines was truly extraordinary. Yet, sometimes for hours on end, he would plaster a particular part of the line, knocking a few already-damaged dug-outs about and piling destruction on destruction—but that was all. There was always the other side, of course, and one unlucky shell would pitch into a dug-out full of men, or on a shelter, killing and wounding more than would have been lost in a small attack.

The preliminary bombardment began on the 12th of September. For three days it never ceased, and the roar of the guns was continuous. From 6 a.m. until 6.30 p.m. the 4·5-in. howitzers pounded the enemy's defences, creating havoc in his trenches, blowing his parapets to bits and tearing great gaps in his wire. Then from 6.30 p.m. all through the night the 18-pounders fired shrapnel for the purpose of causing as many casualties as possible among the enemy's working parties who, when darkness had fallen, would set to work to repair the damage done throughout the day by our howitzers. The latter guns at night fired P.S. gas shell.

Thus, day by day, the unfortunate Bosche was forced to endure a merciless bombardment which often left him dazed and dumb by the time darkness had fallen. There is evidence that, often in sheer madness, the enemy's troops betook themselves to their deep dug-outs, remaining there and caring not at all what happened above ground, praying almost for release from that hell upon earth—the front-line trenches.

The "creeping barrage" was not the only innovation during the Flers-Courcelette battle, for tanks were tried for the first time. These ungainly steel monsters created the greatest interest (and amusement) among our troops, who were not aware of the existence of these strange "animals" until they saw them lumbering along, creating a tremendous noise, almost human in their movements and terrifying in action against the enemy. Gasping with astonishment, our infantry watched the tanks move across wire and trenches, knock down buildings, fall upon, and crush out of existence, machine-gun emplacements, and generally show the utmost disdain for every obstacle encountered during their advance.

This first trial was for experimental purposes, the 50th Division having only two tanks, which the Narrative states "worked on the left flank of the Division, moving up between our flank and the village of Martinpuich."

By 2.30 a.m. on the 15th of September all moves had been carried out in good order and there was very little shelling. During the night, however, the 5th Green Howards had lost their C.O.—Lieut.-Colonel J. Mortimer—who was killed in Pioneer Alley.

At 6.10 a.m. there was a buzz of excitement in the front line. With a "whir-r-ing" sound two tanks were seen approaching in rear of the left of the 149th Brigade, and at 6.18 these gigantic monsters reached, and lifted themselves over, the assembly trenches of the 7th Northumberland Fusiliers and started off across No Man's Land towards the enemy's trenches.

The German soldiery had received warning of the use of these tanks; nevertheless, when the latter appeared they produced terror and consternation. S.O.S. signals went up from the enemy's front line, and numbers of his troops bolted from their trenches back towards their second line. Four minutes later the hostile barrage fell but, as the 7th Northumberland Fusiliers record, "our men got away before a heavy fire was opened on them."

At 6.20 a.m. the Divisional barrage fell, and the 4th and 7th Northumberland Fusiliers of the 149th Brigade, and the 4th East Yorkshires, 4th and 5th Green Howards of the 150th Brigade, advanced in good order close up to the screen of fire and quickly gained the first objective, *i.e.*, Hook Trench.

At this stage the Divisional Narrative states "at once it became clear that the 47th Division would fail to get High Wood *alone*"!

On the high ground at the north-western corner of High Wood the enemy had a very strongly-defended position, part of his defence system which commanded the whole of the ground held by the 50th Division.* This strong point had been repeatedly attacked before the Division took over the line, but without success. It was known to contain a large number of machine-guns.

No sooner had the 149th Brigade begun to dig in on the line of the first objective than galling machine-gun and rifle fire was opened on the 4th and 7th Northumberland Fusiliers. The advance to the second objective was timed to begin at 7.20 a.m., and until that hour battalions made every effort to take shelter from the devastating fire coming from their right. It was apparent that the 47th Division, on the right, had not taken High Wood, and that the left brigade of that division was held up. All the more urgent, therefore, was it for the 149th Brigade to push on and outflank the enemy in the Wood, thus compelling him to evacuate his position.

At zero plus one hour, *i.e.*, 7.20 a.m., the 149th and 150th Brigades advanced and captured the second objective, consisting of the Starfish Line, The Bow and Martin Trench. But from both flanks the enemy's fire caused very heavy casualties amongst the attacking troops. The 4th Northumberland Fusiliers of the 149th Brigade, unsupported on their right by the 47th Division, were driven back to Hook Trench which, with Bethel Sap, was strengthened and made secure. Both the 5th and 6th Northumberland Fusiliers were by now involved in the battle.

On the left, the 150th Brigade had experienced similar opposition from Martinpuich, very heavy fire coming from the ruins of the village as the three attacking battalions advanced. Nevertheless, by 6.42 a.m. the East Yorkshires reported the first objective taken, and by 7.58 a.m. "B" and "D" Companies of that battalion report, "Second objective reached and taken with very few casualties."

The 7th Northumberland Fusiliers, on the right of the East Yorkshires, however, had not advanced in line with the latter and, although Martin Alley and Martin Trench were in the hands of the 150th Brigade, no further advance could take place to the Starfish Line until the 149th Brigade had advanced. The 7th Northumberland Fusiliers give very logical reasons why they were held up. Hook Trench lay along the top of a

---

* It was part of the German Switch Line which the enemy had begun during the first week in July.

ridge, while the second and third objectives were in a valley beyond and nothing could be seen of them from the assembly trenches. The Battalion was, therefore, marching on compass bearings. Touch had been lost with the East Yorkshires between the first and second objectives, and when "near the second objective our lines had to halt as our barrage was holding them up. . . . Several attempts were made to get forward, but we lost so heavily from our own barrage that the remainder of the Battalion was forced to wait until it lifted. We should have reached our second objective at 7.25 a.m.,* but it was 8.35 a.m. before we could move forward." There was another difficulty—a very real one—not mentioned in the Battalion Diary. The ground was dry and had already been pulverised by previous bombardments. So that now the Northumberland Fusiliers found themselves fronted by clouds of dust and smoke, which hung in a pall-like fog over the battlefield.

Eventually (by 8.30 a.m.), the 7th reached the sunken road just south of The Bow, where they captured about thirty men of a *minnenwerfer* battery† and killed several others besides taking four trench mortars.‡

At 9.57 a.m. the 150th Brigade reported the capture of the final objective. At that hour the situation along the Brigade front appears to have been: the East Yorkshires in Martin Trench (second objective), 4th and 5th Green Howards holding some thirty yards of the extreme left of Prue Trench and about a hundred yards of the extreme left of the Starfish Line.

---

* The barrage on the second objective fell at 7.20 a.m., so that to reach the second objective by 7.25 a.m. would hardly have been possible.

† The following amusing incident is related by Capt. F. Buckley, of the 7th Northumberland Fusiliers: "The prisoners, more numerous than ourselves, were sent to the rear in charge of Private Martin, a diminutive signaller. He caused much consternation among his flock by deftly severing their trouser buttons before the journey began. It made an imposing procession—the prisoners with their hands deep in their pockets followed by Private Martin smoking an enormous souvenir cigar and mumbling, 'How way, you blinking beggars.'

‡ At about 12.35 p.m. D/252 Battery, R.F.A., fired 4·5-in. *shrapnel* for the last time and with singular effect. Noting that a machine-gun post in the Swayles High Wood was being stubbornly held and that an enormous quantity of high explosive would have been required to get a direct hit, Major R. M. Knolles ordered the last 12 rounds of shrapnel to be fired. The 11th round was a beautiful low burst which totally destroyed the machine-gun detachment, and from the O.P. the 1st Division infantry were soon seen making good the north-western face of the wood.

The whole Divisional front at this period ran in a north-westerly to south-easterly direction between High Wood, on the right, and Martinpuich, on the left. It is obvious, therefore, that the 149th Brigade met with the greatest opposition and had had the most difficult task, the gap on the right flank uncovering the whole of the Brigade's attack.

The Divisional Narrative concludes with the following remarks: "Both Brigades lost very heavily and became considerably disorganised, especially the 149th Brigade.

"However, by their splendid dash and gallantry they enabled High Wood and Martinpuich to be subsequently occupied by the flank divisions. The 47th Division, on our right, lost very heavily in front of High Wood before the enemy finally surrendered, but the 15th Division occupied Martinpuich without difficulty, thanks to the co-operation of the 50th Division."

Martinpuich had fallen to the 15th Division just before 10 a.m. and by 1 p.m. High Wood had been cleared of the enemy by the 47th Division.

At about 4 p.m. the 150th Brigade reported that their troops had been driven out of the Starfish Line, but still held Martin Trench and Martin Alley. At 6.20 a.m. the 150th Brigade again gives its dispositions: "The 4th East Yorkshires were consolidating in Martin Trench, the 4th and 5th Green Howards in their third objectives, Martin Alley and Tangle North respectively." The 8th and 5th Durham Light Infantry (151st Brigade) were on a line roughly about half-way between Martin and Hook Trenches.

The dispositions of the 149th Brigade at 6.55 p.m. are thus given in the Brigade Diary: "Scout officers have been in touch with a body of men, strength unknown, holding part of Starfish in M.34.a (second objective on right of Divisional front). About one hundred men consolidated strong point M.33.D.26 (this was the sunken road between the first and second objectives, occupied by the 7th Northumberland Fusiliers). Two Vickers dug in about M.33.D.3.8 (the north-western end of the sunken road) with a few men at intervals. Whole of first objective held by portions of Brigade with one battalion headquarters. Two battalion headquarters and about one company in Clark's Trench. No word of teams of two mortars and two Vickers in Bethel Sap. Men in first objective reported very exhausted and heavily shelled. Battalion of 9th

Durham Light Infantry in Clark's Trench and assembly trenches of left sub-sector. Estimated casualties up to 6 p.m.: 31 officers, 1,265 other ranks."

At 6.5 p.m. the 151st Brigade received orders to attack Prue Trench, the assault to be made from Hook Trench. The Brigade at that hour was not concentrated. At 9.25 a.m. the 8th Durham Light Infantry (Lieut.-Colonel J. Turnbull), having been placed at the disposal of the 150th Brigade, moved "C" and "D" Companies up to Eye and Swansea Trenches respectively (under the orders of the 5th Durham Light Infantry) where they remained all day, heavily shelled. During the afternoon "A" Company also moved up to Eye, "B" remaining in the O.G. line. The 9th Durham Light Infantry (Lieut.-Colonel R. B. Bradford) and the 6th Durham Light Infantry (Lieut.-Colonel J. W. Jeffreys) were already in Hook Trench, but the 5th Border Regiment (Lieut.-Colonel J. R. Hedley) did not leave Mametz Wood until 6.30 p.m. and then their guides lost direction, the Battalion finally reaching Eye and Hook Trenches about half an hour after the attack had gone forward.

The attack on Prue Trench, first ordered for 7.30 p.m., then altered to 8 p.m., next to 8.30 p.m. and finally to 9.40 p.m., failed.

The 9th Durham Light Infantry, on the right, and the 6th Durham Light Infantry, on the left (they would have been the centre battalion had the 5th Border Regiment reached the assembly positions in time), went forward gallantly enough. They advanced in direction due north but, reaching a line about five hundred yards north of Hook Trench, were held up by very heavy machine-gun fire. Portions of the 9th Durham Light Infantry from the first two waves of the attack crossed the Starfish Line and pushed on to about twenty yards from Prue and dug in there, but gradually they were killed, all but four wounded men who crawled back. Eventually the Battalion dug in on a line running south-east from The Bow. With the exception of a statement that the Battalion attacked the Starfish Line and Prue Trench, the Diary of the 6th Durham Light Infantry contains no further details.

The 5th Border Regiment, late through no fault of their own in reaching the jumping-off line, received orders at 11 p.m. to make good their objective—a portion of Prue Trench —and gain touch with the 6th and 9th Durham Light Infantry.

But in the darkness it was almost a hopeless task. To move over ground, churned up by shell fire, pock-marked with huge gaping holes, cut across by broken and battered trenches, across belts of wire entanglements and still keep direction was beyond human capabilities. The Battalion did go forward some six hundred to seven hundred yards, but eventually dug themselves in, in The Bow. Some Headquarters details, who had been ordered to move forward in support of the Battalion, eventually got into touch with "B" Company and part of the 6th Durham Light Infantry. With the latter, they pushed on almost to the Starfish Line, but were driven back by machine-gun fire, and finally dug in between The Bow and Crescent Alley.

This attack cost the Division further heavy casualties, the Borders alone losing over one hundred killed and wounded, all ranks. Many officers had fallen.

Thus, the operations of the 15th September so far as they concerned the 50th Division and (in a lesser degree) the 47th and 15th Divisions. The official despatches are not very fair; they do not give credit to the 50th Division[*] for the very great assistance given to the 47th and 15th Divisions. The 47th Division is praised for the capture of High Wood but, as this narrative shows, the capture was very largely due to the G.O.C., 50th Division; to General Wilkinson for his decision not to wait until the two flanking divisions came up into line, but to attack straight away with the intention of making easier the capture of High Wood and Martinpuich; and to those battalions who fought most gallantly in carrying out his orders.

During the night of the 15th–16th of September the Division was ordered by III Corps to resume the attack at 9.25 a.m. on the 16th and seize Prue Trench; the 151st Brigade was to capture Prue Trench east of The Crescent; the 150th Brigade Prue Trench west of The Crescent. The 151st was to attack with three battalions (all of which had already suffered heavy losses), *i.e.*, 5th Border Regiment, 6th and 9th Durham Light Infantry.

The attack was made after fifteen minutes' intense bombardment and, on the right, did not succeed. The attacking troops of the 151st Brigade were met by very heavy machine-gun fire from front and flanks and could not get on.

---

[*] The Division is not even mentioned.

On the left, the 150th Brigade attacked with the 5th Durham Light Infantry, supported on the right by one company of the 1/4th East Yorkshires, and on the left by one company of the 4th Green Howards; the 5th Green Howards held two companies in reserve, in the bend at the western end of Hook Trench. Four bombing parties (two from each battalion) from the 4th and 5th Green Howards, supported by the 5th Durhams, who also had the assistance of two machine-guns, and who were to establish themselves in Martin Alley. The bombers of the 4th Green Howards were to bomb down Prue Trench eastwards, those of the 5th Green Howards down Starfish Line in the same direction. The 150th Machine-Gun Company and a trench-mortar battery were to co-operate. The whole attack by the 150th Brigade was under the command of Lieut.-Colonel G. Spence, O.C., 5th Durham Light Infantry.

The results of the attack were the occupation of a short portion of Prue Trench and about one hundred yards of the Starfish Line nearly as far as The Crescent, though the enemy appears to have maintained his hold on the latter.

Again there was a long list of casualties.

Official records of the attack are very brief, but the following from *The Fifth Battalion, The Durham Light Infantry* is an excellent summary: "Companies were so scattered that it was impossible to collect them together [the Battalion had only received orders for the attack at 7.30 a.m.] in the time available and, when the time arrived, both 'A' Company of our Battalion and the company of East Yorkshires were missing. 'B,' 'C' and 'D' Companies, however, formed up in Martin Trench and attacked in three waves. The enemy trench was four hundred yards away, and the frontage allotted to the Battalion was five hundred yards. As guiding mark they were given the Church of Le Sars on the left, and an old barn on the right. The attacking companies, gallantly led by Lieut. F. E. S. Townsend, came under enfilade fire from machine-guns and casualties were fairly heavy. Unfortunately, they lost direction and swung away towards the left. Consequently, they only captured the western parts of their objective and many men found themselves in the northern end of Martin Alley. Most of Prue and Starfish, including the strong point known as The Crescent, still remained in the hands of the enemy. Parties of bombers were quickly despatched along

Prue and Starfish, but were driven back. Blocks were then made and the trench consolidated. . . . About 11 a.m. the Germans put down a heavy barrage on Martin Trench and Martin Alley, and casualties came thick and fast. . . . Lieut. Townsend* was, unfortunately, mortally wounded. He had gone to an exposed part of the line to see some wounded men and the next lot of shrapnel got him. He had done very good work in the attack."

During the afternoon of the 16th the 149th Brigade was placed in Divisional Reserve, and gradually battalions were withdrawn to Mametz Wood, but it was nearly midnight before the last of them reached their destination.

The losses sustained by each battalion of the Brigade, from the 14th to the 16th of September, were as follows: 4th Northumberland Fusiliers—17 officers killed or wounded; other ranks, 110 killed, 229 wounded, 143 missing. 5th Northumberland Fusiliers—5 officers wounded; other ranks, 10 killed, 54 wounded, 8 missing. 6th Northumberland Fusiliers—1 officer killed, 8 officers wounded; other ranks, 279 killed, wounded or missing. 7th Northumberland Fusiliers—3 officers killed, 9 officers wounded; other ranks, 40 killed, 219 wounded and 74 missing. Total: 43 officers and 1,164 other ranks.

The general situation and disposition of the 50th Division at 2 p.m. on the 16th was that the Divisional Line ran from the eastern end of Hook Trench (the Divisional right boundary point)—The Bow; part of Crescent Alley; Martin Trench; Prue Trench and Starfish Line; west of Crescent Alley; Martin Alley, inclusive; the 151st Brigade was on the right and the 150th Brigade on the left. The last-named was re-organising in the Starfish Line west of Crescent Alley; the 149th Brigade was on the point of moving back to Mametz Wood.

At 8.20 p.m. that night the 5th Durhams were ordered to make another attack on Starfish Line and Prue Trench, but it was not until noon on the 17th that anything was known of the result, and then the enemy was found still in possession of most of Prue and part of The Crescent. A patrol, pushed up Starfish, was bombed back.

At 5.30 p.m. (17th) yet another attack was made by bombers of the 5th Durhams with the object of capturing the remainder

* Lieut. F. E. S. Townsend died of wounds 30th of September, 1916.

of Prue and Starfish Trenches, as far as The Crescent and also The Crescent itself.

"Our bombing sections had suffered heavy casualties, and the Brigadier decided to reinforce them with bombers from the other battalions in the Brigade but, owing to the heavy barrage, these reinforcements did not reach us in time and our bombers carried on the attack by themselves. The advance began at 5.30 p.m., the men working their way methodically along Prue and Starfish towards their objective. Thanks largely to the leadership of Lieuts. E. G. Jones and H. Green and the good work of Sergeants Luke and Brabran, Prue and Starfish, as far as The Crescent, were captured and consolidated. The attack on The Crescent was repulsed, however, and a simultaneous attack up Crescent Alley by men of the 151st Brigade suffered the same fate."*

The enemy then counter-attacked, but was at once driven back by Lewis-gun fire.

The attack of the 151st Brigade mentioned above was made by some bombing squads from the 8th Durham Light Infantry, but as they were advancing they were heavily barraged by the enemy and their attack was completely disorganised. Both at 8.36 p.m. and 9.24 p.m. bombing attacks were also made, but failed owing to barrage and machine-gun fire. The 9th Durham Light Infantry took part in this attack and, although they succeeded in establishing a series of posts in shell-holes about one hundred yards in front of their line, it was all that could be accomplished in the face of the murderous fire of the enemy.

The 5th Border Regiment state that they remained in position about The Bow throughout the 17th improving their position. Their Diary also records the death of their gallant Medical Officer—Capt. M. R. Inglis—who was killed whilst attending the wounded out in the battlefield during the night.

During the evening of the 17th the III Corps ordered the 50th Division to capture Prue Trench at 5.50 a.m. on the 18th.

But once again failure had to be recorded, machine-gun fire from Starfish breaking up the attack, and at 8.40 a.m. the 151st Brigade reported the attacking troops back in their own lines. The Brigade was then ordered to consolidate and link

---

* "The 5th Battalion, The Durham Light Infantry."

up with brigades right and left, the 8th Durham Light Infantry to take over the front line on the night of the 18th.

The weather now took a hand in the operations; heavy rain had fallen all day and very soon the trenches, which had been dry and dusty, became thick in mud. The communication trenches especially were by nightfall almost impassable. These adverse conditions, coupled with the enemy's violent barrage and machine-gun fire, had robbed the Durham Light Infantry of success in their attack.

On the morning of the 19th the 69th Brigade, 23rd Division, relieved the 150th Brigade in the left sub-sector; the 1/4th East Yorkshires had already gone back to the O.G. Line, and there they were joined by the three other battalions, after relief.

The 1/4th East Yorkshires had lost during the operations from the 14th to the 17th inclusive 2 officers killed and 10 wounded; in other ranks their losses were 30 killed, 195 wounded and 13 missing. No casualties are given by the 4th Green Howards; the 5th Green Howards record the loss of 4 officers killed, 11 wounded; 48 other ranks killed, 162 wounded and 27 missing. No casualties are given by the 5th Durham Light Infantry, but Major A. L. Raimes states that: "When the roll was called on the 19th only 4 officers and 88 men answered to their names." Many more had, however, only been slightly wounded and soon rejoined, others had become intermixed with other units and reported themselves during the next two or three days.

Only the 151st Brigade now remained in the front line.

Dawn broke on the 19th on a dismal scene, impossible of adequate description. For a week (including the three days' preliminary bombardment by our guns) the area in which the Brigade was maintaining itself had been swept by violent and almost unceasing shell fire; débris, human and otherwise, littered the whole battlefield. Great gashes in the earth filled rapidly with water, hiding the poor remains of friend and foe; the trenches, hastily dug, were mud channels, blocked here and there with the bodies of the dead, or wounded awaiting evacuation. And still the rain fell. Twice on the 18th the 8th Durhams had tried to reach The Crescent, but the mud had proved an impassable obstacle. Even ration parties had great difficulty in getting food up to the half-starved men in the front line. No fires could be lighted. Like a pall, desolation and misery hung over the whole area.

During the evening another attack on The Crescent was projected and finally ordered, but the bombers of the 8th Durham Light Infantry could not even reach the sunken road, much less The Crescent.

The 5th Border Regiment tell the same story. The 9th Durham Light Infantry had been relieved and were back in Clark's Trench—they were terribly weak in numbers. The 6th Durham Light Infantry, back in Sixth Avenue, Intermediate Trench and Jutland, spent the 19th in salvage work and in repairing their trenches.

The 20th found the 8th Durham Light Infantry holding practically the Divisional front, *i.e.*, from The Bow to Martin Trench; *they were standing in mud two and a half feet deep along the whole trench.* At 11.30 a.m. Corps Headquarters ordered "a defensive attitude to be maintained," which put an end for the time being to all local attacks. And at last, during the evening, the 151st Brigade was relieved and moved back to Mametz Wood, taking over from the 149th Brigade, who had relieved them in the front line.

The total casualties suffered by the 151st Brigade from the 15th to the 20th of September (inclusive) were 43 officers and 903 other ranks. Of this number the 9th Durham Light Infantry had 3 officers killed, 1 died of wounds and 9 wounded; in other ranks their losses were 43 killed, 219 wounded and 27 missing—a total of 302, *i.e.*, 44 per cent. of the Battalion's strength which went into action. The other three battalions do not give the actual number of their casualties.

Although Corps Headquarters at 11.45 a.m. on the 20th had ordered "a defensive attitude to be maintained for the present and positions strengthened," Divisional Headquarters (in the light of further information concerning the enemy's dispositions coming to hand) issued orders that the 149th Brigade, on taking over the front line from the 151st Brigade, "will dig jumping-off trenches for attack on Starfish and Prue Lines."

The relief of the 151st Brigade by the 149th Brigade was completed at 12.30 a.m. on the 21st, and at that hour the 4th Northumberland Fusiliers were on the right—three companies in Hook Trench and one company in Vaux Post (described in the records as the Strong Point at S.3.b.9.5); the 7th Northumberland Fusiliers held the front line, *i.e.*, Bow Trench, the sunken road in rear of it and Hook Trench on the left of the 4th Battalion; the 5th Northumberland Fusiliers were in

Clark's Trench, and the 6th Battalion in Sixth Avenue East and Intermediate Line.

These dispositions remained unchanged throughout the day of the 21st, but during the evening orders were received for the attack on Starfish and Prue Lines.

As the attack was practically a bloodless affair (excepting a few casualties from shell fire), these orders need not be detailed, for information had been received that the enemy had retired. This was so, and finally the 4th and 5th Northumberland Fusiliers occupied both the Starfish and Prue Lines without opposition, the 6th and 7th Northumberland Fusiliers being on the left; touch was obtained with divisions on right and left.

The Diary of the 4th Northumberland Fusiliers gives brief details of the Divisional front early on the morning of the 22nd: "4th Northumberland Fusiliers, with two companies of 5th Northumberland Fusiliers in Prue Trench; 6th Northumberland Fusiliers in Starfish Line; 7th Northumberland Fusiliers in their original front line and support positions, and 5th Northumberland Fusiliers Headquarters and remaining company in Clark's Trench."

Thus, after a week's fighting, the 50th Division had reached its final objective, *i.e.*, the Blue Line, or Prue Trench.

The positions the Divisional infantry had been called upon to assault were very strong; not merely hastily-dug trenches of an enemy "on the run," but carefully selected and well-prepared defences, held for several weeks before the assault took place. The possession of the high ground about Martinpuich was most essential, for it was about the centre of the enemy's line beyond which the ground sloped down towards Le Sars and Lebarque, rising thence towards Bapaume.

The dogged determination and tenacity in the attack displayed by the 50th Division won praise from the Corps Commander, and General Wilkinson had every reason to be proud of his men who had so well acquitted themselves in their first "set" battle.*

But, before closing the narrative of the Battle of Flers-Courcelette (which officially ended on the 22nd of September),

---

* The official despatches state that: "The result of the fighting of the 15th of September and following days was a gain more considerable than any which had attended our arms in the course of a single operation since the commencement of the offensive," and the 50th Division contributed its full share to this success.

something must be said of other units who, though not fighting troops, nevertheless contributed in no small degree to the success of the operations.

The Divisional Pioneers and Field Companies, R.E., have so far been mentioned only in connection with the original operation orders. But their gallant work figures specially in the Narrative written by the G.O.C., Division.

The work of the 7th Field Company, R.E., and the 1st and 2nd Northumberland Field Companies, R.E., and the 7th Durham Light Infantry (Pioneers) is too technical to describe in full, but these four units were engaged all over the battlefield. On the afternoon of the 15th they were at work in the forward area, digging communication trenches, repairing roads and digging gun emplacements. They worked always under shell fire and with none of the opportunities afforded the infantry of "hitting back" at the enemy. For twelve hours on end companies of the Pioneers and Sappers worked throughout the 16th in Martin Alley, Crescent Alley and Bethel Sap. On the 18th they were congratulated by the C.R.E. on the fine work done.

All four units worked throughout the whole operations, and from the records it is apparent that there was scarcely a part of the front line in which the men of the pick and shovel were not assisting their comrades, the fighting infantry, in making the line more secure and in repairing the roads so that transport could move up and down from the forward positions.

Both the Divisional Royal Engineers and Pioneers suffered many casualties, and the 1st Northumberland Field Company alone, on the 16th of September, had 29 killed or wounded.

Similarly, the devotion of the medical units of the Division should not be forgotten for, if the infantry found difficulty in getting forward over country filled with shell-holes, broken and blasted by shell fire, encumbered with wire-entanglements and all the débris created by the enemy's artillery, how much more difficult was it to carry out the evacuation of the wounded and get them safely back to the Dressing and Casualty Clearing Stations.

Nor should the efforts of the Army Service Corps in keeping the troops supplied with the necessary rations and supplies be overlooked. In a great battle it was always the infantry and gunners who received most praise, but unless *all* units of a division did their part well the operations were bound to suffer.

The Divisional Narrative gives the total casualties suffered between the 15th and 24th of September as "about 3,750 all ranks."

They were not in vain.

Events in the 50th Divisional area up to the night of the 24th of September may be summarised briefly: at nightfall on the 22nd the 149th Brigade held the front line, *i.e.*, Prue Trench. The 150th Brigade had sent up two battalions, one to Clark's Trench, the other to Swansea Trench; the two remaining battalions were in the O.G. Line. The 151st Brigade was in Divisional Reserve in Mametz Wood.

The 23rd was a fine, warm day—a boon and a blessing to all ranks, for the men were able to dry their clothes; the muddy trenches also became much drier. Consolidation of the line captured continued, whilst the Pioneers and Sappers were busy on road repairs.

Patrols were pushed out to Prue Copse and in front of Prue Trench towards Eaucourt L'Abbaye to establish a line of posts roughly on a line of the road in front of Prue Trench. On the night of the 23rd–24th the 150th Brigade began the relief of the 149th, the relief being completed by 9 a.m. on the 24th. The 149th then moved back into Divisional Reserve and the 151st Brigade moved forward to support positions.

THE BATTLE OF MORVAL: 25TH–28TH SEPTEMBER, 1916

On the morning of the 24th of September a general bombardment of the enemy's defences was opened all along the line between the Somme and Martinpuich, and at 12.35 p.m. on the 25th the French (on our right) attacked north of the river, while the Fourth British Army assaulted Morval and the German line thence to north of Martinpuich, *i.e.*, roughly on a front of about three and a half miles. The objectives on the British front were "Morval, Les Bœufs and Gueudecourt, as well as a belt of country about one thousand yards deep, curving round the north of Flers to a point midway between that village and Martinpuich."* The New Zealand, 1st, 50th and 23rd Divisions (in that order from right to left) lay between Flers and Martinpuich.

---

* Official Despatches.

The attack had originally been planned to take place on the 21st, but had to be postponed owing to weather conditions and other circumstances.

It will be remembered that the 150th Brigade had relieved the 149th in Prue Trench and posts already established on the road some three hundred to four hundred yards in front of the line.

The Brigade had taken over the line with the 1/4th East Yorkshires on the right and the 5th Durham Light Infantry on the left; the 4th and 5th Green Howards, on the right and left respectively, supported the two front-line battalions from the Starfish Line and Hook Trench; the 4th Green Howards also occupied Vaux Post.

During the morning of the 25th the 5th Durham Light Infantry pushed out a post down Crescent Alley. This "Alley" ran some distance north from Prue Trench, then curved in a north-easterly direction to Eaucourt L'Abbaye. Rutherford Alley was another long communication trench running from Prue to the same village. Both Crescent and Rutherford Alleys originally started from Hook Trench.

Orders issued by Divisional Headquarters at 4.15 p.m. on the 24th gave the final objective of the III Corps in the attack to take place on the 25th. It was a somewhat irregular line starting on the right from the Flers Line, thence westwards past the north of Martinpuich. But the 50th Division, with that energy which had by now become characteristic, had by pushing out patrols already occupied its objectives, though orders stated that if any portion of the objective line, as laid down in Corps Orders, had not been occupied patrols were to do so at zero hour on the 25th. They were also to push forward along the Flers Line and also up Crescent Alley and Twenty-Sixth Avenue (the latter on the left of Crescent Alley) communication trenches.

At zero hour, which had been fixed for 12.25 p.m., the 1st Division, on the right, and the 23rd Division, on the left, advanced to the attack, but the 50th Division, being already on its objective, had little to do. Patrols were, however, constantly on the watch for opportunities of pushing forward the line of posts, and by 4 p.m. the 5th Durham Light Infantry had reached a point in Crescent Alley north-east of the bend towards the Flers Line.

The 150th Brigade was then ordered to dig a "jumping-off" trench out in front of the "Road Line" (*i.e.*, the line of posts) during the night of the 25th–26th. This line was dug, and the 26th was spent by the Brigade in strengthening the posts put out in front of Prue Trench. It was not, however, until the night of the 26th–27th that the Brigade, in conjunction with the 2nd Brigade (1st Division), on the right, attacked what is described as "a new German trench," probably part of the Flers Switch.

The 4th and 5th Green Howards, on the right and left respectively, carried out the attack; the 4th East Yorkshires and the 5th Durham Light Infantry were in support on the right and left.

The night was intensely dark and the 2nd Brigade, new to the ground, lost direction and (so the Diary of the 4th Green Howards states) "lost themselves" as well. The 5th Green Howards also lost direction, but fetched up in Crescent Alley, where they remained. The 4th Green Howards penetrated the enemy's trenches but, their flanks being in the air, they were bombed out again, losing two officers killed, five wounded and about one hundred other ranks killed and wounded. The Battalion then fell back to the Starfish Line to re-form.

The following day (27th) at noon the 5th Durham Light Infantry sent a battle patrol up Crescent Alley and gained the objective of the previous evening.

The Divisional front line was now within a comparatively short distance of the Flers Line, which ran west from Eaucourt L'Abbaye. At 7 p.m. the 5th Durham Light Infantry were ordered to extend their left towards the 23rd Division and push out patrols towards the Flers Line. An incorrect report that Flers was clear of the enemy caused the Durhams to send forward "D" Company to occupy it; but on approaching closer the Line was found to be still strongly held; the Company, therefore, established a block in a communication trench leading northwards towards the Line.

These small "piece-meal" advances, interesting to those actually engaged, make rather dry reading. The 50th Division by its energy was already much in advance of the 1st and 23rd Divisions on its flanks, and had, therefore, to be careful of both flanks, and anything in the nature of a big attack could not take place until Corps Headquarters issued the necessary orders.

On the 28th of September the 151st Brigade relieved the 150th in the front line, the latter going back into support and the 149th remaining in Divisional Reserve. On the right of the 50th Division the 47th Division also took over the line of the 1st Division.

The Battle of Morval ended on the 28th of September, Combles, Les Bœufs and Gueudecourt all falling into our hands.*

THE BATTLE OF LE TRANSLOY: 1ST–18TH OCTOBER, 1916

By the end of September the high ground from Morval to Thiepval had been wrested from the enemy, Gueudecourt being our farthest point pushed into German territory.

But north-east of Martinpuich and Courcelette the Flers Line, running in front of Eaucourt L'Abbaye and Le Sars, had still to be captured. On the 29th the 23rd Division had taken Destremont Farm, south-west of Le Sars, which greatly assisted the attack on the Flers Line on that flank.

Orders were then issued for an attack on Eaucourt L'Abbaye and the enemy's defences east and west of that village. Four divisions were to be engaged, New Zealand, 47th, 50th and 23rd, in that order from right to left.

The 50th Division was well placed to carry out the attack though, as may be imagined, the infantry, after a fortnight of heavy fighting, were tired and badly needed a rest.

"Z" Day had been fixed for the 1st of October and the hour of attack at 3.15 p.m.

Divisional operations orders detailed the 151st Brigade as the attacking brigade, with the 149th in support and the 150th in reserve. But early on the 1st of October the orders affecting the attack were slightly modified. The original scheme was for the 151st Brigade to attack with the 6th Durham Light Infantry on the right, 5th Border Regiment in the centre and the 8th Durham Light Infantry on the left; the 9th Durham Light Infantry were to be in reserve. But the right and centre battalions were so weak in numbers that they were ordered to form one composite battalion, and two battalions of the 149th Brigade were attached to the 151st, *i.e.*, the 5th Northumberland Fusiliers, to be left attacking battalion, with the 4th Northumberland Fusiliers in close support.

---

* On the left of the Albert–Bapaume road the Battle of Thiepval had been in progress from the 26th to the 28th of September, Courcelette and Thiepval, at ast, being captured.

Wire-cutting by the Divisional Artillery began on the 30th of September, and during the night of the 30th September–1st October the guns bombarded the enemy's trenches and communications. Between 4 and 7 p.m. on the 30th of September hostile artillery fire was exceptionally heavy but eased off during the night, the enemy's guns firing intermittently.

After darkness had fallen, work on the "jumping-off" trenches, *i.e.*, North Durham Trench, South Durham Trench and Blaydon Trench and on Rutherford Alley, was carried out by the Pioneers and infantry. Dumps of bombs and ammunition and water were formed, and everyone was busy preparing for the attack.

The infantry had received orders to attack in four waves. In the centre, where the 5th Border Regiment and the 8th Durham Light Infantry formed, for the time being, a composite battalion, the Borders were to form the first and second wave and the Durhams the third and fourth.

Dawn on the 1st still found battalions digging hard or carrying up stores.

As zero hour approached, the troops, in the order and disposition already given, assembled for the attack in North and South Durham Trenches. At 2.35 p.m. the C.O. of the 6th Durham Light Infantry (Major G. E. Wilkinson) was wounded and Lieut.-Colonel R. B. Bradford, commanding the 9th Durham Light Infantry, assumed command of the 6th as well as of his own battalion.

During the morning from 10 a.m. until noon the enemy had barraged the Divisional front line, but at 3.15 p.m. his guns were practically inactive.

At 3.15 p.m. the attack began, but the narratives of operations are not very full. The Diary of 151st Brigade Headquarters, however, gives the following brief description of the initial assault: "The advance was carried out in perfect order, all men moving forward at the correct time and creeping up to the barrage. Our barrage was a perfect wave of fire without any gaps."

Other diaries also mention the very excellent barrage put down by the Divisional Artillery.

Report on operations on the 1st, as seen from the air: "At 3.15 p.m. the steady bombardment changed into a most magnificent barrage. The timing of this was extremely good.

Guns opened simultaneously and the effect was that many machine-guns opened fire on the same order. As seen from the air the barrage appeared to be a most perfect wall of fire, in which it was inconceivable that anything could live. The first troops to extend from the forming-up places appeared to be the 50th Division, who were seen to spread out from the sap heads and forming-up trenches and advance close up under the barrage, apparently some fifty yards away from it. They appeared to capture their objective very rapidly and with practically no losses while crossing the open.

"The 23rd Division I did not see so much of owing to their being at the moment of zero at the tail-end of the machine.

"The 47th Division took more looking for than the 50th, and it was my impression at the time that they were having some difficulty in getting into formation for attack from their forming-up places, with the result that they appeared to be very late and to be some distance behind the barrage when it lifted off the German front line at Eaucourt L'Abbaye, and immediately to the west of it. It was plain that here there was a good chance of failure and this actually came about, for the men had hardly advanced a couple of hundred yards, apparently, when they were seen to fall and take cover among shell-holes, being presumably held up by machine-gun and rifle fire. It was not possible to verify this owing to the extraordinary noise of the bursting shells of the barrage.

"The tanks were obviously too far behind, owing to lack of covered approaches, to be able to take part in the original attack, but they were soon seen advancing on either side of the Eaucourt L'Abbaye–Flers Line, continuously in action and doing splendid work. They did not seem to be a target of much enemy shell fire.

"The enemy barrage appeared to open late, quite five minutes after the commencement of our own barrage, and when it came it bore no resemblance to the wall of fire which we were putting up. I should have described it as a heavy shelling of an area some three to four hundred yards in depth from our original jumping-off places.

"Some large shells were falling in Destremont Farm, but these again were too late to catch the first line of attack, although they must have caused some losses to the supports.

"Thirty minutes after zero the English patrols were seen entering Le Sars. They appeared to be meeting with little or no opposition, and at this time no German shells were falling in the village. Our own shells were falling in the northern half.

"To sum up: the most startling feature of the operations as viewed from the air was:

"(1) The extraordinary volume of fire of our barrage and the straight line kept by it.

"(2) The apparent ease with which the attack succeeded where troops were enabled to go forward close under it.

"(3) The promiscuous character and comparative lack of volume of the enemy's counter-barrage."

On the right of the attack the 6th Durham Light Infantry captured the front German line but could not obtain touch on the right with the 47th Division, which had not succeeded in taking its first objective and Eaucourt. The enemy counter-attacked and drove the Durhams from the front Flers line. During the evening, however, the Battalion again attacked and partially regained their objective. By 7.41 p.m. they had again captured the front Flers line on their front, though the 47th Division had still not succeeded in advancing in line with the Durhams. The latter, therefore, had to build a block in the trench, as the right flank was in the air.

Meanwhile the 5th Borders and the 8th Durham Light Infantry, the centre battalions, had gained both the first and second Flers lines.

The 5th Border Regiment thus relates their part in the battle: "When the bombardment lifted at the time stated (3.15 p.m.) the first wave left the assaulting trench (North Durham Trench) and followed close up to the barrage line, followed by the other three waves at intervals of fifty yards. The two lines were captured before the enemy realised that we were in possession. A very small number only of the battalion on our right (6th Durham Light Infantry) reached the first objective, the result being that the composite Battalion of the 5th Border Regiment and the 8th Durham Light Infantry had a very strenuous and responsible time in clearing their right flank and forming blocks thereto. An enemy machine-gun was captured on the first objective, as it was beginning to cause trouble."

The records of the 8th Durham Light Infantry do not differ materially from those of the 5th Border Regiment. The Battalion advanced in good order, "close under our barrage, which was most successful." The smoke from bursting shells acted as a smoke barrage, so that the troops took the first objective practically without a casualty.

The Durhams captured about twenty-five prisoners, but the German garrisons generally are described as "retiring running."

On the left the 5th Northumberland Fusiliers report that at 3.15 p.m. the "whole line disappeared over ridge and was obscured by smoke of bursting shells. Our barrage opened very intense and, we afterwards heard, with excellent results. Enemy's artillery opened promptly, but the battalions had already passed their barrage zone."

Soon after 4 p.m. both front-line companies reported the capture of their second objective, *i.e.*, the second Flers line, and began consolidating.

Meanwhile the supporting battalions had taken their share in the battle.

The 9th Durhams on the right in support of the 6th Durham Light Infantry, when the latter met with stiff opposition, reinforced the front line, and at about 9.30 p.m. two companies were reported with the 6th Battalion in the enemy's first line, the remaining two companies at work on the communications.

The 9th Battalion, however, in their diary reports the capture of the second objective by 1 a.m. on the 2nd of October.

It was during the attack by the 9th Durham Light Infantry that their C.O., Lieut.-Colonel Roland Boys Bradford, won the Victoria Cross. The official citation* was as follows:

"For most conspicuous bravery and good leadership in attack, whereby he saved the situation on the right flank of his brigade and of the division.

"Lieut.-Colonel Bradford's battalion was in support. A leading battalion having suffered very severe casualties and the commander wounded, its flanks became dangerously exposed at close quarters to the enemy. Raked by machine-gun fire, the situation of the battalion was critical. At the request of the wounded commander, Lieut.-Colonel Bradford asked permission to command the exposed battalion in addition to his own.

"Permission granted, he at once proceeded to the foremost lines.

"By his fearless energy under fire of all descriptions and his skilful leadership of the two battalions, regardless of all

---

* The citation is given in full as there is no narrative apart from it.

danger, he succeeded in rallying the attack, captured and defended the objective and so secured the flank."*

The 6th Northumberland Fusiliers, who supported the 5th Battalion of that regiment, also say little concerning the operations, merely giving the objectives of the attack.

The 4th Northumberland Fusiliers, during the night of the 1st–2nd of October supplied carrying parties. The 7th Battalion moved up to the Flers Switch and Spence Trench during the evening of the 1st, but next morning returned to Prue Trench and Starfish Line.

On gaining the Flers Line, patrols had been pushed out towards a maze of trenches called the Tangle, two hundred to three hundred yards north of Flers Support. A report had been received that these trenches were unoccupied, but they were found held by German machine-guns and, as the right flank of the Division was in the air, no further advance could be made.

Thus, the Division had again captured its objective line, on this occasion with very little loss.

On the morning of the 2nd of October rain began to fall and a heavy downpour followed throughout the next twenty-four hours. Several trenches, freshly dug, had, of course, no duckboards, existing trenches had been battered to dust by the guns of both sides and the dust now turned to thick clinging mud, later becoming more liquid and of the consistency of soup.

In the midst of these horrible conditions, which further exhausted the already tired-out infantry, the relief of the 151st Brigade by the 149th was ordered.

The 7th Northumberland Fusiliers relieved the 6th and 9th Durham Light Infantry. The 6th Northumberland Fusiliers took over the line held by the 5th Battalion early on the morning of the 3rd of October, the latter unit recording that "mercifully there was a thick mist which enabled them [companies] to get out without being seen, though the last company had a machine-gun turned on to it coming down Twenty-Six Avenue." The 4th Northumberland Fusiliers took over the line held by the 8th Durhams and 5th Border Regiment: "The weather was appalling and the mud fearful. A large number of bombs had to be carried up and the men

---

* *London Gazette*, dated 24th November, 1916.

were absolutely exhausted, and the relief was not completed until about 9 a.m. on the morning of the 3rd."*

But at night troops of the 23rd Division relieved the worn-out 50th, and by 12.50 a.m. on the 4th the 149th Brigade was on its way back to Mametz Wood.

During the 4th the Brigade moved from the Wood to Albert, the 150th marching from Albert to Baizieux Wood and the 151st from Bécourt via Albert to Hénencourt. The 149th marched to Millencourt on the 5th, where Divisional Headquarters had been established.

Only the Divisional Artillery, three Field Companies, R.E., and the 7th Durham Light Infantry—the Pioneers—remained in the line attached to the 23rd Division. Their services were so valuable that they could not be given a rest. It seemed hard to penalise efficiency!

On coming out of the line General Wilkinson issued the following Order of the Day to his officers and men:

"Nobody could be prouder than I at commanding such troops as you of the 50th Division.

"Within a few days of landing in this country you made a name for yourselves at the Second Battle of Ypres. Since that battle you have gained a great reputation on account of your magnificent defence of a portion of the Ypres Salient during the worst months of the year.

"From the 15th of September to October 3rd you have had another chance of showing your qualities in attack, and it is not too much to say that no division in the British Army has, or could have, done better.

"You have advanced nearly two miles and have taken seven lines of German trenches.

"Your gallantry and determination on every occasion since you joined in the Battles of the Somme have been worthy of the highest traditions of the British Army.

"I deplore with you the loss of many of our intimate friends and comrades.

"I thank you all for the excellent and cheerful way in which you have undertaken every task put to you."

Back in the Millencourt area all units first carried out refitting and (wherever necessary) reorganisation before settling down to a short period of training. And, in between drill

---

* Battalion Diary, 4th Northumberland Fusiliers.

and exercises, recreation was not forgotten; indeed some form of relaxation was essential for mind as well as for body.

THE BUTTE DE WARLENCOURT, 1916

Eaucourt L'Abbaye had fallen to the 47th Division as the 50th Division was being relieved from the front line on the 3rd of October; Le Sars and the strongly-fortified quarry north-west of the village were taken by the 23rd Division on the 7th. We were, therefore, well forward on the downward slopes of the ridge and (as the official despatches state): "Pending developments elsewhere, all that was necessary, or indeed desirable, was to carry on local operations to improve our positions and to keep the enemy fully employed."

But east of the Les Bœufs–Gueudecourt line it was important to gain ground, for here the enemy still possessed strong defences covering Le Transloy, Beaulencourt and Bapaume, and in feverish haste he was engaged in preparing other formidable trenches. His last completed trench system ran generally in a north-westerly direction, from before Le Transloy, but the village was screened from the west by a ridge which ran east of Les Bœufs and Gueudecourt, and the possession of this high ground was essential.

Both on the 12th and 18th of October* further gains were made east of the Les Bœufs–Gueudecourt line and east of Le Sars. But the battle had ended in less mud—the weather had taken a hand in the operations and for some days rain put an end for the time being to attacks on a large scale.

The first winter on the Somme was fast approaching. The battlefield, under torrents of rain, had already assumed that forlorn and desolate appearance which ever after remained, burnt in upon one's brain—a vision of living torture. Every village wrested from the enemy since the 1st of July was now but a mass of tumbled or tottering masonry, each day and night witnessing further ruination; every road had been wrecked by mines or was pock-marked by shell-holes; every wood had been so torn, disfigured and disintegrated that "wood" was but a misnomer. The ingenuity of Man had rendered Nature abortive, for the very face of the earth was changed, and was ever changing, becoming more brutal, more

---

* The official despatches state "September," not October, but the former must be incorrect.

savage than in its primeval state. Farms, quarries, windmills had gone the way of the villages and the woods—wrecked and ruined by the awful holocaust of high explosive and shrapnel. The very earth stank of gas and was discoloured by the fumes from the bursting of gas shells. The countryside (if so it could be named) was a vast mass of shell-holes overlapping each other in tens of thousands; already they were full of noisome water, putrid from the dead bodies of friend or foe to whom no burial had been given. The fœtid stench from the rotting carcases of horses, or the poor remains of Briton or German torn from their hastily-dug graves by shell fire and tossed here and there to await the mercy of fresh interment, filled the nostrils as one passed to or from the front line.

But as yet (though conditions were bad enough) the full horrors of that first winter on the Somme had not been experienced; *towards the end of October the mud in many front-line and communication trenches was only some two feet in depth*; duck-board tracks (in those divisional areas where the staff had been lucky enough to obtain the materials to build them) had not yet begun to sink out of sight; men and horses and mules had not yet been drowned in mud and shell-holes as some were later; and troops coming out of the line still had the appearance of soldiers, not erstwhile Robinson Crusoes who, burrowing in the earth, had become sodden through and covered in mud from tip to toe.

The 50th Division went back into the line during the third week in October. Verbal orders had been received from III Corps Headquarters on the evening of the 23rd to relieve the 9th Division in the right sector of the Corps front on the 24th and night of the 24th–25th. Command was to pass to General Wilkinson at 9 a.m. on the 25th. On the 26th the Division was to attack the enemy.

At 11 p.m. that night Divisional Operation Orders were issued; the 149th Brigade was to relieve the 26th Brigade on the right, and the 150th, the 27th Brigade on the left; the 151st Brigade was to be in Divisional Reserve in Mametz Wood.

These reliefs took place during the night of the 24th of October. Of the 149th Brigade the 6th Northumberland Fusiliers took over the front line, the 4th Northumberland Fusiliers were in support in the Flers Line, the 7th, in reserve, in the neighbourhood of High Wood and the 5th in Bazentin-le-Grand.

The 4th and 5th Green Howards of the 150th Brigade took over the front-line sector from the 27th Brigade, the 4th East Yorkshires moving into the south-western part of High Wood, and the 5th Durham Light Infantry to the valley north of Bazentin-le-Grand. The relief was completed just before midnight on the 24th.

A deluge of rain had fallen on the night of the 23rd–24th and continued all the morning of the latter date, but ceased about 3 p.m. on the 24th. The condition of the communication and front-line trenches by nightfall, when the two brigades moved up to relieve the 9th Division, can be better imagined than adequately described.

On the morning of the 25th, Divisional Headquarters opened at Fricourt Farm, the 149th and 150th Brigade Headquarters being at Bazentin-le-Grand.

Four Field Artillery brigades of the 9th Division covered the 50th Divisional front; the 50th Divisional Artillery was split up, two brigades covering the 15th Division on the left, and two were "at rest."

The operations ordered for the 26th were postponed until the 28th, but throughout the 25th preparations were carried out, posts in the front line being linked up and the trenches cleared and improved. But this work had to be done warily, for the Bosche was ever on the alert and working parties received, if discovered, heavy punishment.

On the 26th the attack was again postponed, on this occasion until the 30th.

An entry in the Divisional Diary on this day summarises very briefly conditions in the line: "Cold, damp day; mud sticky and plentiful."

Already No Man's Land had become a quagmire—a death trap for advancing troops, and it was necessary to wait until the water had subsided, or a friendly wind had to a certain extent dried up the surface of that ghastly waste.

The sector taken over by the Division on the 24th lay east and south-east of Le Sars and in the fork formed by the Martinpuich–Warlencourt, Eaucourt and Martinpuich–Le Barque roads. The left Divisional boundary followed the former road and the right the latter to just north of Eaucourt L'Abbaye.

The front line when taken over was very irregular. Snag Trench, the front line of the right sub-sector, zig-zagged a good deal; in the left sub-sector there was a series of posts which had to be joined up to make a continuous line. The support and communication trenches in rear of the front line were similarly incomplete—Abbaye Trench and Abbaye Lane (both support trenches) being joined to trenches running in all directions.

The enemy's front line was Gird Trench, Gird Support being immediately in rear. These trenches ran from north-west to south-east across the Divisional front, but in rear of (on the left) the Butte de Warlencourt.

Because of the grim and bloody struggle which took place early in November, 1916, the Butte de Warlencourt looms large in the history of the 50th Division.

The Butte closely resembled a South African kopje, though of a smaller size. Its appearance, and the area around it, is thus described by Major E. H. Veitch:

"The Gird Trench ran east and west from the Albert–Bapaume road towards Gueudecourt. On the left lay the Butte de Warlencourt, a mound or tumulus some forty feet high, reported to be an ancient burial-place similar to those found on Salisbury Plain. This, in September, when the Battalion first entered the Somme fighting, stood out from the surrounding country a green, conical-shaped hill. Of little or no strategical importance, except that it provided observation of all ground towards High Wood, Martinpuich and east of that village, it had been so battered by the daily shelling that all signs of vegetation had now disappeared and it stood a shapeless, pock-marked mass of chalk. Beyond the Gird lay a stretch of undulating country with Bapaume clearly visible in the distance, and midway, almost hidden in a small valley, Le Barque. The remainder of the attack frontage held no special feature except a considerable amount of dead ground to the rear of the objective."

On the 28th of October "Z" Day was again changed to the 1st of November. The weather had cleared considerably on the morning of the former date; the day was finer and there was a drying wind. But at night down came the rain again and conditions became worse.

The 151st Brigade had for the past few days furnished large working parties and the men were getting tired, while the two brigades in the line were hard put to it to keep body and soul together amidst the mud and filth and awful desolation and conditions of the trenches.

Warmer weather, heavy rain storms with a gale of wind at night, characterised the 30th and 31st. Mud in the front line had by now become so thick and deep that an attack was impossible. So once again Zero Day was postponed, and it was not until the 3rd of November that the attack was definitely fixed for 9.10 a.m. on the morning of the 5th of November.

But the 149th and 150th Brigades had been so long in the line that the 151st Brigade was ordered to carry out the assault, and by the early hours of the 4th the latter brigade had relieved the 149th, who moved back into close support on the right flank, having relieved the 7th Northumberland Fusiliers. The relief was carried out without incident.

Divisional and Brigade Operation Orders were issued on the 3rd of November. The 151st Brigade was to attack with three battalions (already in the line) supported by two battalions of the 149th Brigade, *i.e.*, the 4th and 6th Northumberland Fusiliers.

"The objective allotted to the 50th Division is the Gird and Gird Support Lines within a line drawn along the Gird Support Line from M.18.a.3.0 to M.M.b.c.8 and thence due west to M.16.b.9.8."*

From right to left the three attacking battalions were the 8th, 6th and 9th Durham Light Infantry, who were to assemble for the attack in Snag Trench and Snag Support, Maxwell Trench and Tail Trench.

The objectives of the 6th and 8th Durham Light Infantry were Gird and Gird Support; the 9th Durham Light Infantry were to capture the Butte de Warlencourt and the Quarry just west of the Butte. The 4th and 6th Northumberland Fusiliers were to be right and left support battalions respectively. The remaining battalion of the 151st Brigade, *i.e.*, the 5th Border Regiment, was to be in Brigade Support in Prue and Starfish Trenches.

The 151st Machine-Gun Company was to have two guns with each assaulting battalion, six in support and four in reserve. Four guns of the 149th Brigade Machine-Gun Company were to support the right flank of the 151st Brigade. The 151st Light Trench-Mortar Battery was to support the 9th Durham Light Infantry with five guns and the 8th Durham Light Infantry with two.

---

* 151st Brigade Operation Orders.

Of the Pioneers (7th Durham Light Infantry) one company, under Capt. N. R. Shepherd, was to be attached to the right of the Brigade in order to continue Pioneer Alley from Maxwell Trench via Hook Sap to Gird Trench; and one company on the left to continue Tail Trench due north to join Butte Trench; Butte Trench ran in front of Gird Trench.

Zero hour was to be 9.10 a.m., 5th November.

Australian troops were to attack on the right of the 50th Division.

All the available artillery were to support the attack, which was to begin under an intense barrage put down at zero two hundred yards in front of the "jumping-off" line.

The night of the 4th-5th November was a horror. Heavy rain again fell and a gale of wind howled about the trenches making the "going" even more difficult as, staggering under their equipment and usual heavy loads, the troops detailed for the attack floundered through mud and water to their assembly positions. In some parts of the line the mud was now thigh-deep; it is impossible to describe the physical and mental agony of waiting for hours on end, drenched through, caked with dirt, shivering with cold and with clothes rain-sodden, for zero hour.

The 6th Durham Light Infantry are reported to have had several men drowned in the trenches before the attack began.

The rain ceased towards the morning of the 5th and when dawn boke a fine, but cold, day seemed probably. It was a Sunday. As zero hour approached daylight revealed the further ravages caused by the wind and rain of the previous night; to say nothing of the destructive shell fire of the enemy's guns, which had never ceased firing from sunset to sunrise; it was a dismal picture—the lines of waiting men, chilled to the marrow, standing in mud and water.

At zero hour the barrage fell and at once the troops began to crawl out of their trenches. Crawl is an apt description, for the greatest difficulty was experienced in getting "over the top" owing to the deep mud. The men who were first out pulled and dragged their comrades over the parapet. Then, forming up in line as well as the conditions and the mud and water in No Man's Land would allow them, they started off under the barrage.

The enemy's barrage fell in front of Snag Trench, but was not intense. From both flanks, however, murderous machine-gun fire swept the advance and men began to fall at once. The "going" in No Man's Land was very heavy and progress was slow, for it was impossible to advance at little more than walking pace through the mud and water.

What was left of the waves of the 8th Durhams reached a point about thirty yards from Butte Trench, which was strongly held by the enemy. Capt. A. N. Clark and Lieut. W. Boyd* had both fallen wounded, the latter mortally. The few men left in front of Butte Trench, fired at from front and flank by the Bosche and suffering casualties from short shooting by British "Heavies" and the Stokes Mortar Battery (which knocked out a complete Lewis-gun section), found a further advance impossible and they withdrew, under orders, to Snag Trench. The enemy's fire was so severe that both wounded and unwounded lay out all day in shell holes hoping to get back after darkness had fallen.

On the right of the 8th Durhams the Australians had failed completely to get on. Their own guns had unfortunately put down a barrage some seventy yards *behind* the Colonials' front-line trench, while their machine-gun barrage was so erratic that bullets were striking the parapets of the Durhams' trenches. The failure of the Australians undoubtedly added to the cause of failure of the 8th Durhams.

In the centre the attack by the 6th Durhams was both unsuccessful and successful. Their right suffered in the same way as the 8th Durhams had suffered, but the left, owing to the complete success of the attack by the 9th Durham Light Infantry, swept on and over the enemy's front line (Gird Trench) and established a block. But this battalion also suffered heavy casualties.

On the left the 9th Durhams advanced magnificently and carried all their objectives. The following account is taken from their Battalion Diary:

"9.10 a.m. 'A,' 'B' and 'C' Companies crept forward under the artillery barrage and assaulted the enemy's trenches. The assault was entirely successful. By 10.30 a.m. we had taken the Quarry and had penetrated the Gird Line, our objective. A post was established on the Bapaume road at M.16.b.9.8.†

---

* He died later.

† Where the left Divisional boundary cut across the Bapaume road, *i.e.*, north-west of the Quarry.

A machine-gun in a dug-out on the north-eastern side of the Butte held up our advance somewhat, and we attempted many times to bomb this dug-out. Telephonic communication with the Quarry was established.

"By noon our line was as follows: Gird front line from M.11.c.2.1 to M.17.a.4.7 with a post in Gird Support line at M.11.c.4½. The enemy still had a post on the north side of Butte. We held Butte Alley and the Quarry strongly, telephonic communication with the Quarry still holding. On our right the 6th Durham Light Infantry had been held up by machine-gun fire and could not advance much beyond Maxwell Trench.

"Independent witnesses stated that our advance was very finely carried out and that our men could be seen advancing very steadily. They passed right over the Butte and straight on to the Gird Line, where our artillery discs were immediately put out.

"From noon up to 3 p.m. the position remained unchanged, the enemy delivered several determined assaults on the Gird Line but these were all repulsed. Fighting still continued on the Butte, where we tried to capture the fortified dug-out on the north side.

"At about 3 p.m. the enemy, strongly reinforced, again counter-attacked and at 3.30 p.m. we reported as follows: 'We have been driven out of Gird front line and I believe my posts there were captured, and have tried to get back but the enemy is in considerable force and is still counter-attacking. It is taking me all my time to hold Butte Alley. Please ask artillery to shell area north of Bapaume road in M.10.d and M.11.c, as Germans are in considerable force there. Enemy is holding Gird front line strongly on my right, and in my opinion a strong advance to the right of the Butte would meet with success.

" 'I have a small post in a shell hole at the north-western corner of the Butte, but the enemy still has a post on the Butte on the north side. I am just going to make another effort to capture this post.'*

"Desperate hand-to-hand fighting continued all the afternoon, and at 7.15 p.m. the following message was sent back to the Brigade:

---

* Written by Colonel R. B. Bradford, commanding the 9th Durham Light Infantry.

"'We are holding Butte Alley from M.17.a.5.5 to M.16.b.9.8. We have a post on the north side of Butte at M.17.a.3.7. The enemy still has a post on northern slope of Butte, but I am hoping to scupper this. I am now endeavouring to establish a post in Gird front line at M.17.a.7.6 and another one at M.17.a.3.8. Germans are still attacking and a good deal of hand-to-hand fighting is taking place. We killed large numbers of enemy on the Butte and in the Quarry and, owing to heavy fire, could not take so many prisoners as we might otherwise. If another battalion were attached to me I could probably take the Gird front line from M.17.a.7.7 to M.17.b.3.4. The work on the communication trench to Butte is progressing.'"

But the first entry in the Battalion Diary of the 9th Durham Light Infantry on the morning of the 6th of November tells the following tragic story:

"At 12.20 a.m. (6th) we had to report as follows: 'We have been driven out of Butte Alley by a strong counter-attack, and the 9th Durham Light Infantry and the 6th Durham Light Infantry are now in Maxwell Trench. Enemy was in great force and we cannot get back to Butte Alley. All our posts were captured or driven back. The enemy's counter-attack was delivered from the front (from the Gird Line), from the left flank (from the direction of M.16.b.8.9) and from the right flank (from the Gird Line). The Germans, still holding out in the Butte dug-out, came out and advanced over the Butte. The enemy advanced throwing bombs.'

"A party of about twenty Germans worked round our left flank and attacked the Quarry in the rear.

"The enemy was in great strength. His attack was perfectly organised and was pushed with the greatest energy and determination.

"Our men resisted heroically, but after a desperate stand they were driven back to Maxwell Trench, so that by 1 p.m. on the 6th we were in the same position as on the morning of the 5th, prior to the assault."

The 9th Durhams had killed large numbers of the enemy and had sent back seven prisoners.

The 151st Brigade Machine-Gun Company also fought most gallantly. It will be remembered that the Machine-Gun Company had two guns with each of the attacking battalions. Those with the 8th Durham Light Infantry were held up with that battalion and were withdrawn with slight casualties. The guns with the 6th and 9th Durham Light Infantry saw heavy fighting, and the narrative of operations, as contained in the Diary of the 151st Machine-Gun Company, is well worth giving:

"The left battalion alone reached its objective and captured the Butte de Warlencourt. Corporal Rutherford ('B' Section) established his gun in a post on the north side of the Bapaume road. He and all his team became casualties. This gun is missing. Corporal Mewes's gun, 'B' Section (second gun attached to left battalion), was early put out of action and replaced by Corporal Watson's gun of 'A' Section. Later, as both flanks of the left battalion were in the air, Sergeant Clennell's gun, 'A' Section, and Corporal Butler's gun, 'C' Section, were sent up to hold left flank. These three guns did extremely good work, repelling the first counter-attack by the Germans early in the night. In the second counter-attack, which took place about 11 p.m., the three guns kept in action, firing hard until both flanks had been surrounded by enemy bombers when the three guns were forced to be withdrawn, the teams suffering very heavy casualties.

"The two guns of 'B' Section, attached to the centre battalion, went forward with the third wave, but the battalion was held up by machine-gun fire, and the two guns were stranded in No Man's Land. Sergeant Leith's gun was knocked out with all its detachment, who did excellent work getting the wounded back to our old front line. Private Hay took charge of his gun when the N.C.O. was killed, and brought his gun back to our old front line, where he kept it in action all day, supported by only one man."

The 149th Brigade Machine-Gun Company give no details of the part taken by their gunners in the attack, and merely state that the four guns in action co-operated by means of intense fire on the enemy; four more guns being in reserve in the Flers Switch Line.

The Divisional Pioneers (7th Durham Light Infantry) were unable to carry out the work allotted to them, but nevertheless suffered heavy casualties. "B" Company had been attached to the 8th Durham Light Infantry, and "C" Company plus one platoon of "D" Company to the 9th Durham Light Infantry. They took up their positions in Abbaye Trench and Hexham Road, but, before zero hour, came under heavy shell fire and had considerable losses, Capt. N. R. Shepherd being amongst those killed; Capt. A. R. Williamson and Second-Lieuts. J. McLeman and A. H. Polge were wounded. On the failure of the attack of the 8th Durham Light Infantry, "B" Company of the Pioneers cleared Pioneer Alley, which had been badly damaged by shell fire; they then withdrew to the Flers Line. "C" Company made gallant efforts to link up with the 9th Durham Light Infantry, but were forced to withdraw owing to the successful German counter-attack. On the 5th the Pioneers had eight other ranks killed and twenty-three wounded.

The support battalion of the 151st Brigade, *i.e.*, the 5th Border Regiment, took no part in the fighting other than to occupy Snag Trench and Snag Support after the 8th Durham Light Infantry had gone forward, but fell back again to support positions when the Durhams returned to their old front line.

Similarly, neither the 4th nor the 6th Northumberland Fusiliers were called upon to attack the enemy. Though reinforcements were badly needed they could not be moved up during the day, for a very heavy and accurate German barrage was falling on the communication trenches and the whole of the forward area.

The artillery did good work in dispersing numerous parties of the enemy, who were moving up to reinforce, and caused many casualties.

By the morning of the 6th the 50th Division was back in its original front line,* *i.e.*, Snag, Maxwell and Tail Trenches. Orders were then issued for the 150th Brigade to take over the line from the 151st Brigade on the night of the 6th–7th; the 149th Brigade to be in close support. Another attack had been ordered for the morning of the 6th, but it was cancelled.

---

* The A. and Q. Diary, 50th Division, gives the following approximate casualties: 8th Durham Light Infantry—9 officers killed, wounded or missing; 37 other ranks killed, 100 wounded, 83 missing. 6th Durham Light Infantry—11 officers killed, wounded or missing; 34 other ranks killed, 114 wounded, 111 missing. 9th Durham Light Infantry—17 officers killed, wounded or missing; 30 other ranks killed, 250 wounded and 140 missing. 151st Brigade Machine-Gun Company—3 other ranks killed, 1 officer and 19 other ranks wounded, 8 other ranks missing. Total—38 officers and 929 other ranks. Other units suffered casualties which brought the total of other ranks roughly up to one thousand.

Showers of rain had fallen throughout the day and the relief of the 151st Brigade, carried out in darkness, was a veritable nightmare. Of the 150th Brigade the 4th East Yorkshires had been ordered to take over the right sub-sector and the 5th Durham Light Infantry the left; the 4th and 5th Green Howards were to be in close support on the right and left respectively.

Battalions had been forbidden (owing to the enemy's shell fire and observation) to pass over the High Wood Ridge until after dusk; the consequence was that the relief was a late business.

An officer of the 5th Durham Light Infantry thus describes the relief as carried out by that battalion:

"It was a very rotten job. Approaches to the line were completely water-logged, and one was continually meeting stretcher parties and walking wounded, which made going up a slow and tedious business. 'C' and 'D' Companies, taking over the front line, experienced a heavy barrage after passing the 'Pimple.' This barrage set on fire an ammunition dump near Company Headquarters, and we thought that another Bosche attack was coming. However, some of us went ahead and found things all right and, after what seemed an awfully long time, we were able to send 'relief complete' to Battalion Headquarters. But all that night, whilst trying to reorganise and make a fairly continuous front line, one came across isolated posts of the outgoing battalions who knew nothing of the relief. No Man's Land was an equally weird sight. Patrols came across wounded men just sitting absolutely exhausted and unable to move, most of them having been there since the start of the attack. They were, of course, got back to our lines. This was a miserable time and the last straw was when one of the company commanders gallantly arrived at the posts with the rum jar—imagine everyone's horror when he 'dished it out'—the first man who tasted it said it was *whale oil*!"

Another officer of the same battalion said: "Snag Trench was full of mud and water with bodies sticking out all along. In fact it was no exaggeration when I say that in our part one had to tread from body to body to get past. Dead from all regiments were there, including our Divisions, South Africans and 'Jocks' of the 9th Division, and hands, arms and legs were sticking out of parados and parapet where the dead had been hastily buried."

A pen picture which may well make coming generations shudder!

The 1/4th East Yorkshires are very brief about the condition of the trenches they took over: "Trenches in a deplorable condition owing to heavy rain and lack of revetting material . . . from six inches to two feet six inches deep in mud and water; officers and men are feeling effects."

Very early on the 7th the relief was completed.

The 9th of November was a fine, sunny day, and thereafter, for several days, bright and even frosty weather continued; frosts were beginning to cover the ground at night.

Under these conditions it was possible to clear some of the mud and water from the trenches and communications; but life on the Somme during the winter was always more or less a mud bath.

During the night of the 11th–12th of November the 149th Brigade relieved the 150th, the latter moving back into support.

On the 13th the Fifth Army attacked north of the Ancre, and the 50th Divisional Artillery, with other artillery of the III Corps, "demonstrated."

The weather still continued fine. All units of the 50th Division were by now very tired, for they had been in the line for twenty days, but on the 13th, also, orders were received that the 1st Division would relieve the 50th between the 17th and 19th of November.

(THE SOMME)
GIRD TRENCH AND HOOK SAP

However, between the 13th of November, 1916, and 10.30 a.m. on the 19th, when General Wilkinson handed over command of the sector to the G.O.C.s, 1st and 48th Divisions, attacks were made by the 50th Division on Gird Trench and Hook Sap.

The attack was made by the 149th Brigade.

Since the operations of the 5th of November the enemy had spent much time on improving his defences. Butte Trench, which ran from the Quarry, thence in front of the Butte in an irregular line to Hook Sap, had been considerably strengthened. The Sap formed one side of a salient, jutting out into No Man's Land, but was strongly defended; for between the point of the Sap and Gird Trench beyond, the enemy had dug another trench parallel with Gird, known as Blind Trench. The whole German line in front of the Division was one from which it was possible to bring enfilade fire, from almost any point, to bear upon attacks from the British trenches.

Operation orders issued by the 149th Brigade at 6.30 p.m.* on the 13th of November, stated that the attack would be carried out by the 5th Northumberland Fusiliers on the right and the 7th Northumberland Fusiliers on the left. The 4th Northumberland Fusiliers were to be in support with two companies in Hexham Road and two (with the 5th Green Howards attached) in the Flers Line; the 6th were to hold the front line from the left of the 7th Northumberland Fusiliers to the Brigade boundary on the left and support the attack by Lewis-gun and rifle fire.

Zero hour was 6.45 a.m. on the 14th.

The 150th Brigade was to be in support, and subsequently both the 4th East Yorkshires and the 4th Green Howards were involved in the operations.

The objective of the 5th Northumberland Fusiliers was Gird Trench from the right of the Divisional boundary to the junction with Hook Sap; the 7th Northumberland Fusiliers were to capture Hook Sap and Gird Trench, also Blind Trench.

The diaries of both attacking battalions are well written and full of detail.

The 5th Northumberland Fusiliers relieved the 4th Battalion in the front line on the night of the 13th, the relief being completed by 11.45 p.m. The 7th also took over their line on the same night.

By this period the weather had again broken and all trenches were water-logged once more. "Mud was everywhere," records Capt. F. Buckley in his interesting history of the 7th Northumberland Fusiliers, "in parts up to the waist, and what was worse, the thicker, more tenacious kind that just covered the boots and clung in heavy masses. The exertion of forcing our way step by step in an already heavily-burdened state during our various moves about this line remains in my mind as some of most strenuous and exhausting times of the whole War."

---

* All units had, of course, received previous warning orders for the attack before 6.30 p.m. on the 13th.

The dispositions of the 5th Battalion at zero hour were: "B" and "D" Companies forming the first two waves in New Support Trench, "A" and "C" in Abbaye Trench, the latter forming the third wave; "A" Company moving up to occupy Snag and Snag Support Trenches as the attacking troops went forward.

The 7th Battalion disposed "A" and "B" Companies in Snag Trench, "D" and "C" in Abbaye, "D" moving forward at zero hour to occupy Snag Trench when vacated by "A" and "B" Companies.

" 'C' Company," said Capt. Buckley, "was also in Abbaye Trench. Their particular job was for half a company to follow up 'A' and 'B' with the water and bombs to the final objective, and the other half were to remain in support. This half company, I well remember, were inclined to congratulate themselves on their simple duties, but they, poor chaps, had not reckoned with the intensity of the Bosche barrage. . . . Eventually a grey line appeared in the eastern sky, and slowly the low outline of the Butte de Warlencourt took shape half-left of our position. Suddenly the sky seemed to split as our barrage came over. Pencils of golden rain, the German S.O.S., rose all along the opposing line. Machine-guns opened out from all directions and crash came the German barrage."

The attacking troops started off across No Man's Land.

At 8 a.m. Battalion Headquarters, 5th Northumberland Fusiliers, received a message from Capt. Gill (commanding "D" Company on the right), who had been wounded, that they had reached Gird Trench with but few casualties. At 8.45 a.m. news was received that "C" Company had reached their objective but had no officers left. At 10 a.m. there was a report: "Men of 'B' Company, coming down wounded, say that their company got up all right, but we have as yet received no definite news." An hour later Capt. Easton sent a note saying that "part of 'A' Company had got up to Butte Trench."

The first definite news did not arrive until 3 p.m., when Second-Lieut. Armstrong reported that he was now commanding "D" Company and was occupying about one hundred yards of Gird Trench with about one hundred and fifty men of "B," "C" and "D" Companies; that he had established a strong point.

Turning now to the left of the attack: the 7th Northumberland Fusiliers had also made good progress. Their Diary begins as follows: "Four minutes before zero the enemy opened an intermittent rifle fire on our right, which gave the impression that he had detected movement. Troops went forward punctually, and only the fourth wave encountered enemy barrage before reaching Snag Trench. The first three waves met the same barrage almost immediately after leaving Snag Trench and casualties were caused; they pushed straight on and were lost in the mist."

An hour later wounded men began to arrive, and all were satisfied that they had been successful and had got into the enemy's trenches. Next, at 9 a.m., Second-Lieut. Woods ("D" Company, then holding Snag Trench, the front line) reported that he could see men of the Battalion consolidating in Hook Sap. Then an N.C.O., Sergeant Dryden, who came in wounded, stated that he had crossed Hook Trench[*] and had seen men making to the left to establish a post (No. 6); he also saw men working up Hook Sap and a "good few" men, under Second-Lieut. Lawson, going towards the Gird Trench, though almost immediately he saw that officer fall.

At 9.45 a.m. Capt. Morris reported that a wounded man said that his machine-gun was in position in Post No. 7, and simultaneously Second-Lieut. Woods stated that he could hear it firing.

More wounded, who arrived at 10 a.m., said that hand-to-hand fighting was going on on the left, presumably in Snag Trench. On receipt of this news a sap was begun running out from Snag Trench to Hook Sap, the men digging hard. This sap was begun by "D" Company of the 4th Northumberland Fusiliers, who had been detailed for the work in operation orders. But at 11.30 a.m. they had to cease digging as the enemy's machine-gun fire was too heavy.

Meanwhile, at 10.30 a.m., the enemy was reported to have counter-attacked on the left of the 7th Northumberland Fusiliers, but had been beaten off.

But there are no further entries in the Battalion Diary until 2.45 p.m., when Second-Lieut. Woods reported that the machine-gun, previously reported as firing from Post No. 7, had "not been heard firing for some time." No further information was received from the attackers and shortly after-

---

[*] Probably "Blind Trench" was meant, as "Hook Trench" does not appear on the map.

wards Brig.-General R. M. Ovens (G.O.C., 149th Brigade) arrived at Battalion Headquarters, 7th Northumberland Fusiliers, and discussed the situation. The conclusion arrived at was "that we occupied Posts Nos. 4, 6 and 7 and probably also 5; that Post No. 5 and neighbouring part of Gird Trench was counter-attacked by the enemy. This attack was repulsed; that later an attack was made on the same position from both flanks and succeeded, and that Hook Sap was then rushed and taken; that the whole of our position was then surrounded and taken, even the machine-gun in Post No. 7. During the day it was impossible for runners to cross from Snag to Hook Sap owing to machine-gun fire and sniping; the mist also prevented observation."

That, so far, is a fairly accurate account of what had happened to the attack made by the 7th Northumberland Fusiliers, and this conclusion is supported by the Diary of the 5th Battalion, which at 10 o'clock that night reported that "a party started to dig a communication trench from Pioneer Alley to the Hook, but was bombed from the apex of the Hook," so the Germans had managed to get back into their end of the Hook.

At 11 p.m. Lieut.-Colonel N. I. Wright (5th Northumberland Fusiliers) and Lieut.-Colonel B. D. Gibson (commanding 4th Northumberland Fusiliers) arrived in the line to organise a fresh attack. They had for this one company of 7th Northumberland Fusiliers and one company of the 4th Northumberland Fusiliers on the left, and one company of the 4th Northumberland Fusiliers and the remains of "A" Company (7th Northumberland Fusiliers)—about thirty men.

Three strong bombing patrols were then (12.30 a.m. on the 15th) sent out, two on the left of Pioneer Alley and one on the right, but they were exposed by Very lights which had been blown by the wind right over Snag Trench and, meeting with very heavy machine-gun and rifle fire, were forced to return.

A very heavy barrage was put down by the enemy just after midnight, and it was evident that he was holding Hook Sap in strength. "This shows conclusively," records the Diary of the 5th Northumberland Fusiliers, "that the enemy are holding the Blind Trenches and that they have somehow got in between us and our men, who must therefore be in the Gird Line."

Lieut.-Colonel B. D. Gibson and Major N. I. Wright then organised Snag Trench for defence, and returned to Battalion Headquarters as nothing more could be done for the present.

All the morning of the 15th the enemy's shell fire was exceedingly heavy, and Snag Trench and Snag Support were very much damaged.

At about noon word was received from Second-Lieut. Armstrong that the enemy had been seen massing on his left and right front for an attack, and that bombs and ammunition were urgently required. A carrying party of thirty-five men was then obtained from the 5th Green Howards and sent over during the afternoon with supplies.

At 3 p.m. the Signalling Officer and an N.C.O. of the Battalion Scouts sent up from Headquarters to find out the exact position, reported that the situation was unchanged, and that Second-Lieut. Armstrong and his men were still in the Gird Line, about one hundred and fifty yards on the left of the Sunken Road.

Nothing further happened on the front held by the 7th Northumberland Fusiliers. About thirty of their men were with Second-Lieut. Armstrong and his party, which had been reduced to about sixty by casualties. The Diary of the 7th Battalion, however, gives the interesting news that reports of Second-Lieut. Armstrong's position had been brought back by carrier pigeon.

At 7 p.m. the 5th Northumberland Fusiliers in the Snag front line and support were relieved by the 4th Green Howards without difficulty, the same battalion also taking over the line held by the 7th Northumberland Fusiliers.

The 4th East Yorkshires had received orders at 2.15 p.m. to send two companies across No Man's Land to take over Second-Lieut. Armstrong's position in the Gird Line. This they did, the relief being completed by 3 a.m. on the 16th. The 5th Northumberland Fusiliers then report that all that is left of the Battalion returned to the Flers Line—a total of 7 officers and 270 other ranks. The 7th Northumberland Fusiliers also moved back after relief to the Flers Line. Dawn on the 16th broke on the 4th Green Howards holding the front line, "A" and "D" Companies of the 4th East Yorkshires in the Gird Line, and "B" and "C" Companies in the Flers Switch.

Throughout the day the enemy maintained a heavy artillery barrage on the front line and Hexham Road which, at about 4.15 p.m., developed into an intense bombardment. At 5 p.m. he attacked the East Yorkshires in the Gird Line "and drove our two companies out by a combined attack from west (along the trench), north (frontal) and north-east (the Australians falling back in face of a heavy attack). Remainder of 'A' and 'D' Companies, after heavy casualties, held the support line between the Gird Line (continuation of the Snag Trench) and returned directly afterwards, relieved by Australians, to Flers Switch."

As a result of losing the position in the Gird Line another attack on Hook Sap, which had been ordered by 149th Brigade Headquarters, was cancelled.

The Divisional Diary thus sums up the situation: "50th Division and 2nd Australian Division are both back in original 'jumping-off' trenches, and British do not occupy any portion of Gird Line, from which we were driven by German counter-attack."

On the night of the 17th–18th of November the 1st Division began the relief of the 149th Brigade in the right sub-sector of the front line, and during the night of the 18th–19th the 48th Division relieved the left sub-sector.

By the morning of the 20th of November the 50th Division was in III Corps Reserve, Headquarters of the Division at Albert. The 149th Brigade was at Albert, the 150th at Bécourt Camp and the 151st Brigade at Millencourt and in Mametz Wood.

The Divisional Artillery had been relieved on the 14th of November, the C.R.A. opening his Headquarters at Bavincourt Château, near Montigny, and the artillery brigades and Divisional Ammunition Column in the area Bavincourt–Béhencourt–Fréchencourt. But what a terrible job it was getting the guns out! "It was found impossible to pull our own guns out," said Major C. H. Ommanney, "so 'B' and 'C' collected those of 'B' and 'C'/71, their relieving batteries. 'A' was relieved by 'A'/103 and pulled out three of 'D's' guns. One stuck in a large shell-hole and had to be left until next day, when it took fifty men an hour and a half to get it out."

En route to Béhencourt the 250th (Northumbrian) Brigade, R.F.A., was inspected by the C.R.A.

"A more pathetic sight I never saw. The senior Sub. (or Captain I had better call him) and I* were the only ones with horses; all the others were needed for teams. Two horses

---

* Major C. H. Ommanney.

fainted when they were hooked in, and we moved off with four horses per vehicle, all men and officers dismounted, and a heterogeneous of crippled horses and men tailing behind. I remember the water-cart horses, two staunch old veterans, who were so weak that they leant against each other as they staggered along."

Faithful animals; and it is to the credit of our soldiers that the horse was looked upon as a good comrade!

"Constant work over a country, the condition of which only those who saw it can realise, exposure for days and nights to pouring rain and bitter cold; a forage ration cut down to the lowest possible scale, and with never any sort of variety; lack of good water, and drivers very often too dead beat to attend to the wants of their beasts—such were the conditions of life for our poor 'Hairies.' It is not surprising that many of them succumbed, and that still more were sent away to the Veterinary Section, worn out and broken down. The drivers were really splendid, not only for the way they brought up ammunition in the wretched conditions in which they had to work, but for their constant efforts to tend and care for their horses. But the thing was beyond any man's capacity. You cannot groom a horse with an inch or two of thick coat all over him, caked up to the trace-line with solid mud, and with nothing but a semi-liquid dung heap to stand him on."*

On the 16th of November the Artillery of the 50th Division was once more reorganised; the 250th, 251st and 252nd Brigades, R.F.A., were re-formed each into three six-gun 18-pounders and one four-gun 4·5-in. (Howitzer) Batteries. The 253rd Brigade, R.F.A. (Howitzer), was broken up and its gun personnel distributed amongst the three other brigades.†

As far as can be gathered from the A. and Q. Diary of the Division, the casualties sustained during the operations from the 14th to the 16th of November were as follows: 5th Northumberland Fusiliers—2 officers killed, 5 wounded, 1 missing; others ranks: 33 killed, 144 wounded, 85 missing. 7th Northumberland Fusiliers—2 officers killed, 7 wounded, 1 missing; other ranks: 19 killed, 95 wounded, 104 missing. The severity of the enemy's shell fire is shown by the casualties

---

* *War History of the 1st Northumbrian Brigade, R.F.A.*

† For full details of the reorganisation of the 50th Divisional Artillery on the 16th of November, 1916, see Appendices.

of the 6th Northumberland Fusiliers (who, it will be remembered, assisted in the attack by Lewis-gun and rifle fire from the front line), who lost 2 officers killed, 1 wounded; 9 other ranks killed and 112 wounded. The 4th Northumberland Fusiliers lost 16 other ranks killed, 56 wounded and 10 missing. The 4th East Yorkshires had 1 officer wounded, 37 other ranks wounded and 27 missing.

The above were the principal casualties amongst those battalions which took part in the actual infantry attack; there were small casualties amongst other units. In all, the Diary of the A. and Q. shows a loss of 37 officers and 852 other ranks, killed, wounded and missing.

The Division had seen its last fight of the momentous year 1916. From September, when the Flers-Courcelette operations were begun, to the middle of November, the Division had won its way forward in trench-to-trench fighting to a depth of about three and a half miles—no mean achievement. All units had suffered heavily, and yet it is some satisfaction to read in Sir Douglas Haig's despatches that:

"The three main objects with which we had commenced our offensive in July had already been achieved, at the date* when this account closes: in spite of the fact that the heavy continuous rains had prevented full advantage being taken of the favourable situation created by our advance, at a time when we had good grounds for hoping to achieve yet more important successes.

"Verdun had been relieved; the main German forces have been held on the Western Front, and the enemy's strength had been very considerably worn down.

"Any one of these three results is in itself sufficient to justify the Somme Battles. The attainment of all three of these affords ample compensation for the splendid efforts of our troops, and for the sacrifices made by our Allies."

Coming generations and military critics may disagree with Sir Douglas Haig—yet subsequent events proved his statements: within a few weeks of writing this despatch complete proof of the correctness of this claim, *i.e.*, that the enemy's strength had been worn down, was to be amply demonstrated by the German Retreat to the Hindenburg Line.

---

*The 23rd December, 1916.

CHAPTER VI

THE WINTER OF 1916–1917

WINTER had now set in: frosty mornings and frosty nights had begun: only snow remained to fall and hide with a white pall the ghastliness of the Somme battlefields. The 50th Division had, for the time being, turned its back upon the front line: the human machine had almost broken down, and needed rest and repair. The tired and weary men who tramped back to Mametz and Bécourt, and Albert, came out of the trenches thoroughly exhausted. The limit of endurance had almost been reached: nothing but their indomitable pluck and wonderful cheerfulness kept many of them from total collapse—so awful were the conditions under which they had lived and fought.

What a picture they had left behind them! As the last of the troops to be relieved filed out of the muddy, battered trenches and company commanders had given a cheery "good luck" to their relievers, they began that weary tramp back to billets, and reserve positions: back, first down communication trenches, choked in places with the bodies of rotting corpses, thick in mud, halting every now and then to let a stretcher party, bearing a moaning and maimed body, pass on to an aid post. Free of the trenches, staggering and slipping over bog-like ground, or squelching in deep, clinging mud, they slowly wend their way back, perhaps lucky enough to strike a duck-board track a little less treacherous than the sodden earth. As they get further and further from the front line they come every now and then upon the ghostly form of a gun: maybe with a sudden jar to the senses there is a crash, and the dark night is illuminated by the flash of a gun sending its message of hate and death over to the enemy. The lines of silent, plodding men get ever further from the front line, until presently a halt is called and they are formed up once more by companies and platoons on a damp and muddy road: at last they are out of range of the incessant fire from the enemy's field guns.

And now it is that hearts are light again, for soon, as they get going again, the murdered countryside rings with the tune of a marching song—away with care, for the time being, they are

BATTLE OF FLERS-COURCELETTE.
German prisoners coming in from Morval, 15th September, 1916.

(Imperial War Museum Photographs, Copyright Reserved)

free from the horrible nightmare of the front-line trenches. Dawn is coming: and here and there the marching troops pass a cottage or a farm, still sheltering French civilians who, turning uneasily in their beds, murmur "*C'est la guerre, c'est la guerre!*"

Mametz Wood! A pleasant-sounding name, but what attractions the place possessed must have been in far-off pre-war days, for when the 5th, 6th and 8th Durhams, and the 5th Borders of the 151st Brigade moved back there on the 16th of November, it was a pestilential spot. Like other woods on the Somme, "wood" had become a misnomer, for in November, 1916, only gaunt, charred stumps of trees remained, affording little or no shelter, beggared even of branches. The "Wood" had been turned into a camp—a tented camp—pitched in seas of mud, knee-deep in places. Those semi-circular iron contraptions called Nissen Huts had not yet been issued to the troops, and in the bitter weather, rain and frost and snow, with the wind howling around, the poor fellows crowded together over the braziers (if they were lucky enough to possess them) in vain endeavour to get, and keep, warm.

The 9th Durhams with Brigade Headquarters had gone off to Millencourt where (they record) there was an "excellent tent camp and plenty of accommodation," the three battalions left behind in Mametz Wood being detailed for working purposes.

These three battalions, *i.e.*, 6th and 8th Durhams and 5th Borders, were employed until the 30th of November in working parties, being employed chiefly in road making, camp draining, and path making, etc. Occasionally other jobs came their way, while there were periodical inspections of rifles, bayonets and ammunition. The "specialists" continued their training, but little of the latter was possible for companies unless battalions were moved further back where parade grounds were possible.

The 9th Durhams, in Millencourt, however, passed the remainder of the month in training and absorbing reinforcements: this battalion supplied working parties two days a week only.

On the 30th of November, the 151st Brigade, *i.e.* Headquarters and all four battalions, moved to Warloy.

The 149th Brigade with the four Northumberland battalions, after reaching Albert on the 19th of November, promptly ordered "bathing and refitting" for all units. And what a godsend baths were, for the dirt and mud of the trenches had penetrated everywhere. Equipment had to be taken to pieces before it could be properly cleaned. It was not until the 22nd that this "cleaning business" was over, and the first working parties were supplied to the Town Mayor for the purpose of cleaning streets. More men from the battalions were supplied daily for work on new transport lines, erecting stabling and overhead cover, huts for transport personnel, for work on R.E. stores, unloading coal and other duties such as guarding German prisoners at work.

Albert was not beyond range of the enemy's guns and big shells fell occasionally in the town, creating havoc, while the golden image of the Virgin Mary, toppled over from her upright position by the German guns, looked down from the red church tower on to the further destruction of the town. This figure of the Holy Mother, holding the infant child Jesus, her arms suspended over the town in that curious position, was held by the French inhabitants in great superstition: they believed that when the figure fell the War would end.

There is little in the diaries of the 4th, 5th, 6th and 7th Northumberland Fusiliers to record, for they contain nothing but matters referring to duties and work carried out.

On the 30th the 149th Brigade began to pack up for a move to the Bresle area, which move was to take place on the following day, *i.e.*, the 1st of December.

In Bécourt Camp the 150th Brigade was more comfortably situated than the 151st, for accommodation was in "hutments."

The supply of working parties, their numbers and various duties absorbs the whole of the Diary of the 150th Brigade until the end of November, while the Battalion Diaries of the 4th and 5th Green Howards, 1/4th East Yorkshires and the 5th Durham Light Infantry are not informative.

On the last day of the month the Brigade moved to the Contay–Baizieux area. These moves were the outcome of instructions from III Corps Headquarters that the 50th Division was to go into training in the Baizieux area.

On the 30th of November, Divisional Headquarters in Albert packed up, and on the 1st of December moved to Baizieux in which, and in the neighbourhood of which, most of the Divisional units had arrived, the exception being the Divisional Artillery which had gone back into the line on the 23rd of November, and the Field Companies, R.E., and

Pioneers (7th Durham Light Infantry), for whom there seemed to be but little rest.

On the 5th of December, the III Corps Commander inspected the 151st Brigade at Warloy, two battalions of the 150th Brigade at Contay, and two at Baizieux, and the 149th Brigade at Bresle on the 6th. To all these he expressed his great appreciation of the fine fighting qualities of the Division and its good work generally on the Somme since the 10th of September.

In every kind of weather training continued until at last, on Christmas Eve, orders were received at Baizieux Château, where 50th Divisional Headquarters were established, that on the 28th the Division would move back to the front line and relieve the 1st Division in the right sector of the III Corps front, the relief to be completed by the 1st of January, 1917.

Christmas Day was kept up in style: pigs took the place of turkeys, and battalion bands played carols. From home, the kind folk in the north sent the Division many "extras" and, altogether, the Festivities were a great success. This was the second Christmas spent by the Division in France.

Boxing Day over, everyone began to think of the return to the front line—not a pleasant prospect: but the five or six weeks out of the line had done all ranks a world of good and the training had given the reinforcements a good insight into the technique of fighting—actual experience was now to come.

The 149th and 151st Brigades were the first to move, and on the 28th the former marched from Bresle to Bécourt, relieving a brigade of the 48th Division, while the 151st moved from Warloy to Albert, taking over billets held by another brigade of the 48th Division. On the 29th the 149th Brigade moved up closer to the line, taking over positions in Bazentin and High Wood, while two battalions of the 150th Brigade marched from Contay and Baizieux to Bécourt. On the night of the 30th–31st of December, the 149th Brigade relieved four battalions of the 1st and 3rd Brigades (1st Division) in the front line, and on the night of the 31st December–1st January, two battalions of the 151st Brigade took over the front-line trenches from the 2nd Brigade of the same Division.

On the 1st of January, the G.O.C., Division, assumed command of the new front-line sector at 9 a.m., and Divisional Headquarters opened at Fricourt Farm.

The sector taken over by the 50th Division was immediately on the right of that held in the previous November, and from which the Butte de Warlencourt was attacked. The 151st Brigade was on the right, the 149th on the left.

Active operations had, for the time being, ceased, for neither side could withstand weather conditions, and it was all one could do in the front line to keep body and soul together.

The first few weeks of 1917 were, therefore, something in the nature of a battle with the elements rather than with the enemy. Conditions in the front line and support trenches were still terrible—"trench foot" caused many a casualty, for it was impossible to keep the men supplied with dry socks, and rubbing the feet with whale oil was only partly preventive: "gum boots, thigh" also were not always effective.

Back at Mametz a small town of Nissen huts had arisen since the Division was relieved in the Line in November. These semi-circular corrugated iron huts certainly kept out the rain and snow, but they were very cold in winter and hot as Hades in the summer.

The Divisional Headquarters Diary describes the weather on the 1st of January as damp and warm with showers of rain—conditions which prevailed for several days until, about the middle of the month, snow fell again, followed by sharp frosts. The whole countryside was now under a white pall, with here and there the stumps of trees or a lonely wooden cross. The hardened ground made the going up to, or coming down from, the front line much easier, but it had the disadvantage of showing up more clearly tracks to and from the trenches and the outline of the trenches themselves: and as a consequence the enemy's artillery had good targets. For, if the infantry in the front line had for the nonce abandoned attacks, the guns of both sides knew no rest, but pounded their opponent's trenches regularly, and with varying degrees of violence. Patrols usually wore white coats in order to make themselves less conspicuous.

None of the divisional diaries during this period in the line are particularly interesting, but the following extracts from letters written home by various officers give some idea of life in the line early in the New Year:

"I was in the underground passages and vaults of an old abbey (Eaucourt L'Abbaye) the other night. The top part is blown to bits and two of our tanks lie wrecked nearby. Underneath, however, it is quite safe, and you can get sixty feet or more, if you like, underground. The cellars are big enough to hold five hundred men comfortably, and they are full of German leavings. There are hundreds of pounds of biscuits, coffee, etc., and our fellows are now peacefully sleeping in beds recently occupied by Germans."

It was on the Somme in 1916 that we first learned how to construct dug-outs, for never before had we seen such deep and secure underground shelters as those we found after we had captured the German trenches.

Another officer, writing on the 14th of January, gives the following description of life in the front line:

"For an hour or two it was fine, but soon it began to rain and the water steadily rose. We couldn't make the pump work, and to make matters worse, I found a hole in my gum boots which rapidly filled with water. Fortunately Fritz was in much the same plight and did not bother us. He was only about two hundred yards away, and almost any hour of the day we could see two or three of them standing about on the top. We did not snipe at them and they left us alone except to the extent of throwing some fish-tail bombs near us, and we retaliated with rifle grenades. You have no idea of the state of the ground near these advanced posts. Wherever one looked, one saw the same endless extent of black mud and water, christened all over the place with the remains of old trenches, and wherever one walked, one slipped or slithered about among the innumerable shell holes. Almost every day both British and Bosche lose their way and get into the enemy lines .... Wandering about in the mud at night was rather an uncanny business as there were a great many dead bodies lying about, some already half sunk in the mud. The mud will have swallowed them all up before the winter is over."

And the same officer in another letter said: "We found two men sitting in the mud four or five hundred yards from the ruins (of the Abbey). Their gum boots had been sucked off by the mud, their feet had gone wrong and they were absolutely 'done' to the world .... They both went to hospital next day with 'trench feet'."

Patrol work and the maintenance of the defences in the front line when in the forward trenches, and the supply of working parties and training when in the back areas sums up the life of the 50th Division for nearly the whole month of January, for on the 28th the G.O.C. handed over command of the front-line sector to the 1st Australian Division, and Headquarters of the former moved to the Ribemont–Méricourt area, in which all units of the Division were subsequently collected by the end of the month.*

The weather by now was snowy and frosty and, with fairly comfortable billets, all ranks had an opportunity of recuperating after the rough time spent in the front line. Training and sports occupied the men during the day, and that game of all soldiers' games—football—provided much fun and amusement as well as many keen contests.

But early in February rumours circulated that in a little while the Division was to take over a portion of the French line. Operation orders were issued on the 7th of February stating that on the nights of the 13th/14th and 14th/15th the 50th Division was to relieve the 35th and 36th French Divisions in front of Belloy en Santerre and Berny en Santerre. These two places were south-west of Péronne and north and south (respectively) of that long straight road between Villers-Bretonneux and Vermand.

The transfer of British troops to south of the Somme was thus explained by Sir Douglas Haig: "To meet the wishes of our Allies in connection with the plan of campaign for the Spring of 1917, a gradual extension of the British front southwards as far as a point opposite the town of Roye was decided on in January, and was completed without incident of importance by the 26th of February, 1917."

By the 16th of February the Division was settled in the line, the 150th Brigade on the right and the 149th on the left, with the 151st Division in reserve in Foucaucourt.

The trenches were in very poor condition, some of the communications being impassable. But it was not long before working parties, aided by the Pioneers and directed by the Divisional Field Companies, R.E., improved matters. Warmer days, but cold, frosty nights, characterised the weather: but still "trench foot" caused units in the line many casualties.

Of infantry action there was little or none, but the opposing artilleries kept up intermittent shell fire which occasionally blazed up into a regular bombardment. The

---

*There is a note in the Headquarters Diary of the 50th Division, which states that the casualties suffered by the Division during the tour averaged twelve *per diem*.

enemy used a good deal of gas. Berny and Belloy,* and every now and then Estrées, received much attention from the opposing guns. In the third week of the month, the cold weather seems to have broken and the trenches again became mud channels: reliefs were carried out in great discomfort. And again the records speak of the terrible conditions of that first winter on the Somme:

"We came out of the line last night. In the ordinary way we should have been relieved by 8 p.m. We left the trench at 3-30 a.m. this morning (21st of February) and it is now 2 p.m. and I do not think we have got all the men out yet. You cannot imagine the mud. And no Mother's son would recognise him. They are really plastered from head to foot, and soaked through and through. There is such a maze of trenches about here (mile upon mile of them) that we are constantly losing people. They wander about for hours in old disused trenches: and that is no joke with mud up to the knees and German shells chasing you all the time."†

On the 25th of February, Divisional Headquarters received the startling information that the enemy had begun to retire: he had evacuated Pys, north-west of Le Sars, that morning. At night a further message stated that the British had occupied Pys, Irles and Serre. The German Retreat to the Hindenburg Line had begun. The 50th Division, however, was not destined to follow up the enemy as he fell back to his well-prepared defences in the Hindenburg Line, for it was after the Division had been relieved early in March, that he evacuated his defences south of the Somme.

The Division was ordered to keep a close watch on the enemy's trenches, but patrols found his line strongly held.

On the 1st of March, battalions in the line reported a quiet day in the trenches with nothing of interest. On this date also Divisional Headquarters reported that on the nights of the 6th/7th, 7th/8th and 8th/9th of March, the 59th Division, less artillery, would relieve the 50th Division. The next day III Corps Headquarters sent information that the enemy intended to withdraw from his present positions, and that the

---

*Berny and Belloy by this time were practically only places on a map; one officer speaks in the following terms of one of them: "All you could see of the town were a few odd bricks lying here and there."

†An officer of the 7th Northumberland Fusiliers.

Division was to assist the operations of the XV Corps, which was going to attack, by making a "smoke and artillery demonstration." But the 3rd was another "quiet day," indeed the enemy's inactivity, or at all events that of his infantry, was getting more pronounced.

On the 4th, therefore, two raiding parties "went over" to test the enemy's strength and obtain identifications. Both raids took place from the right sub-sector held by the 151st Brigade. The story of these two raids is thus briefly, but sufficiently, related in the Diary of Brigade Headquarters:

"At 2.35 a.m.* a party of two officers and 70 other ranks of 9th D.L.I. left our line at T.9.C.3.O with the intention of raiding enemy line on the western edge of Dragon Wood. The party crossed No Man's Land without causing any alarm and entered enemy trench at T.15.a.55.40 just as our artillery opened its barrage. Our machine guns, Lewis guns and trench mortars co-operated. The enemy trench was entered in two places, one of the parties going to the left, one to the right. One German was found on sentry and five others in a deep dug-out. They belonged to the 10th Grenadier Regiment. These were captured and sent back. Our party withdrew at 3.55 a.m. without any casualties. Enemy machine guns and artillery did not reply.

"Another raiding party, 5th Borders, left our line about T.4.C.5.5. and reached the enemy wire. It succeeded in getting through the first row, but was held up by the second row. Attempts were made to cut a way through but an enemy machine-gun on the left opened fire, and the party withdrew as the element of surprise was gone."

These two raids were the only incidents of more than ordinary interest which happened while the 50th Division was south of the Somme.

On the 5th of March, the relief of the 50th Division, less artillery, by the 59th Division, less artillery, began and continued until the 9th when at 10 a.m. on that date General Wilkinson handed over command of the sector to the G.O.C., 59th Division. The 149th Brigade was then in the Warfusée area, the 150th in Bayonvillers and the 151st in Méricourt-sur-Somme, Divisional Headquarters being established in the latter place.

---

*The time should obviously be 3.45 a.m.

Training began immediately. On the 17th the Division received information that the enemy had begun to withdraw from his position opposite the III Corps front. The relief of the Divisional Artillery began on the 21st and was completed by the 23rd.* On the 25th orders were received from Fourth Army Headquarters that the Division was to concentrate in the Talmas–Villers Bocage–Molliens area by the 31st of March, the Divisional Artillery being transferred to the VII Corps. By the last day of the month these moves had been completed.

The 50th Division had, however, received orders to move up to the Arras area, where final preparations were being made for the great battle which was to open on the 9th. On the 2nd, therefore, further moves took place and were continued for several days until, on the 8th, all three infantry brigades were in the Avesnes area under orders to move "at six hours notice."

---

*Reorganisation had again been busy in the Divisional Artillery. Between the 16th and 20th of January, 1917, the 252nd Brigade, R.F.A. was broken up, "A" Battery going complete to 242nd Artillery Brigade, "B" complete to 72nd Army Brigade, half of "D" to 250th Brigade, and the remaining half of the same Battery to the 251st Brigade. The 50th Divisional Artillery now consisted of the 250th and 251st Brigades, R.F.A.

CHAPTER VII

THE BATTLES OF ARRAS, 1917

AVESNES, to which area the three infantry brigades of the 50th Division had moved on the 8th of April, lay roughly some ten miles west of Arras. Divisional Headquarters were at Le Cauroy. The *rôle* allotted to the Division in the great attack, to open on the 9th at 5.30 a.m., was to push through after the enemy's line had been breached by the assaulting troops and follow up the retiring enemy. For the moment the Division was in reserve.

The Battles of Arras were the first of the Allied Offensives of 1917 and, so far as the British Armies were concerned, Sir Douglas Haig's plans were as follows:

"In the spring, as soon as all the Allied Armies were ready to commence operations, my first efforts were to be directed against the enemy's troops occupying the salient between the Scarpe and the Ancre, into which they had been pressed as a result of the Somme Battle.

"It was my intention to attack both shoulders of this salient simultaneously, the Fifth Army operating on the Ancre front, while the Third Army attacked from the northwest about Arras. These converging attacks, if successful, would pinch off the whole salient and would be likely to make the withdrawal of the enemy's troops from it a very costly manœuvre for him if it were not commenced in good time.

"The front of attack on the Allied side was to include the Vimy Ridge, possession of which I considered necessary to secure the left flank of the operations on the south bank of the Scarpe. The capture of this ridge, which was to be carried out by the First Army, also offered other important advantages. It would deprive the enemy of valuable observation and give us a wide view over the plains stretching from the eastern part of the ridge to Douai and beyond. Moreover, although it was evident that the enemy might, by a timely withdrawal, avoid a battle in the awkward salient still held by him between the Scarpe and the Ancre, no such withdrawal from his important Vimy Ridge positions was likely. He would be almost certain to fight for this Ridge and, as my object was to deal him a blow

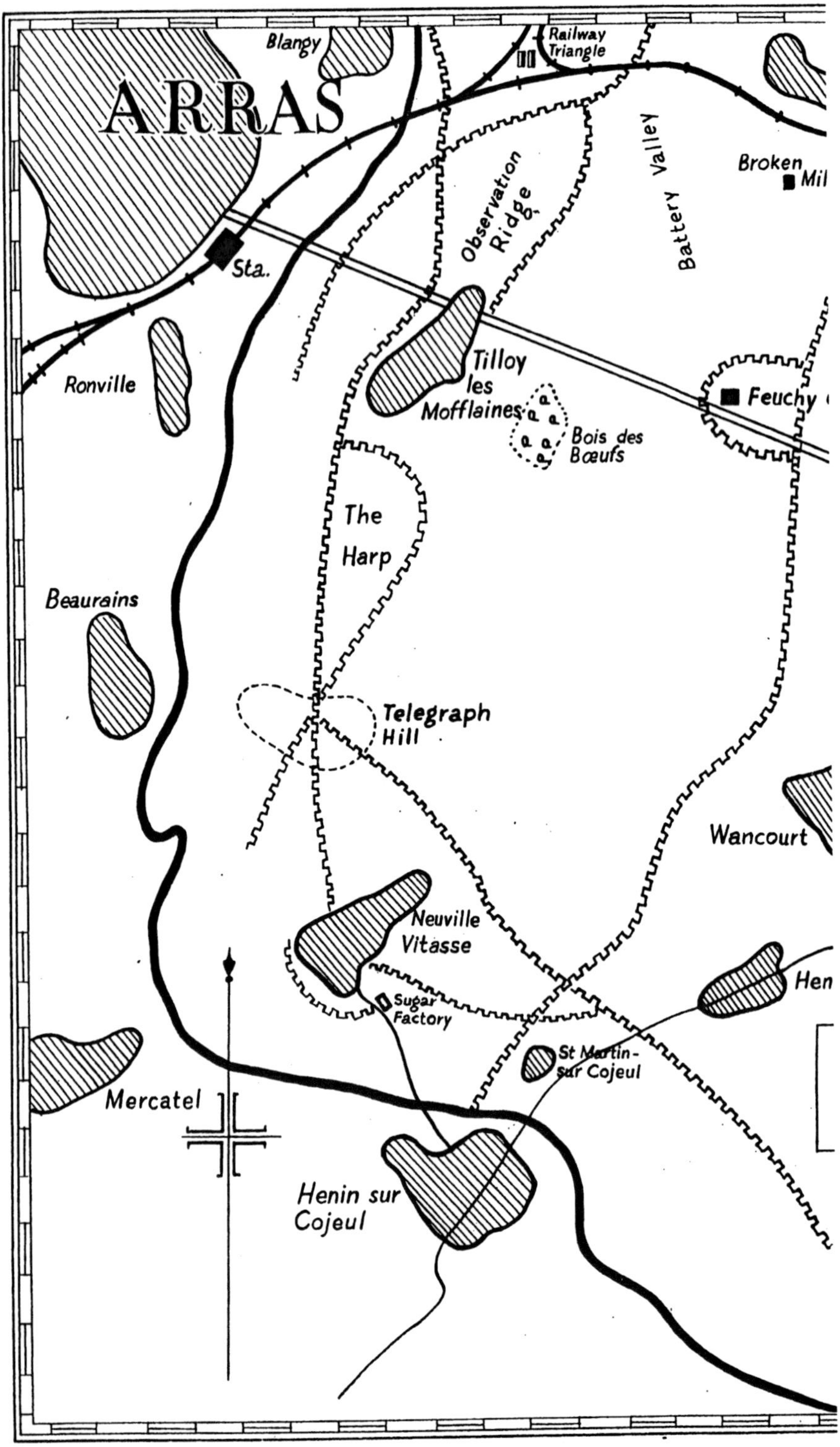

ARRAS
Blangy
Railway Triangle
Observation Ridge
Battery Valley
Broken Mil
Sta.
Ronville
Tilloy les Mofflaines
Bois des Bœufs
Feuchy
The Harp
Beaurains
Telegraph Hill
Wancourt
Neuville Vitasse
Sugar Factory
Hen
St Martin-sur Cojeul
Mercatel
Henin sur Cojeul

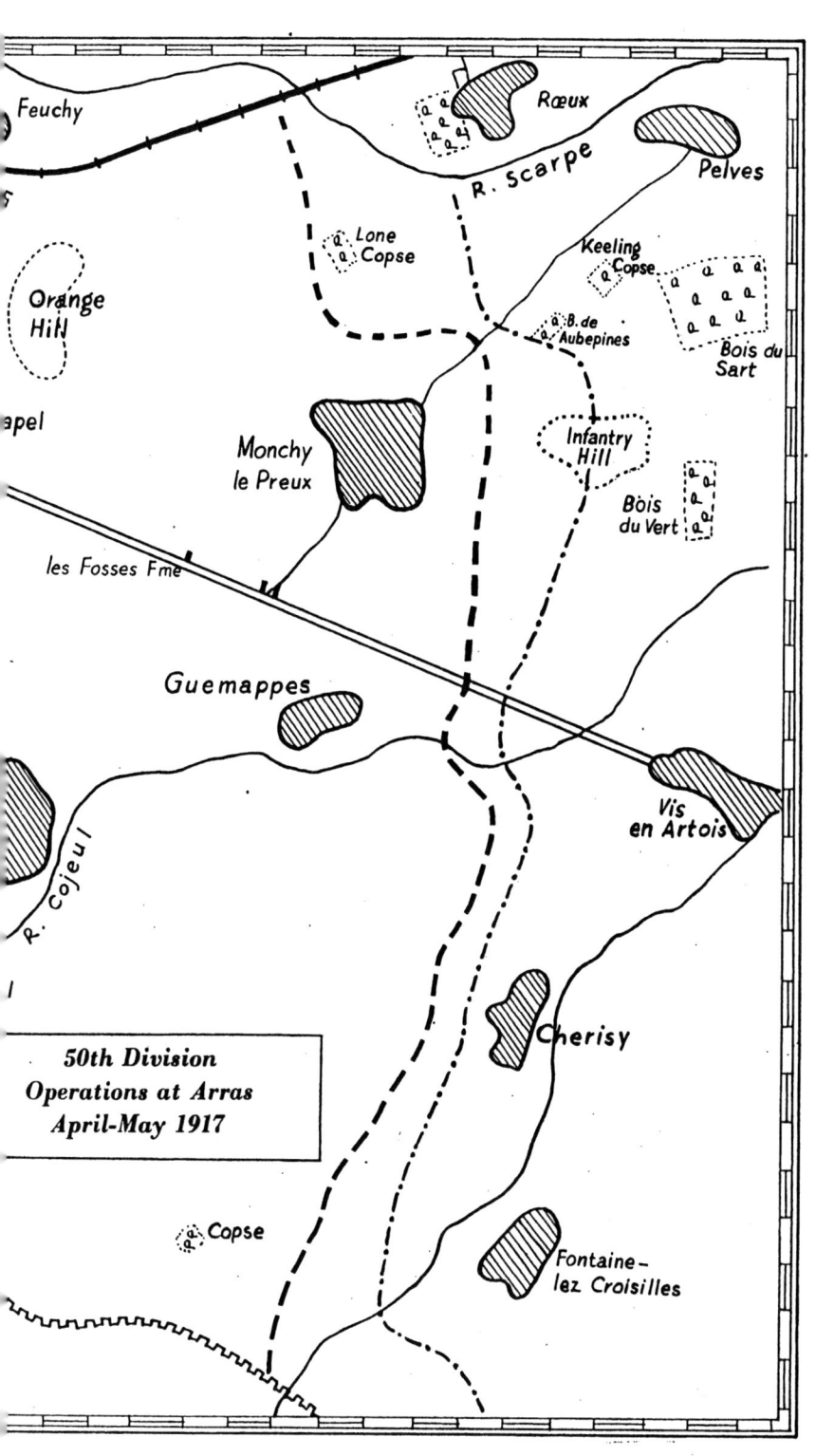

**50th Division
Operations at Arras
April-May 1917**

which would force him to use up reserves, it was important that he should not evade my attack."

Sir Douglas Haig's plans were the outcome of a conference of military representatives of all the Allied Powers held at French General Headquarters in November, 1916, when it was decided to launch "a series of offensives on all fronts, so timed as to assist each other by depriving the enemy of the power of weakening any one of his fronts in order to reinforce another."

The "fronts" mentioned above included not only France and Flanders but Italy and Russia.

But early in 1917, the situation became very different from what it had been when the Allied Conference was held. Russia had been torn by revolution; the Italians could not be ready until some time after the date fixed for Sir Douglas Haig's attack; even the French, who were to launch great attacks farther south, were delayed; while on the British front, the German Retreat to the Hindenburg Line changed somewhat (though not seriously) the *rôle* of the British Armies. The Fifth Army had merely to follow up the retirement of the enemy and establish itself in front of the Hindenburg Line, instead of attacking. The Third Army having made all preparations for advancing and attacking from the front line south of the Scarpe, had to first occupy the enemy's old front line and dig more assembly trenches and secure new gun positions before the 9th of April.

"My task," continues Sir Douglas Haig's despatches, "was, in the first instance, to attract as large hostile forces as possible to my front before the French offensive was launched, and my forces were still well placed for this purpose. The capture of such important tactical features as the Vimy Ridge and Monchy-le-Preux by the First and Third Armies, combined with pressure by the Fifth Army from the south against the front of the Hindenburg Line, could be relied on to use up many of the enemy's divisions, and to compel him to reinforce largely on the threatened front."

The importance of one paragraph in the official despatches must not be overlooked: indeed, from that paragraph one may deduce what is undoubtedly a fact, *viz.*, that had circumstnceas allowed the British Commander-in-Chief to keep to his original intention there might have been no "Bloody Passchendaele," for the Ypres Battles of 1917 would have begun in better weather, before the whole area east of the battered city had become a sea of mud. The significance of this paragraph must not be overlooked.

"With the forces at my disposal, even combined with what the French proposed to undertake in co-operation, I did not consider that any great strategical results were likely to be gained by following up a success on the front about Arras, and to the south of it, beyond the capture of the objectives aimed at as described above. *It was, therefore, my intention to transfer my main offensive to another part of my front after those objectives had been secured.*"

"Another part" meant the Ypres Salient.

To all those divisions and regiments which took part in the Arras Battles of 1917, those significant words will supply a reason why many of those same units found themselves a few months later floundering about in mud and morass east of Ypres in foul and vile weather—in a seemingly hopeless task: and the 50th Division was one of those units.

But to return to Arras.

The enemy's defences were formidable:

"Prior to our offensive the new German lines of defence on the British front ran in a general north-westerly direction from St. Quentin to the village of Tilloy-lez-Mofflaines, immediately south-east of Arras.* Thence the original German trench systems continued northwards across the valley of the Scarpe River to the dominating Vimy Ridge which, rising to a height of some 475 feet, commands a wide view to the south-east, east and north. Thereafter, the opposing lines left the high ground and, skirting the western suburbs of Lens, stretched northwards to the Channel.... The front attacked by the Third and First Armies on the morning of the 9th of April extended from just north of the village of Croisilles, south-east of Arras, to just south of Givenchy-en-Gohelle at the northern foot of the Vimy Ridge, a distance of nearly fifteen miles. It included between four and five miles of the northern end of the Hindenburg Line which had been built to meet the experience of the Somme Battles. Further north the original German defences in this sector were arranged on the same principle as those which we had already captured further

---

*This was after the Retreat to the Hindenburg Line had taken place, of which the official date is 14th March–5th April, 1917.

south. They comprised three separate trench systems, connected by a powerful switch line running from the Scarpe at Fampoux to Liévin, and formed a highly-organised defensive belt some two to five miles in depth."

Three weeks prior to "Z" Day (the day of the attack) the artillery opened a heavy bombardment of the enemy's wire, back areas, communications, trenches, strong points and billets: a merciless hail of shell swept the hostile positions till the days immediately preceding the attack, when the general bombardment opened. In those few days the whole German line appeared to be a mass of smoke from bursting shells, with sharp stabs of flame. So terrible was that bombardment, that the enemy's ration parties were unable to approach the front lines and the unfortunate German soldiery holding the trenches were compelled to seek the shelter of their deep dug-outs where, shaken and almost demoralised, they awaited death or capture as a happy release from their awful position.

In this bombardment the 50th Divisional Artillery took part, for on the 25th of March, the Brigades had been temporarily transferred to the VII Corps and began to move north towards the Talmas–Villers Bocage–Molliens area, where they had been ordered to concentrate by the 31st. On the 30th of March, the 250th and 251st Brigades moved to the Wagon Lines at Wailly where they came under the orders of the C.R.A., 56th Division. On the 31st both brigades moved up into action to positions between Beaurains and Agny.

Both brigades were now in for a strenuous time: "The weather was a succession of storms and bitter gales with snow. Horses died like flies from exposure .... The roadsides were lined with dead horses at intervals of a hundred yards or so round Arras."

The 1st of April was spent mostly in getting up ammunition and in registering targets, but on the 2nd the guns joined in the general bombardment which continued up to "Z" Day.

On the night of the 8th-9th the 50th Divisional gunners used gas shell for the first time.

THE FIRST BATTLE OF THE SCARPE, 1917: 9TH–14TH APRIL

The attack began at 5.30 a.m. on the 9th of April under cover of a most effective artillery barrage, the despatches stating that, "Closely following the tornado of our shell fire our gallant infantry poured like a flood across the German lines, overwhelming the enemy's garrisons." Indeed, the latter were mostly sheltering in their deep dug-outs against the awful avalanche of shell in which it seemed impossible for anything to live.

General Wilkinson with some of his staff went up to a position south of Arras in the neighbourhood of Ficheux, from which he witnessed the attacks of the 14th, 56th and 30th Divisions of the VII Corps.

In the meantime orders had been received on the 4th of April for the Division (less artillery) to move eastwards on the 6th and 7th, the 149th and 151st Brigades to the Rollecourt area, and the 150th Brigade to Houvin–Houvigneul on the 6th, and all three brigades to the Avesnes area on the 7th.

News of the successful operations on the 9th reached the 50th Division a few hours after zero, but it was 11.30 p.m. that night before orders were issued to the three infantry brigades to move to the Habarcq–Wanquetin area on the 10th. On conclusion of their moves the 149th Brigade occupied the Wanquetin–Hauteville area, the 150th was located at Habarcq, and the 151st at Agnez, Gouves and Montenescourt: the 7th Durham Light Infantry (Pioneers) moved into Arras.

Divisional Headquarters opened at Berneville at 4 p.m.

On the 11th the Division was transferred from the XVIII to the VII Corps and began the relief of the 14th Division.

The 149th Brigade was first into the line and began to move off at 5.15 p.m. A heavy snowstorm was in progress and the men had been ordered to "dump" their great coats, taking only their blankets as protection against the weather. All ranks, therefore, were soon in a wretched condition. The route followed by the Brigade lay through Warlus, Dainville and Arras, thence eastwards to the trenches south of Tilloy, held by the 42nd Brigade (14th Division). These trenches bestraddled Telegraph Hill. The right of the line was taken over by the 6th Northumberland Fusiliers, the left by the 7th Battalion; the 5th Northumberland Fusiliers were back in the old German front line, while the 4th were in reserve in Ronville Caves. The relief was completed by 3.35 a.m. on the 12th. The relief was apparently without incident.

Meanwhile the 151st Brigade moved up and relieved the 43rd Brigade (14th Division) in Ronville Caves. The 150th Brigade remained at Habarcq.

On the 12th the relief of the 14th Division was continued. The 150th Brigade moved up to the Ronville Caves, the 151st Brigade relieved the 41st Brigade in the front line during the night of the 12th-13th, and the 149th took over the support trenches in the Telegraph Hill area.

At 12 midnight the G.O.C., 50th Division, assumed command of the front-line sector and Divisional Headquarters opened in Arras.

The new sector occupied by the 50th Division was on the ridge immediately east of the villages of Wancourt and Héninel. The river Cojeul ran through the latter village, continuing north-east past the eastern outskirts of Wancourt. Here, however, it took a sharp turn eastwards, south of Guémappe. The left flank of the Divisional front rested on the river east of Wancourt, the right on the well-defined building known as the Wancourt Tower, which stood upon the ridge east of Wancourt and Héninel. South-east, but beyond the Divisional right boundary lay Chérisy, while directly ahead was Vis-en-Artois. Guémappe, also in the German lines, was north of the Cojeul on the left front of the 50th Division: machine-gun fire from the village could rake the Divisional front line in enfilade.

The 56th Division was on the right of the 50th and the 3rd Division on the left.

The whole of the area taken over by the 50th Division had only recently been captured, indeed, both Héninel and Wancourt had only been captured on the 12th after a hard struggle. The situation therefore, east of the Cojeul was none too clear, and especially about Wancourt Tower some doubts existed as to the exact extent of the line.

Early on the 13th, therefore, patrols were pushed out eastwards, and at 4.10 a.m. Lieut.-Colonel Bradford, of the 9th Durham Light Infantry, reported that he had two companies east of the Cojeul, and two in the river bed (which was dry). Soon after mid-day patrols were reported as having dug in fifty yards east of the Tower, but heavy machine-gun fire from Guémappe was sweeping the area. Two companies of this Battalion, however, which tried to reach the Tower were held up, and had to dig in fifty yards west of it.

At night on the 13th the position appears to have been that two companies of the 9th Durham Light Infantry were holding the front line from Wancourt Tower northwards for about six hundred to seven hundred yards, and two companies were in a sunken road just east of the Cojeul River. Guémappe was attacked by the 3rd Division at 7 p.m., but the operation failed.

Meanwhile orders had been issued that the VI and VII Corps would again advance on the 14th.

The 151st Brigade of the 50th Division was to attack in conjunction with the divisions on right and left. At about 2 a.m. on the 14th, however, these orders were changed: the 50th Division and the 56th Division (on the right) only were to attack the enemy, no attack being made by the 29th Division (which had relieved the 3rd Division) on the left, until the ridge south of Guémappe had been captured. The 56th Division, on the right, was to capture Chérisy; the 50th Division was to advance abreast of, and protect the left flank of the 56th Division, and form a defensive flank facing north along the high ground roughly just south of the 80 Contour, with their left in Wancourt Tower.*

The original plan of attack had been to send an order to the 3rd Division to attack Guémappe, but that Division having been relieved, the 29th Division was not ready. But to advance was imperative.

The plan adopted by the G.O.C., 151st Brigade, was as follows: the 9th Durham Light Infantry were to remain stationary in their position as a guard against counter-attack from Guémappe. The advance was to be made by "the 6th Durham Light Infantry, 8th Durham Light Infantry, and the 5th Border Regiment, to assemble in succession in the dry bed of the Cojeul River from N.29 a.5.8. to N.23.c.9.2."†

The three battalions were already moving up to positions laid down in the original order but were stopped in time. The change in orders had to be explained verbally to battalion commanders, for there was no time to circulate the later orders.

The 6th Durham Light Infantry, accompanied by one section of the 151st Machine-Gun Company, was told to start at zero, abreast the 169th Brigade (56th Division), while the C.O.s of the 8th Durham Light Infantry and the 5th Border Regiment

---

*As a landmark the Tower disappeared on the night of the 13th, having fallen down at 10 p.m.

†Just north-east of Héninel.

were told to report personally at Advanced Brigade Headquarters as soon as their respective battalions had assembled on the Cojeul River, to receive orders from the G.O.C. when to advance.

The O.C., 6th Durham Light Infantry, was ordered to deploy on a two-company front, the third company to cover the left leading company, the fourth company to cover the third. The two leading companies were to advance hugging the left flank of the 169th Brigade (56th Division) as far as they went. When the 169th Brigade came to a standstill, the two leading companies of the 6th Durham Light Infantry were to halt also, and refuse their left flank; the 3rd and 4th companies were then to prolong the refused flank.

Orders to the 1st, 2nd and 3rd companies of the 8th Durham Light Infantry* were similar to those of the 3rd and 4th companies of the 6th Battalion, *i.e.* they were to prolong the refused flank formed by the 6th Durham Light Infantry. If the three companies of the 8th Durham Light Infantry were unable to carry the refused flank back to the right of the 9th Durham Light Infantry at Wancourt Tower, the 5th Border Regiment would then be put in to fill the gap.

Zero hour on the 14th was 5.30 a.m.

Brigadier-General Cameron (G.O.C., 151st Brigade) had established Advance Brigade Headquarters just west of the Cojeul River and here, at 5 a.m., it was reported that there was a considerable gap between the right of the 9th Durham Light Infantry, and the left of the 56th Division. He therefore ordered the 6th Durham Light Infantry to deploy with their left on Wancourt Tower, or rather the spot where it had stood. A few minutes after 5 a.m. this movement was begun, and completed by 5.20 a.m.

From Brigade Headquarters all which could be seen were the banks of the sunken road east of the river, and beyond the ridge on which the Tower had stood, but at Zero, the leading lines of the 6th Durham Light Infantry were observed cresting a bank which ran from north-east to south-west on the lower slopes of the ridge. But in the half light it was difficult to make out whether they were exactly abreast of the 56th Division. The O.C., 6th Durham Light Infantry stated they were and,

---

*The 4th Company, 8th Durham Light Infantry, had been on detachment and only rejoined the Battalion on the afternoon of the 14th of April.

as he was on the bank mentioned above, he was in the best position to judge.

The enemy's barrage had fallen almost immediately the attack began, but the 6th Durhams were seen to pass through it successfully, then top the ridge and disappear over the crest. The time was by now 5.55 a.m. and the 8th Durham Light Infantry were then ordered forward. It was 6.10 a.m. when the second company of the 8th Battalion crested the bank.

The O.C.s, 6th and 8th Durham Light Infantry, had established combined Headquarters in a sunken road just east of the Cojeul, from which the signallers of the 6th Durhams had carried a wire back to Advanced Brigade Headquarters.

At about 7 a.m. news was received that the 6th and 8th Durham Light Infantry had passed the cross tracks some distance south-east by east of the Tower, and the 5th Borderers were, therefore, ordered down to the Cojeul. The G.O.C. was then ordered to send one battalion up as the reserve to Niger Trench (west of Wancourt). But no confirmation had been received that the 6th and 8th Durhams had passed the cross tracks mentioned and the Borderers were not ordered forward from the River.

Between 7 and 9 a.m. reports came in that the 56th Division was established along a north and south line, just west of a small tangle of German practice trenches, south of, and almost up to, the Tower, but no further advance could be made owing to intense machine-gun fire. It was also apparent that the 6th and 8th Durham Light Infantry were much intermixed with troops of the 56th Division. An effort was made to re-organise these units, but hostile machine-gun fire made movement on the plateau impossible and all parties, big and small, began consolidating where they were.

Reports to Brigade Headquarters began to pour in: a party of 6th Durhams, east of the Tower, had been cut off by a strong party of Germans; directly south of the Durhams, troops of the 56th Division had similarly been surrounded; considerable machine-gun fire from the direction of Guémappe was harassing the 9th Durham Light Infantry. Neither of the first two reports were confirmed, but on receipt of the latter the G.O.C. ordered the artillery to deal with certain definite points in the village and, for the time being, the gunners succeeded in silencing the machine guns. Guémappe was evidently strongly held by the enemy, for considerable bodies

BATTLE OF ARRAS, 1917.
Infantry moving up in artillery formation, 9th April, 1917.

(Imperial War Museum Photographs, Copyright Reserved)

Facing page 210

of German troops were observed on the roads leading westwards, and hostile infantry could be seen moving from a north-easterly direction on the village: and one time a counter-attack from the village appeared imminent. But the Divisional Artillery broke up these forward bodies of troops and caused considerable casualties among them.

There are very few reports of the operations of the 14th of April and none in detail. A "situation map" with the Diary of 151st Brigade Headquarters, however, gives the positions at 6 p.m.: a small party of 6th Durhams had reached the tangle of practice trenches south of the Tower; the 6th Durham Light Infantry, as a whole, were extended along a sunken road running roughly from west to east, south-west of the Tower; three companies of the 8th Durham Light Infantry were in line from the left of the 6th Durhams to just west of the Tower; from the latter point one-and-a-half companies of the 9th Durham Light Infantry, with their right on the ruined building, faced north-east; the remaining two-and-a-half companies were just east of the Cojeul; the 5th Border Regiment was still in position west of the River.

The G.O.C., 151st Brigade, in concluding his report, states in his opinion all four battalions of the Brigade and the 151st Machine-Gun Company played their parts very well. "The difficulties of the operation fell with special force on the 6th Durham Light Infantry (and the Machine-Gun Section attached), as they led the advance, and had to deploy in the dark. The dash and spirit with which they advanced does them great credit. All four guns of the Machine-Gun Section were, I regret to say, put out of action.

"The work of one of the companies of the 8th Durham Light Infantry came prominently to my notice. This company (under the command of Captain Williams) occupied and consolidated an important German work. It handed over the work to a unit of the 169th Brigade early on the night of the 14th-15th April. That unit was to be relieved again later by one of the 168th Brigade, and I have just heard that Captain Williams remained behind till 7 a.m. on the 15th so that the unit which was to hold the post would have the benefit of hearing at first hand, from one who had been there in daylight, all about the post and its surroundings. I think this shows the spirit which animated the Company."

The 6th Durham Light Infantry had had hard luck. They reached their objective, but had to fall back again owing to the failure of the 56th Division to take Chérisy. There is little more to be said of the attack other than, again, the 50th Division had carried out its orders to the letter, and only evacuated the line gained owing to the inability of other troops to reach the line allotted to them.

The Division is mentioned in the official despatches[*] in the following terms:

"In the centre a Northumberland brigade of the 50th Division (Major-General P. S. Wilkinson), advancing in open order, carried the high ground east of Héninel and captured Wancourt Tower. Three counter-attacks against the position were successfully driven off and further ground was gained on the ridge south-east of Héninel."

Of the three counter-attacks, however, there is no mention in any of the official diaries, indeed, as already stated, the narratives of operations are meagre and lack detail, but the 50th Division may be proud that "The Capture of Wancourt and Ridge" was sufficiently important to be included under the heading of "Tactical Incidents" of the Battle by the Battles Nomenclature Committee.

The First Battle of the Scarpe, 1917, officially ended on the 14th of April, and during the night of the 14th–15th the 151st Brigade was relieved by the 149th Brigade, the former moving back into support, the 150th Brigade still remaining in reserve.

During this Battle the 50th Divisional Artillery again came under their own C.R.A. and supported the attack on the Wancourt Ridge. Major Ommanney says: "In the early morning of the 14th the batteries again moved forward to support the attack on Wancourt Tower and Chérisy. The move began at 4 a.m. and was completed by 7 a.m. at which hour fire was opened. The positions were quite in the open, with no cover of any sort and in full view of the Bosche from Wancourt Tower. The batteries were all jammed up close together in a small valley which runs westwards along the north side of Wancourt, and Brigade Headquarters moved up and took over B's old position at Neuville Vitasse. Wancourt Tower was taken, but the attack was then held up by machine-gun fire from the flank."

---

[*] Boraston's edition.

By early morning of the 15th of April the 149th Brigade had relieved the 151st. The 6th Northumberland Fusiliers had taken over the trenches held by the 9th Durham Light Infantry, but record in their diary that, "Contrary to information received, it was discovered that the line ran fifty yards *west* of Wancourt Tower which was occupied by the enemy." While the Diary of 149th Brigade Headquarters states: "The Tower, commanding a view of all our approaches from Telegraph Hill, was destined to become the scene of continual fighting during the next few days."

The 7th Northumberland Fusiliers were in support—two companies in Nepal Trench, and two along the bank east of the Cojeul; the 5th Northumberland Fusiliers were in Niger Trench, and the 4th in the Cojeul Switch.

At daybreak on the 15th the 6th Northumberland Fusiliers pushed out a bombing party of four men, and established a post in the ruins of Wancourt Tower (which was apparently only occupied by the enemy at night) so as to enable the Battalion to include it in the front-line system and consolidate it.

The events of the 15th are related in the Diary of the 6th Battalion: "At 3.30 p.m. the enemy were observed digging a sap with the intention of re-occupying the house. A platoon was at once ordered to occupy the Tower and prevent the enemy from reaching it. This was carried out after a brief hand-to-hand combat, and consolidation was begun. The position was held in spite of a very heavy hostile barrage and two bombing attacks which were both repulsed. Organisation for the defence of the position was commenced and a communication trench from the front line to the north of the Tower dug."*

The day of the 16th was spent in improving the positions about the Tower, for the 56th Division, on the right, had not joined up a "T" sap round the ruins as had been arranged. Orders were also issued to the 7th Northumberland Fusiliers to relieve the 6th that night. But at 10 p.m., shortly after the beginning of the relief, the enemy, after an intense bombardment, attacked in force and, overwhelming the garrison of the Tower, succeeded in occupying a small portion of the original

---

*The Diary of Divisional Headquarters records that casualties on the 14th of April were estimated at 16 officers and 213 other ranks, killed, wounded and missing.

front line. Bombing attacks were at once launched but, owing to the darkness and uncertainty of the dispositions, were unsuccessful. The remainder of the night was spent in reorganising and preparing for a counter-attack on a larger scale.

The relief by the 7th Northumberland Fusiliers was postponed; "A" and "C" Companies were preparing to move up when the enemy's counter-attack was launched. For the bombing attack by the 6th Northumberland Fusiliers (described above), "D" Company of the 7th Northumberland Fusiliers sent up bombs and had two officers and two other ranks killed, one officer and eleven other ranks wounded and one officer and one other rank missing.

On the morning of the 17th the 7th Northumberland Fusiliers were ordered to recapture the lost position. Man by man, "A" and "B" Companies moved up to the place of assembly, *i.e.*, the bank behind the ridge, "B" on the right, "A" on the left. At 11.53 a.m., assisted on the flanks by the bombers of the 6th Northumberland Fusiliers, the attack began under an intense artillery barrage. The hostile garrison bolted before the first man of the attack reached the objective. The whole of the front line was reoccupied, the Tower recaptured together with a small section of trench north of the Tower, which had been used by the enemy as a bombing post.

At night both the 6th and 7th Northumberland Fusiliers were relieved by the 5th Northumberland Fusiliers, the 6th proceeding to gun pits north of Neuville Vitasse and the 7th to Nepal and Niger Trenches.

On the 18th, at 6.30 a.m., a wounded German stated that the enemy intended attacking at 2 p.m. with a new battalion. At 11 a.m. his troops were observed massing but were completely dispersed by the Divisional Artillery, and information received later stated that a German relief had been badly cut up by our fire.

During the next few days nothing of outstanding importance happened on the Divisional front.

THE SECOND BATTLE OF THE SCARPE, 1917: 23rd–24th APRIL

That we should have been compelled in April 1917 to continue the operations east of Arras, after the objectives laid down by Sir Douglas Haig in the First Battle of the Scarpe, was one of the tragedies of the War. The British line had been rolled four miles further east—all the dominating features considered necessary had been captured from the enemy—we were in a fine position on the heights looking eastwards; our casualties had been light and the enemy's heavy.

"So far, therefore," said the British Commander-in-Chief, "as my own plans were concerned, it would have been possible to have stopped the Arras offensive at this point and, while maintaining a show of activity sufficient to mislead the enemy as to my intentions, to have diverted forthwith to the northern theatre of operations the troops, labour, and material required to complete our preparations there. At this time, however, the French offensive was on the point of being launched.* It was important that the full pressure of the British offensive should be maintained in order to assist our Allies. Accordingly, active preparations were undertaken to renew my attack."

The intervening days between the First and Second Battles of the Scarpe had been of great value to the enemy. He had had time to bring up reserves and recover from the temporary disorganisation our first attack had caused him:

"Both the increasing strength of his resistance and the weight and promptness of his counter-attacks made it evident that, except at excessive cost, our success could not be developed further without a return to more deliberate methods."†

It was therefore evident that our next attack would meet with strenuous opposition and that if we gained our objectives we should do so only after heavy casualties.

The front selected for the Second Battle of the Scarpe extended from Croisilles to Gavrelle—a distance of about nine miles.

Operation orders were issued early on the 20th from 50th Divisional Headquarters; they may be summarised briefly. The advance eastwards was to continue on the 23rd of April; the 50th Division, with the 30th Division and the 15th Division on the right and left respectively, was to occupy as the first objective (Blue Line) the whole of the ridge east of Wancourt Tower and (roughly) a north and south line, 1,600 yards west of it, and as the second objective (Red Line) a south-west to north-east line from the southern end of the Blue Line

---

*The French attack had been planned originally to follow within two or three days of the first British attack on the 9th of April, but was postponed until the 16th, and met with only partial success.

†Official Despatches.

to the right bank of the Cojeul River, north-west of Vis-en-Artois and just short of Rohart Factory.

The attack was to be carried out by the 150th Infantry Brigade, with the 151st in support and the 149th in reserve. The 50th and 14th Divisional Artilleries, with an Army Brigade, were to put down a "rolling" barrage and, during the pause between the advance from the Blue to the Red Line, *i.e.*, seven hours, four 18-pounder batteries were to move forward east of the Cojeul River.

The 149th Machine-Gun Company and two sections of the 151st Machine-Gun Company were also to support the attack with barrage fire. Two tanks were to co-operate. The Divisional Royal Engineers and Pioneers were to begin work as soon as possible after the attack on the ruined Wancourt Tower–Marlière–Guémappe.

At Zero Hour (4.45 a.m.) the three infantry brigades were to be in position as follows: two battalions ready to assault, two in Nepal and Tiger Trenches; 151st—three battalions in the Harp, one in Ronville; 149th—four battalions in Ronville. Each objective, when captured, was to be consolidated at once; on capturing the Red Line, outposts were to be pushed out beyond it.

The 151st Brigade was to detail two companies to occupy and consolidate the German trenches east of the Tower; these companies were to reach the bank, west of the Tower, at Zero plus 6½ hours, and at Zero plus 7 hours were to move forward to the trenches mentioned. Two hundred portable knife rests were to be provided by the C.R.E. so that each man of the two companies could carry one forward, and place it at once in front of the trench.

Of the 150th Brigade, the attack was to be carried out by the 4th East Yorkshires on the right, and the 4th Green Howards on the left, each battalion keeping one company in support; one section of the 150th Machine-Gun Company was to be attached to each battalion and, in addition, one gun and a carrying party from the 150th Trench-Mortar Battery was to be attached to the Green Howards. Of the two battalions in reserve (the 5th Green Howards and the 5th Durham Light Infantry) the 5th Green Howards were to move at zero from Nepal Trench to the hillside west of Wancourt Tower and, fifteen minutes after zero, the 5th Durhams were to move to the hillside north of the Tower.

Strong points were to be constructed by both assaulting battalions and garrisoned by a platoon drawn from the supporting companies.

One important item in the Operation Orders was: "In the event of the Brigade on our left (of the 15th Division) not getting on, a defensive flank will be formed by the 4th Green Howards, facing north. On no account is the right of the attack to be stopped."

The supporting brigade (151st) detailed the 5th Border Regiment to support the two companies who were to consolidate the German trenches east of the Tower, and of the other battalions, the 9th Durham Light Infantry were to move from Ronville to The Harp, the 5th Border Regiment (less two companies) to Nepal Trench, the 8th Durham Light Infantry to Niger Trench, while the 6th Durham Light Infantry were to remain in The Harp.

With the exception of the 4th Northumberland Fusiliers (ordered to move to the old German line north of Beaurains) and two sections of the 149th Machine-Gun Company who were to support the attack of the 150th Brigade, the 149th Brigade was to remain in billets at Ronville.

At 4.15 a.m. on the 23rd the front-line battalions were reported in position and "O.K."

Of the 4th East Yorkshires, companies were in line from right to left as follows: "B," "A" and "D" forming the first and second waves, "C" the third wave. On the left of the East Yorkshires, the 4th Green Howards disposed "W," "X" and "Z" in the front line, from right to left, and "Y" in position behind "X" and "Z." The 5th Green Howards (right support) and 5th Durham Light Infantry (left support) were in Nepal and Niger Trenches respectively.

About five minutes before the attack the two tanks attached to the 50th Division nosed their way to the front and moved slowly in a north-westerly direction. Next, at 4.45 a.m., there was a crash as the eighty-four 18-pounders and thirty 4.5 in. howitzers opened fire simultaneously. At once the advance of the infantry began. They had scarcely started forward when red stars began to burst in the sky—the German S.O.S. to their artillery.

At about one hundred yards distance from their own trenches the attacking troops ran into their own barrage, which had been calculated and was moving at too slow a rate. Although suffering heavy casualties from their own guns it was essential to push on. But in the two flank companies of the East Yorkshires it was not long before every officer and many N.C.O.s had been killed or wounded. The flank companies, therefore, were in some confusion and there was a loss of direction. Nevertheless, those upon whom the task now fell of leading the men forward carried out their duties splendidly. "A" Company, in the centre pushed on unchecked and reached a point about one hundred yards east of a small wood along the Guémappe–Chérisy road. Heavy losses had been suffered by this company, but eventually the survivors dug in east of the wood. A party of "B" Company (right) had reached the first objective and had dug in facing south-east towards Chérisy.

Meanwhile a mixed party of all three front companies had encountered and captured a German battery of 77 mm. guns just south-east of the wood. But the situation of the East Yorkshires was by this time serious, for only three officers and about two hundred other ranks remained. The Battalion was out of touch with the 4th Green Howards, whilst neither on the right nor left of the Division had the 30th or 15th Divisions made progress. The 4th East Yorkshires (and, as it turned out later, the 4th Green Howards also) were in the air and exposed to counter-attacks which would certainly be made ere long.

About 7 a.m. the enemy launched vigorous counter-attacks from the direction of Chérisy and Vis-en-Artois.

The Diary of the 4th East Yorkshires records that: "The Battalion was quickly surrounded," but apparently not all were captured, for not only does the Brigade record state that: "The 1/4th East Yorkshires are back in original line," but a subsequent casualty list gives 17 officers and 352 other ranks killed, wounded and missing, and on the 25th of April the trench strength of the Battalion was 10 officers and 215 other ranks.

The remnants of the Battalion appear to have been drawn back to the original front line, where they came temporarily under the orders of the 8th Durham Light Infantry.

Meanwhile, on the left, the 4th Green Howards had also passed through heavy fighting. Their diary records first that our barrage was "very good, heavy and accurate" and that the German barrage fell twenty seconds after ours.

The Green Howards suffered several casualties from our own guns during the first few minutes of the advance, as the troops ran into the barrage which was moving at the rate of twenty-five yards a minute.

"W" Company, on the right, met considerable opposition from rifle and machine-gun fire from the enemy's front line, and had to take to the shelter of shell holes about fifty yards from the hostile trenches. Not until the company had established superiority of fire, and a tank had passed through, was it possible to rush the trench which was found strongly held. But the Green Howards beat down opposition and many prisoners were taken. Many dead and wounded Germans littered the trench which, however, was not in bad condition, and had not been battered out of recognition as many were.

In the centre, "X" Company had reached the enemy trench a little earlier than "W" and had less opposition, but had some thirty casualties from machine-gun and artillery fire before reaching their opponents.

On the left, "Z" Company, which had been facing north-east at zero hour, swung round, aligned themselves with "X" Company, and reached the German front line with few casualties and less opposition than the other companies.

All companies had had a rich harvest of prisoners in the enemy's front line.

The records then state that: "The Battalion, by now considerably thinned out but still a continuous line, then moved east to the German support trench which did not run parallel with, but was a switch (south-west to north-east) of, the front line. This was reached by 5.25 a.m. It was found to be a broad trench literally filled with dead Germans, except for the occupants of two deep dug-outs on "X" Company's front: no prisoners were taken here. By this time our line had become very thin; no East Yorkshires were observable on the right and the 44th Infantry Brigade appeared not to have progressed on the left. The Battalion, however, moved forward, captured a three-gun howitzer battery in O.19.a. (north-west of the little wood previously mentioned) and proceeded to dig itself in, along a line one hundred to two hundred yards west of the first objective. Enemy rifle and artillery fire had practically ceased, but machine-gun fire was increasing in intensity, and a particularly deadly stream of bullets was directed on to our left flank from the direction of O.14.a. (a farm north of the Cojeul River and east of Guémappe).

Captain Hirsch, who by now was the only officer left, therefore formed a defensive flank with half of "Y" Company, who dug in along a line above, and parallel with, the river just south of Guémappe. With the remainder of the Battalion (about one hundred and fifty men) he decided to hold on, and sent back for reinforcements and S.A.A.

At 6.30 a.m. a company of the 5th Durhams was sent up for the purpose not only of carrying up a fresh supply of S.A.A., but in order to extend the right of the 4th Green Howards across the railway, and so gain touch with the 4th East Yorkshires. The Durhams reached the railway line and established themselves astride it, but their right was in the air and touch with the East Yorkshires was not obtained.

By 7.15 a.m. Captain Hirsch (who had previously been wounded) was killed and Lieut. W. Luckhurst of the trench-mortar battery took charge of the Battalion for a short time. What happened to this officer is not known, the Battalion Diary recording that: "His fate is now uncertain."*

For an hour-and-a-half the 4th Green Howards appear to have maintained their position, but by 7.30 a.m. the Germans were seen massing for a counter-attack. One party was observed creeping down the low ground along the Cojeul, others were coming from the trenches in front of Vis-en-Artois, and a thick *bloc* advancing on the right rear (previously taken for East Yorkshires) were now seen to be Germans.

With no officer and only some half-a-dozen junior N.C.O.s a retirement was made, first to the enemy's second line, then to his front line, and finally back to the original "jumping-off" line. The movement was carried out under heavy machine-gun fire, but the N.C.O.s stated that the line was always under control and that sections of riflemen constantly fought rear-guard actions to cover the retirement of the rest.

By 8.10 a.m. the 4th Green Howards were finally back in their old line. They give their losses as three officers killed, seven wounded and one missing, and 352 other ranks killed, wounded and missing.

The records of the two battalions in support of the East Yorkshires and 4th Green Howards are all too brief, for where casualties were so heavy, there must have been fighting and

---

*He is reported as killed on the 24th of April, 1917, in *Officers died in the Great War*.

both the 5th Green Howards and the 5th Durham Light Infantry suffered heavily.

The 5th Green Howards (who supported the East Yorkshires), on the right, sent up reinforcements during the first advance, and later the whole Battalion was moved up to meet the enemy's counter-attack. The Battalion remained in the front line until 6 p.m., when the second attack was launched against the enemy in conjunction with two battalions of the 151st Brigade, and the line gained held all right. The 5th Green Howards give their losses on the 23rd of April as three officers and fifteen other ranks killed, five officers and 118 other ranks wounded and two officers and 55 other ranks missing.

The 5th Durhams (as already stated) had sent off one company ("D" Company) to reinforce the 4th Green Howards; an hour later "B" Company moved off to support the left of the latter Battalion. When the enemy counter-attacked at 11.30 a.m. the Durhams took up positions in the front-line trenches. In the second attack later, the 5th Durham Light Infantry were in support of the 9th Durham Light Infantry, and were later relieved by the 8th Durham Light Infantry.

The casualties of the 5th Durhams on the 23rd were four officers and 23 other ranks killed, three officers and 137 other ranks wounded, and one officer and 96 other ranks missing.

The Diary of the G.S., 50th Division, at this stage of the battle, *i.e.* when the attacking troops were finally back in their original "jumping-off" trenches, is interesting: "By 1 p.m. report received that the 15th Division, on our left, and the 30th Division, on our right, had also been forced back to their original positions by strong hostile counter-attacks. After so brilliant a success in the morning it was the more disappointing that the ground captured was re-taken by the enemy, and with it the battery of 7.7 cm. guns.... At 3 p.m. orders received from VII Corps that the attack would be resumed at 6 p.m. and that the Blue Line was to be taken. Two battalions, 151st Infantry Brigade, were therefore placed at the disposal of the G.O.C., 150th Infantry Brigade, for the attack."

But possibly the order from Corps Headquarters was only a confirmation of a proposal by the G.O.C., 50th Division, that he should attack again, for the Headquarters Diary of the 150th Brigade records that it was at 2.20 p.m. that the G.O.C. arranged over the telephone with Divisional Headquarters to renew the attack with two battalions of the 151st Brigade, in conjunction with brigades of the 30th and 15th Divisions, on the right and left respectively, also that the 5th Green Howards, on the right, and the 5th Durham Light Infantry, on the left, would support the attack by the 5th Border Regiment and the 9th Durham Light Infantry, who would attack on the right and left.

It will be remembered that the original orders to the 5th Border Regiment stated that two companies were to move up to a bank west of the Tower, draw knife rests and place them in front of the German line when captured. But owing to the enemy's counter-attack these two companies were kept back and did not move up.

On receipt of orders for the attack the Borderers and the 9th Durham Light Infantry moved up to the front line, taking over the right and left respectively.

Zero hour for the attack was 6 p.m.

This counter-attack equalled in brilliance the initial operations in the morning. Under a splendid artillery barrage the attacking troops advanced in fine style. The Border Regiment modestly report the action in a few brief words: "At 6 p.m. the Battalion, with the 9th Durham Light Infantry on the left, attacked and re-took the objective; five enemy machine-guns, several trench mortars, and about two hundred prisoners were captured, also many of our (150th Infantry Brigade) wounded, taken in the enemy counter-attack, were recovered. In our attack "A" Company remained in echelon to defend the flank, as the division on our right did not reach its objective. A platoon of the left company ("D") got well forward and occupied part of an old German trench, and were subsequently absorbed by the 9th Durham Light Infantry, under whose orders they remained until time of Battalion relief."

The 9th Durham Light Infantry attacked with two companies in the first wave and two in the second: "The companies carried the front trenches by storm, making considerable captures and firing on the retreating enemy, not one of whom escaped. Without pausing the advance continued for several hundred yards when further enemy machine-guns were encountered, and several played on us from the northern side of the Cojeul River. After a short struggle, our men using their Lewis-guns, rifle grenades and rifles, these were overcome and the enemy, abandoning their positions, were either killed or captured.

On arriving at the objective, a partly-constructed trench was found, lightly held by the enemy. This was immediately occupied by all four companies and the work of consolidation commenced.

"Throughout the attack all ranks showed determination and enthusiasm . . . . We advanced 1,600 yards on a five-hundred yard frontage. Both flanks were held up, and we did not get in touch until the 24th when the 15th and 30th Divisions attacked. Our casualties were slight."

The Durhams speak of the artillery barrage as being "Particularly good." A Colonel, a doctor, four other officers and about two hundred other ranks were captured by the Durhams, as well as three guns, eleven machine-guns and much other material.

The Headquarters Diary of the 151st Brigade has some further notes on the attack at 6 p.m.: "Our men repeatedly got in with the bayonet, and on one occasion bayonetted the teams of two machine-guns, which they rushed in a frontal attack. The most magnificent spirit was shown by all ranks, and the attack was pressed home in the most gallant fashion, notwithstanding an intense hostile barrage of 5.9 and 8-in. shells and concentrated machine-gun fire."

The Brigade Diary also throws a further light on the attack by the 5th Border Regiment: at 7 p.m. observers reported that the right flank was held up and the Borderers were, therefore, ordered to be prepared to form a defensive flank on the right to secure the right of the 9th Durham Light Infantry. The 5th Border Regiment then refused their flank.

The disquieting situation of the right flank of the 50th Division was, however, cleared up before the morning of the 24th, for during the night the 2nd Green Howards of the 30th Division gained touch with the 5th Border Regiment.

The fine fighting by the 50th Division did not pass unnoticed by the higher command, for the VII Corps Commander (Lieut.-General T. D. O. Snow) spoke on the telephone to General Wilkinson, congratulating him on the result of the day's operations.

The Division had suffered during the fighting on the 23rd, casualties numbering 66 officers and 1,400 other ranks.

During the early morning of the 24th the 151st Brigade relieved the 150th Infantry Brigade, who moved back into reserve in The Harp area; the 4th Northumberland Fusiliers of the 149th Brigade were attached to the 151st Brigade, the remainder of the 149th being in support.

At about 11.30 a.m. the enemy was reported retiring in front of the 30th Division, and the G.O.C. of that Division stated he was going to push on to the Blue Line. At 12.30 p.m. orders were received from Corps Headquarters that the advance was to be continued and that the Blue Line was to be made good by nightfall. In accordance with these orders the G.O.C., 151st Brigade, was instructed to advance at 4 p.m. under an artillery barrage. But, meanwhile, the 30th Division had already reached the Blue Line, and was digging in on it, and the 151st Brigade was, therefore, ordered to conform immediately to the movement of the 30th. The 5th Border Regiment swung up their right flank and obtained touch at about 4 p.m. But the 9th Durham Light Infantry, in the centre, with a company of the 4th Northumberland Fusiliers attacked, and had a sharp tussle with the enemy before occupying the Blue Line. This company ("B") had received orders to push forward patrols and then capture the German trench astride the railway. A platoon of the Company carried out these orders most gallantly as stated in a wire from the O.C., 9th Durham Light Infantry, to Battalion Headquarters, 4th Northumberland Fusiliers: "A platoon of your company has just captured enemy trench from O.20.7.6. to O.20.C.1.9 (astride the railway) and is holding the trench. Only three casualties incurred. Fine piece of work."

The Blue Line was now being consolidated and, the objectives of the 50th Division having been occupied, Corps Orders for another attack became inoperative.

"As the result of these two days' very severe fighting," states the Diary of Divisional Headquarters, "our line was advanced a mile further east and very considerable casualties inflicted on the enemy . . . . Thus ended another glorious day for the 50th Division, the traditions of the British Army upheld to the full."

Some 17 German officers and 793 other ranks had been captured, as well as three guns, fifteen machine-guns, two trench mortars and twelve football trench mortars, and there was evidence also that two German divisions had been very severely handled.

In the narratives of the great battles of the War it is inevitable that the front-line troops, *i.e.* the infantry, almost completely

BATTLES OF ARRAS.
Part of the broad wire entanglement in front of the Hindenburg Line, near Héninel, 3rd May, 1917.

(Imperial War Museum Photographs, Copyright Reserved)

Facing page 224

absorb the attention, but it must not be forgotten that the front-line troops depended very largely on the assistance and co-operation of other units of the division, whose efforts were just as strenuous and self-sacrificing, though their work is seldom detailed in official reports.

The infantry of the 50th Division were most faithfully served always by their artillery, Royal Engineers, Pioneers, machine-gun companies, trench mortar batteries, medical units and Army Service Corps; the Veterinary sections are seldom referred to, and yet the strenuous and successful efforts of the Veterinary officers to keep the horses and mules of a division in good condition were worthy of the highest praise. Even poor worried "D.A.D.O.S." deserves more mention than he frequently receives, for on him depended the replacement of equipment.

The infantry of the Division themselves (as already quoted) paid tribute to their artillery and the splendid barrages put down by the gunners.

The C.R.E. pays tribute to the excellent work carried out by the 7th, 446th and 447th Field Companies, R.E., during the operations. The reconnaissance and repair of roads, the locating and clearing of dug-outs and cellars, the wiring of trenches, digging of trenches in the front line—all these tasks took place under shell fire and, as the C.R.E. states, the work was arduous and involved a fair number of casualties.

The Signal Company, R.E., whose labours were to keep open communication by telephone, mention one cable which was constantly being destroyed by the enemy's barrage, which shows that the Signallers were in no safe quarters. But throughout the operations, communication was maintained with all units, and the Company well deserved the compliments paid to it by the G.O.C. after the Battle was over.

The 7th Durham Light Infantry (Pioneers) give no details of their work other than the brief statement that two companies worked on strong points in the reserve line, made infantry shelters and carried out wiring in front of the reserve line: another company was at work on the road in Wancourt, having to cease periodically as hostile shell fire was heavy.

The medical diaries are interesting. That of the A.D.M.S., 50th Division, is more interesting than the usual diary, for he gives a running commentary on the operations, and even a map.

The chain of communications of the medical units of the Division during the operations of the 23rd and 24th of April is given in full. Just east of the Cojeul River, and sheltering under a bank was the Advanced Bearer Post with a staff of two doctors and thirty-two other ranks. Next came the Relay Post, west of the Cojeul, and on a road running north-west, in charge of thirty-two N.C.O.s and men. The Advanced Dressing Post was still further north-west on the Wancourt–Tilloy road, where two doctors and sixty other ranks were engaged. The Advanced Dressing Station was on the Neuville Vitasse–Mercatel road, five doctors and one hundred and twenty other ranks officiating here. Finally, there was a Collecting Post for walking wounded, with a staff of five doctors and sixty-five other ranks, on the road at the north-eastern end of Mercatel. In addition to the above, one N.C.O. and eight men of the R.A.M.C. were attached to each Battalion Regimental Aid Post in the front line.

The A.D.M.S. also gives the information that two officers and one hundred men of the 5th Northumberland Fusiliers were held in reserve as stretcher bearers. One diary (that of the 1st Northumberland Field Ambulance) records that: "German prisoners were utilised for carrying wounded. Some of these, about sixty, were employed all day at this work, but these were not sent further forward than Command Dressing Post, and were all escorted to Prisoners' Cage at 7 p.m. They did this work willingly and cheerfully and seemed eager to be so employed."

During the heavy fighting the A.D.M.S. records that "the stretcher bearers worked splendidly under heavy shell fire."

The 2/2nd Northumberland Field Ambulance Diary states that "1,650 cases were dealt with during the day, and of these, 1,397 were evacuated to the C.C.S. by motor buses, charabancs and lorries, of which there was an unlimited supply."

At about 4 p.m. on the 24th orders received at Divisional Headquarters stated that the Division (less artillery) was to be relieved by the 14th Division, and during the night a brigade of the latter took over reserve positions held by the 150th Brigade, the latter moving back to billets in Arras.

Heavy artillery fire characterised the 25th, our guns raking the enemy's positions, and causing him many casualties. During the morning another brigade of the 14th Division relieved the 149th Brigade in support, the latter moving to The Harp: the

151st Brigade was placed in support. On the 26th the 149th Brigade moved to Arras and the 151st to The Harp, and at 5 p.m. General Wilkinson handed over command of the sector. Divisional Headquarters then opened in the Couturelle area where, by the 28th, all three infantry brigades were concentrated, *i.e.*, 149th—Pommera–Mondicourt; 150th—Halloy–Famechon–Grenas, and 151st—Humbercourt–Warluzel–Coullemont.

As usual the guns remained in the line—theirs was a hard existence, for they seldom knew a really good rest out of the forward area.

"Cleaning up" kept all ranks busy for several days and, with the advent of warm and sunny weather, life once more took on a different aspect. It was always wonderful to see how quickly men recovered their lively spirits once they were away from all the discomforts of the front-line trenches.

CHAPTER VIII

THE SUMMER OF 1917

ON the last day of April, Divisional Headquarters received orders that on the 1st of May the Division would move eastwards again. These orders were disappointing, for after the very severe fighting the Division had passed through, everyone hoped that ten days rest at least would be given them. But on the 1st the 149th Brigade Group moved to Souastre and Fonquevillers, the 150th Brigade Group to Coigneux and Bayencourt, and the 151st Brigade Group to Berles-au-Bois, Pommier and Bienvillers-au-Bois. Divisional Headquarters, however, still remained at Couturelle.

The Divisional Artillery was still detached and working under the 14th Division.

Another move took place on the 2nd of May, the 149th Brigade Group marching to Mercatel, the 150th to Ficheux, Blairville and Ransart, and the 151st to Grosville, Bellacourt and Bailleulval; Divisional Headquarters also moved, Advanced Headquarters being established in a camp near Neuville Vitasse.

The reasons for these moves were now made known: on the 3rd, the First, Third and Fifth Armies were to attack the enemy, and the original intention was to use the 50th Division to exploit any success gained. Owing to modifications in the plan of operations the Division was placed in Army Reserve instead.

The attack which took place on the 2nd of May was unsuccessful. The Division did not move and the day was employed in resting the men.

The following day Divisional Headquarters went back to Couturelle Château and the three infantry brigades began to move westwards again, and by the 5th the 149th were in the Pommera–Mondicourt area, the 150th in Halloy and Grenas and the 151st at Warluzel, Coullemont and Humbercourt.

In fine, sunny weather, the Division's interrupted training was resumed until the 15th of May when Divisional Headquarters Diary records the arrival of orders for the Division to move up to a forward area on the 17th, 18th and 19th, and that one infantry brigade would be put at the disposal of the

33rd Division for an operation to be carried out by the latter on the 20th.

When darkness fell on the 19th the 149th Brigade was concentrated in the Boiry St. Martin–Ayette area under the orders of the 33rd Division, the 150th Brigade at Douchy-les-Ayette, and the 151st Brigade at Monchy-au-Bois; Divisional Headquarters had opened at Beaumetz-les-Loges.

On the 20th the 149th Brigade moved up to St. Leger and the valley west of it during the attack by the 33rd Division. This attack was partially successful and, the enemy making no counter-attack, the 149th were not required. On the 22nd, however, the Brigade moved up during the night and relieved the 19th and 100th Brigades, 33rd Division, in the Hindenburg Line, the 150th and 151st Brigades receiving orders to move back to the Couin–Souastre–Bayencourt–Fonquevillers area, which move took place on the 23rd. On the 26th the 149th was relieved and moved back to Moyenneville, and on the 28th to Monchy-au-Bois, reverting again to the 50th Division.

June the 1st still found the 50th Division in training, and on the 2nd, 3rd, and 4th, parties of officers were allowed to visit the Somme battlefields of 1916, particularly the ground between Bazentin and Butte de Warlencourt over which the Division had fought its way eastwards.

The G. S. Diary for the 5th of June records the award of the K.C.M.G. to General Wilkinson.

In the middle of June the Division returned to the front line. Early on the 15th the 150th and 151st Brigades (less the 5th Border Regiment and the 9th Durham Light Infantry) marched out of Bayencourt and Souastre to relieve the 55th and 53rd Brigades respectively. The two Brigades of the 50th Division first took over reserve and support areas, but on the 16th the 151st relieved the 53rd Brigade in the left sub-sector of the front line, while the 150th took over reserve and support positions in the right sub-sector. On the night of the 17th–18th of June the 150th relieved the 55th Brigade in the front-line right sub-sector, and by the morning of the 18th the Division was once more in the line, the G.O.C. taking over from the G.O.C., 18th Division, at 11 a.m. Divisional Headquarters were in a camp half-a-mile south-west of Boisleux St. Maré.

The front now held by the Division was approximately three thousand yards in length and approximately one thousand yards west of the villages of Fontaine-lez-Croisilles on the right and Chérisy on the left front. The German trenches were about five hundred yards west of the two villages, but the enemy's defences were difficult to observe for they were dug on the reverse slope of the ridge west of the Sensée Valley.* Indeed the Diary of 151st Brigade Headquarters records that "at no point can our front line see enemy's front line, both being on reverse slopes."

On both sides artillery fire was heavy, the enemy's guns being most active during the mornings.

At 9.30 p.m. on the 18th, after a ten-minutes artillery preparation and to the accompaniment of fire from trench mortars and "fishtails," the enemy rushed a sap running eastwards from Bullfinch Trench (front line). A party of about thirty Germans then appeared all round the sap into which they flung showers of bombs, wounding the whole of the garrison.

The 6th Durham Light Infantry held the front line of the 151st Brigade at this period, and an immediate counter-attack from the front line was organised. Stokes mortar bombs and rifle grenades were fired into the sap, but the counter-attack failed, for the enemy was too strong. A second counter-attack was organised, led by Second-Lieuts. Aubin and Richardson, but on reaching the sap they found that the enemy had gone back to his own trenches, leaving three dead behind him.

This small affair was the first incident after the 50th Division returned to the line. The weather was now warm and sunny and ideal for raids and patrol work; there was, therefore, considerable activity on both sides.

The 50th Divisional Artillery had once more come under their own command, but the C.R.A. also had under him a brigade of guns of the 33rd and 56th Divisions, and all the artillery of the 18th Division.

On the 20th the installation of Livens gas projectors began, the 151st Brigade furnishing large carrying parties to bring up the cylinders. It was obvious that something was afoot, and later the 150th Brigade was informed that they were to advance their right.

Operation orders were issued on the 22nd of June. The front line of the Brigade was very irregular, consisting of many saps.

---

*The 33rd Division was on the right and the 56th on the left of the 50th.

The German front line, however (Fontaine and York Trenches) was continuous and well dug and wired. About half-way in the enemy's line there was a trench (Wood Trench) which ran in a north-westerly direction to the 150th Brigade front line, most of which was also occupied by the enemy. This was the trench the Brigade was ordered to capture and consolidate, also the southern portions of Fontaine Trench opposite Fontaine Wood. It was certain, however, that the enemy would put up a stout fight and would not relinquish hold easily.

As one portion of the German line to be attacked ran from south-west to north-east, and the other from south-east to north-west, there were to be two simultaneous and converging attacks, that on the right by the 5th Green Howards to be known as Attack "A," and that by the 5th Durham Light Infantry, on the left, known as Attack "B." The 4th East Yorkshires were to place two companies at the disposal of each assaulting battalion on receipt of orders from Brigade Headquarters. The 4th Green Howards were to be in reserve. One company of the 7th Durham Light Infantry (Pioneers) was to assemble in Swift Trench (which ran north-east from Wood Trench) and at zero hour was to open Wood Trench from the eastern end of that portion occupied by the 150th Brigade to its junction with Fontaine Trench.

Both the Green Howards and the Durhams were to assault the enemy's trench with two companies each of two platoons, each platoon fifty-two strong. Major A. L. Raimes commanded the Durhams, and Second-Lieut. E. G. Stewart-Corry the Green Howards.

Zero hour was to be 12.30 a.m., 26th of June.

By 11 p.m. on the 25th, the 5th Green Howards were assembled astride the lower end of York Trench, the 5th Durham Light Infantry in a new trench which had been dug and camouflaged between Wood Trench and Rotten Row, just in front of the posts.

The Green Howards' account of this small operation is brief but sufficient: "At 12.30 a.m., in conjunction with the 5th Durham Light Infantry on the left, the Battalion attacked the German position north-west of Fontaine. Objectives were Rotten Row and the cross roads at U.1.d.7.9 (immediately north-west of Fontaine). Attack was carried out by 'A' Company (under Second-Lieut. E. G. S. Corry) with 'D' Company in support. 'C' Company was in reserve in Shaft

Trench. The objective was gained at once and several dug-outs in Rotten Row were successfully bombed. Casualties were slight but included Second-Lieut. Corry who was missing after the first few minutes of the attack.* The Company then proceeded to dig in, using an old German trench along the western side of Rotten Row, but the attack had moved too much to the left and the cross-roads were included in the objective gained. When daylight came the Company was completely isolated from the supports who had moved up to the assembly trench, and at 5 a.m. the Germans attempted to counter-attack from the direction of the River Road. The counter-attack was dispersed by machine-gun fire and bombs, and the company maintained its position all day, being relieved at night by a company of the 4th East Yorkshire Regiment. Captures during the operations—four prisoners, one machine-gun. Casualties—four killed, eleven wounded, one (officer) missing."

The 5th Durham Light Infantry do not give a very intelligible report, but the following is apparently what happened: "A" and "B" Companies advanced under Major Raimes and captured all their objectives but a small portion on the left. A large section of the German trench was consolidated and a strong point established near Rotten Row. The Durhams suffered only about ten casualties.

The Germans counter-attacked heavily in the morning but were beaten off two or three times. The Durhams handed over the new line to the 4th Green Howards and 4th East Yorkshires at night. The Battalion captured twenty-seven prisoners and a machine-gun, and lost, all told, twenty-two men killed or died of wounds.

On the 27th the Germans turned their artillery on to the newly-captured line and completely flattened out Fontaine Trench.

The net result (after the loss of the débris known as Fontaine Trench) was a line of shell holes just west of the old trench.

The 1/4th East Yorkshires, who had taken over the line at dusk on the 26th, lost during the following day four officers and 101 other ranks, killed, wounded and missing.

It had been decided to project gas into Fontaine-lez-Croisilles at about 2 a.m. on the night of the 27th–28th, and for this

---

*Afterwards reported killed.

purpose large carrying parties of the 149th Brigade were employed in carrying up the drums. The last of these parties, however, was heavily shelled and one of the gas drums received a direct hit, with the result that one officer was killed, and about thirty other ranks gassed.

At about midnight (28th) the enemy attempted to raid a sap in the 149th Brigade area (left), but were driven off in disorder; a German officer was killed and one other rank captured.

On this date the Duke of Connaught visited the 50th Division and General Wilkinson conducted His Royal Highness round the battlefields in the neighbourhood of the Butte de Warlencourt, and the ground over which the Division had fought.

The next three months—July, August and September—were strenuous in the front line. There were no more big attacks on the Arras front after June, but trench warfare was vigorous and the guns of both sides were always more or less active. Constant patrol work, varied now and then by a raid, much work in repairing the defences of the front line or in digging new ones, kept all ranks busy. Activity in the front line was all the more necessary, because of great offensive actions to take place in the Ypres Salient towards the end of July. In that month five raids occurred along the front of the 50th Division, *i.e.*, one by the 151st Brigade, two by the 150th Brigade, and three were made by the enemy; in August the 149th Brigade raided the enemy, and later the enemy raided the 5th Durham Light Infantry. Only one raid (by the 9th Durham Light Infantry on the enemy) took place during September.

The first of these raids took place on the 13th of July when the 9th Durham Light Infantry raided an isolated enemy trench in front of Jackdaw Trench, the left sub-sector. But the Durhams "drew a blank" as the trench was unoccupied. Six days later the enemy, after an intense bombardment, attempted to raid the 6th Durham Light Infantry. At six places the Divisional front was raided, but everywhere the attackers were stopped by wire and Lewis-gun fire. Only one German entered the trench and he was immediately shot dead. This was a big raid, the enemy's forces being estimated at the strength of six platoons. The Division had eighty casualties from shell fire. The prompt action of the Durhams in repelling this raid drew congratulations from General Sir T. D'O. Snow, the Corps Commander. Three days later the enemy attempted to raid a post held by the 4th Northumberland Fusiliers. Hand-to-hand fighting took place, but with the exception of leaving several dead behind, the Germans obtained no advantage.

On the night of the 25th the 4th Green Howards (one officer and fifteen other ranks) attempted to cut out an enemy post. The post was found surrounded by no less than five rows of barbed concertina wire, and no gap could be found. The raiders then climbed the wire and got into the enemy's trenches, but found them deserted. Finally, the Green Howards were fired on by machine-guns and suffered a few casualties.

At 3.45 a.m. on the 27th a small party of Germans, from ten to fourteen in number, attempted to raid a post on the 149th Brigade front, but they were discovered crawling towards it and rifle fire soon drove them back, one *unter-offizier* being killed.

That night the 5th Durhams attempted a raid. The raiders numbered two officers and twenty other ranks. They advanced in two waves for about one hundred yards without seeing signs of the enemy. Then suddenly, after advancing a few more yards, a volley of some twenty stick-bombs met the raiders, and put the leading seven men, including one officer, out of action. The party then withdrew carrying all their wounded.

The next raid took place on the 3rd of August when two officers and thirty-six other ranks of the 6th Northumberland Fusiliers left the trenches to raid some gun pits, but as the latter had been evacuated by the enemy, the attempt was without result. The following night one officer and twenty-three other ranks of the 5th Northumberland Fusiliers set out to raid an enemy sap, but lost direction and finally had to retire.

On the 10th of August the enemy raided a listening post held by five men of the 150th Brigade—three were wounded and two were missing.

Two abortive raids were carried out by the 151st Brigade during August—one on the 8th by the 5th Border Regiment, and the other on the 11th by the 6th Durham Light Infantry.

But by far the most important raids were two which took place on the night of the 15th–16th of September, as part of a very successful "minor operation" carried out by the 151st Brigade on the enemy's trenches west of Chérisy. The operation took place in two phases: first a raid at 4 p.m. by three companies of the 9th Durham Light Infantry and, finally, a gas attack with projection at 4 a.m. on the 16th.

The 9th Durhams' account of this raid is as follows: "Quiet morning. At 4 p.m. heavy creeping barrage came down and 'A,' 'B' and 'C' Companies raided the German front and support line in front of Chérisy. 'A' was left, 'C' centre, and 'B' right company. Flank parties each of six other ranks under Second-Lieut. A. Hall and Second-Lieut. D. Inham, covered the flank. Raid a complete surprise to enemy. About seventy Germans were killed and twenty-five prisoners brought back; eleven dug-outs were bombed* and one machine-gun brought back. Raiders remained in enemy trenches for half-an-hour before returning. A hostile counter-attack was repulsed. Raid a great success. Congratulations from all sides."

But that success had to be paid for and rather dearly too, for Second-Lieut. Hall and seven other ranks had been killed, two officers and ten other ranks wounded and evacuated to hospital, and three officers and eight other ranks wounded but "at duty."

Shortly after the retirement to their own lines the raiders were relieved and moved back to the Brigade Reserve Camp.

The second raid began according to scheduled time (7.40 p.m.), "C" Company of the 8th Durham Light Infantry attacking in four waves and proceeding to their objective behind an equally effective barrage. Very few Germans were found in the trenches, but these (numbering about twelve) were killed. Three prisoners were taken, but two were killed by the enemy's barrage as they were being brought back. Two machine-guns were captured. The raiders withdrew at 8 p.m.

Finally, at 4.4 a.m., 552 gas drums were successfully projected into the enemy's lines and ten minutes later the 18-pounders opened intense fire for ten minutes; the 4.5-in. howitzers then took a hand and poured lethal shell on to Sun and Moon Quarries.

Altogether the "minor operation" was a great success.

The 9th Durham Light Infantry again raided the enemy on the 27th of September, when at 10.15 p.m. Second-Lieut. Gibson and twenty-one other ranks of "D" Company crossed No Man's Land and, by means of mats thrown across the enemy's wire, entered his trench, killed six men and brought back one wounded prisoner—all at the small cost of one man

---
*By the Divisional R.E.

slightly wounded. On the 29th the Battalion was relieved by the 4th Northumberland Fusiliers and returned to Durham Lines.

This is the final incident of outstanding importance during the month of September.

The final entry in the General Staff Diary of the 50th Division for September gives some idea, though brief, of what was happening along the Divisional front:

"Sunday, September 30th, 1917: Dispositions unchanged. Our artillery directed harassing fire on Hill Top Work, Communication Trench O.21.C.6.8, and numerous tracks. Several concentrations were fired on Neva and Otter Lines in reply to *minnenwerfer* fire. The enemy's artillery was more active than usual. The front line of the right brigade, Shikar Avenue, Kestrel Avenue, Avenue Trench, Wancourt and area O.25 were shelled during the day. Hostile *minnenwerfer* were active, firing on Mallard Reserve and the front line in O.26.C and O.31. b. Much work done in repairing our line and revetting. Weather cold and misty early, but hot and clear later. Wind south-east."

A bald enough statement, for death and destruction were always present, and yet it was not possible to record the hundred-and-one incidents which took place day after day, night after night; the gamble between life and death was incessant.* But the mere mention of dates and names of trenches or areas will be sufficient to raise once again in the minds of those who were there, visions of gallant deeds, of happenings long forgotten, of the immortal things of those months of trench warfare in front of Chérisy and Fontaine.

October began with the 149th Brigade in the front line on the right, the 150th on the left, and the 151st in Divisional Reserve. With the exception of the 1st the enemy's artillery was not active and life in the line was comparatively quiet: a good thing for the Division, for on the 4th the relief of the 50th Division by the 51st began, the 151st Brigade in reserve marching to Gomiecourt, while the 149th Brigade, having been relieved from the front line, took over the reserve area. On the 5th the 149th Brigade marched to Courcelles and the 150th came out of the front line into the reserve area. At 10 a.m. on

---

*The casualty list of the 50th Division for September shows 4 officers killed and 22 wounded, 38 other ranks killed, 271 wounded and 2 missing.

the 6th the G.O.C., 50th Division, handed over command of the sector to the G.O.C., 51st Division, the 150th Brigade marching to Achiet-le-Petit where Divisional Headquarters had been opened.

The weather had changed and in rain and strong winds training was begun, but it was not for long, for on the 16th the Division began to entrain for the Zeggers Cappel area.

Several days were then taken up in various moves, but on the 22nd of October, the Division was disposed as follows: Divisional Headquarters—Proven No. 1 area; 151st Brigade Group—Corps Staging Area No. 1. On that day, however, orders were issued to all units of the 50th Division that on the 23rd the Division was to relieve a portion of the 34th Division in the front line; the 149th Brigade was to take over the trenches, the 150th was to move up in support, to between Elverdinghe and the Ypres Canal, and the 151st Brigade was to remain at Corps Staging Area No. 1.

In accordance with orders the relief began on the 23rd, and by the 25th the 149th Brigade held the front line with the 150th Brigade in support.

The General Staff Diary for the 25th ends with the following words: "The 149th Infantry Brigade will attack the German positions to-morrow 26th October at 5.40 a.m. in accordance with Operation Order No. 133."

The 50th Division was about to take part in the last of the Battles of Ypres, 1917, known as the Second Battle of Passchendaele.

CHAPTER IX

THE BATTLES OF YPRES, 1917

THE SECOND BATTLE OF PASSCHENDAELE:

24TH OCTOBER–10TH NOVEMBER

TO all those who took part in the operations east of Ypres during the autumn and early winter of 1917, the word Passchendaele has an evil sound: it conjures up visions of seas of mud, of incredible conditions beyond adequate description, of almost superhuman efforts of infantry and artillery to "carry on" despite the desperate situations in which they often found themselves; and of courage, tenacity and a cheerfulness (wonderful to see) inconceivable to those who were not there. For the latter stages of the battle were almost as great a struggle against the elements as against the enemy.

Even the German Chief of the Imperial Staff* said of Passchendaele: "Enormous masses of ammunition, such as the human mind had never imagined before the War, were hurled upon the bodies of men who passed a miserable existence scattered about in mud-filled shell holes. The horror of the shell-hole area of Verdun was surpassed. It was no longer life at all. It was mere unspeakable suffering. And through this world of mud the attackers dragged themselves slowly but steadily, and in dense masses. Caught in the advanced zone by our hail of fire they often collapsed and the lonely man in the shell hole breathed again. Then the mass came on again. Rifle and machine-gun jammed with the mud. Man fought against man, and only too often the man was successful."

For "the man" read "British": and this admission by General Ludendorff is a tribute to the unspeakable suffering and heroism of our troops.

The official records, concerned only with presenting the official point of view, contain little or nothing of the agonies through which all were passing; and only from private diaries is it possible to glean the true nature of the fighting and conditions under which the gigantic struggle was continued, and

---

*General Ludendorff in *My War Memories*, 1914-1918.

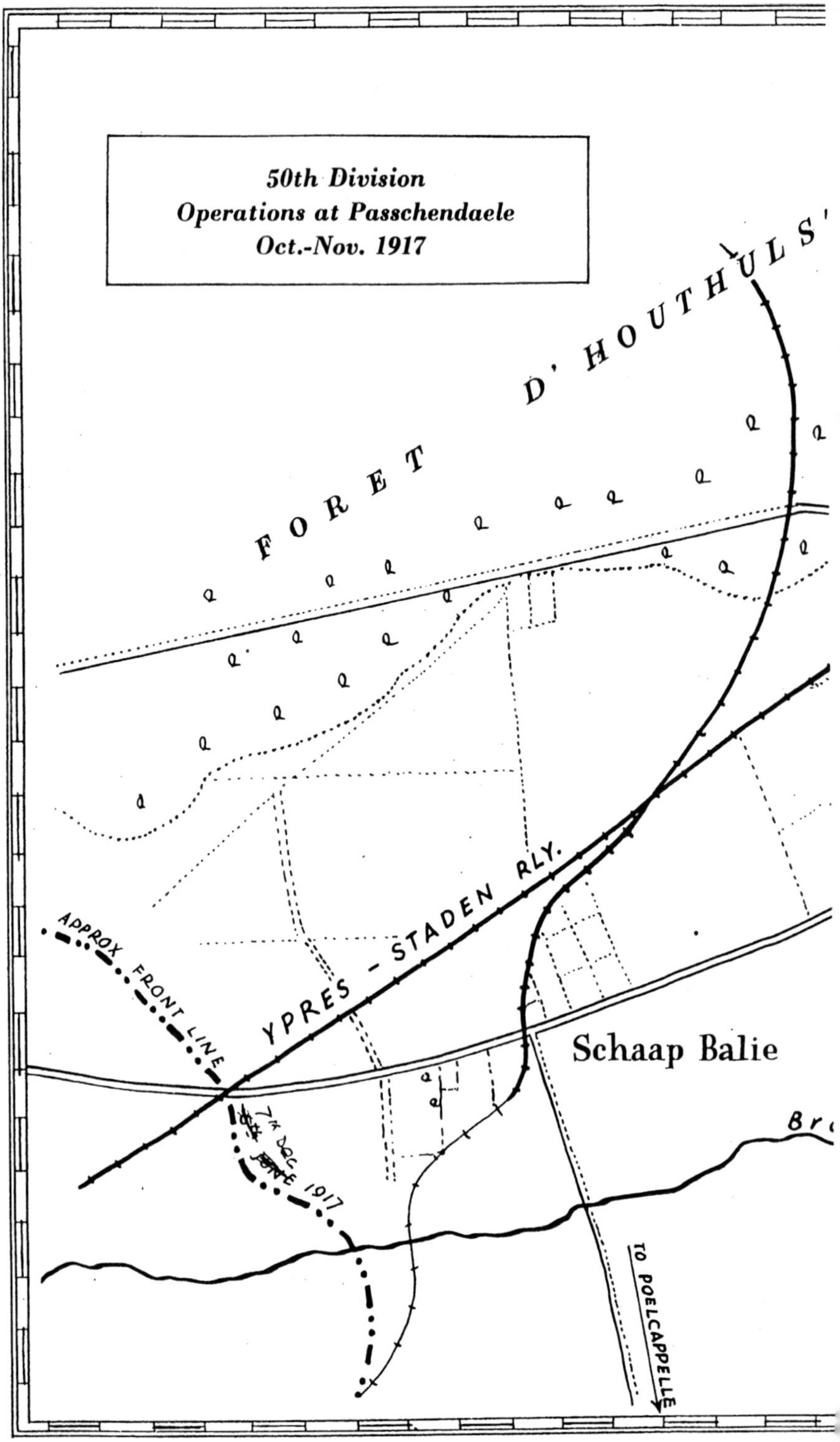

50th Division
Operations at Passchendaele
Oct.-Nov. 1917

Vijfwegen

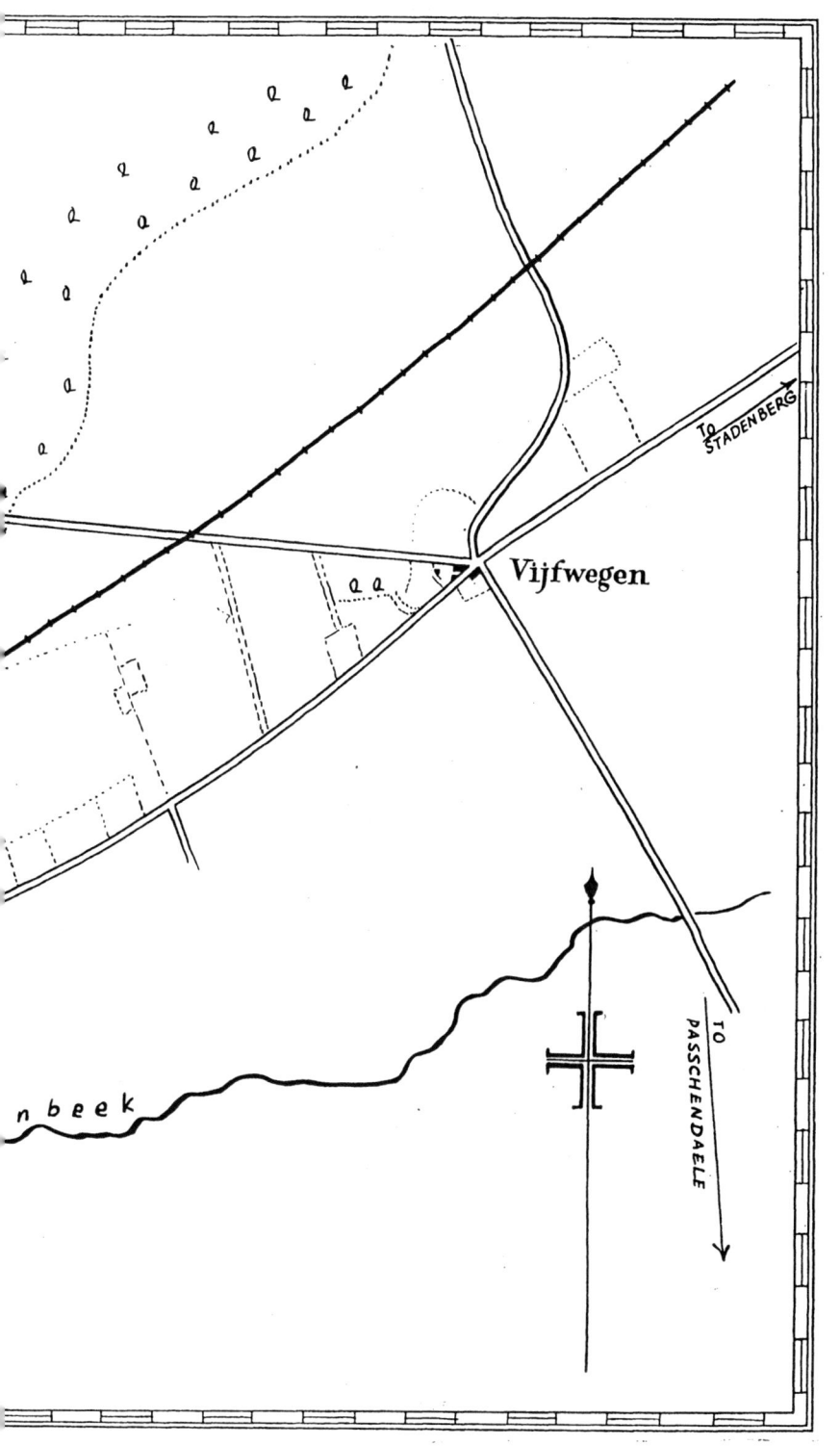

TO STADENBERG

TO PASSCHENDAELE

n beek

facing p. 238

the almost piecemeal advance across seas of mud, when the gain of a few hundred yards was a splendid achievement, though the cost was heavy indeed.

At the period when this story begins, *i.e.*, towards the end of October, the whole Salient was a dreary, desolate area, pock-marked with countless shell holes (those in the forward area being inhabited by small garrisons who constituted the "front line"), lines of water-logged, battered shell-torn trenches, evil-smelling and rat-infested cellars beneath a rubble of bricks, which once marked the dwelling place of farmer or villager in pre-war days, and burrowed holes in the sodden earth, dignified by the name of dug-outs. Thick, clinging mud covered duck-board tracks and the few remaining roads to the front line; to slip from the former (a common experience) was to be engulfed in a shell hole feet deep in stinking water which often hid the poor remains of man and beast. Away from the trenches and "roads" the Salient presented an almost endless conglomeration of shell holes, stretches of water and morass; a patch of dry ground was a rarity. And this dismal state of the ground extended almost for miles beyond the front line, back west of Ypres and the Yser Canal, to where the guns were in action, "camouflaged" as much as possible, but always under a hail of shell of all calibre which the enemy's artillery poured upon the Salient, covering almost every yard so that none were safe, even miles behind the front line. And *our* guns were just as persistent (even more so, for we were attacking) in searching out every hole and corner of the desolate area over which were scattered the enemy's troops, eking out an existence not less precarious and vile than that under which we were living.

The 50th Division, it is true, entered late into the operations, but early into the full horrors of the battlefield, for by the end of October, anything more terrible than conditions in the front line and the ground over which the 149th Infantry Brigade attacked, cannot be imagined, while the Divisional Artillery, longer (as usual) in the line than any unit of the Division, faced conditions which appalled even the stoutest-hearted gunner.

"Fifty square miles of slime and filth from which every shell that burst threw up ghastly relics, and raised stenches too abominable to describe; and over all, and dominating all, a never-ceasing ear-shattering artillery fire and the sickly reek of the deadly mustard gas. Such was the inferno into which, after a long journey by train and road, the Colonel led the four

Battery Commanders* in the early morning of the 23rd of October, 1917."

The line taken over from the 34th Division by the 50th Division lay south of the Houthulst Forest and astride the Ypres–Staden Railway, which ran from north-east to south-west through the sector occupied by the centre Battalion (5th Northumberland Fusiliers) of the 149th Brigade. Just in front of the 5th Northumberlands' line there were forked roads, one of which crossed the railway: this point was known as Tourenne Crossing. From the latter the Brigade portion of the front line ran in a south-easterly direction for about five hundred yards; the line on the northern side of the railway curved with a slight bulge inwards east of Aden House to a point about four hundred yards east of Colombo House; the latter portion of the line was about 900–1,000 yards in length. The left and centre of the sector were on the outskirts of the Forest, though by this time only blackened stumps of trees remained. On the extreme right of the 149th Brigade, just within its area, a small stream ran in a north-easterly to south-westerly direction, named the Stadendrevebeke.

When the Brigade relieved the 34th Division the 4th Northumberland Fusiliers held trenches on the right sub-sector, the 5th Northumberland Fusiliers the centre, and the 7th Northumberland Fusiliers the left; the 6th Northumberland Fusiliers were in support and about Pascal Farm.

The relief on the night of the 24th–25th of October was carried out without serious interference, though difficulties beset the relieving battalions. Guides provided for the 4th Northumberland Fusiliers did not know the ground and were, therefore, useless, but despite this the Battalion (less a few men who were stuck in the mud and lost themselves) found its way to the front line. The 7th Northumberland Fusiliers, however, during the latter part of the relief were caught in a hostile barrage, Captain R. A. Brown and six other ranks being killed, and thirty-two other ranks wounded.

Operation orders for the attack had been issued during the evening of the 24th, and are well summarised in the Diary of 149th Brigade Headquarters:

"The XIV Corps" (to which the 50th Division belonged) "in conjunction with the XVIII Corps, on the right, and the

---

*Of the 250th (1st) Northumbrian Brigade, R.F.A. (T.F.)

BATTLE OF PASSCHENDAELE.
General view of battlefield, showing derelict 6-inch 26-cwt. howitzer. Passchendaele Ridge, October 1917.

(Imperial War Museum Photographs, Copyright Reserved)

First French Army on the left, will renew the attack on the 26th of October, 1917. The 50th Division will attack with the 57th Division on its right, and the 35th Division on its left. The attack on the 50th Divisional front will be carried out by the 149th Infantry Brigade with three Battalions, the 4th Northumberland Fusiliers on the right, the 5th Northumberland Fusiliers in the centre, and the 7th Northumberland Fusiliers on the left, the 6th Northumberland Fusiliers being in Brigade Reserve and the 4th Green Howards from the 150th Infantry Brigade being placed at the disposal of the Brigade in case of emergency."

The Brigade was to attack in a north-easterly direction between the southern borders of the Houthulst Forest and the Broembeek. The principal objective included "Hill 23," Colbert Cross Roads, and a ground for huts some seven hundred yards south-west of Schaap Ballie.

The Brigade Diary then has the following note: "Aeroplane photographs were unfortunately not very clear, but they revealed an area that was capable of obstinate defence, and one that might be rendered impassable by heavy rain. The chief obstacles being a double row of concrete huts or 'pill boxes' and ground that was already dangerously full of water holes."

These "pill boxes" were new to the 50th Division. They are thus described in the official despatches, which also give the reason these field forts were used by the enemy:

"The difficulty of making deep mined dug-outs in soil where water lay within a few feet of the surface of the ground had compelled the enemy to construct in the ruins of farms, and in other suitable localities, a number of strong points or 'pill boxes,' built of reinforced concrete. These field forts, distributed in depth all along the front of our advance, offered a serious obstacle to progress. They were heavily armed with machine-guns and manned by men determined to hold on at all costs."

Our ingenious enemy, indeed, scored heavily in introducing this new method of defence, for he was able to shoot down our men, floundering in mud and water as they advanced to the attack, without being exposed himself to our fire. For only "heavy" shells could reduce them by direct hits, and the Bosche had carefully concealed his "pill boxes" so that to locate them from a distance was a difficult matter.

Other points in operation orders were: each battalion was to attack on a three-company frontage,* each company on platoon fronts, the fourth company being in battalion reserve. Platoons were to "leap-frog"† one another, special parties being told off to deal with each point or locality known to be occupied by the enemy. These points, or their neighbourhood, were to be prepared immediately for defence and garrisoned by the troops who had captured them; when the final objective had been gained organisation in depth for defence was to be completed.

The last point was very important as it was expected that the enemy would counter-attack rapidly from the direction of Vijfwegen along the line of the Schaap Ballie road and the Staden Railway.

In order to assist in consolidation the 149th Machine-Gun Company was to detail two guns and teams to each of the three attacking battalions.

The 149th Trench Mortar Battery was to allot two mortars to each attacking battalion. These mortars were to be in position to fire on any known strong point at zero hour and cover the advance of the infantry.

There were to be five barrages: (*a*) a creeping barrage, (*b*) standing barrage, (*c*) a back barrage of 6-in. howitzers and 60-pounders, (*d*) a distant barrage of heavy howitzers and 60-pounders, and (*e*) finally a machine-gun barrage.

One officer, writing subsequently of these barrages, stated that it seemed as if the British and Germans had concentrated all their artillery in the Ypres Salient, so violent was the shell fire.

The 446th Field Company, R.E., was to be at the call of the G.O.C., 149th Brigade, for any urgent work required, but though the Pioneers do not figure in orders, it may be assumed that they were busy not far from the front line.

Zero hour for the attack was fixed for 5.40 a.m.

The 25th of October was spent in completing preparations for the attack, and Brigade Headquarters established a report centre at Pascal Farm, where also were the Regimental Aid Posts.

---

*This formation was subsequently changed by the 4th Northumberland Fusiliers who found that, owing to the swampy state of the ground on their right, there was only sufficient room for a one-company frontage.

†This "leap-frog" system of advance, *i.e.*, platoons passing through each other to further objectives, had been practised while out of the line, and was new to the Division.

SHELLED GROUND OVER WHICH TROOPS WENT IN THE PASSCHENDAELE ATTACK.
February 1918.

(*Imperial War Museum Photographs, Copyright Reserved*)

Facing page 242

Between 7 and 9 p.m. companies began to move forward to their assembly positions, *i.e.*, shell holes where they dug themselves in. Hot food was brought up to the line by pack animals, the food containers being packed tightly with hay.

At 4.5 a.m. on the 26th the 4th Northumberland Fusiliers reported assembly complete.

The 5th Northumberland Fusiliers reported they were formed up at 11 p.m. when they were served out with rations and hot tea, carried up by the 6th and 9th Durham Light Infantry.

The 7th Northumberland Fusiliers reported "all ready" at 5 a.m.

It is interesting to note what the C.O. of the 4th Northumberland Fusiliers reported of the conditions on his front when he asked permission to alter the formation of his Battalion, for his report gives first-hand evidence of the difficult nature of the attack:

"From reports received from 11th Suffolks," says the C.O., "the right of my Battalion front is a swamp. Even if it is possible to assemble the right company, I do not consider they would be able to advance, *but would have to be dug out*. I propose with your permission to attack with two companies" (subsequently changed to one company) "only in the front line, one in support, and to keep the fourth company in reserve in Tranquille House area. Conditions on rest of the front are such that if a man steps off a firm piece of ground into the slightest hollow he has to be dug out. There are very few firm pieces of ground away from the railway and roads."

Heavy rain began to fall again at 3 a.m. and the "very few firm pieces of ground" became even less in number; the water, trickling at first down the muddy sides of shell holes, soon became small streams, filling the occupants of the shell holes with gloomy prospects of success in the attack; pools of water widened almost to small lakes. Even in the darkness it was possible to discern stretches of water out in No Man's Land across which the attackers would have to pass. And when the artillery opened fire an hour before zero, with a preparatory bombardment of great intensity, the flashes from the guns, the fitful glare of Very lights and the burst from the enemy's shells disclosed an ominous picture to the troops as they crowded in their wretched positions—benumbed and wet through—with only the fire of their indomitable pluck and courage in endurance to keep their souls alive until zero hour.

Who imagined that the attack could be successful? Only the Higher Command! The Division had received orders to attack and the attack would be carried out; but not one of those gallant fellows, who watched for the grey dawn to appear, ever imagined that, with the Bosche safely ensconced in his numerous "pill boxes", ready with rifle and machine-gun to shoot down the attackers as they floundered through mud and water almost at snail's pace, they could successfully hold, even if they captured, their objectives, because their numbers would be so thinned out in the attack that at the best the line would be very weakly held. Nevertheless, there was a sporting chance if, in the first place, the guns did their work well, that Jerry would "take a knock"; and it was just that "sporting chance," small though it was, which so often turned the probability of failure into success. With all the odds against them, therefore, the three attacking battalions of the 149th Brigade awaited zero hour.

Punctually, at 5.40 a.m. the creeping barrage fell. It was to move forward at the rate of one hundred yards in eight minutes. Had the "going" been good the slow "creep" would hardly have restrained the troops, who lay close up under the barrage waiting for the first "lift"; so close, indeed, that several casualties were suffered. But at the first "lift" of the guns the attackers rose to their feet and advanced. The rain had, however, done its deadly work, for all the gallant fellows could do was to drag themselves along through the thick clinging mud and water at a much slower pace than the barrage which soon got ahead. Then from "pill box" and shell hole a murderous fire was poured upon them. Many fell dead; some of the wounded fell into the gaping holes of water and were drowned; fortunate were those who escaped. But on went the survivors.

The story of that very gallant attack is thus told in the diaries of the three attacking battalions:

4th Northumberland Fusiliers: "The Battalion moved forward to the attack . . . in good order and were all clear before the enemy's barrage was put down. Barrage ("ours") consisted entirely of shrapnel which was quite useless against lines of concrete huts, which were our first objective. In addition to this, rain fell heavily and the conditions of mud and water were perfectly appalling. Our attack was held up about eighty yards west of the line of huts, and machine-gun fire and sniping were so severe that movement of any kind was quite impossible."

The 4th Battalion finally consolidated on the original line held before the attack. The advance had been made very gallantly but the odds were too heavy. The Battalion Runners and the Signalling Officer and his men did splendid work.

The 5th Northumberland Fusiliers report their attack in time-table form:

"5.40 a.m. Barrage commenced. Companies go over well. Enemy barrage on road U.12.b.2.9 to U.12.d.9.1 within three minutes of zero hour. 'A' Company in V.7.a.5.8 heavily shelled. 7.10 a.m. Report from wounded that all companies have taken their first objective. 7.40 a.m. Report from wounded that 'B' Company, on the left, are on Hill 23, and being heavily fired on by machine-guns from direction of wood. 9 a.m. Report that 'C' Company are held up by machine-gun fire from huts V.1.d.1.6. 11.30 a.m. One platoon of 6th Northumberland Fusiliers moved forward and occupied line Aden House–Tourenne Crossing with remains of 'A' Company. 2.15 p.m. Lieut. Lewis and remains of 'C' Company retire to Turenne Crossing and get in touch with 'A' Company. 4.15 p.m. Remains of Battalion back on original line."

The wounded gave the following information:

" 'B' Company (left Company) advanced well from assembly point, taking first objective easily, until they reached the road in V.1.c.5.3. which was found wired between the trees. When the first and second waves reached this and attempted to cut the wire to reach enemy trench situated about V.1.C., which was full of enemy, they were enfiladed by machine-guns firing from V.1.b.9.0 and practically wiped out. The other waves were unable to advance on account of intense machine-gun fire. 'C' Company and 4th Northumberland Fusiliers, on their right, advanced as far as huts in V.1.d but were unable to advance further on account of machine-gun fire. 'D' Company having taken first objective, advanced under heavy fire. No further news can be obtained of this Company."

The 7th Northumberland Fusiliers record their part in that terrible attack in the following words:

"Troops advanced and enemy machine-guns immediately opened fire and enemy barrage came down at zero plus one minute on line 5 Chemins, Angle Point, Aden House, and raked backwards towards our advancing troops. Enemy observed to be running back. Companies on either flank made progress for some two thousand yards, but 'B' Company, in centre, was immediately held up by heavy machine-gun fire from the front and probably from the left, about one hundred yards from their "jumping-off" line.

" 'B' Company eventually surrounded and passed these concrete huts, but suffered considerable casualties in doing so. One platoon of the reserve company was sent to their help and soon after another platoon to 'A' Company who were held up by machine-gun fire and very accurate sniping from the right flank.

" 'D' Company, on the left, quickly gained their objectives, but were being constantly sniped at and machine-gunned from their front. They, however, managed to hold on to their objective all through the fight.

" 'A' Company, in the meantime, with the help of the platoon from the support company, struggled on under heavy machine-gun fire, suffering heavy casualties. At the road junction in V.1.a.5.1 they encountered a trench strongly held by machine-guns which had been untouched by our barrage. Second-Lieut. Thompson and his platoon put up a great fight for this trench, he himself and most of his platoon being killed in the attempt.

"Second-Lieut. Shaw and his platoon and Second-Lieut. Temperley and platoon pressed on to keep in touch with the company of 5th Northumberland Fusiliers on the right, suffering such heavy casualties that another platoon of 'C' Company was despatched to their aid. Second-Lieut. Shaw was killed and Second-Lieut. Temperley wounded, but very gallantly led his platoon on, he himself going forward alone, again being wounded whilst doing so, to light a flare at a position where it could be seen by aircraft. Whilst crossing the German wire to get back to his men Lieut. Temperley was killed by a sniper.

"Second-Lieut. Strong, the Company Commander, was also killed by a sniper when pressing forward to reconnoitre and rally the remainder of his company. All four officers and most of the N.C.O.s of this company were killed, and as the enemy were being reinforced the few men left were compelled to fall back on a line with the centre company which was still held up and suffering considerable casualties; two of their platoon officers—Second-Lieut. Tucker and Second-Lieut. Brown were killed.

"The third platoon of 'C' Company, in support, had lost their officer and had many casualties in going to the help of the right company and could be of little use.

"Owing to very heavy machine-gun and sniping fire, the centre and right companies, being practically without leaders, were unable to hold on to the ground gained and orders were sent out to consolidate as far in front of the tape line as possible—about 150 yards.

"The right flank of the left flank company, being consequently unprotected, it was decided to swing it back into line with the other two companies. The enemy had very soon re-occupied the ground temporarily won by us, but all wounded, as far as it was humanely possible, were brought in. The communication was perfect throughout the whole day with all companies."

The Support Battalion (6th Northumberland Fusiliers) gives but few details of the attack, though one company was sent up to support the 7th Northumberland Fusiliers and a platoon of "A" Company to assist the 5th Northumberland Fusiliers.

The 4th, 5th and 7th Northumberland Fusiliers were relieved at about midnight by the 150th Brigade and, but a skeleton of their former selves, marched back to the Rose Cross Roads (4th and 5th Northumberland Fusiliers) and Marsouin (7th Northumberland Fusiliers) areas.

Roll call revealed appalling casualties in the three battalions: Of the 4th Northumberland Fusiliers, who went into action with a strength of 20 officers and 578 other ranks, 10 officers and 256 other ranks had been killed or wounded, or were missing; the 5th Northumberland Fusiliers lost 12 officers and 439 other ranks; the 7th Northumberland Fusiliers reported the loss of 11 officers and 246 other ranks.

Further casualties from hostile aircraft were suffered by the 5th Northumberland Fusiliers* at Rose Cross Roads and altogether the Diary of 149th Brigade Headquarters puts the losses during the 26th–27th October at 38 officers and 1,080 other ranks.

The commanding officer of one of the attacking battalions, when he knew the extent of his losses, is reported to have said:

---

*The 7th Northumberland Fusiliers in one of these aircraft raids lost Captain R. P. Neville, their Quartermaster, who was killed. He was an old soldier with a wonderful record of service, and a first-class quartermaster. His death was keenly felt by all ranks.

"This has fairly done me," the while tears trickled down his weather-beaten face.

This very gallant attack by the 149th Brigade was foredoomed to failure. No troops in the world could have done more: they advanced with great courage against an almost invisible enemy, but were mown down by machine-gun and rifle fire.

The Divisional Artillery had a terrible time: "The enemy's artillery was very active, especially at night when he deluged us with mustard gas. So intense was this gas that everything one touched was infected with it. Nobody had a voice left after the first few days."

The action of mustard gas was insidious: "We did not at first realize the full danger of this, and just laughed because no one had a voice: but when people began to blister and swell, and two men of my old Battery died horribly from eating bread which had been splashed with this stuff, we got wind up thoroughly. The whole area was tainted: one could touch nothing with safety; even our own doctor, who came to see us, slipped in the mud and was so badly blistered by it that we never saw him again. The gas casualties were bad enough, but oh! the shell casualties were pathetic. I lost many of my greatest friends in the Battery, horribly mutilated in the mud, and towards the end was as near a raving lunatic as possible... Our guns were in the open; the only protection for the gunners the piles of high explosive; and the mud was over everything and tainted with mustard gas."[*]

The 4th and 5th Green Howards of the 150th Brigade, which relieved the 149th Brigade on the night of the 26th–27th October, make no comments on the relief; the 5th Durham Light Infantry were at Pascal Farm in support, and the 1/4th East Yorkshires at Marsouin Farm in Brigade Reserve. On the 30th, however, the latter Battalion moved up to the front line and relieved the 5th Green Howards, having received orders to atttack the enemy at 2 a.m. on the 31st, with the object of gaining a new line which ran in a convex semicircle from Turenne Crossing to Colombo House. Two companies, in the centre, were to advance and establish a line with posts in front along the road some four to five hundred yards north of the line of assembly. The flanking companies were to

---

[*] Colonel Shiel.

(Imperial War Museum Photographs, Copyright Reserved)

THE PASSCHENDAELE SALIENT. HUMP ON HORIZON IS PASSCHENDAELE CHURCH.
Photograph shows waterlogged state of ground with impassable shell holes.

Facing page 248

protect the flanks of the two centre companies. Two companies of the 5th Green Howards were to be in support.

At 2 a.m. on the 31st, under a very heavy barrage, the East Yorkshires advanced, but the centre companies, subjected to violent machine-gun fire, were held up. The flanking companies, however, pushed on gallantly and gained their objective; finally a line, only a hundred yards or so short of the objective, was established and consolidated, the Battalion handing over the line at night to the 6th Durham Light Infantry.

In this attack the East Yorkshires lost one officer and six other ranks killed, two officers and twenty-eight other ranks wounded.

The early days of November, save for shell fire, which periodically was very heavy on both sides, were comparatively quiet, *i.e.*, so far as the 50th Division was concerned, for no more attacks were made on, or by, the enemy.

On the 9th of November, the Division, having been relieved by units of the 17th Division, gradually began to move to the Eperlecques area, and by the 13th the 149th Brigade was established in the Serques area, the 150th Brigade in and about Tournehem, and the 151st Brigade at Houlle.

Training was begun and continued until the 8th of December, on which date the Divisional Athletic Meeting was held. The next day the Division began to move back towards the front line, having been ordered to take over the Passchendaele sector from the 33rd Division.

CHAPTER X

THE WINTER OF 1917–1918

A MONTH had passed since the close of the Second Battle of Passchendaele, but the heavy guns of both sides still pounded with merciless vigour front lines and back areas. The enemy feared another outburst of the battle, while we were uncertain as to whether our opponents might not launch an attack; so, for a time the concentrated artillery of British and Germans shelled each other heavily until, at last, it was obvious that neither side, owing to exhaustion, could continue the attack. Trench warfare then intervened.

By the 13th of December, the 50th Division was back again in the front line, holding a sector which ran just east of (and including) Passchendaele, and south of the ruined village. The 150th Brigade held the front line with two battalions; the other battalions were in support and reserve. The 149th Brigade was in support in Potijze, and the 151st in reserve at Brandhoek, where also Divisional Headquarters were established.

The front line was held by a series of posts: those east of Passchendaele were not so bad, but parts of the line south of the village defy adequate description. Indeed, between the Passchendaele Ridge and Potijze, the state of the ground was so terrible and the signs of battle so horrible as to scar the minds of all who passed that way.

An officer moving up to support positions at Seine (nearly a couple of miles south-west of Passchendaele) speaks thus in his diary of the move forward: "Our first journey into this sector was a strange and eerie experience, though we reached our positions without casualty, and without much shelling. To those officers who had just recently joined us, it must have been an uncanny "breaking in," for they were suddenly transported from conditions of civilization to conditions and environments totally different from any they had ever before seen, or been able to conceive—*conditions where was nothing anywhere to suggest life in any form or civilization in any degree.*

"Passing the White Château on the outskirts of Potijze, we proceeded along the Ypres–Moorslede road until at length we came to a notice-board bearing the one word, 'Frezenberg.' It had a geographical interest only, for not a trace of the village remained. The very ruins were indistinguishable from the rest of the clay. The road along which we passed was in fairly good condition, thanks to the work of various labour units continually employed upon it. It was an important one for, except when the visibility was very good, motor and horse transport took up supplies almost as far as the line of the Ypres–Roulers railway. On either side was black waste. The ground had been so churned up that no green thing remained; everywhere were shell holes, mud and water; wreckage of every description was strewn about. Occasionally we came upon the wrecked vehicles which had fallen a prey to enemy shelling, and had been swept off the road and abandoned. Frequently we came upon sadder sights: the badly-mutilated and rotting bodies of horses and mules—servants of man, whose innocent lives he had taken to further his own ends. Here and there along the route a trench-board track led off from the left-hand side of the road into the mist and obscurity. Occasionally a 'pill box,' which had weathered the storm, loomed into view. The only signs of life in this region of death were weary parties, scarcely recognisable as human beings, slowly making their way down from the line. Our guns, of all calibres, barked viciously on each side of us.

"When we had almost reached the point where the road meets the railway we turned to the left down a plank road, known as the Mule Track. For some distance we followed roughly the line of the railway, and then deviated slightly to the left. We were now proceeding straight for the Passchendaele Ridge though, owing to the mist, we could not see it. Everywhere the scene was grim, black, charred and most unnatural, and the strange appearance of everything was accentuated by heavy black clouds which lowered overhead, and cast a peculiar light over the landscape. The ground was patched here and there with islets of ground mist and the higher ground east of us was quite hidden from view."

After a march of some two or three hours the writer of the above and his men arrived at Seine, the support position. Having seen his men "settled in," he then set out "to investigate the neighbourhood before darkness completely set in." He thus describes the approach to the front line: "In front of us was a slight valley which had at one time been wooded, but which now resembled the rest of the countryside, being nothing more than mud and water with charred and very shattered logs lying about. One or two still stood erect like large daggers pointing to the sky, but most were pounded up with the clay. The valley was almost entirely under water, but we discovered a somewhat precarious trench-board track across it. The ground rose more steeply and here and there we saw one or two 'pill boxes.' To our right was a rising expanse of mud; to our left was lower ground consisting also of mud and much water. There seemed to be an almost entire absence of landmarks in the drab landscape. To find one's way in such a region would be bad enough in daylight; by night—impossible—unless there were special methods of guidance."*

It would be possible to give many first-hand descriptions of the Salient, such as the above, from private diaries, but they would all tell the same tale—death, mud, desolation—conditions which could not be imagined—the foulness, the vileness of war in its most terrible aspects. The one word "Passchendaele" brings back to the minds of those who served in the Salient during the winter of 1917–1918 the most awful memories of an existence scarce human but, thank God, it brings also the remembrance of the British soldier's pluck and endurance—of courage unparalleled in all the wars which the Army fought before 1914–1918.

The Divisional Artillery lived and served their guns also in mud; all units of the Division in fact worked and carried out their various duties in mud; it was mud, mud, mud and little else, though the bedraggled appearance of officers and men sometimes caused merriment.

As already stated the Division was established in the line by the 13th, the 150th Brigade having taken over from the 98th Brigade (33rd Division), the relief being completed shortly before midnight on the 12th. Each infantry brigade did four days in the front line, four in support and four in reserve. The 150th, therefore, handed over to the 149th on the 16th, and the latter Brigade to the 151st on the 20th.

Previously (on the 18th) the 149th Brigade captured four machine-guns, one officer, one N.C.O. and eleven other ranks who had apparently lost their way in No Man's Land; they

---

*From the private diary of Lieut. A. Hodgson, 1/5th Battalion, The Border Regiment.

provided a valuable identification. But this incident and the occasional heavy bursts of artillery fire are the only items of interest in the records. The 149th was the Brigade in the front line on Christmas Day.

None could foresee that the winter of 1917-1918 was to be the last of actual warfare; indeed, some had almost forgotten that there was once a time when war was not. But the optimists were vastly in the majority, and kept up the tired and flagging spirits of those who were war-worn.

The last day of the old year was signalised by a heavy burst of hostile artillery fire at 6 a.m. The front line and back areas as far back as Brigade Headquarters were swept by a hurricane of shell. This lasted for ten minutes, then ceased. The Bosche was suitably replied to, and one of his dumps near Moorslede set on fire. There was some gas shelling during the night.

New Year's Day, 1918, broke fair but cold. The General Staff Diary records that, "No great activity on either side marked the coming of the New Year, the only incident which could be assumed to be in connection with it being the sending up of a large number of coloured lights by the enemy about midnight, 31st–1st. Nothing in the nature of artillery or infantry action resulted."

On the 4th of January, the 33rd Division began to move up to the support area (Hamburg and Seine) and the following night took over the front line from the 151st Brigade. The relief of the 50th Division was completed on the 6th and Headquarters opened at 10 a.m. at Steenvoorde, in which area all units were situated by the morning of the 7th. On the 15th a move was made to Tilques, and on the 19th to the Wizernes area. The 26th of January, however, saw the Division on the move again, back to the front line and three days later the 149th Brigade took over the right of the VIII Corps sector at Passchendaele from the 33rd Division. On the 9th of February, the 50th Division handed over a portion of the front to the 29th Division, and took over a new sector from the 66th Division.

On the 11th of February the reorganisation of the Division took place. Nothing caused more heart-burning in France and Flanders than these reorganisation orders, especially in those divisions in which the spirit of brotherhood was very strong, as it had always been in the 50th Division. The hard necessity which forced Sir Douglas Haig to reduce the number of infantry battalions in a division from twelve to nine* is explained in his despatches and, as he stated, "the fighting efficiency of units was to some extent affected." Reinforcements from home had dropped off. Instead of being sent out to fill the gaps of divisions which had lost heavily during the hard fighting of 1917, they were kept back in England. This necessitated the disbandment of a certain number of divisions in order to make up losses in others. Battalions were disbanded, or transferred to other divisions.

The three unfortunate Battalions to be transferred from the 50th Division were the 7th Northumberland Fusiliers to the 42nd Division, the 9th Durham Light Infantry to the 62nd Division, and the 5th Border Regiment to the 66th Division. These three Battalions had done splendid work for the 50th Division. The 9th Durham Light Infantry had been commanded by that splendid young soldier, Lieut.-Colonel R. B. Bradford, V.C., who became a Brigadier at twenty-five years of age, in command of an infantry brigade of the 62nd Division; they were a first-class fighting unit but were made Pioneers in their new division. The 7th Northumberland Fusiliers and the 5th Border Regiment both had fine records. The 5th Borders were also turned into a Pioneer Battalion.

After the reorganisation the three infantry brigades were formed as follows: 149th—4th, 5th and 6th Northumberland Fusiliers; 150th—4th East Yorkshires, 4th and 5th Green Howards; 151st Brigade—5th, 6th and 8th Durham Light Infantry.

The 149th Brigade was still commanded by Brigadier-General E. P. A. Riddell; the 150th Brigade had a new Brigadier on the 25th of February, *i.e.*, Brigadier-General H. C. Rees taking over from Brigadier-General J. E. Bush, who had commanded the Brigade from just before the Somme Battles of 1916 began; the 151st Brigade was commanded by Brigadier-General C. F. Martin.

Major-General P. S. Wilkinson (G.O.C., 50th Division) went home on leave on the 24th of February, and temporary command of the Division was taken over by Brigadier-General C. Coffin, V.C. As will be stated later, to the very great regret of all ranks, General Wilkinson did not again join the Division. The B.G., R.A., was Brigadier-General A. V. Stockley.

---

*Not counting the Pioneer Battalion.

"Everybody is coming to see us and to say good-bye," records the War History of the 7th Northumberland Fusiliers. "Major-General Wilkinson comes nearly every day: he feels the loss of one of his best battalions keenly. The Brigadier (General E. P. A. Riddell) said good-bye to the Battalion two days ago. He told us that we were leaving when we were at our best."

Both the 7th Northumberland Fusiliers and the 9th Durham Light Infantry moved to their new divisions on the 12th of February, and the 5th Borders on the following day; all had a tremendous "send-off." This reorganisation scheme was a great mistake, though forced upon the Commander-in-Chief for the reasons already given.

On the 20th the relief of the 50th Division by the 33rd Division began again, and by the 23rd all units were located in the Wizernes area, Divisional Headquarters being in the town. None knew it, but the Division had turned its back for ever on the Ypres Salient.

Training was carried out in the Wizernes area until the 7th of March when, orders having arrived to proceed to a new area, everyone began packing up in preparation for the move. Entrainment began on the 8th, and by the 9th the transfer of the Division to the Fifth Army had been completed, the 50th Division being located in the Moreuil area which, however, proved but a halting place, for on the 11th the Division moved by road to Proyart, Divisional Headquarters opening at Harbonnières; the 149th Brigade was at Mézières, the 150th at Guillaucourt and the 151st at Marcelcave. These places were south of the Somme. The 50th Division was now in Army Headquarters Reserve, at twelve hours' notice to move in the event of emergency.

CHAPTER XI

THE GERMAN OFFENSIVE ON THE SOMME, MARCH, 1918

THE new Divisional area lay south of the Somme and west of the Somme Canal, about half-way between the latter and Amiens. On the 12th special training began, and the reconnaissance of areas of probable operations continued, for by this date it was clear that in the near future, the enemy intended launching a great offensive, though the exact date could not be ascertained.

The official despatches state that: "Towards the middle of February, 1918, it became evident that the enemy was preparing for a big offensive on the Western Front."

The balance of man-power in March was with the enemy. The Russian *débacle* had released guns and troops from the Eastern Front and the enemy had, as early as November, 1917, begun to transfer them to the west. By March no less than twenty-eight divisions had been reported by our Intelligence as having arrived from Russia, and a very large number of guns had accompanied them.

On the other hand, the British forces were at a low ebb, both in training and in numbers, for the British Army had practically taken all the heavy fighting of 1917 on its shoulders and, though the casualties had been very great, reinforcements only in negligible numbers had arrived to fill up the depleted ranks. America, though now "in the War," could not get her troops to France in time to meet the German attack, nor had they had sufficient training. The French Army in 1917 had been shaken by mutiny, and our Allies, therefore, were hardly in a position to afford a great deal of assistance; indeed, to add to his difficulties, Sir Douglas Haig had had to take over from the French an additional front of twenty-eight miles, and by the end of January, 1918, when the "taking over" was completed, the British Armies held an active front of some 125 miles. It was too much.

Moreover a vast amount of work had to be done in the construction of the defences, old systems having to be re-modelled and new ones created. The necessity for providing large

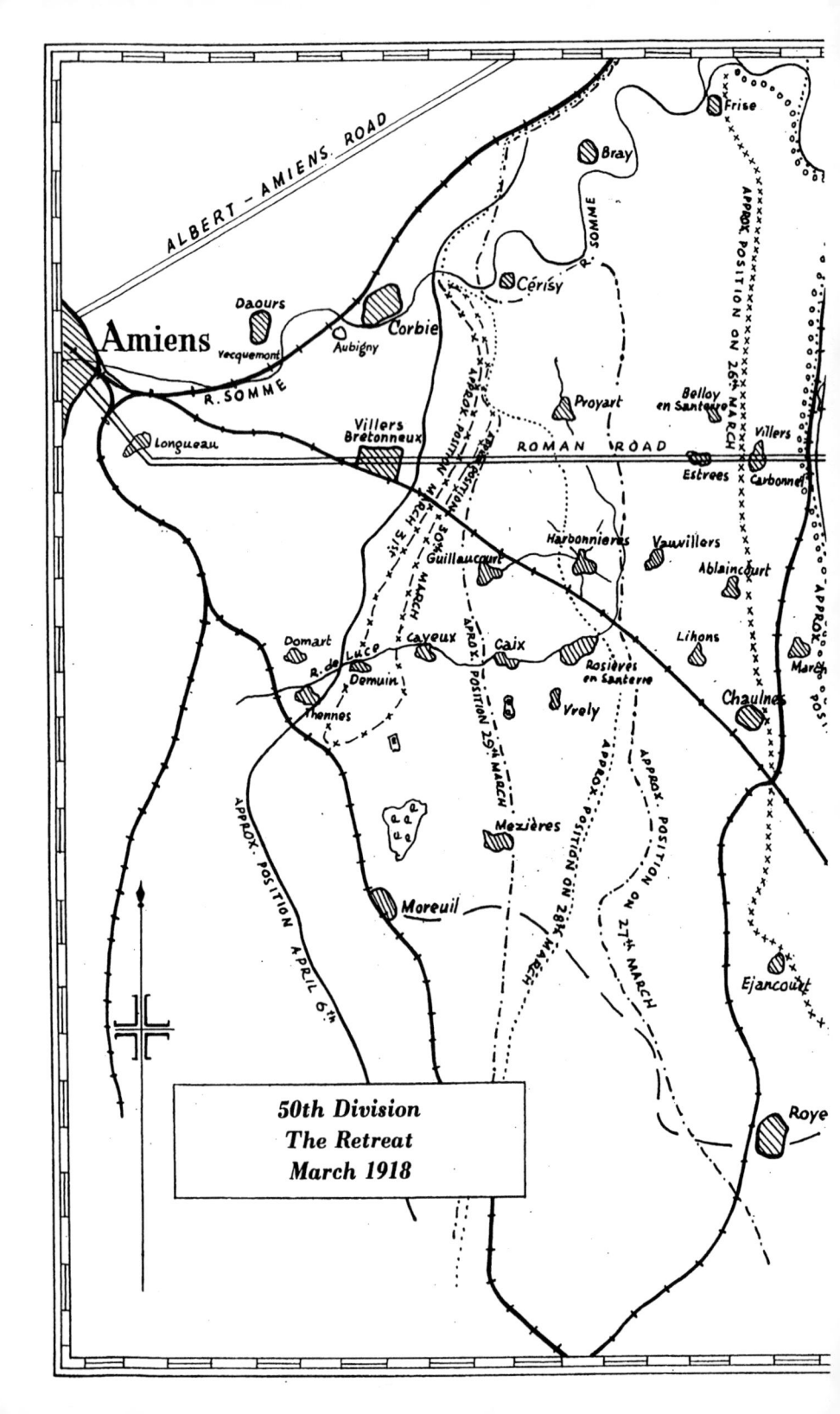

**50th Division
The Retreat
March 1918**

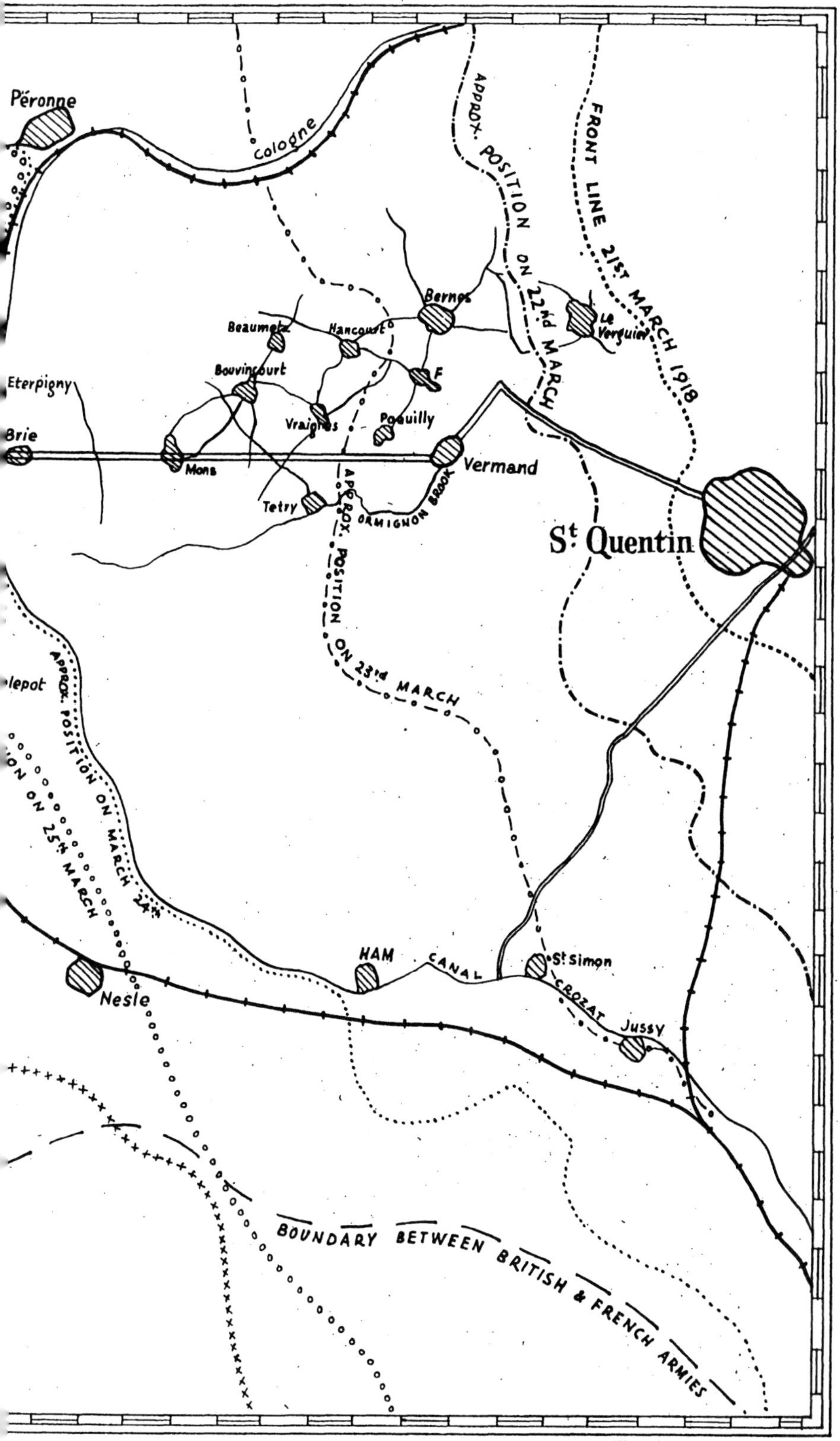

Péronne
Cologne
APPROX. POSITION ON 22nd MARCH
FRONT LINE 21ST MARCH 1918
Bernes
Le Verguier
Beaumetz
Hancourt
Bouvincourt
F
Eterpigny
Vraignes
Poeuilly
Brie
Mons
Vermand
Tetry
OMIGNON BROOK
APPROX. POSITION ON 23rd MARCH
St. Quentin
APPROX. POSITION ON MARCH 24th
25th MARCH
HAM
CANAL
St Simon
CROZAT
Jussy
Nesle
BOUNDARY BETWEEN BRITISH & FRENCH ARMIES

working parties constantly left battalion commanders with few troops for training purposes—a very serious position.

In spite of all these difficulties, however, the British Armies "carried on" and awaited the impending Bosche attack with equanimity and even high spirits, for that was the way of the Army! But soon the 50th Division, tried in many a hard-fought battle, was to undergo further tests of its fine fighting qualities, for the Division was one of only four British divisions* which took part in all three phases of the great German offensive of 1918, *i.e.*, on the Somme, on the Lys, and on the Aisne.

For several days training continued, during which the C.O.s of all units and their company commanders and senior N.C.O.s reconnoitred the forward areas, and the battle zone over which fighting would take place in the event of a retreat being forced upon the Fifth and Third Armies.

None could foresee the enormous number of troops the enemy would launch against us. He had massed for the attack three huge Armies, the Seventeenth, Second, and Eighteenth, totalling in all some seventy-six divisions, of which, state the official despatches: "at least sixty-four German divisions took part in the operations of the first day of the battle."

Against such a huge concentration of troops, aided by an overwhelming majority in artillery of all calibre, Sir Douglas Haig could muster on the first day of the operations only thirty-four divisions, many being under strength and containing a large number of only partially-trained men.

The selected areas for the attack by the three German Armies were: the Second and Eighteenth, the line from and between Villers-Guislain and La Fère, and the Seventeenth from Croisilles to Boursies; the Flésquières Salient, *i.e.*, from opposite Gonnelieu to south of Moeuvres, was to be "pinched off" by the inner flanks of the Second and Seventeenth Armies.

But the position of the Fifth Army area of chief interest to the 50th Division was that which lay between the Cologne River and the Omignon Brook, thence westwards to the Somme Canal at Eterpigny and Brie, the long straight road to Villers-Bretonneux and Amiens, and the country south of it about the River Luce.

On the 15th of March, the Divisional Artillery moved forward,

---
*The others were the 19th, 21st and 25th Divisions.

both the 250th and 251st Brigades, R.F.A., marching to Buire, where they were billeted in Nissen huts. On the same date also the Divisional Engineers and Pioneer Battalion moved up to the XIX Corps area for work in the battle zone.

On the 17th Brigadier-General C. Coffin, V.C., handed over command of the Division to Brigadier-General A. V. Stockley, who thus temporarily ceased to be C.R.A.

On the 18th or 19th of March, two German deserters, taken by the French, gave information concerning the date of the impending attack; it was to take place on the 21st. Both the Fifth and Third British Armies hurried on preparations for meeting the onslaught. Unless Fortune favoured the enemy unduly all ranks were confident that the Bosche would not break through. But the chances of war cannot be foreseen.

The night of the 20th–21st of March was extraordinarily quiet: an uncanny stillness had fallen over the battlefield-to-be, but in the front line, where the troops were ordered to be on the alert for the attack to take place for a certainty on the following day, there were many who treated the order as a joke, the same thing having occurred again and again.

Behind the lines where information concerning the attack was most positive, the same degree of disbelief existed amongst many. "At Mess the previous evening," said the Signalling Officer of the 149th Brigade, "someone had mentioned that the Bosche was expected to attack on the morrow. As we were one of the divisions waiting in reserve to counter-attack this should have been of paramount importance. Actually, no one paid much attention to the statement—we had heard that story so often before."

To the great dismay of the British soldiers dawn broke on the 21st in a dense white fog which covered the whole countryside, blotting out everything but objects a few yards away. Unless the fog lifted, artillery and machine-gun fire would be restricted to registered targets and the guns "blinded" to the massing and advance of the enemy's troops. But that was exactly what happened.

Between 4.30 and 5 a.m. the enemy opened a particularly violent bombardment against practically the whole of the Fifth and Third Army fronts from the Oise to the Scarpe Rivers. Every size of gun was used in this savage hail, trench mortars also joining in. The S.O.S. signals sent up from the front line were unseen owing to the fog, and all that our guns could do was to fire on previously-registered positions. Nor could any assistance be given by our airmen.

As the 50th Division was not in the front line at the time of the enemy's assault, the official despatches may again be quoted as they give an admirable summary of the Bosche advance:

"The hour of the enemy's assault varied in different sectors, but by about 9.45 a.m. a general attack had been launched on a battle front of fifty-four miles between the Oise and the Sensée Rivers. Later in the day, as visibility improved, large numbers of low-flying aeroplanes attacked our troops and batteries.

"Favoured by a thick white fog, which hid from our artillery and machine-gunners the S.O.S. signals sent up by our outpost line, and in numbers which made loss of direction impossible,* the attacking German infantry forced their way into our foremost defensive zone. Until 1 p.m. the fog made it impossible to see more than fifty yards in any direction, and the machine-guns and forward field guns, which had been disposed so as to cover the zone with their fire were robbed almost entirely of their effect. The detachments holding the outpost positions were consequently overwhelmed or surrounded, in many cases before they were able to pass back information concerning the enemy's attack."

From messages received, from the rumbling of guns which sounded like a terrific thunder-storm, though as yet distant, and from those who had come back from the front line and near it, the divisions in reserve knew that at last the great Bosche attack had been launched, though with what result few could tell, as the fog blotted out everything.

As early as 4.30 a.m. the 50th Division had received warning from Fifth Army Headquarters to move at twelve hours' notice. This was confirmed at about 9.30 a.m. But already more urgent orders had been issued to the infantry brigades, the 149th Brigade at Mézières being ordered at 5.30 a.m. to move at three hours' notice, and the 150th Brigade a little later receiving orders to move at four hours' notice. Yet all day long, although everyone waited anxiously, no move was made until evening when the Brigades left billets and marched to Guillaucourt, the Division having been ordered to support the 66th Division (XIX Corps). Some of the battalions had a considerable distance to march before reaching the entraining

---

*It was said that the enemy advanced "shoulder to shoulder."

station (Guillaucourt), the 5th Green Howards, for instance, not entraining until about 11 p.m. The three Brigades moved in the following order, 151st, 150th, 149th.

They had received orders to assemble in the Green Line (or rear zone of defences) which ran from Villevecque to Boully and covering Fléchin, Bernes and Nobescourt Farm.

The march from Brie to the Green Line was a weary business, for already everyone was tired. Thick mist, darkness, heavy traffic on the main road, delayed progress. The men were carrying their packs and, on reaching their bivouacs soon after dawn, were in an exhausted condition. Hot food did not arrive until 8.40 a.m., just as orders were received to man the defences immediately.

By about 8 a.m. on the 22nd the Green Line was occupied throughout its length, the order of Brigades from right to left being 149th, 150th and 151st. This Line was well wired but only from one to two feet in depth.

In the front line the 149th Brigade disposed the 4th Northumberland Fusiliers on the right, the 6th Northumberland Fusiliers on the left and the 5th in reserve in St. Martin. The 149th Machine-Gun Company (less two guns in reserve) were also in the line. Brigade Headquarters were at Tertry. The line occupied by the Brigade ran from the cross-roads one mile south-west of Villevecque to Pœuilly (inclusive).

In the centre the 150th Brigade, holding a line covering Fléchin, Bernes and Nobescourt Farm, had placed the 4th East Yorkshires on the right (Fléchin and Bernes) and the 4th Green Howards on the left; the 5th Green Howards were in reserve about Hancourt where Brigade Headquarters were established at about 6.30 a.m. The left Brigade (151st)* had the 5th Durham Light Infantry on the right, the 8th Durham Light Infantry in the centre and the 6th Durham Light Infantry on the left covering Boully.

The 5th Durham Light Infantry, however, at about 10 a.m. were lent to the 66th Division and were sent forward to take up a position in order to prevent the enemy debouching from Roisel. Later in the morning the 24th and 66th Divisions received orders to retire through the 50th Division, and the 5th Durham Light Infantry returned to the Green Line,

---

*The 151st Brigade Narrative of Operations does not begin until the 24th of March.

resuming its place as right Battalion of the 151st Brigade. It was not an easy business for the Durhams to find their old position, for the constant stream of men, horses, tanks, guns and limbers, all belonging to the divisions retiring through the 50th, made the location of the line difficult. However, all ended well, and companies settled themselves down to await the coming of the enemy, for now the Green Line, so far as the 50th Division was concerned, was the front line.

The general situation on the morning of the 22nd of March, was that the enemy had all along the front of the Fifth Army occupied the forward trenches of the latter; the Flésquières Salient still held, and only a retirement to conform with the movements on both flanks had taken place; on the Third Army Front the enemy had also penetrated the front line, but not to such an extent as in the south.

Heavy fog from dawn to midday had again assisted the enemy by covering his advance, and denying targets to our machine-gunners and artillery; for frequently the appearance of waves of Germans right in front of our men was the first indication they had that the enemy was again advancing, the massing of his troops having been hidden by the mist. Thus aided, the enemy, having pierced parts of the line, was enabled to turn the flanks of battalions who still imagined that their right and left were safely held.

Meanwhile the Divisional Artillery had come into action, and the manner of the entry of at least one battery of the 250th Brigade, R.F.A., into the fight is worthy of special record. "On the morning of the 21st we were roused by a distant cannonade which increased in fury as day grew and which, to our expectant ears, seemed to come nearer and nearer each hour. Nevertheless football went on, and that afternoon we played the final of the Brigade Cup between 'A' Battery and the S.A.A. Section. We had been ordered to stand to at eight o'clock and all was ready."[*]

"At about 4 p.m. with ten minutes to go and no score, the Colonel was summoned to Headquarters. Nine minutes later he returned and said to me, 'Come on, my lad, I want you.' I replied: 'I cannot go, I have money on this.' At the same moment my Battery scored a goal and the whistle went. I collected my five francs and fled after the Colonel."[†]

---

[*]An officer of the Division.   [†]Colonel Shiel.

The game finished, there was then a scramble to limber up the guns, and so urgent were orders that the team of "A" Battery actually went into action in their football "togs."

The 250th Brigade, R.F.A., moved off eastwards through Tincourt towards Hesbécourt and took up position to cover the 66th Division, or all that remained of it. The 251st Brigade, R.F.A., marched via Cartigny and Bouvincourt to Vraignes, and at 2 a.m. on the 22nd went into action east of Pœuilly (C/251), east of Sailor's Wood (D/251), west of Soyécourt (A/251) and west of Sailor's Wood (B/251) covering the zone near Caubières Wood.

On the 22nd the enemy began to advance at about 6 a.m. and the 250th Brigade opened fire on S.O.S. lines, but no observation was possible owing to fog. The 251st Brigade similarly fired bursts on S.O.S. lines from 9 a.m. onwards, but batteries were blinded by the fog.

The action of the three infantry brigades on the 22nd of March is described from right to left, *i.e.*, 149th, 150th, 151st.

The 4th Northumberland Fusiliers were on the extreme right flank of the 50th Division, having the 24th Division on their right. The Northumberlands state that it was 4 p.m.* when the enemy attacked. He came on in eight waves, providing splendid targets for rifle and machine-gun. South of the Omignon Brook he broke through the left of the 24th Division and, a little later (the 149th Brigade Diary puts the time at 5 p.m.) broke also the left of the 4th Northumberland Fusiliers. Thus with both flanks turned, the Northumberlands were forced back to Caulaincourt.

On the left of the 4th, the 6th Northumberland Fusiliers held the enemy, broke up his attack, and even took a number of prisoners, some of whose pockets were full of packets of English cigarettes—so rapid had been his advance. As night fell, the enemy's attack became more determined but the 6th held their ground though, as the night wore on, it became clear that something had gone wrong on the right of the Battalion. At midnight orders were received that, as the enemy was half-a-mile past the right of the Battalion, the latter was to retire at

---

*Battalion, Brigade and Divisional Narratives all differ as to the time the attack began. The first-named place the time as 4 p.m., the brigade at 3 p.m., the division 5.45 p.m.

2 a.m. (23rd) to a new line about two miles in rear. Covered by Lewis guns, this retirement was carried out successfully.

The 5th Northumberland Fusiliers, in reserve, received orders at 12.45 p.m. to send forward two companies to report to front-line battalions: the companies despatched were "C" and "D." The 5th Battalion apparently counter-attacked the enemy, but the only account of this attack is contained in the Diary of the 149th Brigade: "5.15 p.m. 5th Northumberland Fusiliers counter-attacked from St. Martin and drove enemy over the Caulaincourt–Pœuilly road (the 6th Northumberland Fusiliers co-operating) and retook the greater part of Caulaincourt; 5.30 p.m. Enemy again drove us out of Caulaincourt, but the second counter-attack by one company 5th Northumberland Fusiliers partially restored the situation." The Diary then states that the 24th Division had been driven over the Caulaincourt–Beauvois road west of Trefcon, exposing the right of the Brigade. In order to secure the latter, details of Brigade Headquarters and two sections of R.E., being the only available forces, were posted to secure the two bridges east of Tertry and the one south of it, the latter being prepared for demolition. The new line resisted all attacks. The Divisional Artillery had withdrawn about four thousand yards and in such a position were unable to cover the infantry. The 250th Brigade, R.F.A., had moved to positions one thousand yards west of Nobescourt Farm at about 10 a.m., but were hardly settled in before the guns were ordered back to near Cartigny, though the enemy was not near Nobescourt. The Diary of this Artillery Brigade states that Nobescourt Farm was captured by the enemy at about 7 p.m. but only after several attempts.

On the left of the 149th Brigade, the 150th appear to have been attacked at about 6 p.m., the 4th Green Howards being forced to give ground to a position about eight hundred yards west of the Green Line. It was here that their gallant C.O., Lieut.-Colonel Charlton, and his Adjutant, Capt. J. S. Bainbridge, who had gone up to rally the left company of the Battalion, were killed. Companies had lost touch with one another, but fortunately the enemy's attack stopped short, and no further advance was attempted.

Of the 4th East Yorkshires, the right of the 150th Brigade, there is little to record, their Diary summing up the happenings of the 22nd of March in the following brief sentences: "In the Green Line in reserve to 66th Division. At 4 p.m. they retired through us, and we became the front line and had patrols out; we captured seven prisoners."

The 5th Green Howards, in reserve, having dug in on their arrival, sent one company to fill a gap which existed between the left of the 4th Green Howards, and the right of the 151st Brigade.

At nightfall, the position of the Brigade was: the 4th East Yorkshires were holding their original positions in the Green Line, covering Bernes and Fléchin. Although heavily attacked, they had held their ground and had inflicted heavy losses on the enemy. But considerable bodies of hostile troops were reported to be digging in "close up to our wire." The 4th Green Howards, with one company near Bernes, were in touch with the 4th East Yorkshires, but were no longer in the Green Line, having fallen back about eight hundred yards as already described. The 5th Green Howards, in reserve, had sent one company to fill a gap between the 150th and 151st Brigade, otherwise the Battalion had not been disturbed.

The right Battalion (5th Durham Light Infantry), as already stated, had been moved up on arrival to trenches near Nobescourt Farm in support of troops of the 66th Division, but on the latter falling back, the Durhams had retired to the Green Line. But the enemy having attacked and broken the line of the Battalion on the left of the 5th Durham Light Infantry, the latter had to withdraw to the outskirts of the farm, with "B" Company in support behind the farm. Here the Durhams hung on until orders were received to withdraw to a line in front of Cartigny.

The 8th Durham Light Infantry (the centre of the 151st Brigade) record that the Green Line was only in a spit-locked condition but a good belt of wire protected the position. A few casualties occurred when the enemy shelled the trenches at 5 p.m. and hostile aeroplanes flew low over the line.

At about 5.30 p.m. the enemy's snipers became active and small bodies of his troops were observed in the Cologne Valley: these were fired on. At 6 p.m. machine-gun fire, in enfilade from the north, began to sweep the line. But what was even more disconcerting was the fact that the Divisional Artillery was firing very "short," shells falling just behind the line and in the wire. All companies were forced to withdraw their standing patrols, as it was impossible to obtain communication with the Artillery, or even with Brigade Headquarters. It was not until an artillery F.O.O. reported at Battalion Headquarters that the "short-shooting" was stopped.

At dusk the 8th Durham Light Infantry were in touch on their right with one company of the 5th Durham Light Infantry, and on their left with the 6th Durham Light Infantry.

There is little in the Diary of the 6th Durham Light Infantry, which merely states: "Remained in Green Line. Slight encounters with enemy patrols and fire opened on masses of enemy at long ranges. Evacuated the line about 9 p.m. and withdrew to Cartigny Ridge."

During the night orders were issued from Divisional Headquarters for all three Brigades to retire to a line running from Monchy-Lagache–Vraignes–east of Beaumetz to Brusle and "to defend it at all costs." All units immediately began to move in order to get dug in before dawn. But while the withdrawal was in progress fresh orders were received at Divisional Headquarters from Corps Headquarters: the 50th Division was to withdraw as rapidly as possible to the line of the Somme during the 23rd, crossing to the west bank by the St. Christ, Brie and Eterpigny Bridges.

Here and there amongst the official and private diaries the wisdom of these continual retirements is criticised. The writers of course, could not possibly have known what compelled these withdrawals, nor of the situation on their flanks, nor the true situation of the Fifth Army, but the complaint is so insistent at times from units who were in a perfectly good position for defensive action, that there seems to be good reason for the contention that so many quick retirements were often premature and unnecessary.

Divisional orders were issued at 7.30 a.m. on the 23rd. Brigades were to withdraw first of all to the line Le Mesnil–Athies, at the discretion of Brigadiers, but from that line the withdrawal to the Somme was to be carried out under orders from the Division. The 149th Brigade was to cross the bridge at St. Christ, the 150th at Brie and the 151st at Eterpigny "for infantry—in file only—who *must break step*."

A significant statement then occurs in the order: "The whole movement will be carried out as rapidly as possible consonant with steadiness and control." It was probable that, having received orders to retire rapidly, some units got "wind up," but there was, in reality, very little "panicking" during the March Retreat. Just as in the Retreat from Mons, both officers and men could not understand the repeated orders to retire, so in March, 1918, similar orders were received with a certain amount of ill grace: the British soldier does not like retiring.

The Divisional Narrative states that the line Athies to Le Mesnil having been prepared by the 7th (Pioneer) Battalion, Durham Light Infantry, all units fell back to it, and had taken up their positions by 11.30 a.m.

The enemy meanwhile, at 6.30 a.m., had delivered a heavy attack preceded by violent artillery fire on the vacated Green Line, the morning mist having again covered his advance. Finding the Line empty, he pressed on and various rear-guard actions took place.

The 149th Brigade reached the line Athies–road junction west of Brusle only after fighting the whole way. But only one Diary (that of the 6th Northumberland Fusiliers) gives anything like a detailed account of that desperate rear-guard action. The Diary begins:

"Second day of battle: The retirement from the Green Line was carried out in perfect order along the whole battalion front, and at 4.30 a.m. the troops arrived on the new ground and, after being supplied with hot tea and rum from the Battalion cookers, commenced digging in on a line of posts running south from the Mons–Vermand road. In a couple of hours our troops had dug in sufficiently to secure the line, and dispositions were made to hold it. At 8.30 a.m., however, operation orders were received to commence a retirement at 9 a.m. to which the whole line would conform. By the time these orders could be repeated to companies, the front line had become involved in close contact with the enemy who also advanced in large numbers and in mass formations. The 150th Brigade, on the left, counter-attacked along their front and commenced a retirement, but on the Battalion front 'A' and 'C' Companies were too involved with the enemy to get clear, and three platoons of 'A' Company and part of 'C' Company were unable to free themselves and were afterwards missing. Lieut. Balden, with part of 'A' Company, was last seen fighting in a hand-to-hand encounter with the enemy. Lieuts. Oswald and Hamilton were both seen wounded and were afterwards missing. In the meantime 'B' Company covered the retreat of the remainder of the Battalion, and fought a brilliant rear-guard action as far as Mons, where it was relieved by another company. The whole retirement was carried out in perfect order, although the enemy pressed forward with machine-guns, artillery and aeroplanes, and kept up a gruelling fire from all these weapons. In this retirement Lieut. S. J. R. Stanton was wounded, but was able to continue with the relieving forces; Second-Lieut. Milligan was also wounded and carried down with the retirement. The line of retirement was due west. It was a summer-like morning with hot sun and as the battle went on hour after hour unceasingly, with the enemy artillery becoming more and more pressing, the fatigue of marching and fighting was more and more felt. At 12.30 p.m. Brie was reached, the troops being in good order and passing a covering force of the 8th Division. In and around Brie enormous fires were burning and ammunition dumps which could not be removed were blown up. Huts, camps, aerodromes, etc., on the eastern side of the Somme Canal were also burning during the retirement. From the Green Line the Battalion fought and retired a distance of ten-and-a-half miles in eight hours, the greater part of the distance being covered in extended order over open country, and with rear-guard actions taking place from time to time to relieve enemy pressure. The Battalion (less 'D' Company), which occupied trenches on the western bank of the Somme Canal, rested in trenches east of Villers-Carbonnel, and at night supported 'D' Company."

Presumably the 5th Northumberland Fusiliers also fought a rear-guard action, though only a brief reference in the Battalion Diary leads to that supposition, *i.e.*, "11.30 a.m. Battalion outflanked and retirement to the Somme commenced."* The 5th Battalion up to that period had dug in on a line south-east of Athies. Battalion Headquarters with "C" and "D" Companies crossed the Somme Canal at St. Christ at about 3 p.m., but "A" and "B" Companies had been detached, and did not rejoin until early on the morning of the 24th of March. West

---

*The 149th Brigade Diary states that: "The withdrawal to the western bank of the Somme was begun (at 11 a.m.) covered by the 5th Northumberland Fusiliers holding Ennemain and the high ground immediately east of the village with one company. This rear-guard was heavily engaged, but held its ground while the whole Brigade crossed St. Christ Bridge and took up positions from Cizancourt (exclusive) to Happlincourt (exclusive), order of battle, right to left, 4th Northumberland Fusiliers, 5th Northumberland Fusiliers, 6th Northumberland Fusiliers, with two remaining machine-guns in the line."

of the Somme Canal "C" and "D" dug in and held a line of trenches.

From Monchy-Lagache the 4th Northumberland Fusiliers at 9 a.m. moved back to Devise where they supported the 6th Battalion. Capt. T. A. L. Thompson temporarily commanded the Battalion, Lieut.-Colonel Robb having been wounded at Caulaincourt the previous day. The 4th Northumberland Fusiliers also crossed the Somme Canal at St. Christ and took up a position commanding the bridgehead, "C" Company holding the bridgehead until relieved by troops of the 8th Division.

The 149th Brigade Machine-Gun Company ("A" Company, 50th Machine-Gun Battalion) gave splendid support to the troops retiring. The machine-gunners had held on to their positions in the Estrées-en-Chaussée–Mons-en-Chaussée–Monchy-Lagache line, until 10 a.m. They then withdrew, under orders, the withdrawal being carried out in an orderly manner; they crossed the Somme Canal at St. Christ, having had four officers wounded or missing, one other rank killed, ten wounded and six missing.

At dawn on the 23rd the 150th Brigade held a line Vraignes–Beaumetz, the 4th East Yorkshires on the right, 5th Green Howards on the left, and the 4th Green Howards just east of Bouvincourt. On the receipt of orders for a withdrawal to the western bank of the Somme Canal, orders were issued for the retirement to be carried out in two stages, *i.e.*, to the St. Oren–Catelet road, thence to the Le Mesnil–Athies road: the 4th Green Howards were to cover the withdrawal in the first stage, the 4th East Yorkshires in the second stage, and then establish themselves on the bridgehead position about the line Le Mesnil–Athies. In supplementary orders the 4th East Yorkshires were to hold the outer defences of Brie, the 4th Green Howards to pass through and hold the inner defences of that village, while the 5th Green Howards passed straight on over the bridges and occupied a line on the western bank of the Canal; the 4th East Yorkshires were then to cross and support the 5th Green Howards, the 4th Green Howards being the last to cross and go into reserve.

It is interesting to give the orders as issued from Divisional and Brigade Headquarters, and to observe how impossible it was at times for units to carry them out. For instance, the 4th East Yorkshires received their orders four hours late as shown in the following extract from their Diary of the 23rd of March: "In the early morning withdrew to Vraignes under orders, the enemy having got round our left flank. At 7.30 a.m. the enemy attacked, having got motor machine-guns well forward under cover of a ground mist. Orders to retire being received four hours late our Battalion was almost surrounded and 'B' Company was cut off. Withdrew under orders (5 p.m.) across the Brie Bridge after fighting a rear-guard action. Not in touch with anyone on our flank. Had to retire through a heavy barrage.... Took up a position in support about one thousand yards west of the bridge."

The records of the 5th Green Howards do not throw any further light on the above extract. The Battalion Narrative states that at 8 a.m., when orders were received to withdraw along the main Mons–Brie road, the Green Howards were "engaged with the enemy and the withdrawal (was) difficult, as enemy was coming round right flank. From Mons to Brie fought rear-guard action on north side of Mons–Brie road with 4th East Yorkshires on the right and 8th Durham Light Infantry on the left." The 5th Green Howards crossed the Somme Canal at Brie at about 3 p.m., passing through troops of the 8th Division. They then marched to Villers-Carbonnel.

The 4th Green Howards apparently carried out their orders to the letter, as their Diary records that: "The retirement of the 4th East Yorkshires and 5th Green Howards was covered by the 4th Green Howards, who fought a rear-guard action all the way back to Le Mesnil-Bruntel. On reaching the Somme the B.G.C. ordered one company to hold the high ground east of Brie until all British troops were through Brie. Afterwards this company covered the retirement of the other troops across the River Somme (the Canal) and held the enemy in check until all the bridges except one had been destroyed. They then withdrew across this bridge which was immediately destroyed. The Battalion, less the company which had covered the retirement, joined the rest of the Brigade at Villers-Carbonnel. The other company went to the Transport Lines at Belloy-en-Santerre where they rested for the night."

The 150th Brigade Narrative states that the 4th Green Howards had had to fall back almost immediately the 4th East Yorkshires and 5th Green Howards had retired, as the enemy came on so rapidly after the last Battalion had passed through.

The Brigade then records that the 4th Green Howards "got scattered, one company retiring on Mons, the remaining three on Le Mesnil where they had assisted the 151st Brigade in the defence of that village, withdrawing with that Brigade and crossing the Brie bridges ahead of any other unit of the Brigade."

It is a pity that the 151st Brigade Headquarters Narrative of operations does not begin until the 24th of March, for the three Battalions (5th, 6th and 8th Durham Light Infantry) were involved in the fighting on the previous days during their retirement to the Somme Canal.

The Diary of the 8th Durham Light Infantry contains a good deal of information, but it is mostly concerned with moves of the Battalion, not the actual fighting. The Battalion at about 4.30 a.m. on the 23rd was holding the Beaumetz Ridge with the 6th Durham Light Infantry on the left, and the 5th Durham Light Infantry in support. By 6 a.m. the Durhams had dug themselves in, but it was fruitless work, for orders were received at 6.45 a.m. to assemble the Battalion and retire, fighting rear-guard actions, to the Somme. The 5th Durham Light Infantry were to cover this retirement which began immediately, the 6th Durham Light Infantry, on the left, conforming. By 7.30 a.m. the 8th and 6th Battalions were on the Cartigny Line and at 8 a.m. the 5th Durham Light Infantry withdrew through the 6th Durham Light Infantry in order to cover the next stage of the retirement.

Both the 8th and 6th Durham Light Infantry then withdrew through the 5th Battalion to Le Mesnil without any serious infantry actions on the Brigade front. Enemy patrols had been engaged but no casualties ensued.

As may be imagined, by this period the troops were becoming very exhausted, for they had been marching and preparing defensive positions with little rest since detraining at Brie on the 21st of March. The enemy began to shell Cartigny and Le Mesnil at about midday, and enfiladed the right and left flanks of the Brigade with machine-gun fire. At 12.30 p.m. he developed an attack and by 1 p.m. had succeeded in working round the right flank, where there was a gap caused by the retirement of the 150th Brigade. Orders for a methodical retirement to the Eterpigny Bridge on the Somme Canal were then received, the enemy being then within three hundred yards, his machine-guns enfilading the line.

Again the 5th Durham Light Infantry covered the retirement, and the 8th and 6th Durham Light Infantry fell back in extended order to the plank bridge at Eterpigny, and by 2.30 p.m. the 8th Durham Light Infantry were assembled on the western bank of the Canal, one hundred yards south of Eterpigny Church.

The 6th Durham Light Infantry in their Diary record that the Battalion was ambushed in Le Mesnil but, owing to successful rear-guard actions, extricated themselves and crossed the bridge with slight casualties.

The 5th Durham Light Infantry, who probably saw more fighting than the other battalions of the Brigade, give no details but record only the various stages of the retirement to the Somme where, from the eastern bank they covered the crossing of the 8th and 6th Battalions at Eterpigny. The last of the 5th Durhams having fallen back across the Canal the bridges were blown up at about 3 p.m. The Battalion then moved to the neighbourhood of Barleux, changing position to north of the village on coming under the orders of the 66th Division at 10 p.m.

Meanwhile, what had happened to the Divisional Artillery? On the 22nd at 10 a.m. the 250th Brigade, R.F.A., had taken up positions one thousand yards north of Nobescourt Farm, but moved again at 9 p.m. to near Le Catelet. At 5.30 a.m. on the 23rd orders were received that two batteries of the Brigade were to retire and cross the Somme Canal at Brie to cover the bridgehead, while the remaining batteries fought a rear-guard action. The leading batteries crossed over the bridge at about noon, the remainder at about 2 p.m., the whole Brigade moving then into positions near Barleux.

The Diary of the 250th Brigade has the following interesting entry: "Almost exactly a year ago the brigade had followed enemy across the same bridges in his retreat."*

The 251st Brigade, R.F.A., had gone into action between Mons-en-Chaussée and Devise on the 22nd, but did not open fire. At 5.30 the next morning batteries moved to south of the latter village to cover the infantry of the 24th Division and cavalry who were retiring from the line Monchy-Lagache to Guizancourt. The guns put down a protective barrage,

---

*To the Hindenburg Line. Only the 50th Divisional Artillery was then in the line, the infantry brigades having been relieved.

keeping touch with the infantry by means of officer patrols. The guns were shelled with considerable accuracy by the enemy 10.5 cm. guns, their positions having been given by hostile aeroplanes which were everywhere. The 251st Brigade, R.F.A., then received orders to retire across the Canal at St. Christ. During this retirement batteries were heavily shelled, but successfully crossed the bridge and came into action between 3 p.m. and 4.20 p.m. between Licourt and Morchain. From 5.0 p.m. and onwards during the night, the enemy was shelled, batteries engaging visible targets and areas occupied by the Bosche.

At 4 p.m. on the 23rd, Major-General H. C. Jackson,[*] appointed to command the 50th Division, arrived at Foucaucourt where XIX Corps Headquarters and 8th and 50th Divisions were then established. On reporting at Corps Headquarters, General Jackson was ordered to assume command of the Division as soon as it was concentrated at Foucaucourt. At this period the position of the Divisional infantry was as follows: 149th Brigade holding the line of the Somme Canal from St. Christ bridge (inclusive) to Brie bridge (exclusive), Headquarters at Misery; 150th Brigade from Brie bridge to Eterpigny (exclusive), Headquarters at Villers-Carbonnel; 151st Brigade from Eterpigny (inclusive) to O.9. central, Headquarters at Villers-Carbonnel.

The Battle of St. Quentin officially ended on the 23rd of March, and it will be seen from the records that, although incidents of the fighting are almost entirely missing, the 50th Division carried out its orders with fine devotion to duty. The continued retirements were not to the liking of officers or men, who could have taken far greater toll of the enemy than was done, though very considerable casualties were inflicted on him. Orders, however, had to be obeyed.

A final picture of the close of the Battle of St. Quentin, on the night of the 23rd of March, is given by the 149th Brigade Signalling Officer, who says:

"I went up to a bit of high ground on the left of the village, to see how the lamp to the centre battalion was working. In the valley in front of me a field battery was in action, loosing

---

[*] The loss of General Wilkinson was keenly felt by all ranks, especially during the anxious days of the March Retreat: his guidance in the early stages would have been invaluable.

off salvo after salvo at full speed, the flashes lightening up the darkening sky, the crack of the 18-pounders and the drone of the departing shells filling the air. To my right was a great hog's back of a hill, along the crest of this groups of horsemen were moving: one speculated as to whether they were our calalry or gunners returning, or Bosche cavalry advancing. In front and from either flank came the intermittent crackle of machine-guns and occasionally in the woods a pale Very light sailed upwards. The machine-gunning and the Very lights were the true portents which, throughout the Bosche advance by day or by night, never failed to herald the coming of his patrols. The Very lights were, of course, intended to indicate to his gunners the point reached by the patrol. This was all one could see of the great German offensive on the night of the 23rd of March. Everything else was enveloped in what journalists call 'The fog of war.' From the ordinary subaltern's point of view, the whole world had been turned upside down. The orderly routine of reliefs going into trenches and coming out to the back areas to rest was at an end; the future might hold absolutely anything."

Turning from official records from the 21st to the 23rd of March to private diaries and published histories of units of the 50th Division, there is still a dearth of interesting comment on the first phase of the Retreat, and of stories of individual acts of bravery, there are very few.

One of these published records relates how a gallant N.C.O. (Corporal J. A. Cook), a battalion signaller, climbed a telegraph pole in full view of the enemy and cut down the wire which was needed to complete communication with the centre company. Another records how Corporal H. Smirthwaite of the 5th Durham Light Infantry, having done excellent work in covering the retirement of his company, stayed behind although the enemy was almost upon him, to put out of action a number of Lewis guns which could not be saved. Both these N.C.O.s were awarded the Military Medal.

In a short account of the 4th Northumberland Fusiliers during the German offensive in March, April and May,[*] the following stories of gallant fighting are given:

"Capt. T. W. Gregory of 'B' Company was wounded but continued to fight: was wounded again in several places and

---
[*] By the Rev. R. Wilfrid Callin, C.F.

died in the Field Ambulance in the neighbourhood of the village of Tertry. Capt. A. Finlayson of 'C' Company was wounded in the arm, but refused to go back, fighting with a number of his men from behind the shelter of a broken wall in the village. It is feared that this officer, an unyielding, indomitable Scot, fell at the spot from which not even wounds could dislodge him. Equally gallant is the story of Capt. King of 'D' Company, another officer who never came back, Second-Lieut. Chevreau, a Franco-British officer, holder of the Croix de Guerre, was in charge of an advanced position with a platoon of 'B' Company. He and his thirty-four men fought until they were reduced to eight, of whom several were wounded. Though badly wounded himself he continued to fight in order to cover the escape of his wounded men to the Aid Post. He gave no ground to the last and died at his post."

Yet another officer, Second-Lieut. Tibbs, was last seen heroically defending his position; he was subsequently reported missing.

A very gallant story was told of Capt. Hicks and ninety men of "A" Company. They were cut off by the enemy during his rapid advance, but refused to surrender. A diversion by other British troops (presumed to be cavalry) at that moment weakened the circle closing slowly, but surely, round the officer and his comrades. But, immediately seizing the opportunity, Hicks and his men fought their way out and escaped south towards Nesle. How many were left is not stated.

So far as the Fifth Army was concerned the close of the first phase of the great German offensive appears to have left British and Germans facing each other on the western and eastern banks of the Somme Canal respectively. The struggle for the crossings was likely to be severe.

ACTIONS AT THE SOMME CROSSINGS, 24TH–25TH MARCH, 1918

During the night of the 23rd–24th small parties of the enemy crossed the Canal over broken-down girders and débris, which allowed men in singe file to reach the western bank. But these troops were, for the most part, quickly shot down, or otherwise disposed of.

At 10 p.m. on the 23rd, Divisional Headquarters, at Foucaucourt, had issued orders that early on the 24th the 50th Division would be relieved by the 8th Division, and that the former was to begin withdrawing from the line of the Canal at 3 a.m. The 150th Brigade was, however, placed under the orders of the G.O.C., 8th Division.

Accordingly, at 7 a.m. on the 24th, the command of the Canal Line passed to the 8th Division, and at 10 a.m. the 50th Division was disposed as follows: Divisional Headquarters at Foucaucourt; 149th Brigade (having moved from Misery) at Foucaucourt; 150th Brigade at Belloy-en-Santerre at the disposal of the 8th Division; 151st Brigade (less 5th Durham Light Infantry, who had been placed under the orders of the 66th Division) at Foucaucourt. The Divisional Royal Engineers were also at Foucaucourt, but the Pioneers (7th Durham Light Infantry) were under orders to proceed to Eterpigny and occupy a portion of the line under the G.O.C. 8th Division.

The official despatches record that "with the dawn, powerful attempts were made by the enemy to force the crossings of the Somme, and these attempts were by no means confined to the recognised points of passage. Owing to the dry weather the river and marshes did not constitute a very formidable obstacle to infantry, while the trees and undergrowth along the valley afforded good cover to the enemy and limited the field of fire of the defenders.

In the early morning hostile troops, which had crossed at St. Christ and Béthencourt, were attacked and driven back by the 8th Division. At Pargny, however, the Bosche succeeded in maintaining himself on the west bank of the Canal.

The 50th Division, having been relieved by the 8th Division, saw little actual fighting on the 24th of March.

Of the detached Battalions, the 5th Durham Light Infantry, from north of Barleux, moved "A" and "B" Companies forward in readiness to counter-attack at the bridgehead at Biaches if necessary. At 10 a.m. "C" and "D" Companies were moved to south of La Maisonette, and "A" and "B" Companies returned to their old positions near Barleux. About 6 p.m. "D" Company was sent forward to the assistance of the 2/8th Lancashire Fusiliers to counter-attack on the bridgeheads at Péronne. The Durhams made two attempts to recapture the bridgehead, but it was too great a task for one company.

The 7th Durham Light Infantry (Pioneers), who had been sent to fill a gap on the Canal between the 66th and 8th

Divisions, arrived at about 3 p.m. They also were, apparently, not engaged with the enemy, though the fire of our howitzers worried the Battalion considerably.

The 149th Brigade had a peaceful day; at 5 a.m. falling back to Foucaucourt, and at 5 p.m. taking up a line one thousand yards in length, north and south of Assevillers and the eastern end of the village, the 5th Northumberland Fusiliers being on the right, the 6th on the left and the 4th in reserve. Brigade Headquarters moved to Estrées.

For the 150th Brigade, however, the 24th was anything but a quiet day. As already stated the Brigade had been attached to the 8th Division to assist in the defence of the Somme about Eterpigny, which was due east of Belloy, where Battalions had arrived and bivouacked. During the morning the Brigadier and Brigade-Major visited Headquarters, 23rd Infantry Brigade.* At about 12 noon, as they were on their way to reconnoitre the new position, they were overtaken by Staff Officers of the 8th Division, who had orders that the 150th Brigade was to march at once across country, carrying Lewis guns, to Marchélepot to reinforce the 24th Infantry Brigade, on whose front the enemy had already crossed the Somme.†

These orders could not be carried out. The men were already in an exhausted condition; Marchélepot was at least five miles from Belloy, and the country between the two villages was part of the devastated area with broken ground everywhere. But the Brigadier gave orders that the Brigade should march at 2.30 p.m. with Lewis gun limbers and water carts via Estrées; and he went forward himself to reconnoitre the roads and gain touch with Headquarters, 24th Infantry Brigade.

With long halts to rest the men, who needed it badly, the 150th Brigade marched via Estrées, Déniécourt and Génermont to Marchélepot. Outside the latter village the Brigadier met the Brigade and gave orders that the 4th East Yorkshires were to be attached to 24th Infantry Brigade Headquarters at Marchélepot, and the 4th and 5th Green Howards to 25th Infantry Brigade Headquarters at Pertain. Personnel of 150th Brigade Headquarters were directed on Omiecourt, while the Brigadier and Brigade-Major rode forward to Pertain to meet the two battalions detailed to join the 25th Brigade. It was

---

*The Infantry Brigades of the 8th Division were 23rd, 24th and 25th.

†At Pargny, *vide* quotation from the official despatches.

GERMAN OFFENSIVE. STORES AND HUTMENTS BURNING AT OMIECOURT. Note bustle of departure in the background, and, in the foreground, gun teams going forward to pull out their guns. Omiecourt, 24th March. 1918.

(Imperial War Museum Photographs, Copyright Reserved)

9 p.m. when the Brigadier rode into Pertain, but at 10 p.m. there was no sign of either battalion of the Green Howards. Enquiry was then made over the telephone to 24th Brigade Headquarters, when the Brigadier of the 150th Brigade was told that all three battalions of his Brigade had been stopped by the 23rd Brigade, under orders from 8th Divisional Headquarters, and placed at the disposal of the 24th Brigade. The Brigadier of the 150th then returned to Omiecourt.

The records of 151st Brigade Headquarters (which begin on the 24th of March) state that the Brigade (less the 5th Durham Light Infantry) was ordered to take up a position in a trench system running from Ablaincourt through Estreés to Assevillers, the Brigade sector extending from Estrées (inclusive) to Assevillers (exclusive), the 8th Durham Light Infantry on the right and the 6th Durham Light Infantry on the left.

The 8th Durham Light Infantry sent out standing patrols throughout the night of the 24th–25th, but there is little else worth recording, neither do the records of the 6th Battalion contain any other item than the move to Estrées.

Of the Divisional Artillery on the 24th, the 251st Brigade, R.F.A., had a busy day. The 250th Brigade, R.F.A., records that the enemy made several attempts to cross the river, but did not succeed. His casualties during these attempts were very heavy. Battery positions were moved back towards Belloy to get more cover. All day long there was continuous fighting near the bridgeheads and late at night the batteries of the 250th Brigade, R.F.A., moved across to the southern side of Belloy in order to relieve congestion on the roads.

It will be remembered that on the night of the 23rd–24th the 251st Brigade, R.F.A., had come into action between Licourt and Morchain. At 10 a.m. on the 24th the Brigadier of the 24th Infantry Brigade informed the 251st Brigade that the enemy had crossed the Canal, which was practically dry, and was advancing on Morchain. At once "A"/251 moved in sections on to the crest of a hill and caught the Bosche advancing in large numbers between Morchain and Pargny. So close was the enemy that the gunners fired with open sights. The infantry of the 24th Brigade had begun to fall back, and "C"/251 and "D"/251 retired with them, but it was not until 11.30 a.m. to noon that "B"/251 and "A"/251 drew out of the fight and retired by sections, orders to do so having been received from the C.R.A.

But between Marchélepot and Licourt, "A", "B" and "D"/251 came again into action with "C"/251 west of the first-named village. Batteries began firing on roads near Epanancourt, Falvy and Pargny, which were crowded with hostile troops, guns and transport. The remainder of the day was spent by batteries in these positions, firing whenever a target presented itself. Enemy aircraft, flying low over the batteries, caused a good deal of annoyance; some were brought down by the infantry—by Lewis gun and rifle fire. During the night of the 24th–25th, "A"/251 moved to a position five hundred yards further west.

Both on the 23rd and 24th the 50th Battalion, Machine-Gun Company, had done splendid work in covering the hard-pressed infantry. On the former date two guns were put out of action before the remainder crossed the Brie bridge. But eight more guns were in position on the western bank of the Canal, and forced the enemy to remain behind the ridge east of Brie bridge. On the 24th Nos. 3 and 4 guns moved to Chaulnes, the officer in charge being under the impression that the Division had fallen back in that direction. But eventually a despatch rider, sent out by the O.C., Machine-Gun Battalion, found the guns and the latter marched to Foucaucourt joining up with the Division again.

The Field Ambulances, as may be imagined, experienced the greatest difficulty in attending to, and evacuating, the wounded, while practically on the move. The Advanced Dressing Stations worked heroically, the M.O.s and their staffs doing splendid work. On the night of the 24th the 1st and 3rd Northumberland Field Ambulances had their Advanced Dressing Stations at Foucaucourt and Dompierre respectively; the 2nd Northumberland Field Ambulance was with the 150th Brigade under the 8th Division.

If the infantry of the 50th Division, on the 24th, had a comparatively uneventful day, the 25th was to tell a different story, though narratives are all too brief.

The 149th Brigade had been placed at the disposal of the 66th Division at 8.30 p.m. on the 24th, while the 151st Brigade, at Estrées, had been ordered to be ready to move at short notice.

At 10.30 a.m. on the 25th the 5th Northumberland Fusiliers were ordered forward to south of Barleux, and the 6th Northumberlands to north of that village, where both Battalions were to be under the orders of the 66th Division. The 5th Northumberlands (less one company) were, however, taken by the 8th Division (on the right) without reference either to 50th or 66th Divisional Headquarters.

Unfortunately the records of the 149th Brigade on the 25th of March are all too brief. The 5th Northumberlands record that at 10.30 a.m. they "moved from Assevillers to Villers-Carbonnel line. Enemy attacked 66th Division. Battalion counter-attacked and occupied trenches south of Barleux. Held trenches until 9 p.m. when ordered to withdraw to Assevillers line. Battalion concentrated in Sugar Factory and trenches in immediate vicinity. Battalion in Brigade Reserve."

Of the 6th Northumberland Fusiliers their Diary states: "The Battalion being in support to the 66th Division, was ordered at 5 p.m. to take up positions to cover the retirement of that Division at 9 p.m. This retirement was covered from high ground north of Barleux with the enemy advancing in strength from a south-easterly direction. At night the Battalion acting as rear-guard, fell back on the defensive zone of Assevillers."

The 4th Battalion merely states that at 10 a.m. they moved into the trenches in front of Assevillers.

The 149th Brigade Headquarters Diary records that at 9 p.m. the "149th Brigade Force withdrew fighting."

Meanwhile all three battalions of the 150th Infantry Brigade had been engaged in heavy fighting.

At 3.30 a.m. on the 25th the Brigadier with his Headquarters moved to the western outskirts of Marchélepot where, to his indignation, he was informed by 24th Brigade Headquarters that the 4th East Yorkshires and 4th Green Howards had been detailed to make a counter-attack at 7 a.m. The 150th Brigade Diary states that, "It was too late to make any alteration but the Brigadier entered a strong protest against the use that had been made of his exhausted battalions without any reference to himself." He sent the Brigade-Major back to Divisional Headquarters at Foucaucourt to explain the situation.

The situation of the three battalions early on the 25th was as follows: the 4th East Yorkshires (who had snatched a few hours rest during the night in an evacuated casualty clearing station at Marchélepot) moved at 3 a.m. to a position about one thousand yards north-east of Licourt. The 4th Green Howards were on the right of the East Yorkshiremen. The 5th Green

Howards had two companies in the line, also north-east of Licourt, and one in close support, and the fourth company immediately north of the village.

The East Yorkshires and 4th Green Howards, who had been ordered to make a counter-attack supported by French troops, one tank, some armoured cars and an artillery barrage, of which "nothing was ever seen of any of these," record that zero hour was constantly postponed until, at about 10 a.m., the enemy attacked.

The 4th Green Howards fought very gallantly but the enemy, adopting his usual methods, worked round the flanks and the line had to be withdrawn. One company fought on until surrounded. The remainder fell back about half-a-mile in the direction of Misery, where they held an old trench for seven hours. But about 6 p.m., as touch could not be obtained with any other unit and ammunition was running short, Lieut.-Colonel Wilkinson (commanding 4th East Yorkshires), who had taken over command of the detachment, ordered a retirement to the railway line north-west of Misery, and a further retirement to a line east of Fresnes. Touch was later obtained with 150th Brigade Headquarters and Colonel Wilkinson and his men were ordered to join the remainder of the Brigade, which was at Ablaincourt.

The 4th East Yorkshires, having made all preparations for the counter-attack which was to drive the enemy from Epanancourt, also record the continual postponement of zero hour. And in the meantime the enemy broke through on the Battalion's right and entered Licourt, the 2nd Worcesters (24th Brigade) having fallen back. "A" Company of the East Yorkshires immediately counter-attacked the enemy in the village, but was unsuccessful. It was an uneven fight, for always we were outnumbered. If a German was shot down there were half-a-dozen at least ready to take his place; but we had no reserves.

After this unsuccessful counter-attack the line was withdrawn some two thousand yards to a position east of the Chaulnes–Péronne railway. Absolutely worn out, the East Yorkshires and Green Howards held on to their positions for six hours, heavily shelled the while. They then withdrew to another position two hundred yards west of the railway and finally, at 8.30 p.m., to a line of trenches at Ablaincourt. But "A" Company of the East Yorkshires, which had made the counter-attack referred to, failed to rejoin. The brigade was now formed into a Composite Battalion under the command of Lieut.-Colonel Wilkinson, East Yorkshires.

The 5th Green Howards similarly saw hard fighting. They were attacked at about 9 a.m., and by 10 a.m. the enemy (as already stated) had occupied Licourt. The two companies of Green Howards in the front line, with some Sherwood Foresters on their left, in spite of being hard pressed, defended their positions until forced back. One company ("B") clung with great courage and tenacity to the line until at last only a mere handful got away. The company commander (Lieut. Hepton) and many of his men were wounded and captured.

At about 10 a.m. Battalion Headquarters were established on the Licourt–Villers-Carbonnel road, a defensive flank being formed on the right to conform to the situation. Here the C.O.s of the 4th East Yorkshires and 5th Green Howards met and awaited orders to counter-attack. By 10.30 a.m., however, the enemy had completely occupied Licourt and opened enfilade fire, causing both Battalions to withdraw to the high ground north-west with their left on the St. Christ–Marchélepot road, and their right on a copse on Hill 102. Here the Battalions held on until 5 p.m., but at that hour, their flanks in the air, no orders obtainable, and ammunition almost exhausted, the C.O.s decided to fall back. In Misery they were ordered to take up a position along the railway from the Villers-Carbonnel–Marchélepot road crossing thence northwards. But the situation was obscure, for the enemy was again working round the flanks, so that both Battalions withdrew towards Fresnes, taking up a position from Mozancourt northwards, having on their right the 8th Durham Light Infantry, with whom they were in touch. At 8 p.m., however, under orders, they withdrew to Ablaincourt where all three Battalions—5th Green Howards, 4th Green Howards and 4th East Yorkshires in that order from right to left—occupied trenches immediately east of the village. The 150th Brigade now formed one Composite Battalion.

The Brigadier of the 150th Brigade records that, "From this time (early morning of the 25th of March) onwards to the concentration of the Brigade west of Amiens on the 1st of April, the battalions ceased to fight under the orders of the Brigade, but were attached to 24th Infantry Brigade, and later to 20th Division."

The approximate strength of the three battalions when they were organised into one composite battalion was: 4th East Yorkshires—300; 4th Green Howards—110; 5th Green Howards—140.

The 151st Brigade (less the 5th Durham Light Infantry) had passed the night of the 24th–25th on the Estrées (inclusive)–Assevillers (exclusive) line, the 8th Durham Light Infantry being on the right and the 6th Durham Light Infantry on the left.

At 8 a.m. on the 25th the Brigadier received orders from Divisional Headquarters that his Brigade (less the 5th Durham Light Infantry) had been placed under the orders of the 8th Division. Orders were then received from 8th Divisional Headquarters that the 151st Brigade had been placed under the orders of the 24th Infantry Brigade, and was to move to Marchélepot immediately.

The Brigade (*i.e.*, the 6th and 8th Durham Light Infantry) was collected and marched out of Estrées at about 9 a.m. The Brigade-Major went forward to Marchélepot to obtain orders from the G.O.C., 24th Brigade. He was told that two counter-attacks were to be made (each with one battalion) immediately. One was for the purpose of obtaining a footing on the high ground south-east of Marchélepot between Licourt and Pertain; the other, to obtain a footing on the high ground east of Marchélepot between Licourt and St. Christ. Information as to other British troops in the neighbourhood was vague: indeed all that could be gathered from 24th Brigade Headquarters was that a few troops were scattered round Marchélepot, and that there was an isolated battalion in St. Christ; possibly there were a few troops in Licourt.

The 6th Durham Light Infantry were at once despatched across country in artillery formation to deliver the counter-attack on the right, while the 8th Durham Light Infantry were diverted to make the counter-attack on the left. At the road junction, some four hundred yards west of Fresnes, a forward Brigade Headquarters was established and relay posts pushed out to keep touch with battalions. The Brigadier of the 151st Brigade then joined 24th Infantry Brigade Headquarters at Gomiécourt.

But neither counter-attack materialised, for both the 6th and 8th Durham Light Infantry were stopped by staff officers of the 24th Brigade, the former Battalion being ordered to man a portion of the Hyencourt–Marchélepot railway, and the latter the railway between Misery and Marchélepot stations: it was thought that the enemy held the high ground in front. About 1 p.m. the 6th Durhams side-stepped to the right for about a mile; this left the front line very thinly held and there were no reserves in hand.

About 2 p.m. a reconnaissance on horseback was made of the ground in front of the 8th Durham Light Infantry, and neither on the high ground in front, nor on the north-east side of Marchélepot were there any signs of the enemy. A small isolated party of British troops (150th Brigade), on the outskirts of Licourt, were falling back, but the right flank of the garrison holding the bridgehead at St. Christ was completely in the air.

At 3 p.m.,* before a line in front of Misery, joining up the 8th Durham Light Infantry with the garrison at St. Christ, could be established, the enemy advanced from south-east of Misery and got in between the 8th Durham Light Infantry and St. Christ. The troops falling back from Licourt† were organised as a defensive flank on the left of the 8th Durham Light Infantry, this line being subsequently reinforced by the troops from St. Christ bridgehead, who fought their way back though almost surrounded.

It was now that the enemy had a bad time. He held the high ground on the left, looking down on our troops; the hill appeared to be alive with Germans, offering fine targets to the machine-gunners and Lewis-gunners, who blazed away with terrible effect on the enemy.

At 5 p.m. the troops of the 150th Brigade (on the left of the 8th Durham Light Infantry) fell back under orders which exposed that flank. Again and again the enemy tried to turn this flank, but were held back by machine-gun and Lewis-gun fire. For six hours the struggle went on until orders were received to withdraw on to the Chaulnes–Ablaincourt–Estrées line. The 6th Durhams reached this line somewhere about 10.30 p.m., but the 8th Durhams, having to fight their way back, and also to withdraw over truly terrible country, did not

---

*The time given in the original diaries. It will be remembered, however, that the 150th Brigade states that it was about 10 a.m. when the enemy occupied Licourt.

†These were the East Yorkshires and Green Howards, *vide* text.

march in until 4 a.m. on the 26th. An officer of the 8th Durham Light Infantry thus described the country over which the retirement was made:

"This was the most difficult of all the night marches carried out during this period. The country to be crossed was absolutely unknown to everyone, and the only maps available were on too small a scale to be of much use other than a general guide. All landmarks were obliterated and the ground was intersected in every direction by old French and German trenches, covered by old rusty barbed-wire entanglements and pitted all over with old shell holes of the period prior to the German retirement of twelve months previously. The roads were mere tracks, mostly indiscernible, so overgrown with rank grass and weeds was the whole countryside; to men, already in a very exhausted condition, the night's march was a veritable nightmare of falling into trenches and shell holes, stumbling into barbed wire and groping in the darkness for the new position."

The two battalions detached from the 50th Division, *i.e.*, the 5th and 7th Durham Light Infantry (Pioneers) to the 66th and 8th Divisions respectively, saw much fighting on the 25th.

When dawn broke on the 25th "A" and "B" Companies of the 5th Durham Light Infantry were in bivouacs near Villers-Carbonnel, "D" Company was in the front line with the 66th Division and "C" Company in support some five hundred yards south of La Maisonette.

At 9 a.m. the enemy opened a violent bombardment on the front line, using trench mortars as well as artillery. Simultaneously strong forces of German infantry forced their way across the Canal near Eterpigny, and established a bridgehead north of the village. Patrols of the enemy worked southwards, and cut off a camp of the 2nd Middlesex (8th Division) holding the village, only a few men succeeding in cutting their way out. Reinforcements were at once sent up by the 8th Division, and a line covering Villers-Carbonnel was formed, protecting the flank of the battalions who were holding on to the Canal further south at Brie and St. Christ.

The 5th Durham Light Infantry were ordered to counter-attack and in five minutes "A" and "B" Companies ("C" and "D" being detached), were on the move. The following narrative of this counter-attack is taken from *The 5th Battalion, The Durham Light Infantry:**

"As we advanced we were attacked by five or six hostile aeroplanes flying very low and firing at us with their machine-guns, but they did not appear to cause any casualties. When we reached the open country between Barleux and the Canal, we could see that the troops in front were coming back in large numbers and, as things looked black, it was decided to occupy the high ground immediately in front, commanding the shallow valley leading from the Somme to Barleux.... At about 10 a.m. the enemy attacked near Péronne, but were beaten off. A second attack followed about noon and this time the Germans succeeded in driving back the troops holding the line near the Canal. Our two detached companies withdrew with the men of the 66th Division and ultimately rejoined us. The enemy, who pressed them closely, presented splendid targets for their Lewis guns and rifles, and were severely punished; 'C' Company, in particular, did good work. Their position commanded the ground as far as the Canal and they kept up a steady fire until the German infantry were close to them. They then retired gradually, each platoon taking its turn in holding up the enemy while the others withdrew. No. 12 Platoon, under Second-Lieut. F. Williams, was nearly cut off, and only extricated itself after very close fighting. The two companies had, unfortunately, many casualties.

"It was clear that there were now no British troops in front of us, and that we must expect shortly to be attacked. We therefore took up a good position nearer Barleux, in an old trench with plenty of wire in front of it. During this movement "B" Company were under machine-gun fire and suffered casualties, and Lieut. J. N. Slack was captured while trying to save one of his men who had been hit. We soon settled down and waited for the enemy. We had part of the 7th Durham Light Infantry on our left. A platoon of the same Battalion was immediately on our right, but beyond them our flank was in the air."

For some time the 5th Durham Light Infantry watched the enemy advancing on the right well past the flank of the Battalion, but he came to a standstill about two hundred yards

---

*By Major A. L. Raimes.

in front. Just before dusk his troops in front of the Durhams massed for an attack, but at that period the Battalion was in communication with Brigade Headquarters and signalled back the enemy's position; a battery of field guns then opened fire with such rapidity and accuracy as to dispel any idea the Germans had of attacking.

Darkness fell, and the Durhams still waited. The only order from Brigade Headquarters had been "to hang on to the death." Other troops on the left had been ordered to retire at 7.30 p.m. Two officers of the Durhams then started back to find Brigade Headquarters and explain the perilous situation of the Battalion. "When we had got three or four hundred yards down the road we found a platoon of Northumberland Fusiliers of our own Division: they told us they had been told off to cover the withdrawal of the 5th and 7th Durham Light Infantry, and had wondered what had happened to us, as practically all the other troops had gone. We at once realised what had happened. Orders to withdraw had been sent to us, as to other battalions, but for some reason or other they had not reached us."

Eventually, after some excitement at Barleux, the 5th Durham Light Infantry reached the Estrées–Assevillers line and were attached to the 149th Brigade.

The 7th Durham Light Infantry records are not very illuminating, but they confirm most of the narrative as told by the 5th Durham Light Infantry and, like the latter, the 7th Durhams withdrew under orders to Estrées.

Both the 250th and 251st Brigades, R.F.A., saw heavy fighting on the 25th. Observation was difficult during the morning owing to fog, but later the gunners continually supported the infantry, after remaining until the latter had passed through the gun positions.

"During a long day's fighting such as this, with a constant flow of battle, first backward, then forward, and with continual changes in the situation, our work was necessarily hard, and we were all thoroughly done up by the time we got to Foucaucourt. We had to shorten our ranges so much that day that 'D' Battery hit a tree in front of the guns, and it was this accident that wounded [Major] Angus and his twelve men. The end of a perfect day came when the officers of the whole Brigade fell, rather than marched, into an old deep dug-out near Foucaucourt—and a cold miserable night we had. A very damp sandy floor, practically no food, and dead to such an extent that we could not sleep."

Such were the trials of the 250th Brigade, R.F.A.

The 251st Brigade, R.F.A., from gun positions about Licourt and Marchélepot, fetched up eventually at Vermandovillers under the C.R.A., 24th Division. At one period during the evening batteries found themselves in front of the front line, the infantry having fallen back.

Darkness fell on the 25th of March with the enemy everywhere across the Somme Canal. That part of the line of the Fifth Army which concerns the 50th Division ran from just east of Chaulnes, northwards east of Ablaincourt, Estrées, Assevillers and through Herbécourt to Curlu on the Somme River.

The official despatches give the general line on the night of the 25th–26th March as Hattencourt–Estrées–Frise.

"Except for General Carey's Force* there were no reinforcements of any kind behind the divisions, which had been fighting, for the most part, continuously since the opening of the battle. In consideration of this fact and the thinness of our line, the Fifth Army Commander did not deem it practicable for our troops to attempt to maintain the Hattencourt–Frise positions if seriously attacked.

Accordingly, orders had been given on the night of the 25th of March that, in the event of the enemy continuing his assaults in strength, divisions should fall back, fighting rearguard actions to the approximate line Le Quesnoy–Rosières–Proyart."†

From the above narrative it will be observed that the 50th Division was still split up; Headquarters were at Foucaucourt; the 7th Durham Light Infantry (Pioneers) were in front of Estrées (in touch with the 8th Division on the right) and astride the Brie–Amiens road; the 5th Durham Light Infantry were on the left of the 7th Durhams; the 149th Brigade was on the left of the 5th Durham Light Infantry, the 4th Northumberland Fusiliers on the right, 6th on the left with the 5th Battalion in reserve on the Assevillers–Fay road. All these troops were

---

*A mixed force including details, stragglers, schools personnel, tunnelling companies, Army troops companies, field survey companies and Canadian and American engineers.

†Official despatches.

under the command of Brigadier-General E. P. Riddell. The 150th and 151st Brigades were still detached with the 8th Division.

Orders to retire "if seriously pressed" (*vide* extract from official despatches given above) reached 50th Divisional Headquarters at about 12.30 a.m. on the 26th, the sector allotted to the Division extending from Rosières to Vauvillers, both exclusive.

THE BATTLE OF ROSIERES, 26TH–27TH MARCH, 1918

On the morning of the 26th the enemy recommenced his attack in strength, south-west and west from Nesle, no doubt with the intention of separating the French and British Armies and interfering with the detraining arrangements of the former by the capture of Montdidier.

The 66th Division, on the left of the 149th Brigade, was again strongly attacked and fell back under pressure. Whereupon the 5th Northumberland Fusiliers were ordered to counter-attack and restore the situation. The Battalion (according to 149th Brigade Headquarters) attacked with two companies and restored the left flank of the Brigade, but the 66th Division still continued to retire. Under the circumstances, with his northern flank uncovered, the Brigadier of the 149th Brigade ordered a retirement to the Rosières–Vauvillers line.

Few of the official diaries speak of the exhausted state of the troops at this period; few, indeed, mention the extraordinary tenacity, the marvellous courage of the British soldier as he retired, fighting to the last, from position to position. Little groups of officers and men from several units were frequently to be found "holding on" and taking heavy toll of the enemy as, like a grey cloud, his troops swept over the old Somme battlefields of 1916 and 1917. Remnants of battalions, companies, platoons, even sections, supported one another till the last possible moment; some held on beyond that, and were finally surrounded or shot down. But of panic, of the demoralisation German General Headquarters expected—there were no signs. Stragglers there were, but these for the most part were men who had been cut off from their own units, and were wandering about trying to find them. To the undying glory of the British soldier, let it be remembered of him that in the greatest battle the world has ever known, he carried himself with high honour and courage, fighting the harder as the situation grew more desperate, often preferring death to surrender.

To deal first of all with those units which still constituted the 50th Division: the counter-attack by two companies of the 5th Northumberland Fusiliers has already been mentioned after which the retirement of the 149th Brigade to the Rosières–Vauvillers line began.

The story of the retirement of the 6th Northumberland Fusiliers was thus related, after the War, by a member of the Battalion:

"At 7.30 a.m. (26th March) the enemy attacked again. A storm of machine-gun bullets swept the 6th Battalion and the troops of the 66th Division, and once again hordes of Germans flung themselves upon the thin lines of British soldiers. The 6th Battalion stood fast, but alas! the 66th Division was compelled to fall back. In justice to the Lancashire men it must be said that their retirement was not due to any lack of courage. They had fought desperately through the whole attack since the 21st and were reduced to a mere remnant. They had lost almost all their officers, and their companies were about the strength of ordinary platoons. But the River Somme, which runs here from east to west parallel with, and about four miles to the north of, the Amiens–Vermand road, was between the 66th Division and the troops on their left, and there seems little doubt that a sudden advance of the enemy along the Somme Valley, due to a British retirement north of the Somme, was the cause of the 66th Division falling back.

"To hold Assevillers was now hopeless. At 9 a.m. orders came to withdraw to a line between Rosières and Vauvillers, and the Battalion accordingly retired. A pause was made at Foucaucourt after the first stage of the retirement, which took place over rough country, much broken by wire and old trenches. Rolls were called and stragglers rejoined their sections, and in perfect order, although much reduced by casualties, the Battalion took up its new position.

"As the Battalion passed through Foucaucourt, huts and stores were blazing. If the place could not be held, at any rate nothing of value was to be permitted to fall into the hands of the enemy. At Foucaucourt cross-roads, two runners had been left with a message for all officers who had not yet passed through. Later in the day the writer learned that these runners had waited at the cross roads with the military policeman on duty until the Germans were entering the village a couple of hundred yards away. The policeman then ordered the runners to leave. When they came away the policeman remained. He was standing at his post as cool and calm as the constable who stands at the foot of Northumberland Street. Shells were bursting round him, and the approaching enemy were but a stone's throw from him. Apparently he had no orders to quit his post and he stood fast.

"In the new position between Rosières and Vauvillers all was quiet on the immediate front of the 6th Battalion.... Darkness came on, and the 6th took over the advanced posts with other troops of the 50th Division on the right and left.

"The night passed quietly."

The 4th Northumberland Fusiliers had occupied posts around Vauvillers by 2 p.m. At 4 p.m., however (details do not exist), the Battalion counter-attacked at Framerville and drove the enemy out of the western part of the village. At midnight the 4th withdrew again to the posts at Vauvillers.

In the above counter-attack, the 7th Durham Light Infantry (Pioneers) also took part. "A" and "B" Companies "forced their way through the village twice but, owing to the commanding position held by the enemy with machine-guns, it was impossible to remain, and they were compelled to withdraw to a line about five hundred yards immediately south of the village. At dusk all troops under the 149th Brigade were withdrawn, and occupied posts immediately on the southern side of the main railway."*

Meanwhile what had been happening along the fronts held by the 150th and 151st Brigades who were still with the 8th Division? The Diary of the 8th Durham Light Infantry (151st Brigade) discloses an extraordinary intermixing of units. At 4 a.m. on the 26th of March, the 6th Durham Light Infantry were in trenches south-west of Ablaincourt; the 8th Durham Light Infantry were similarly placed north-east of that village, but in between these two Battalions of Durhams were the 150th Brigade and details of the 24th Infantry Brigade.

Starting from the right: the 6th Durham Light Infantry thus describes the happenings of the 26th, so far as they were

---

*Battalion Diary, 7th Durham Light Infantry (Pioneers).

concerned: "About 9 a.m., after confused orders, the whole line withdrew and the Battalion in artillery formation, passed through Lihons to a line in front of Rosières. A line was dug here and the Battalion remained for the night."

The 150th Brigade Narrative states that: "The battalions at Ablaincourt received the order for the retirement about 8 a.m. Almost at the same time the enemy started to attack. The orders were to retire by battalions from left to right, but as soon as the left battalion (8th Durham Light Infantry) withdrew, the Worcesters (8th Division), on the right of the 150th Brigade, immediately started a retreat.* This made the withdrawal of the Brigade very difficult, and the rear-guard platoon of the 5th Yorkshires (Green Howards) was cut off, and either killed or captured. Retirement was continued through Vermandovillers in artillery formation to the line east of Rosières. There was no rear-guard during the retirement and, owing to the extremely difficult country, the retiring troops were unmolested by the enemy. The enemy were again in touch with our outposts at about 7 p.m."

The 4th Green Howards were in support and were not engaged with the enemy.

The 5th Green Howards withdrew at about 11 a.m. The Battalion was then under heavy machine-gun fire and fell back to a position on the Rosières–Vrely road. The enemy, either from nervousness or exhaustion (for by this time the German troops also were getting worn out, though they should have had sufficient reserves to preserve the momentum of their attack) followed up the retirement in a very dilatory fashion, for it was not until 10 p.m. that he attacked the East Yorkshires in their new position and then he was repulsed. In this attack, however, Lieut.-Col. Wilkinson was wounded, and had to be evacuated.† Lieut.-Col. Thomson (commanding 5th Green Howards) then assumed command of the 150th Brigade Composite Battalion.

On the left of the East Yorkshires the 8th Durham Light Infantry, after some anxiety and difficulty, reached and consolidated a position running from one hundred yards north of

---

*The order of battalions at this period, from right to left, was 2nd Worcesters, 4th Green Howards, 5th Green Howards, 4th East Yorkshires, 8th Durham Light Infantry.

†Lieut.-Col. Martin assumed command of the Composite Group of the 150th and 151st Brigades and remnants of the 24th Infantry Brigade.

Rosières sugar refinery to four hundred yards north-west of Méharicourt. Although the enemy was observed one thousand yards east of this position no infantry attack developed, but from Lihons Halte, two German field guns shelled the Durhams.

On the night of the 26th of March, the British general line south of the Somme extended from Guerbigny through Rouvroy-en-Santerre and Proyart; we were in touch on the right with the French.*

When dawn broke on the 27th of March, units of the 50th Division, by now terribly tired and worn out, occupied the following positions: The 6th and 8th Durham Light Infantry and part of the 150th Brigade were with the 8th Division in the Rosières line; two companies of the 5th Durham Light Infantry covered Rosières station; the 149th Brigade occupied a line from Rosières (exclusive) with five officers and 120–140 men of the 5th Durham Light Infantry in support, and the 7th Durham Light Infantry with the 22nd Entrenching Battalion (attached to the Division) in reserve. The 66th Division was near Framerville, the 39th to the south of Proyart and the remains of the 16th Division near Proyart and Méricourt.

Desperate fighting took place on this date south of the Somme, the enemy's troops, having been given Amiens as their objective, making great efforts to break through the British line, and penetrate between our line and that of the French. But the gallant men who had fought on day after day without relief, with very little food and less sleep, braced themselves once again to the task of beating off the enemy, or holding up his advance until, from sheer exhaustion, he could push on no further.

North of the Somme, the Third Army had practically brought the German advance to a standstill and, had it not been for an unfortunate mistake, whereby the right of General Byng's Army had fallen back five miles behind the left flank of the Fifth Army, it is doubtful whether the enemy would have taken Proyart and turned the line south of the Somme.

At about 8 a.m. the enemy attacked the Rosières line. On the left and in the centre he was driven off, but on the right a

---

*It was on the 26th of March that the momentous decision to place the supreme control of the operations of the French and British forces in France and Flanders under General Foch was made by the Governments of France and Great Britain.

Labour company fell back, involving the right company of the 6th Durham Light Infantry, but "three companies ('W,' 'X' and 'Z') counter-attacked and restored the situation"; that is all the Durhams record of this attack. Short shooting by our artillery caused the 6th Battalion a number of casualties. At night (about 8 p.m.) the enemy made another determined attack. He advanced in no less than twelve waves, but was again repulsed. Large numbers of his troops were shot down by rifle and machine-gun fire.

Of the 150th Brigade Composite Battalion, the 5th Green Howards record that the night of the 26th–27th was quiet except for hostile artillery fire. By 8 a.m. the next morning, the enemy was in possession of Méharicourt, and his machine-guns were sweeping the line of the Composite Battalion. It was, however, 7 p.m. before he launched an infantry attack, which was broken up with heavy loss; he made no more attacks that night.

The 4th Green Howards state that they were engaged with the enemy "throughout the morning" and that they repulsed all his attacks. In the evening, when he attacked north of Rosières, two platoons were sent to reinforce the line of the 8th Durham Light Infantry. "These platoons," the Diary records, "with the exception of one officer and two other ranks, eventually became casualties."

Heavy shell fire and machine-gun fire are recorded by the 4th East Yorkshires on the 27th, and "A" Company, sent up as reinforcements to the front line, carried out a brilliant counter-attack some fifteen hundred yards on the left flank of the Battalion. The East Yorkshiremen, who were also attacked during the enemy's night attack, drove him off with heavy loss.

When dawn broke "A" and "D" Companies of the 5th Durham Light Infantry held a position in front of Rosières station, "B" and "C" being near Vauvillers. At about 11 a.m. "A" and "D" Companies received orders to withdraw and fell back to the railway bridge between Rosières and Guillaucourt. While this withdrawal was taking place "C" Company counter-attacked to delay the enemy in his advance. No official details exist of this gallant effort, the 151st Brigade Headquarters Diary omitting all mention of it, and the Battalion Diary merely stating that Major Raimes and other officers were wounded.

This counter-attack by the 5th Durhams was necessitated by one of those mistakes which sometimes occur in great actions and retreats, *i.e.*, the wrong reading of orders. The 5th Northumberland Fusiliers, on the left of the 5th Durhams, who had received "provisional orders" for a further withdrawal, misread them as "definite orders" and fell back accordingly. Part of the 6th Northumberland Fusiliers also acted on the supposed orders, and Battalion Headquarters, 5th Durham Light Infantry, being close to those of the 5th Northumberlands, the latter passed on what they believed were the right orders, *i.e.*, to withdraw. Before long a considerable section of the line was falling back towards Harbonnières.

The 4th Northumberland Fusiliers, at Vauvillers, stood fast, but the 5th, part of the 6th, and the 5th Durham Light Infantry (as already stated) were on the move back. Steps were now taken by the Brigadier, 149th Brigade, to prevent a disaster. The 22nd Entrenching Battalion was moved forward, while the 7th Durham Light Infantry (Pioneers) were ordered to counter-attack towards Framerville. In the north the 66th Division assisted by counter-attacks, also the 8th Division near Rosières, which attacked in a north-easterly direction. No records exist as to the result of the counter-attack by the 7th Durham Light Infantry.

The retiring troops were stopped and posted along the light railway at Harbonnières.

Meanwhile, the enemy seeing the retirement, attacked vigorously, took Vauvillers and forced the 6th Northumberlands, near Rosières, back to the light railway; the situation was dangerous.

The 5th Durham Light Infantry (who supply details of the retirement and counter-attack in their Regimental History) record that: "There was no panic, and on receipt of orders, we quietly took up our position, and watched with interest the counter-attack which we could see developing a mile or more away from us on the left. A few shells were fired at us, but dropped behind our line, and eight or nine enemy aeroplanes came swooping at us, firing with their machine-guns, but did not appear to do any damage. After a while orders from the Brigadier were passed along from officer to officer instructing us and the Northumberland Fusiliers to advance in line with the counter-attack on our left, and recapture the position, which we had held during the night. We accordingly pushed on, platoon by platoon, and section by section, in quite the old field-day style, the men firing freely at the Germans who could now be seen advancing towards us five or six hundred yards away. We came under machine-gun fire, and the bullets were kicking up the dust all along our line. We had many casualties and, as we looked back over the level ground behind, we could see the motionless forms of men who had fought their last fight, while here and there were wounded men trying to make their way to the rear. After a while it became very exciting, as we could see the enemy halt and turn back through the trees near Vauvillers. Our men gave a sort of grunt and advanced ten times as quickly as before . . . . Eventually the resistance of the enemy broke down, and the Northumberland and Durham men swept forward together, and re-occupied their old positions, while our field guns from behind fired salvo after salvo at the retiring Germans."

But alas! the ground so gallantly recaptured could not be held. The troops were exhausted, they had lost many of their leaders, their ammunition had almost run out. So that when again the Germans came on in great force, Vauvillers fell once more into their hands, and the thin line of British infantry was forced back to the line of the light railway where they remained, still fighting, till dusk fell. At 7 p.m., under orders, the 5th Durham Light Infantry moved to near Rosières station, under the command of the 8th Division.

An interesting comment on the withdrawal which had taken place during the 27th is contained in the 50th Divisional Narrative of Operations:

"The retrograde movements which became so general on this date were not directly due to enemy action. They appear to have been begun by the men owing to the observed, or imagined, movements of troops on the flanks. There were no signs of panic: the movements were carried out at a steady pace, and the men readily responded to the instructions of Regimental and Staff officers to face about and re-occupy the vacated positions. It is possible that by this time the continued retirement in the face of the enemy, and the abandonment of strong positions for reasons outside the ken of the men themselves, had produced a habit of withdrawing which needed more vigilant and strong leadership to overcome than was within the compass of the Regimental officers then remaining with their units."

The 8th Durham Light Infantry, at about 9 a.m., also made a counter-attack on the enemy, driving him back through Méharicourt, but a heavy hostile barrage during the attack caused a withdrawal of one of "B" Company's posts in front of the Sugar Refinery. At 12.30 p.m. the situation was again quiet. At about 5.45 p.m. Lieut.-Col. H. Martin (commanding 8th Durham Light Infantry) was wounded outside Battalion Headquarters. At 5.5 the enemy developed an attack on the left of the Battalion, but Lewis and machine-gun fire broke up the attack, scores of Germans being shot down. Twice during the evening the enemy was reported massing for further attacks, but they did not materialise. The Diary of the 8th Durham Light Infantry closes on the 27th with the following words:

"The greatest difficulty by day had been lack of orders and difficulty of communication (which was by runners). By night, the difficulty was to keep the troops awake, as everyone was worn out by the recent strain and heavy fighting."

Of the 149th Brigade, the narrative of the 6th Northumberland Fusiliers is by far the fullest and most interesting.[*]

The 6th Northumberland Fusiliers begin their diary of the 27th with the significant words: "Sixth day of battle. Enemy did not get into touch with our outpost line till 8 a.m., when he was seen moving across our front in force in the direction of Rosières, which was being heavily shelled, and the 8th Division front attacked. This attack was beaten off. Large numbers of enemy were seen massing on our front, and Lieut. Brownrigg and a party of N.C.O.s and men attacked and captured party of the Germans who had forced their way between the Battalion left and the right of the 5th Northumberland Fusiliers. Enemy directed main attack on 66th Division front north of Vauvillers, and at 12 o'clock a telephone instruction was received to carry out the retirement in conjunction with the 5th Northumberland Fusiliers on the left. This withdrawal was arranged with O.C., 5th Northumberland Fusiliers, and at 1 o'clock orders were issued to companies to commence retirement. A few minutes later a telephone message was received cancelling retirement and ordering a counter-attack. The troops were already moving along the

---

[*] It is inevitable that these narratives overlap in places, but for historical purposes, where the units are concerned, the full story is given.

whole front and had reached the line of the Rosières–Proyart light railway, with the enemy attacking in force and bringing up machine-guns. The 8th Division, on our right, stood fast. Col. Anstey (50th Divisional Headquarters) rode on to the ground ordering troops back to fight and, at the call of their officers, Battalion Headquarters Composite Company and 'C' Company (Captain Davies) of the 6th Northumberland Fusiliers, portions of 4th East Yorkshires and Entrenching Battalion formed up on the line of the Rosières–Proyart light railway under the command of Lieut.-Col. F. Robinson. The counter-attack was launched with the greatest courage and determination, and the enemy were driven from the ridge, Col. Robinson leading the attack, in doing which he was shot down, badly wounded. Col. Robinson gave instructions for Capt. Armstrong, Adjutant, to take command; Capt. Armstrong, unfortunately, was almost immediately shot down, badly wounded, and Lieut. A. W. Leech took command. The counter-attack had succeeded brilliantly, and a further attack on Long Trench and enemy machine-guns, which were playing havoc along our front, was ordered. Part of Long Trench and two enemy machine-guns were captured, together with parties of the enemy. The 8th Division also supported this further advance and secured a batch of prisoners from Long Trench. Lack of ammunition had considerably hampered the efforts of our men and, by orders of G.O.C., 8th Division, 500 rounds [5,000?] of S.A.A. were handed over to the 50th Division troops. Five minutes after the ammunition had been distributed the Transport Officer of the 150th Brigade arrived with ammunition carried on pack mules, which was dumped behind our front line. The enemy at this time appeared to be in retreat and, as far as could be seen, the line was firmly established and in touch with the 8th Division troops who were lending support. An enemy attack developed from the direction of Vauvillers on our left flank, however, and the left was driven in, in the direction of the Guillaucourt–Rosières railway. Thereupon orders were given for the troops holding Long Trench and forward positions to form a defensive flank to the 8th Division, and this was done, the whole line being subsequently filled in and held. The enemy did not further press his attack and practically all the ground won during the counter-attack was successfully held. All wounded officers and men were evacuated . . . . Casualties in N.C.O.s and men were, unfortunately, extremely heavy in killed. . . . The 6th Battalion Northumberland Fusiliers were most ably supported in their counter-attack by a small party of 4th East Yorkshires under Lieuts. Brown and Elvin; Lieut. Brown was killed."

The 8th Division took over the line held by the 6th Northumberland Fusiliers, and at night the Battalion, which had become a good deal scattered during the afternoon operations, rendezvoused south of Harbonnières under the command of Capt. Leathart, being joined later by Lieut. A. W. Leech and what remained of the counter-attack force—*some twenty other ranks in all!*

The 5th Northumberland Fusiliers report that the enemy made a heavy attack, and that the Battalion counter-attacked; the final line held at night was in front of Guillaucourt with the Battalion partly concentrated on the Harbonnières–Wiencourt road.

The 4th Northumberland Fusiliers state that they held their position at Vauvillers until noon, when they withdrew owing to troops on either flank having done so. But they state also that Brigadier-General Riddell personally commanded the counter-attack during the afternoon, and that the Battalion then occupied positions east of Harbonnières.

Throughout the 27th, the hard-pressed infantry of the 50th Division were splendidly supported by their artillery. The 250th Brigade, R.F.A., during the counter-attack in the afternoon gave great assistance in breaking up the enemy's attack: "The guns, ready and alert, brought down the barrage just east of the Rosières–Vauvillers road, and right on top of several supporting enemy waves. The effect was magical. Our foes trooped away like crowds on a race-course."[*]

This narrative of the terrific struggle which took place on the 27th of March would be incomplete without reference to the Divisional Royal Engineers, who are thus referred to in the 50th Division Narrative of Operations: "At 11.30 a.m. a report was received that the enemy had broken through at Proyart. The 8th Division despatched the 2nd Battalion Devons and 22nd Durham Light Infantry to counter-attack Proyart. These Battalions were supported by R.E. Battalion, 50th Division."

---

[*] History of the 1st Northumbrian Brigade, R.F.A. (T.F.).

The Diary of the C.R.E. records that on the 27th he received orders to assume command of a party of 350 details of the 151st Brigade and form, with the 7th and 447th Field Companies, R.E., a composite battalion for tactical or work purposes. This composite battalion was formed at Wiencourt at 7 a.m., and then marched to Guillaucourt where packs were dumped and the men got into fighting order. They proceeded thence along the railway to a point due south of Harbonnières, where Major Baker, O.C., 7th Company, with about half of the details, and Major Chivers, O.C., 447th Company, with the remaining half details, formed a defensive flank to cover the right of the 149th Brigade in the event of the latter being attacked from the direction of Rosières. But the gallant Sappers were not engaged, for no attack developed. At 12 noon, however, the R.E. Composite Battalion received orders to co-operate with two battalions of the 8th Division in a counter-attack from Harbonnières on Proyart. The force under Major Chivers, before the arrival of the 8th Division troops, or Major Baker's force, was to seize and hold a road about a mile north of Harbonnières before the enemy reached it. This was successfully done. Major Baker's* force and the two battalions of 8th Division troops coming up, the "Composite Battalion" then accompanied the attack in right-rear support to cover its right flank. This counter-attack was, however, held up about 1,200 yards west of Proyart, where existing trenches were occupied in depth, and held during the night of the 27th–28th.†

Thus ended the 27th of March, for ever memorable in the annals of the Division and all units as a day of hard fighting and magnificent courage. Every available man had been rushed up into the fight, and at one time the only troops General Riddell (149th Brigade) had at his disposal for counter-attack was a scratch collection of Brigade staff, cooks, grooms, batmen and signallers.

For the enemy the 27th of March was in several ways a blow to his ambitions, for north of the Somme our line had begun to stabilise, the Seventeenth German Army was worn out, and could get no further and was, indeed, being successfully counter-attacked; all three German Armies had suffered

---

*Severely wounded in Harbonnières.
†The 446th Company, R.E., was in Vauvillers.

enormous losses and all that German General Headquarters could do was to reinforce the Second and Eighteenth Armies in a final attempt to break through to Amiens.

THE FINAL ATTACK

For the fighting on the 28th of March, and on the closing days of the month, when the enemy, spurred on, no doubt, by the bitter disappointment of not being able to break through our thin lines, launched heavy forces against us, there are no official Battle Honours.*

On the night of the 27th–28th the Allied line, south of the Somme, ran from Mesnil St. Georges (west of Montdidier which had been captured from the French during the 27th), thence via Boussicourt–Arvillers–Warvillers–Rosières–Harbonnières, where it bent back to Hamel, just south of the Somme. It will thus be seen that we held an awkward salient which the enemy would be sure to attack heavily on the 28th.

During the night of the 27th–28th the enemy broke into Warfusée and Bayonvillers. Owing to the critical situation created by this advance the G.O.C.s, 8th, 50th and 66th Division, met at about 3 a.m. at Cayeux, at Headquarters of the 8th Division. Corps Headquarters were then rung up, and the G.O.C., 8th Division, suggested to the Corps Commander that the line should be retired during the night to Vrély – Caix – Guillaucourt – Wiencourt – Marcelcave – Villers Bretonneux. At 4.30 a.m. permission was given and verbal orders were at once given: 149th Brigade to hold from Rosières along the line of light railway to Harbonnières, inclusive, with the 50th Division R.E. units and the two battalions of the 8th Division located towards Proyart, as the 39th Division had retired through Harbonnières. The 149th Brigade was then to fall back to the line Caix–Guillaucourt, whence the line was to be continued by the 66th Division to Wiencourt, and by the 39th Division to Marcelcave.

It will be observed that the Divisional Narrative makes no reference to the 150th and 151st Brigades, though the Headquarters Diary of the former Brigade does state that Col. Thomson, commanding the 150th Brigade Battalion, received

---

*Why no Battle Honours were awarded for the heavy fighting south of the Somme from the 28th of March to the 4th of April (exclusive) is inconceivable.

orders from the G.O.C., 24th Brigade, to withdraw his Battalion to trenches immediately in rear, just in front of the Rosières–Vrély road, distributing it in depth from the northern end of Vrély village to the light-railway crossing. The Headquarters Diary of the 151st Brigade records that it was 6 a.m. on the 28th when verbal orders from 24th Brigade Headquarters were received by the Battalion that "in the event of a hostile attack the line was to withdraw, starting from the left, unless the attack was from the right, in which case the withdrawal would take place from the right." It is evident, therefore, that the 150th and 151st Brigades were still definitely under the orders of the 8th Division.

Because of the intermixing of units and the impossibility (from the reader's point of view) of following the fortunes of battalions during the final stages of the Great Retreat, the period from the 28th of March to the 4th of April* will be summarised. For, before the exhausted troops of the 50th Division were withdrawn, they came during the last days of March under the orders of yet another division, *i.e.*, the 20th.

The presence of the enemy in Warfusée and Bayonvillers was indeed dangerous, for he was west of our troops still holding the line in front of Harbonnières.

The 149th Brigade received orders at 6 a.m. to withdraw to the line Caix–Guillaucourt, and five minutes later the line began to swing back to the Rosières–Guillaucourt road, with a rear-guard holding all roads leading into Harbonnières from north-east and west. By 8 a.m. the Brigade (with attached units) was south of the railway and moving into the following positions: 6th Northumberland Fusiliers to Caix, 5th Northumberland Fusiliers to Guillaucourt, 4th Northumberland Fusiliers on the right of the 5th Battalion, and the 7th Durham Light Infantry joining up the 4th and 6th Northumberlands. The 22nd Entrenching Battalion was ordered back to the right bank of the River Luce, south of Guillaucourt; only two companies, however, marched back to the River.

Units were scarcely settled in the Caix–Guillaucourt line when, at 10 a.m., the enemy, sweeping down in a southeasterly direction, broke the line at Guillaucourt. The 5th Northumberlands state that they counter-attacked, but the

---

*The infantry of the 50th Division had been withdrawn by the latter date, but the hard-worked artillery were still in the line.

result is not given in the records. The Battalion had formed a picquet line round Harbonnières, and had to fight a stiff rear-guard action in order to get away.

The two companies of the 22nd Entrenching Battalion which had not retired to the Luce, counter-attacked the enemy and restored the situation as far as the Caix–Guillaucourt road,* but their gallant effort was of little use, for both the 39th and 66th Divisions retired on Cayeux. At 1 p.m., therefore, the 50th Division retired to the line Caix–Cayeux, but held Caix and Cayeux bridgeheads until 6 p.m. At the latter hour numbers of British troops could be seen marching along the Caix–Beaucourt road, and the G.O.C., 149th Brigade, ordered the rear-guard to withdraw on Mézières, covering the retirement of his Brigade to Moreuil where, worn out with fighting and marching (the distance from the positions they had held in the morning to Moreuil was from nine to ten miles), all units billeted for the night of the 28th–29th.

The following morning the whole Brigade, plus the 4th East Yorkshires, 5th Durham Light Infantry, 22nd Entrenching Battalion and the 149th Machine-Gun Company, under the orders of the G.O.C., 149th Brigade, was ordered to advance forward in support of the 20th Division, to a road astride the Amiens–Roye road, a mile south of Demuin; the brigade with attached units was to be under the orders of the 20th Division, the latter being then disposed on the line Mézières–Demuin.† At Mézières we were in touch with the French on our right.

---

*The following account of this gallant counter-attack is thus related by Brigadier-General Riddell:—

"A glance towards Guillaucourt showed me the Bosche infantry eight hundred yards away. He was coming our way and would soon reach the crest overlooking Caix through which troops of all sorts were now passing. Below me, to the south, under the shelter of one of those remarkable steep-sided banks which abound in this country, were the 22nd Entrenching Battalion calmly eating their dinner and, as is the custom of the British soldier at meal times, quite oblivious of what was happening around them. I galloped to them shouting, 'Fall in.' Fortunately the men were in extended order in a long line at the bottom of the bank with the officers in a group. I shouted the order to fall in in two ranks, and told them it was a race for the crest of the hill. As they climbed up the steep sides of the bank, away behind me, near Harbonnières, I heard the sound of a hunting horn. It was General Jackson, the Divisional Commander, blowing his 'pack' to him. 'Forrard away' and up the hill and over the crest went the Entrenching Battalion and back into Guillaucourt went the Bosche. For the time being Caix was saved."

†On the night of the 28th of March, the British front line south of the Somme ran from Mézières to Ignaucourt and Hamel.

The 6th Northumberland Fusiliers at 12 noon attacked and captured a wood east of their position. At 4 p.m. an attack, organised by the 20th Division on Mézières, failed and the Division, being heavily counter-attacked, fell back on the line of the Demuin-Moreuil road. This retirement uncovered the right of the 149th Brigade which then launched a second counter-attack. The 4th East Yorkshires, in a brilliant attack, drove the enemy from the high ground north of Maison Blanche, the 6th Northumberlands co-operating. The 5th Durham Light Infantry then attacked the wood immediately north of Villers. These attacks gave the 20th Division time to re-form in their new line. At 7 p.m. the 149th Brigade (and attached troops) began to withdraw to the north of the Amiens—Roye road in order to conform to movements of the 20th Division, now on the right of the Brigade. That night the Brigadier of the 149th Brigade was ordered to hand over all troops under his command to the 20th Division.

The records also state that "all troops of the 50th Division had a hot meal."

Throughout the retirement the "Q" Branch of the 50th Division had "played up" extraordinarily well. It was no light task to feed troops continually on the move, fighting most of the time, and then withdrawing in all directions. But the Administrative Staff appears to have been successful in feeding all units by dumping supplies at places through which the troops would pass.

At 6 a.m. on the 30th the enemy again attacked heavily. At 10 a.m. the 6th and 5th Northumberland Fusiliers received orders to hold Rifle Wood (south of the Amiens-Roye road), but at 11 a.m. the enemy gained possession of the wood. An immediate counter-attack, however, robbed him of his gains and restored the situation.

Demuin was lost on the 30th. During the night of the 29th-30th, the enemy had gained possession of Moreuil Wood, and on the 30th had attacked on both sides of the River Luce. Cavalry had cleared the enemy from the wood, but he retained possession of Demuin. The official despatches record that: "In the evening a most successful counter-attack by troops of the 20th and 50th Divisions re-established our line south of the Luce."

The attack was organised and personally led by Capt. Pollock, 1/4th East Yorkshires (temporarily commanding 150th

Brigade battalions).* Artillery support was obtained from a battery of field guns in rear, and from machine-guns on the right flank. Under heavy machine-gun and rifle fire, the officer and men gallantly and fearlessly advanced to the attack, and cleared both the copse and wood (south of the Domart–Roye road) at the bayonet point, killing and putting *hors de combat* some two hundred odd of the enemy, and capturing some seventy prisoners and eight machine-guns; the latter were immediately turned against the enemy. In half-an-hour the enemy had been cleared out, and the East Yorkshiremen, with their comrades of the Brigade Battalion, were consolidating their gains.

On the 31st the enemy attacked and drove the 20th Division and the French to the northern bank of the Luce, all units of the 50th Division (with the exception of the 6th Northumberland Fusiliers and the 5th Durham Light Infantry) suffering a similar fate. The two Battalions held their ground south of the River, covering Hangard. At 9 p.m. that night the 18th Division, under the impression that they were held by the enemy, attacked Hourges and Hangard.

At the close of the fighting on the 31st of March the British line ran from Moreuil Station to Hangard, thence to the old line west of Warfusée-Abancourt.

On the 1st of April the infantry of the 50th Division were relieved, though small parties still remained with the 20th Division. The 149th Brigade Battalion (strength about four hundred all ranks) on the morning of the 1st was dug in on the crest of a hill 1,200 yards north-west of Domart, in support of the 20th Division. All day long this position was held until, at 6 p.m., the Brigade Battalion was relieved by troops of the 41st Division; the 149th then marched to Longeau and billeted there for the night. On the 2nd the Brigade Battalion marched to Saleux, and at 10 p.m. entrained for Rue *en route* for the Douriez area, where 50th Divisional Headquarters had already been established.

The 150th Brigade Battalion, after remaining all day on the 1st in reserve to the 20th Division, similarly marched to Longeau, billeting for the night and entraining on the following day for Rue. The Brigade was also very weak, the strength of

---

*Lieut.-Col. Thompson (Green Howards) had been wounded on the 29th of March.

units being: Brigade Headquarters—5 officers, 69 other ranks; 4th East Yorkshires—1 officer, 147 other ranks; 4th Green Howards—4 officers, 362 other ranks; 5th Green Howards—4 officers, 230 other ranks.

The 151st Brigade had been relieved and were billeted in Saleux on the night of the 31st of March–1st of April and moved to Rue on the 1st.

Thus the infantry of the 50th Division, with the Field Ambulances, Royal Engineers and other Divisional troops, had by the 2nd of April been relieved, and had been withdrawn to rest and refit to the Douriez area.*

But the artillery of the Division remained behind. When the Great Retreat ended, the 250th and 251st Brigades, R.F.A., found themselves, after many vicissitudes, in the neighbourhood of Gentelles where the gunners stayed until the 8th of April. In front of them there was still a lot of fighting, *i.e.*, attacks and counter-attacks about Hangard Wood as the front line swung backwards and forwards before settling down. In all these actions the Divisional artillery took part, and was heavily shelled, especially on the 4th of April,† when the 250th Brigade suffered a great loss in Lieut.-Col. Chapman, who was hit and wounded very badly in the right arm: "He went home and we saw him no more to our great regret. He had brought the Brigade through many vicissitudes and much hard fighting, with added credit, and we all felt his loss greatly."‡ Two days later the Brigade suffered another loss, Major Wilkinson of "B" Battery being killed as he was walking from a reserve position to his guns. He was very greatly missed.

No one was sorry when, on the 8th, the guns were withdrawn from about Gentelles and the trek northwards began. But the 50th Divisional artillery had played its part in stopping the enemy in front of Amiens, and in robbing him of his objective.§

The results of the Great German Offensive on the Somme in March, 1918, were terribly disappointing to the enemy, who had counted upon a complete break-through. That he *did* not

---

*On arrival in the Douriez area the Division (less artillery) numbered roughly about six thousand all ranks.

†The Battle of the Avre.

‡Extract from The War History of the 1st Northumbrian Brigade, R.F.A.

§ General Ludendorff said: "That we had also failed to take Amiens, which would have rendered communication between the enemy's forces astride the Somme exceedingly difficult, was specially disappointing."

break was due to the splendid courage and tenacity of the British soldier, for the French rendered little or no assistance to the hard-pressed troops of the Fifth Army. Even the Australian troops, who took part in the Battle of the Avre on the 4th of April, though claiming to have "stopped the rot", did not do so, for before that period we had the enemy held.

The fine fighting displayed by all units of the 50th Division received but little notice in the official despatches, nor indeed do the records of the Division give anything in the way of detailed descriptions of the Great Retreat. Major C. H. Ommanney of the 250th Brigade, R.F.A., stated the truth when he said in his book on his Brigade that: "There is no record in the War Diary explaining the why and the wherefore of our various moves, and all we have been able to give in the way of description of the fighting has been culled from sources outside the Brigade proper. It is so with all units; the grim business of fighting kept C.O.s and Adjutants (just as on the Retreat from Mons in 1914) from keeping an adequate diary. And that is why it is not possible to relate the countless deeds of gallantry and daring which everyone knows took place all over that vast battlefield."

"Most of the time we seemed to be on the point of being surrounded," wrote one officer, and his statement accurately describes the position in which infantry and gunners were continually finding themselves. So vast were the enemy's numbers that the whole countryside appeared to be alive with men, yet it was marvellous to see how small bodies of British troops, banding themselves together, held up the grey hordes for hours. The German casualties must have been enormous, for the machine-gunners and Lewis gunners frequently found fine targets, the enemy often advancing in mass formation, wave after wave.

Wonderful to see was the way in which troops, whose normal functions kept them behind the front line, took part in the fighting as infantrymen, and how splendidly they did their job.

A padre of the Division, who went through the Retreat with his battalion, said that: "Apart from heavy casualties, the worst feature of the Somme fighting was undoubtedly the incredible fatigue and lack of sleep. Men simply could not keep awake despite the danger, and the slightest respite found them in deep slumber. Any bed was a good bed—a heap of stones by the roadside, a ditch, an open field, a sloping bank. Cold and hunger were forgotten in Nature's overwhelming clamour for sleep. Passing through Moreuil on the eve of Good Friday, men dropped asleep on doorsteps for three or four minutes at a time, walked a few yards further, slept on another doorstep and so on .... Physically the men had come to the very end of their tether—only sheer will power kept them going. It was not so much a question of muscles being tired—though they were *very* tired—as of the very bones being sore—all reserve force being utterly used up. Nevertheless, what that will power could do the enemy learned to his cost."[*]

---

[*] Rev. R. W. Callin.

CHAPTER XII

THE GERMAN OFFENSIVE ON THE LYS, 1918

THE enemy's attacks of the 4th and 5th of April having ended in failure, his offensive on the Somme ended for the time being, and the opposing forces once again settled down to trench warfare, broken only by occasional local actions by one side or the other.

But in the north the storm clouds had already begun to gather, and the 50th Division, arriving in its new area north and northwest of Bethune, heard with misgivings rumours of another Bosche offensive along the line of the Lys River.

The official despatches state that: "The possibility of a German attack north of the La Bassée Canal, for which certain preparations appeared to have been carried out, had been brought to my notice prior to the 21st of March. Indications that preparations for a hostile attack in this sector were nearing completion had been observed in the first days of April, but its extent and force could not be accurately gauged."

The situation on the British side was far from satisfactory. To meet the urgent demands for reinforcements in the Somme fighting, ten divisions had been withdrawn from the Flanders front and sent south, and were replaced by divisions exhausted by the terrific struggle which took place between the 21st of March and the end of that month; indeed when the Bosche offensive on the Somme ceased, no less than forty-six out of a total of fifty-eight British divisions in France and Flanders had been engaged in the southern area.

It is, therefore, not too much to say that General Jackson, viewing his sadly depleted division on arrival north of the La Bassée Canal, and having received warnings of the impending Bosche attack, must have wondered how his troops would fare in the coming offensive; for although large numbers of reinforcements had arrived to fill the ranks of battalions, the majority were little more than boys, practically untrained, and without any war experience whatsoever. There were, indeed, a number of old soldiers, those who had fought at Mons in the early stages of the War (for there was a great "comb-out" of depôts in England) and Class "B" men who, of necessity, had

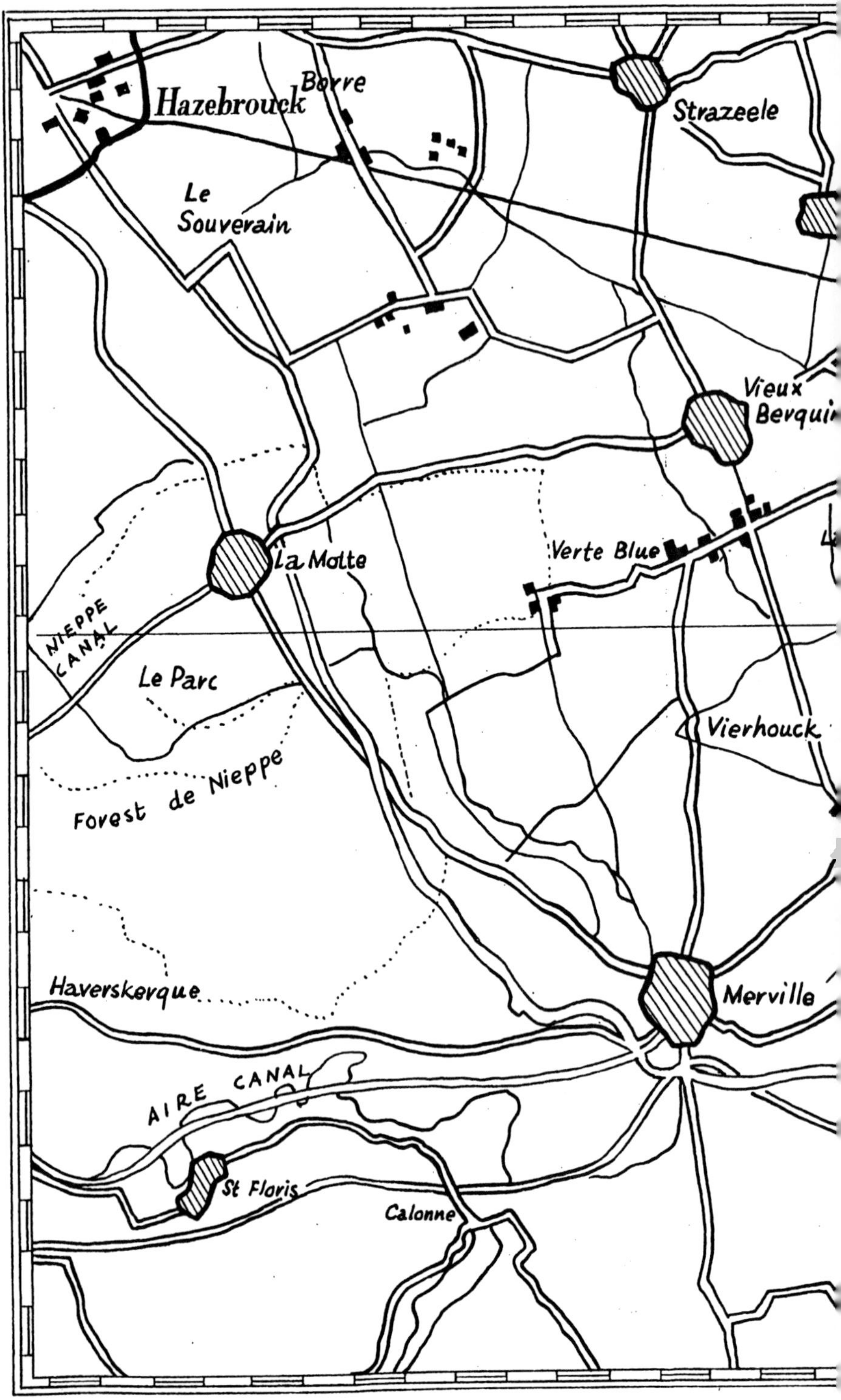
Hazebrouck
Borre
Strazeele
Le Souverain
Vieux Berquin
La Motte
Verte Blue
NIEPPE CANAL
Le Parc
Vierhouck
Forest de Nieppe
Haverskerque
Merville
AIRE CANAL
St Floris
Calonne

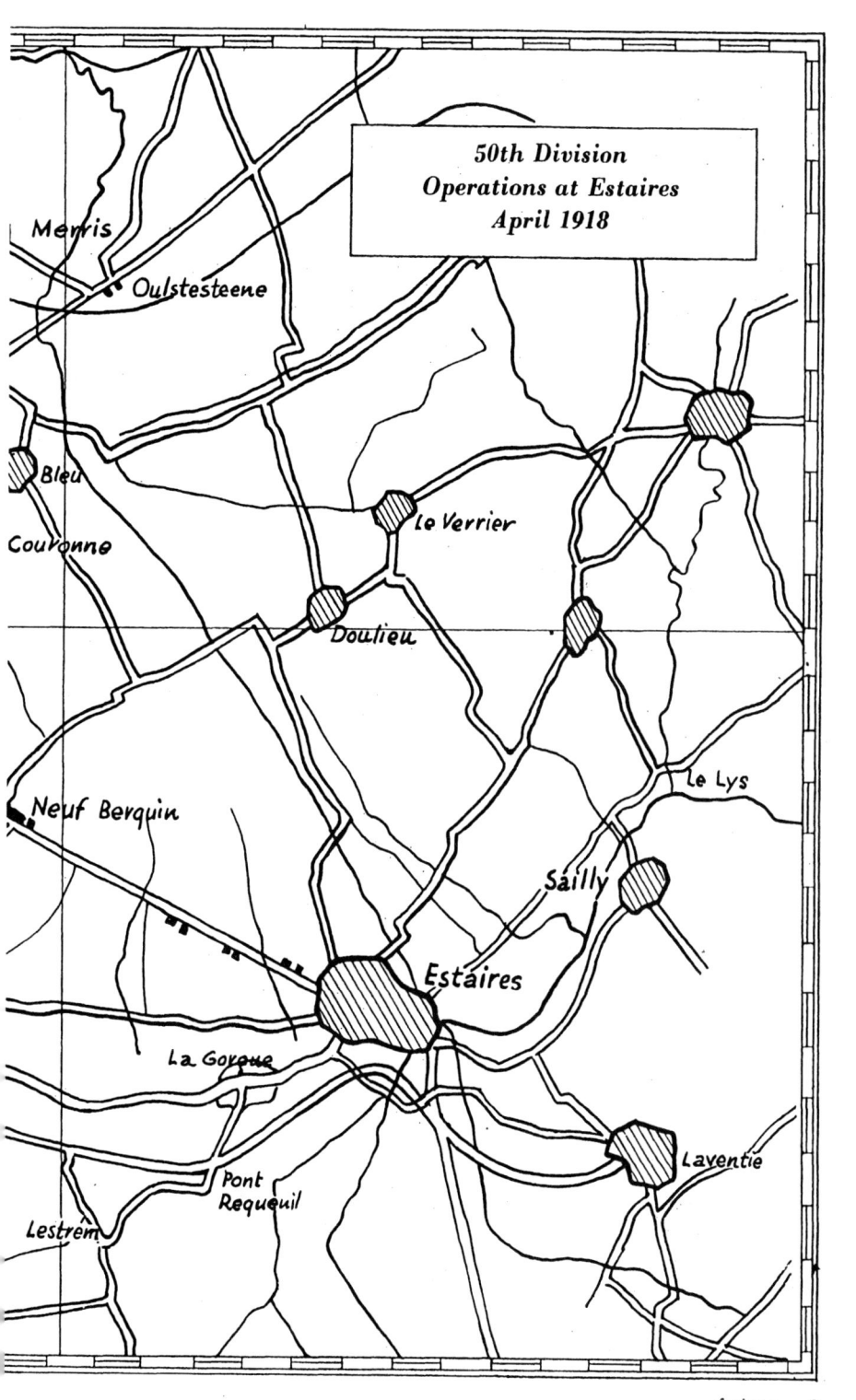

**50th Division
Operations at Estaires
April 1918**

facing p. 308

been re-classed "A." The most difficult of all to replace were the senior officers and N.C.O.s who had been killed on the Somme. Nevertheless, it will be seen that the young recruits fought splendidly side by side with the seasoned warriors of the Division, and gave a good account of themselves.

By the 4th of April Divisional Headquarters were established at Robecq (Burnes area), the 149th Brigade being billeted in the Gonnhem and L'Eclême area, the 150th Brigade in Locon and Essars, and the 151st Brigade in Vendin and Beuvry. The 50th Division now formed part of the XI Corps of the First Army. But during the next few days the Division was ordered to move to the Estaires area and join the XV Corps of the First Army.

On the 7th of April the 151st Brigade moved by road and light railway to Estaires, and the following day the 149th and 150th Brigades and the remainder of the Division (less artillery which had not yet rejoined from the Somme) moved to Merville.

The front line from Givenchy northwards to the Ypres–Comines Canal was held on this date (8th April) by the 55th, Portuguese, 40th, 34th, 25th, 19th and 9th Divisions: with the exception of the 55th and Portuguese Divisions all those holding the front line had already been engaged on the Somme. Of the four divisions in reserve, *i.e.*, 51st, 50th, 49th and 29th, the two former had also been through the operations of March.

The official despatches state that: "Arrangements for the relief of the Portuguese Division, which had been continuously in the line for a long period and needed rest, were therefore undertaken during the first week of April, and were to have been completed by the morning of the 10th of April."

It was in order to relieve the Portuguese that the 50th Division moved to Merville, and the 151st Brigade to Estaires to begin the relief. If the enemy attacked before the line could be taken over from the Portuguese, the 151st Brigade was responsible for the defence of the crossings of the Rivers Lys and Lawe, above and below Estaires.

Estaires at this period was a busy little town; it had hardly been touched by shell fire, and was full of civilian inhabitants who kept the shops and estaminets in full swing, doing good business with the military.

Brigade Headquarters were in Estaires, and on the 7th the G.O.C. and Brigade-Major reconnoitred the defences of the two Rivers and the outpost line which ran from Lestrem to Laventie, the position which the 151st Brigade had been ordered to take up in the event of an attack on the Portuguese.

A defence scheme was then evolved in which battalions were to be disposed as follows: 6th Durham Light Infantry in a system of redoubts named Clifton Post, Riez Bailleul, Carter's Post, Le Drumez Post and Cockshy House. These posts were to be garrisoned by a platoon with a platoon in reserve, and a company in reserve to the whole Battalion. The 8th Durham Light Infantry were to hold the defences and bridgeheads of the River Lawe from Fosse Post to its junction with the River Lys at La Gorgue (exclusive). The 5th Durham Light Infantry were allotted the bridgeheads of the River Lys in front of Estaires from La Gorfue (inclusive) to Nouveau Monde (exclusive), that at the latter place being known as Pont Levis.

Instructions were then issued that, if a heavy bombardment of our line broke out, all troops were at once to "stand to" and, if it became obvious that an attack was taking place, would at once move to their positions of defence.

On arriving in Estaires the troops had spent a happy evening, thinking themselves fortunate in being quartered in billets in the midst of so much civilian life.

THE BATTLE OF ESTAIRES, 9TH–11TH APRIL, 1918

Very early next morning (it was about 4 a.m.) a furious bombardment broke out all along the line from opposite Bethune to Armentières. Shells plunged into Estaires and La Gorgue and soon houses were tumbling down and fires broke out.

The "stand to" was ordered and all troops were soon on the move to their respective battle positions. The 5th Durham Light Infantry in Estaires were cheered on their way by the Regimental Band. By this time some of the streets were already impassable for transport. One officer was killed at the head of his men before the Battalion cleared the town. The civilians were in a pitiable state, but little could be done for them but advice given them to clear out at once.

In the meantime, the 149th and 150th Brigades had, between 5 a.m. and 5.30 a.m. received orders to "stand to" and be prepared to move at one hour's notice.

Battalions of the 149th Brigade were billeted in the Le Sart–Arrewage–Caudescure area, *i.e.*, just west and north-west of

BATTLE OF ESTAIRES. BRITISH WALKING WOUNDED AWAITING EVACUATION BY LORRIES.
Bethune, 9th April, 1918. 50th and 51st Divisions.

(Imperial War Museum Photographs, Copyright Reserved)

Merville; at 7.30 a.m. they were ordered to move and concentrate at Chapelle Douvelle.

The 150th Brigade, billeted in the areas Doulieu (Brigade Headquarters and 4th East Yorkshires)–Rue Montigny (4th Green Howards) and La Couronne (5th Green Howards), had been ordered to reconnoitre the forward area Fauquissart sector (held by the Portuguese) on the night of the 8th and, if their C.O.s had already made arrangements to do so, on the morning of the 9th.

The fighting strength of the 150th Brigade at this period was 4th East Yorkshires—16 officers, 642 other ranks; 4th Green Howards—11 officers, 787 other ranks; 5th Green Howards—14 officers, 582 other ranks. The Brigade Headquarters Diary adds the following comment: "It should be remembered that battalions had just received large drafts which they had had no opportunity to train or assimilate, while the remainder of the men had barely recovered from the strenuous fighting on the Somme, from which the Brigade had only been withdrawn on April 1st."

At 7 a.m. an order was received for the Brigade to concentrate at Trou Bayard, just north of the Lys and east of Estaires, and by 11 a.m. all three units (as well as the 150th Trench Mortar Battery) had arrived in their allotted positions.

Turning first to the fortunes of the 151st Brigade; at 6.20 a.m. all three battalions were instructed to move to their defence positions. Estaires and the bridgeheads were then under a very heavy bombardment, and unfortunately one shell fell into the billet occupied by officers of the 6th Durham Light Infantry, killing, wounding or burying all these officers, with the result that the Battalion had to proceed into action with only three officers in addition to the Commanding Officer and Adjutant, all platoons and one of the companies being commanded by N.C.O.s. Brigade Headquarters were established in Estaires, and the Forward Report Centre near Pont Riquel, where there was a buried cable. It was afterwards discovered that the cable had been deliberately cut and Brigade Headquarters were therefore cut off from telephonic communication with Report Centre.

At 10 a.m. reports were received that the Portuguese were being attacked; a steady stream of Portuguese flowing westwards confirmed this information. Cyclist patrols were therefore sent forward down all roads leading to the front line and observation posts were established.

By 11 a.m. the worst fears had been confirmed; the enemy had broken through the lines of defences along the whole front held by the Portuguese, and had then turned north and south attacking respectively the flanks of the 40th and 55th Divisions. By this time also the last of the Portuguese had passed through the 151st Brigade; they had left all their guns, from 9·2's downwards, in the hands of the enemy.

The position held by the 151st Brigade thus became the front line and patrols, both infantry and cyclist, were pushed forward to gain touch with the enemy.

Earlier, 151st Brigade Headquarters had received intimation that the 51st Division was moving up as fast as possible to the right flank of the Brigade, and that the 150th Brigade was also on the way to man the bridgehead over the Lys on the left. Dispositions were also received from the 40th Division which stated that their reserve line of defence had been captured, and that their reserve brigade held a line from Cockshy House through Laventie to Sailly Station with two battalions, thus continuing the outpost line of redoubts to the north.

At 12 noon touch was obtained with the enemy. He was then reported to be within six hundred yards of the outpost line as well as advancing in force on Laventie.

The disposition of the three Durham Battalions was now as follows: the 6th held a line of fortified farms and posts about two miles south-east of Estaires; the 8th Battalion held the bridges over the Lawe near Lestrem with detached posts in front; the 5th Durhams held the bridges at La Gorgue, Pont Levis and Pont de la Meuse (east and west respectively) at Estaires.

The 6th Durhams must have become involved with the enemy shortly after noon, but their Diary records only that "After fighting all day the Battalion withdrew to a line running north from Lestrem."

But from the Brigade Headquarters' Diary it is possible to gather something of the gallant fight put up by the 6th Durham Light Infantry before they were practically wiped out, as the records show.

Patrols returned to Brigade Headquarters with the information that Laventie was being evacuated, and that there were no British or Portuguese troops on the left flank of our outpost line; also that the enemy had already reached the western outskirts of Laventie. They also reported Cockshy House (held by the 6th Durhams) as smashed in by shell fire, and the garrison of that post destroyed. The 151st Trench Mortar Battery (the only reserve in the Brigade at that time) was immediately sent forward (at 1.30 p.m.) to reinforce Le Drumez Post (also held by the 6th Durhams) and endeavour to delay the enemy's drive, obviously heading for the crossings over the Lys between Pont de la Meuse and Nouveau Monde. But all there were in the outpost line to oppose the driving wedge of the enemy in this direction were two platoons.

Though the gallant garrison put up a splendid resistance to the very last, Le Drumez Post and Carter's Post (6th Durhams) fell to the enemy at 1.45 p.m.

The 151st Trench Mortar Battery had been unable to arrive at Le Drumez to save the post and took up an isolated position astride the La Bassée road.

The 6th Durham Light Infantry were then ordered to move their reserve company to the left flank and establish a refused flank, joining up their outpost garrison at Riez Bailleul with the garrisons of the Lys and Pont Levis bridgeheads. The 5th Durham Light Infantry were ordered to move supports forward to assist at this junction.

The enemy was now advancing rapidly in two columns, the first heading for the bridgeheads, and the second swinging out from Le Drumez with the obvious intention of rolling up the outpost line of redoubts, and securing the crossings of the Lawe River at Lestrem.

The enemy's first column reached the Lys at Nouveau Monde some time before 3 p.m. The information was at once passed on to the 5th Durham Light Infantry, that they were to hold Pont Levis "at all costs." The same Battalion was also ordered to deliver a counter-attack in the direction of Laventie with one of their reserve companies with the idea of strengthening the refused flank south-east of Pont Levis.

There is no information concerning this counter-attack.

At 3.30 p.m. the 8th Durham Light Infantry (in front of Lestrem) reported that they were in touch with the 152nd Brigade (51st Division) on the right; they also reported that the last two posts held by the 6th Durhams, *i.e.*, Riez Bailleul and Clifton Post, had fallen, the garrison of the former having been surrounded, and that of the latter having been driven back by the enemy. At 4 p.m. therefore, the remnants of the 6th Durham Light Infantry (four officers and sixty men) were ordered to fall back to a position and fill a gap between the 8th and 5th Durham Light Infantry. One company of the 7th Durham Light Infantry (Pioneers) was sent also to this gap to come under the orders of the O.C., 6th Battalion.

The 151st Brigade Headquarters Diary, which at this point is very explicit, states that: "The battle zone had now reached bridgehead defences of Rivers Lawe and Lys, and the battle concentrated into two main attacks, one attack being thrown against river east of Lestrem, with the obvious objective of obtaining a crossing over the River Lawe, and the second being thrown between Pont Levis and Nouveau Monde with the idea of obtaining a crossing over the River Lys. These two attacks were definite and isolated from each other and will therefore be treated separately as far as possible."*

The Battle for the Crossings over the Lys will be dealt with first: the situation at 6 p.m. at Pont Levis was serious, and two companies from Brigade Reserve were sent up to take up a position in front of Pont Levis and fire down the La Bassée road. Cyclist patrols reported that the enemy had forced back the garrison of Pont Levis to the northern bank of the River. The 5th Durhams had by now used up all their available reserves and the 151st Trench Mortar Battery, situated on the northern bank of the River behind Pont Levis, was ordered to counter-attack and re-establish the bridgehead. This counter-attack was launched immediately and the bridgehead re-established.

At 5.15 p.m. the 4th Northumberland Fusiliers (149th Brigade) were placed at the disposal of the 151st Brigade for the purpose of counter-attacking the enemy, if he obtained a crossing over the Lys. The Northumberlands moved at once to a position on the northern side of Estaires, and an hour later were placed under the command of Lieut.-Col. G. O. Spence (5th Durham Light Infantry), commanding defences of the River Lys, with instructions that they were to be used for counter-attack purposes only.

Fighting continued at Pont Levis. The enemy, supported by artillery, trench mortar and machine-gun fire, again

---

*It must be remembered that for the moment the operations of the 151st Brigade (and attached troops) are being described; those of the 149th and 150th Brigades will follow. For the sake of clarity it is necessary to adopt this method.

attacked and again drove the garrison over the bridge. It now looked as if the Germans would succeed in holding the bridge, but two gallant men—Privates T. Tweddle and E. Dean—volunteered to try and rush the position. Others then came forward and, in spite of heavy fire and a desperate defence by the enemy, the bridge was re-captured and held until voluntarily relinquished during the night.

At 7 p.m. the position was such that it was deemed more satisfactory to hold the northern bank of the Lys, and blow up the bridgeheads, for the enemy had brought up his field guns and was systematically smashing up the bridgehead garrisons at point-blank range. He had also established machine-gun posts in houses in Nouveau Monde which were firing in enfilade at the garrisons. Accordingly orders were issued for the 5th Durham Light Infantry to withdraw to the northern bank of the River; also for the withdrawal of the 6th Durham Light Infantry, reinforced by one company of the 7th Durham Light Infantry (Pioneers) and one company of the 4th Northumberland Fusiliers, to the northern bank of the River Lawe, obtaining touch with the 5th Durham Light Infantry southwest of La Gorgue, and with the 8th Durham Light Infantry at Lestrem.

The 8th Durham Light Infantry were still to hold the eastern bank of the River re-entrant in front of Lestrem, *i.e.*, Pont Riquel and the Le Marais Posts. This withdrawal began at dusk and was successfully carried out during the night.

The Pont de la Meuse was successfully blown up, but the charge at Pont Levis failed to destroy the bridge completely. A further effort during the night was also unsuccessful. The bridge at La Gorgue was also blown up.

At 3.30 a.m. on the 10th orders were received at 151st Brigade Headquarters from Divisional Headquarters that the line was to be re-adjusted before dawn, as follows: The 51st Division would side-step west and relieve the 8th Durham Light Infantry up to Lestrem Bridge (inclusive); the 149th Brigade would take over the defences of Pont Levis from the 5th Durham Light Infantry. The relief of the Durhams was to be carried out by a portion of the 4th Northumberland Fusiliers, the remainder of that Battalion passing back to the command of their own brigade. The 8th Durham Light Infantry, on relief, were to be withdrawn to the neighbourhood of Beaupré to be in Brigade Reserve for counter-attack purposes. These orders were circulated at once, but Brigade Headquarters' Narrative records: "As 51st Division would not move up to relieve the 8th Durham Light Infantry this Battalion had to remain where they were and hold the River re-entrant in front of Lestrem."

The story of the 8th Durham Light Infantry on the first day of the Battle of Estaires is one of hard fighting, for the Durhams were engaged in the second of the enemy's attacks, *i.e.*, the Battle of Lestrem.

The position held by the Battalion was east of the Lawe, a sharp salient consisting of a series of detached posts in the form of redoubts covering the crossings over the River. On the left flank was Pont Riquel Post, in the centre (in front of Lock de la Rault) Le Marais Post East, Le Marais Post West and Le Marais Post South; there was also a garrison, about one thousand yards south-west of Le Marais Post South, holding a footbridge and an R.E. bridge crossing the Lawe.

The posts were held by two companies ("A" and "B") with "D" Company in support on the banks of the Lawe about five hundred yards north-west of Le Marais Post West; "C" Company was in reserve near Battalion Headquarters, some five hundred yards west of Lock de la Rault.

Apparently Le Marais Post East was the first to fall, the enemy capturing the Post at about 1 p.m. At 1.40 p.m. the officer in command of Le Marais Post South stated that the enemy was then attacking his position, but he was being held up by the fire of machine-guns which had been placed on the Canal bank, causing him heavy losses.

Following the capture of Le Marais Post East, the enemy working round Le Marais Post West from the north captured the Post and its garrison, and then advanced in a south-westerly direction. This Post was lost shortly before 3 p.m.

The enemy now threatened Lock de la Rault, the garrison of which was very weak; two platoons were, therefore, sent forward at once with orders to counter-attack immediately if the enemy succeeded in obtaining a footing.

By 4.30 p.m. Le Marais Post South, which had, up to then, put up a most gallant resistance, was almost surrounded; the garrison therefore withdrew, fighting a rear-guard action to near the foot and R.E. bridges, where a line was dug in conjunction with the garrison at that point. A platoon was sent up to strengthen this line and another to Lock de la Rault.

At 5 p.m. the Germans, under cover of a heavy artillery barrage, advanced and a few gained the crossing at Lock de la Rault, but they were then held up and a counter-attack by three platoons was organised by the Durhams. It was not successful, being broken up by the enemy's intense machine-gun fire. A line was then established on the western side of the Lock. In this position the 8th Durham Light Infantry had units of the 51st Division on both flanks.

The situation was that, at 11 p.m., one of the above-mentioned units was withdrawn into reserve, and the other side-stepped southwards, leaving the 8th Durham Light Infantry almost holding a salient, the 7th Gordons (51st Division) holding the R.E. bridge and footbridge.

Thus the operations of the 151st Brigade on the 9th of April.

Turning now to the 150th Brigade: just after 12 noon the Brigadier had received orders from Divisional Headquarters to hold the line of the River Lys east of Estaires. He then set out personally to see all units of the Brigade placed in position. On arrival at a redoubt near Trou Bayard the enemy's shell fire was so heavy in that area that it was obvious he intended attacking. The 4th Green Howards were the first unit met by the Brigadier, and were given orders to move to the left flank of the line to be held. The Battalion reached its allotted position at about 2 p.m., and began digging in on a line which ran from Rouge Maison Farm, on the right, to the temporary bridge south of a factory, on the left and north of Sailly. Three companies took over this line with one in reserve. The 4th East Yorkshires were on the right of the 4th Green Howards, and the 21st Middlesex (40th Division) on the left. The Green Howards destroyed a footbridge over the Lys on their front, and the Royal Engineers had a demolition party ready to blow up the bridge at Sailly.

Having given orders to the 4th Green Howards, the Brigadier then found the C.O. of the 4th East Yorkshires and 5th Green Howards. The East Yorkshires were ordered to proceed to the right of the line, their left resting on Rouge Maison Farm where they were in touch with the 4th Green Howards; on their right they gained touch with the 5th Durham Light Infantry defending Pont Levis.

The 5th Green Howards were ordered to a line between Farms de Bretagne and Quennelle.

Both the East Yorkshires and the 4th Green Howards were hardly in position before the enemy's troops reached the eastern bank of the Lys. Opposite the right flank of the East Yorkshires, on the eastern bank of the River, was a small place—Nouveau Monde—and here the enemy's machine-guns were firing from houses overlooking a bridge which spanned the Lys. Desperate fighting took place for the possession of this bridge. The Germans, covered by their machine-guns and advancing in rushes, tried to cross. But at each attempt they were driven back. With rifle and machine-gun fire the enemy was repulsed, the fire control of the East Yorkshiremen being excellent—a very praiseworthy thing considering that officers and men were practically new to one another. The new drafts were doing wonderfully well. This bridge was successfully "blown" by the R.E. during the late afternoon. At 6.55 p.m. the Battalion was ordered to push out posts, with Lewis guns, to the River's edge in order to patrol the western bank during the night.

Away on the left of the 4th East Yorkshires, the 4th Green Howards record that, by 4 p.m., all British and Portuguese troops had withdrawn from the eastern bank of the Lys. The R.E. tried to blow up the bridge at Sailly, but failed to do so. The bridge, however, was held by posts of the Green Howards, and the enemy suffered heavy casualties in attempting to cross. During the late afternoon the enemy crossed the Lys some distance north of the Green Howards and formed a line at right-angles to the Battalion front; this line ran—road from Bac St. Maur–Croix du Bac–Pont Vanuxeem. The enemy was held on this line throughout the night.

With the exception of patrol work, the 5th Green Howards had a comparatively quiet night. Battalion patrols, finding a gap existing between the right of the 4th East Yorkshires and the left of the 5th Durham Light Infantry, put a company into the space between the two Battalions. This Company ("A") was, however, relieved by the East Yorkshiremen at 10 p.m., but kept in close support.

At 3.45 p.m. the Brigadier of the 150th Brigade had received a message from Divisional Headquarters stating that the 149th Brigade was moving up in support with orders to counter-attack immediately should the enemy succeed in crossing the River. Headquarters of the Brigade were established, with those of the 150th Brigade, at Pont de Poivre, at 2.30 p.m.

At 3.15 p.m. the 5th and 6th Northumberland Fusiliers moved up into position in support of the 150th Brigade "with orders to counter-attack any portion of the line which may be pierced. The line of the River Lys and River Lawe to be held at all costs."

The 6th Northumberlands moved to the left to protect that flank of the 150th Brigade and patrol the stream which ran almost due north to Steenwerck. At 9.10 p.m. the 5th Northumberlands were ordered to take up position in strong points near Trou Bayard where they joined up with the 4th Northumberlands.

At 5.30 p.m. the 4th Northumberlands had sent a platoon and two Lewis guns to report to the 5th Durham Light Infantry on the far side of Pont Levis. The platoon took up a position covering the approach to the bridge. A portion of "A" Company then went forward to hold the house on the near side of the Canal bank between Pont de la Meuse and Pont Levis.

The Diary of the 4th Battalion thus reports (from 7 p.m. onwards): "The remainder of the night was quiet. The enemy was reported to have crossed the Canal further north, but no definite information was obtained regarding this." The Diary then adds (a tribute to the "Q" Branch): "Rations were received in good time and distributed to companies."

Thus, so far as the 50th Division was concerned, ended the first day of the Battle of Estaires. The enemy, for the little advance he had made along the Divisional front, had lost very heavily. Several Divisional units also had suffered severe casualties, but battalion commanders had noted with great satisfaction the behaviour of the beardless youth, who had come fresh to the Division. One officer wrote of them: "The youths from home, conquering inexperience and the first fright of battle, vied with our veterans in tenacity, resolution and faithfulness."

By the night of the 9th of April, the original British line from Givenchy to Bois Grenier had given way, and when darkness had fallen ran roughly—Festubert–Le Touret–Le Cason–Vieille Chapelle–Pont Rigneul, thence round the north of Lestrem–La Gorgue–just east of Estaires along the western bank of the Lys, to west of Sailly-sur-la-Lys to Croix du Bac–north of Fleurbaix–to just north of Bois Grenier. A big dent, on a front of about ten miles, had thus been made in our line, creating dangerous salients north and south.

The official despatches, which describe the heavy fighting on the 10th of April, and the struggle for Estaires, twice mention the 50th Division:

"Early in the morning of the 10th of April the enemy launched heavy attacks covered by artillery fire about the river crossings at Lestrem and Estaires, and succeeded in reaching the left bank of both places; but in each case he was driven back again by determined counter-attacks by the 50th Division.

"The enemy continued to exercise great pressure at Estaires, and fierce street fighting took place in which both sides lost heavily. Machine-guns, mounted by our troops in the upper rooms of houses, did great execution on his troops as they moved up to the attack, until the machine-guns were knocked out by artillery fire. In the evening the German infantry once more forced their way into Estaires and, after a most gallant resistance, the 50th Division withdrew at nightfall to a prepared position to the north and west of the town."

The above general view of the fighting on the 10th of April summarises in excellent terms the fine work done by all units of the Division.

Throughout the night of the 9th–10th Estaires was shelled heavily by the enemy; in all directions buildings were toppling down and already the town was a mass of ruins.

At 1.55 a.m. (10th) orders were issued for a re-adjustment of the Divisional front: the 151st Brigade to hold from Lestrem Bridge (exclusive) to Pont Levis (exclusive); the 149th Brigade from Pont Levis (inclusive) to the Lys, opposite Rue de la Lys, with one battalion in the front line and two in reserve; the 150th Brigade thence to the junction of the Steenwerck with the Lys, with reserve battalions so placed as to be able to counter-attack rapidly towards Sailly, or continue the defensive flanks on the Stillbecque.

Soon after daybreak fighting began again. The 5th Northumberland Fusiliers,* who were now holding Pont Levis, were heavily attacked under cover of violent artillery fire. In spite of the fine resistance put up by the Fusiliers the enemy forced his way across the bridge, though a dozen machine-guns, firing from Trou Bayard, gave him a warm reception. Only his prodigious numbers carried him through.

---

*They had relieved the 4th East Yorkshires very early on the 10th of April.

Ferme Quennell had also fallen to the enemy as he forced his way into the south-eastern part of Estaires and captured some of the houses on the north side of the main street.

The Brigadier of the 149th Brigade at once organised a counter-attack; the 6th Northumberland Fusiliers were detailed for this operation.

Covered by the fire of four Howitzers and twelve 18-pounders (the only guns available), with the machine-guns at Trou Bayard co-operating, the Fusiliers deployed under the trees near Trou Bayard with their right flank on the Estaires–Neuf Berquin road.

Of this gallant counter-attack there is no official record, and only a few particulars, gathered from private sources, can be given. For in place of the Diary of the 6th Northumberland Fusiliers for April, 1918, there is a letter, dated the 3rd of May, written by the O.C. of that Battalion to Brigade Headquarters:

"Owing to the exceptional volume of the heavy casualties suffered by this Battalion lately, which include the C.O., Adjutant and Intelligence Officer, great difficulty is being experienced in obtaining authentic data for the continuous history of the operations in which this unit has taken part during the period covered by the War Diary in question. Major J. G. Leathart, at present at Le Touquet, is the only surviving officer who can supply certain necessary facts, and as he will not be returning to the Battalion until the end of the present week, I fear that it will not be possible to submit the War Diary for April at the stipulated time. It will be forwarded at the earliest possible moment."

"The earliest possible moment" never came, for the 6th Northumberland Fusiliers moved down to the Aisne, and there shared the tragic fate of other units of the 50th Division.

With great determination the Battalion advanced, forcing their way through the gardens and houses north of the main street of Estaires. But they found the enemy holding the cemetery and approaches to Pont Levis, and further progress in the face of a murderous fire was impossible. The Battalion had, however, cleared the enemy from a considerable portion of the town, and he now held only the eastern edge to within two to three hundred yards of Pont Levis, which was never cleared. By 10.30 a.m. the 6th Northumberland Fusiliers had gained touch with the 5th Durham Light Infantry, who were holding the river bank at Pont de la Meuse. There were two or three factories near the river and in the upper floors of these the Fusiliers mounted their machine-guns which swept the approaches to both bridges and caused the enemy south of the river, very heavy losses. But as the day wore on the position became more and more difficult.

Despite the repeated efforts of the 149th Brigade to turn him out, the enemy still held on to the cemetery, and at about 4.30 p.m. hostile artillery was concentrated on to the houses and factories in which machine-guns had been mounted. Very soon these places were smashed to bits and many of our machine-guns and Lewis guns put out of action—an end which must have been foreseen by the gallant men who had manned the ruined buildings, to which they clung with so much tenacity and courage.

Under cover of this fire the Germans in large numbers crossed the river at Pont Levis and to the west of it. Concentrated machine-gun fire from Trou Bayard was directed on to the bridge but, although suffering very heavy casualties, the enemy succeeded in working through the houses and cemetery on the northern edge of the town, and the 6th Northumberland Fusiliers were withdrawn to the neighbourhood of the Water Tower.

The enemy was now firmly established among the houses between the church and Pont Levis. At 4 p.m. an advance by him towards Trou Bayard was stopped by machine-gun fire from Pont Poivre. At 6 p.m. he was still pressing, but was held. At 7 p.m. the 6th Northumberland Fusiliers, owing to heavy casualties, had to evacuate a portion of Estaires. At 9 p.m. the enemy was still held.

Meanwhile, both the 150th and 151st Brigades had also been involved in heavy fighting all day long.

On the right, where the 151st Brigade held the Pont Rigneul salient (a front of nearly three thousand yards), the 8th Durham Light Infantry* were attacked under heavy trench mortar fire, and forced back on to the line held by the 51st Division (on the right of the 50th). Some mingling of units occurred here and the situation about Lestrem was for a while in doubt. But in conjunction with troops of the 51st Division,

---

*"The 8th Battalion Durham Light Infantry" gives the position of the Battalion at 5 a.m. on the 10th as Pont Levis (not the Estaires bridge)—western bank of the River Lawe at Pont Rigneul—line of posts west of Lock de la Rault and Lestrem Post.

the Durhams counter-attacked and Lestrem Post was recaptured, and a line of posts established east of Lestrem village. Lestrem Post, however, had to be evacuated during the night when, badly outflanked and shelled unmercifully, the garrison had to withdraw. Very late that night the 8th Durhams were relieved, and withdrew into Brigade Reserve at Beaupré.

The situation of the remnants of the 6th Durham Light Infantry with one company of the 7th Battalion (Pioneers) on the right, ran along the western bank of the Lawe from a little south of the railway bridge, thence along the northern bank of the canal to the Estaires–Chapelle Douvelle road, where touch was obtained with the 5th Durham Light Infantry. The latter, after heavy fighting throughout the day, were withdrawn at 8 p.m. to a position south-east of Vierhouck, where the Battalion dug in. During the day their C.O. (Lieut.-Col. G. O. Spence) and several more officers were wounded.

The fortunes of the 150th Brigade are difficult to follow for, time after time, the situation became obscure, the enemy on the left of the Brigade continually outflanking units.

At dawn on the 10th the Brigade was disposed in the following positions: on the right, two companies of 4th East Yorkshires held the western bank of the Lys from opposite Rue de la Lys to Rouge Maison Farm; the remaining two companies were along the road in rear of the Farm.

The 4th Green Howards were on the left of the East Yorkshires from Rouge Maison Farm (exclusive) to the junction of the Lys with the Steenwerck, and the 5th Green Howards, protecting the left flank of the Brigade, faced north-east and south-east, west of Pont de la Boudrette.

Along the Brigade front, the night of the 9th–10th had been comparatively quiet; rations and ammunition had been issued, and some of the men had succeeded in getting a few hours rest.

Orders for the readjustment of the line, which had been received at 3.30 a.m. at 150th Brigade Headquarters, were sent out to units; so far as the Brigade was concerned these orders meant the relief of the right and centre companies of the 4th East Yorkshires by the 149th Brigade, and the moving of the 5th Green Howards in rear of the 4th Green Howards, where they would be in a position to protect the left flank of the Division. The 5th Green Howards completed their move before dawn, but the two companies of East Yorkshires were not so lucky, and one company was scattered by machine-gun and shell fire.

At 7.45 a.m. the enemy was reported in La Boudrelle. The 5th Green Howards were then ordered to patrol vigorously in the direction of the village, but it was 11 a.m. before Colonel Thomson (5th Green Howards) was able to confirm the report that the enemy was in La Boudrelle in strength. His battalion was then disposed as follows: two companies were in line facing south-east, each forming a defensive flank with elements of Scottish Fusiliers on their right, and no one on their left; one company was supporting the 4th Green Howards and one was held in reserve. For the time being the left flank, though threatened, appeared to be fairly secure. But on the right of the brigade, the fact that the enemy was in Estaires and held Pont Levis, made the situation on that flank somewhat obscure—"Brigade was, in fact, being threatened from both flanks, and the only redeeming feature of the situation was the arrival of the 29th Division in support."[*]

A report, timed 10.10 a.m., received at Brigade Headquarters from the 4th Green Howards, disclosed no change in the situation, but their position, covering the bridge at Sailly-sur-la-Lys, was rapidly becoming untenable. The enemy was advancing from the direction of La Boudrelle across the rear of the Battalion and by noon it was necessary to withdraw from the advanced positions or be cut off. The 4th Green Howards, in their records, state that troops holding the line opposite Pont Vanuxeem (at right-angles to the Green Howards) were driven back and their retirement eventually exposed the left flank of the Battalion. Heavily attacked in front as well as from the left, the Green Howards were compelled to fall back to a new line which the troops on their left had taken up. This line ran from one hundred to three hundred yards east of, and parallel with, the Trou Bayard–Le Pt. Mortier road. The 4th Green Howards then had the 4th East Yorkshires on their right and the 5th Green Howards on their left. The line was held throughout the night of the 10th–11th April. During the withdrawal Major Graham, who commanded the 4th Green Howards, was wounded.

---

[*] Narrative of 150th Brigade.

The withdrawal of the 4th Green Howards involved the 5th Green Howards, whose defensive flank became heavily engaged. Large bodies of the enemy attempted to press back the line, but the battalion, with fine tenacity, stuck to their position. "Great contest for fire superiority developed," records the 150th Brigade Diary, "and Colonel Thomson recorded it as his opinion that it was the arrival of a limber (seventeen boxes) of ammunition at about 4 p.m. that decided the battle, and enabled the Battalion to hold its ground for the day. This S.A.A. was sent up in a machine-gun company limber, the normal battalion system of supply having entirely broken down."

The Brigade Narrative then states that: "The fortunes of the 4th East Yorkshires during the afternoon are more difficult to follow," but from the Battalion Diary it is evident that they were badly cut up, though putting up a splendid resistance.

It will be remembered that early in the morning two companies of the 5th Northumberland Fusiliers had relieved "A" and "B" Companies of the 4th East Yorkshires, who had suffered heavy casualties. In this relief two platoons of "A" Company went astray, and they were reported as "lost"; a similar fate overtook the company commander who went off to find them. "A" Company had been scattered by heavy artillery and machine-gun fire. "B" Company, with the two remaining platoons of "A," withdrew to the Estaires–Croix du Bac road, behind their old position, and dug in, where they formed a counter-attack force if called upon.

At about 12 noon, the company commander of "B" Company (Capt. Ruthven) observed that there were no British troops in front of him and that the line had retired, evidently to a flank. For the enemy had appeared not only on a ridge about 150 yards on his right flank, but also in front of him. He therefore sent two platoons forward a few yards to hold the position, and for two hours these gallant men maintained their position, when the remnants of "B" Company were withdrawn, though their company commander was later reported as "missing."*

The trouble was that the 4th Green Howards had not informed the East Yorkshires that they were compelled to fall back. On receiving information from "C" and "D" Companies, however, the latter formed a defensive flank, but

---

*Capt. Ruthven was captured by the enemy.

they could not obtain touch on the left with the 4th Green Howards.

The last message received at Brigade Headquarters from Major Jackson, commanding 4th East Yorkshires, timed 2.30 p.m., stated that the enemy was massing in the direction of Rouge Maison Farm; the situation of the two companies was then desperate. They had with them two companies of Northumberland Fusiliers, but these were withdrawn owing to the enemy being round their right flank.

At 4 p.m. the remnants of "C" and "D" Companies, "who had been fighting for thirty hours," were then under the command of Capt. Barr; communication with Battalion Headquarters had been cut off for two hours. Capt. Barr then made a reconnaissance and found that he and his men were nearly surrounded, as the enemy was on his left rear, in front, and coming up on the right rear. There was barely time to withdraw but, posting two Lewis-gun sections on the Trou Bayard–Croix du Bac road to cover them the tired and exhausted survivors of the two gallant companies were successfully withdrawn.

Their safe withdrawal was due to the splendid bravery of the two Lewis-gun sections who covered them. One by one these gallant fellows fell dead or wounded until the last man remained, and presently he dropped too. The whole of the two sections had become casualties, but they had done their duty nobly.

As to Battalion Headquarters of the 4th East Yorkshires, their records state: "Battalion Headquarters, consisting of Major Jackson (C.O.), Capt. Slack (Adjutant), Second-Lieut. Thompson (Intelligence Officer), the R.S.M., and orderly room corporal, had been at their headquarters (a shell hole) all the 9th and 10th until about 3 p.m. (on the latter date presumably), when the enemy had appeared about fifty yards to their front; from which time there is no information concerning them and they are missing."

The line occupied by the 50th Division after dark ran from Lestrem, on the right, to Beaupré, thence along the Estaires Road Defensive Line to Trou Bayard, thence to La Boudrelle.*

---

*The possession of La Boudrelle on the night of the 10th of April is open to doubt.

Officially the Battle of Estaires ended on the night of the 10th of April, but those in the line knew that fighting was practically continuous throughout the night and the next day, and that a Battle Honour should have been awarded for the operations of the 11th, south of the Messines area.

THE OPERATIONS OF THE 50TH DIVISION ON THE 11TH APRIL, 1918

Dawn broke on the 11th on the three infantry brigades holding the line given above: the 151st on the right, 149th in the centre and 150th on the left.

On the morning of the 11th the enemy attacked on the whole front and again made progress. Between Givenchy and the Lawe River, the successful resistance of the past two days was maintained against repeated assaults. But between Locon and Estaires the enemy who, on the previous evening, had established a footing on the western bank of the river in the neighbourhood of Fosse, continued to push westwards despite vigorous resistance.

The official despatches again mention the 50th Division on the 11th of April: "At Estaires the troops of the 50th Division, tired and reduced in numbers by the exceptionally heavy fighting of the previous three weeks, and threatened on their right flank by the enemy's advance south of the Lys, were heavily engaged. After holding their position with great gallantry during the morning, they were slowly pressed back in the direction of Merville."

Of the 151st Brigade, the 6th Durham Light Infantry (still with the company of 7th Durham Light Infantry attached) held a line from a bend in the Canal to the railway, southward, over the Lawe River. The 5th Durhams were on their left in a line of old trenches and redoubts which ran from the Estaires–Neuf Berquin road to the bend already mentioned in the Lys Canal. The 8th Durham Light Infantry were in support, *i.e.*, two companies in Beaupré and two behind the left of the line held by the 6th Battalion.

Early in the morning the enemy gained ground near Lestrem and the 6th Durham Light Infantry, with two companies of the 8th Battalion, formed a line along the railway embankment protecting the flank of the Brigade.

The 5th Durham Light Infantry were attacked as soon as day broke, with trench mortars and field guns brought up to close range and snipers firing from behind iron shields. After this preliminary bombardment the German infantry began to advance from Estaires and La Gorgue and, covered by an intensive fire, were very soon near the trenches and posts held by the 5th Durhams. On the right there was a gap of about one thousand yards between the 5th and 6th Battalions, and into this gap the enemy penetrated to a small wood in rear of "C" Company of the former unit, whom they threatened with envelopment. The 6th and 8th Battalions, also aware of this gap but unable to fill it, prepared to destroy the pontoon bridge over the Lys at Beaupré, and move westwards on Merville to the bridgehead garrisons of that place. This withdrawal (covered by two companies of the 8th Durham Light Infantry) was successfully carried out, and the pontoon bridge destroyed. By 2.45 p.m. the enemy had gained a footing in Chapelle Duvelle. A party of one hundred men of the 7th Durham Light Infantry counter-attacked, but the attack was unsuccessful. The line after this counter-attack ran from the Canal west of Chapelle Duvelle thence to Pont de la Trompe.

Meanwhile the 5th Durham Light Infantry were still being heavily attacked. On the left of the Battalion a gap existed between the Durhams and the 149th Brigade through which the enemy forced his way up the road towards Neuf Berquin, outflanking the 5th who again had to retire; at about 2 p.m. they held a recently-prepared line just east of Neuf Berquin.

The Divisional Narrative mentions this attack on the 5th Durhams in the following words: "The resistance offered along the Neuf Berquin road by the 5th Durham Light Infantry, which consisted mainly of the Battalion Headquarters under Lieut.-Colonel Spence (and a counter-attack delivered about 11 a.m. by the 6th Northumberland Fusiliers), delayed the enemy's advance to such an extent that the troops were not driven back on to the line prepared by the R.E., east of Neuf Berquin, until nearly 2 p.m. The enemy were attacking in masses, but made little impression on the line which commanded an excellent field of fire, until concentrated machine-gun fire and close-range field-gun fire destroyed one post after another."

About 4 p.m. the enemy made another fierce attack near Neuf Berquin. There was still an ugly gap north-west of the road and the German machine-gunners made full use of it. So the gallant little band of 5th Durhams had to fall back again, during which the Colonel was wounded. The line was now composed of small groups of men utterly worn out with continuous fighting and isolated from one another. But the friendly darkness put an end to the fighting, for the enemy stayed his advance as night fell. An officer who was present said: "I think the only thing that saved us that night was the amount of liquor the Bosches found in Estaires and Neuf Berquin, as I have never heard such a noise in my life as they made, singing." It was about 6 p.m. when the enemy gained possession of Neuf Berquin. At 8 p.m. the 5th Durham Light Infantry were withdrawn to a position south-east of Vierhouck where they dug in. The 6th and 8th Durhams had been withdrawn to the west of Merville.

Meanwhile the 149th Brigade, who at 2 a.m. on the 11th held a line from the Estaires–Neuf Berquin road to just west of Trou Bayard, had had a hard day's fighting. The 5th Northumberland Fusiliers held the right sector of the line, and the 4th Battalion the left; the 6th Battalion was in reserve.

At 7 a.m. the enemy was reported to have occupied Trou Bayard.

At 9.35 a.m. the 5th Battalion was heavily attacked and the 151st Brigade, on the right, having by that hour been forced back, thus exposing the right of the 149th Brigade, the 5th Northumberland Fusiliers were withdrawn. The 6th Northumberland Fusiliers were ordered at 11 a.m. to move forward and establish a line running north-east from the Estaires–Neuf Berquin road, but by 1.50 p.m. the Battalion had not progressed very far, the enemy's opposition being too stiff. At 2 p.m. a section of men were reported to be holding out around Trou Bayard.

By 2 p.m., however, the line was being gradually forced back and, although the Brigade was in touch on the left with the 29th Division, the right flank was open. At 4.15 p.m., however the line still held, and at 8 p.m. also, no further withdrawal had been made. At 11 p.m., after a conference between the brigadiers of the 149th and 86th and 87th (29th Division) Brigades, orders were given for the line to fall back to the line Vierhoek–Neuf Berquin road, the 149th Brigade to hold Vierhoek to the cross-roads on the Neuf Berquin–Vieux Berquin road, just south of Pont Rondin.

The move was to begin at 2.30 a.m., 12th April.

Throughout the 11th of April the 150th Brigade saw hard fighting. At dawn, the 4th East Yorkshires held Trou Bayard, from whence the line ran in a north-easterly direction, with the 4th and 5th Green Howards (in that order) on the left of the East Yorkshires. The left of the 5th Green Howards was thrown back to form a defensive flank opposite (west of) the Steenwerck.

At 6.30 a.m. all was quiet along the Brigade front, but two hours later the 4th Green Howards reported that the enemy was advancing against the Battalion's front, in large numbers, with a line of skirmishers thrown out in front. At 9.5 a.m. the 5th Green Howards reported that the enemy's pressure on their front was very great and that a withdrawal to the line held by the 29th Division was imminent. Fighting hard, the Green Howards held on until practically surrounded, and many were captured or left wounded, owing to the impossibility of getting them away. The Brigade Diary records that: "What actually happened on this front remains obscure. It seems, however, certain that the elements of the 40th Division, on our immediate left, withdrew before dawn leaving our flank exposed."* The result was that when the enemy started his advance between 8 and 9 a.m. he managed to work in behind the 5th Green Howards. The greater part of that Battalion was cut off, only stragglers being able to get away. The enemy then worked in behind the 4th Green Howards, and again only stragglers were able to escape. In the meantime, the line of the 4th East Yorkshires through Trou Bayard was still holding firm.

At 9.45 a.m. the 87th Brigade (29th Division) reported to the Brigadier of the 150th Brigade that they had received orders to take over the front held by the latter. The Brigadier immediately went to 87th Brigade Headquarters to fix up details for the relief though, as a matter of fact, the 87th Brigade already held the front line, the 150th Brigade being represented by a few scattered elements. "These," records the Brigade Diary, "it was hoped to withdraw at once, but this could not be done successfully till dark when the situation had completely changed. These elements, therefore, only rejoined after the Brigade had been relieved several days later."

---

*The 40th Division had been relieved by the 31st Division.

At 11.30 a.m. orders for the relief of the Brigade were received from Divisional Headquarters. These orders stated that the Brigade was to concentrate at Pont de la Trompe, south-east of Neuf Berquin. But the Brigadier, in view of the situation, decided that it was better to try to concentrate the Brigade close to Doulieu, and when some men had been collected they would be marched to Pont de la Trompe. The 4th and 5th Green Howards were accordingly ordered to march off towards Doulieu, the 4th East Yorkshires to withdraw as soon as possible, but very few men under Capt. Ralston rejoined the Brigade.

Arrived near Doulieu, the 4th and 5th Green Howards set up a joint Battalion Headquarters, and the remnants of the two Battalions formed a battalion under the command of Colonel Thomson.

At 2.15 p.m. Brigade Headquarters, which had been opened at a farm near Doulieu, moved to Vieux Moulin (on the Neuf Berquin–Vieux Berquin road). About 3 p.m. the Brigadier went out to reconnoitre the position south of the village, and found a line of hastily-dug trenches astride the road about Pont de la Trompe. These were manned by some R. E. companies and a Corps Reinforcement battalion. A thousand yards away the Brigadier saw large bodies of the enemy advancing astride the main road from Estaires; there appeared to be about two regiments advancing in artillery formation with a screen of scouts thrown out. On returning to Brigade Headquarters the Brigadier rang up Divisional Headquarters and reported what he had seen. The Divisional Commander then ordered that the line in front of Vieux Berquin should be held at all costs—a difficult order to carry out, seeing that there were no troops to reinforce or support this line.

The enemy's attack began to develop at about 3.30 p.m., and by 5.15 p.m. the line on both sides of the main road had given way entirely. The Brigadier rallied a certain number of men on the line of Vieux Berquin. The trench mortar battery had already been moved up as reinforcements. At 5.45 p.m., under orders, Brigade Headquarters moved to Vierhoek.

"The position now seemed almost desperate," records the Brigade Narrative. "A wide gap in our line existed from Vierhoek to the main Vieux Berquin road, and it was by no means certain that our line was being held to the east of that road. A certain number of troops were collected at Vierhoek under Lieut. Ginger, and ordered to dig in. It was discovered that Colonel Thomson, with a small party, was holding a position astride the main road about one thousand yards south of Pont Rondin. Darkness was falling fast, and the enemy fortunately were not pressing their advance. Field guns remained in action at Vierhoek till dusk and materially assisted in stopping the enemy's advance." Again Brigade Headquarters moved (after dark), and before midnight were established, with Advanced Divisional Headquarters, north-west of Merville.

Colonel Thomson's gallant little party, numbering in all about fifty, withdrew after dark, and were given a few hours sleep in a barn close to Brigade Headquarters.

A party of men, under Capt. Saltonstall, was ordered by Colonel Pike to hold a position astride the road just south of Vieux Berquin; this party was formed of details from the transport lines, and remained in position until the morning of the 12th.

Meanwhile the 4th Guards Brigade (31st Division) was moving up from Vieux Berquin, and the right flank of that Brigade had to be protected by preventing the enemy debouching from Merville, which he had captured about 9 p.m. But fortunately he did not continue his advance, and for the moment the right flank was safe.

Thus the fortunes of the 150th Brigade throughout the 11th of April. The battalion diaries add little to the details given in the Brigade Narrative, although the latter appears to have lost sight of the 4th East Yorkshires who eventually fetched up in rear of the 4th Guard Brigade support line, south of the Verte Rue–La Couronne road. The strength of this Battalion was now 3 officers and 120 men.

On the night of the 11th of April, the British line at Merville ran roughly north and south, about two miles from the town.

THE BATTLE OF HAZEBROUCK, 12TH–15TH APRIL, 1918

What might have happened had the enemy pushed on westwards through Merville, on the night of the 11th of April, it is impossible to say, but he *may* have broken through our line, for the situation was indeed critical. However, there is evidence that the German soldiery, having entered the town, got out of hand and, instead of pressing their advantage,

BATTLE OF HAZEBROUCK. Troops passing over a railway bridge, which was mined ready to be blown up should it be necessary. 11th April, 1918. Merville.

(Imperial War Museum Photographs, Copyright Reserved)

wasted valuable time in plundering and looting. But on the morning of the 12th he again resumed his vigorous attacks.

The official despatches record that: "At about 8 a.m. the enemy attacked in great strength on a front extending from south of the Estaires–Vieux Berquin neighbourhood. After very heavy fighting . . . he succeeded in the afternoon in overcoming the resistance of our troops about Doulieu and La Becque, forcing them back in a north-westerly direction."

Before it was light the 149th Brigade set out to march to its new position from Vierhouck (inclusive) to the cross-roads on the Neuf Berquin–Vieux Berquin road just south of Pont Rondin. The Brigade marched in three sections (*i*) 4th and 5th Northumberland Fusiliers under Lieut.-Colonel Irwin, providing the flank and advance guards, (*ii*) 6th Northumberland Fusiliers and a few of the 4th Battalion under Major Temperley, (*iii*) Reinforcement Battalion, under the command of the O.C., Corps Troops. At 6.30 a.m. the Brigade was reported as having crossed the road, encountering slight opposition and, half-an-hour later, the 6th Northumberland Fusiliers had occupied Vierhouck, and were forming a defensive flank along the road leading to Pont Rondin, the Battalion line moving from south of the village round the western edge. The Reinforcement Battalion was on the left of the line, and the 5th Northumberland Fusiliers on the left of the Reinforcement Battalion to the Neuf Berquin–Vieux Berquin road. But touch on the left with the 29th Division could not be obtained. The Corps Composite Battalion was on the right, west and south of Merville. The 151st Brigade, whose units were now much intermingled, continued the line along the western bank of the stream opposite the factory north of Merville. Parties of the 150th Brigade, totalling about 150 men, were in position just east of Pont Tournant and towards Vierhouck, where the outposts of the 4th Guards Brigade (now coming up from Vieux Berquin) relieved the remnants of the 5th Durham Light Infantry. The latter then moved via Pont Tournant and reinforced the line opposite Merville.

By 12 noon, the enemy had pressed back the line on the right until it ran from west of Le Sart to the footbridge over the stream east of Pont Tournant. Fortunately the pressure was not heavy, otherwise the line was so thin and disorganised, and the men so exhausted, that little resistance could have been offered to an assault by heavy masses.

At about 4.30 p.m. the enemy succeeded in placing a machine-gun in a house near the Factory, north of Merville, which enfiladed the line. A premature withdrawal began, but the line rallied and stood fast for the remainder of the evening, until relieved by the 5th Division in the early hours of the night. The 150th Brigade was withdrawn about 11.30 p.m. and the 151st by 3 a.m., and the whole Division concentrated in the grounds of La Motte Château by dawn on the 13th of April, the 149th Brigade, after considerable fighting all day, having been relieved by the 4th Guards Brigade.

The 50th Division moved into billets on the morning of the 13th and was employed on the Haverskerque–La Motte Reserve Line until the evening of the 15th. The Division, less the 149th Brigade (lent for digging purposes under the 5th Division) moved into rest billets in the neighbourhood of Aire on the 16th; the 149th Brigade rejoined the Division on the 18th.

It is not possible to obtain from the records the exact number of casualties suffered by the 50th Division between the 9th and the 13th of April, but on the night of the 12th–13th, after the 5th Division had relieved the remnants, the latter numbered 55 officers and 1,100 other ranks. These figures are eloquent of the superb courage and tenacity of the Division.

On the 14th the Corps Commander visited Major-General Jackson, and congratulated him on the splendid work carried out by the Division in fighting the rear-guard action from the 9th of April to the night of the 12th, and stated that the magnificent stand by the Division had gained the necessary time to enable reserves to be brought up, and had saved the situation. And on the 15th a letter was received at Divisional Headquarters from General Sir H. S. Horne (commanding First Army), which was circulated to all ranks of the Division, and contained the following well-deserved praise: "I must write a line to tell you how highly I appreciate the magnificent way in which you and the 50th Division have fought since the 9th, not only against overwhelming superiority of numbers, but under particularly difficult circumstances."

Once again the decimated Division set to work to rebuild its strength. Reinforcements arrived and units filled their ranks, and soon began to take on an "up-to-strength" appearance. These reinforcements were still composed largely of youths, untrained and quite inexperienced in the field—but they were splendid material, as the Battle of the Lys showed.

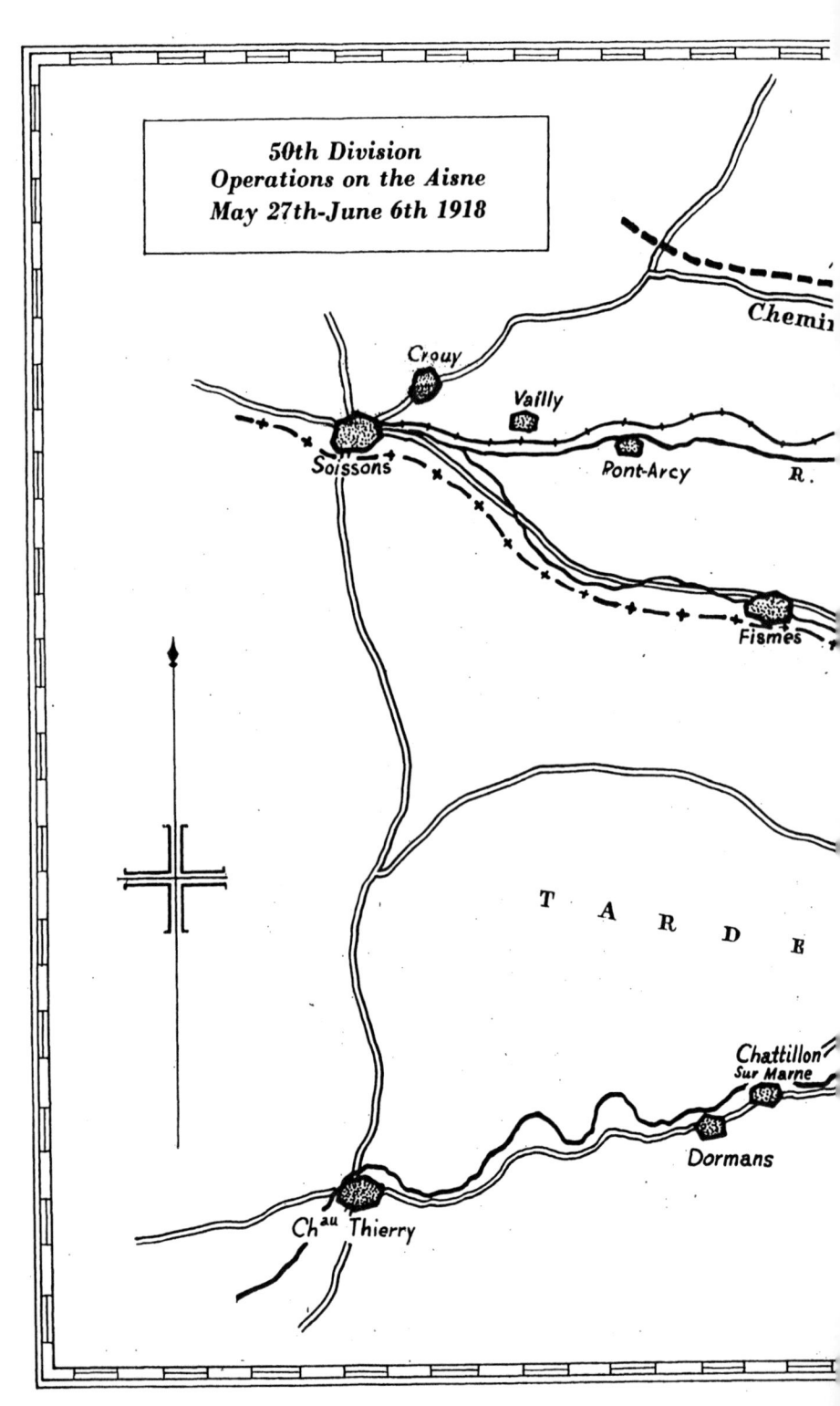

**50th Division
Operations on the Aisne
May 27th-June 6th 1918**

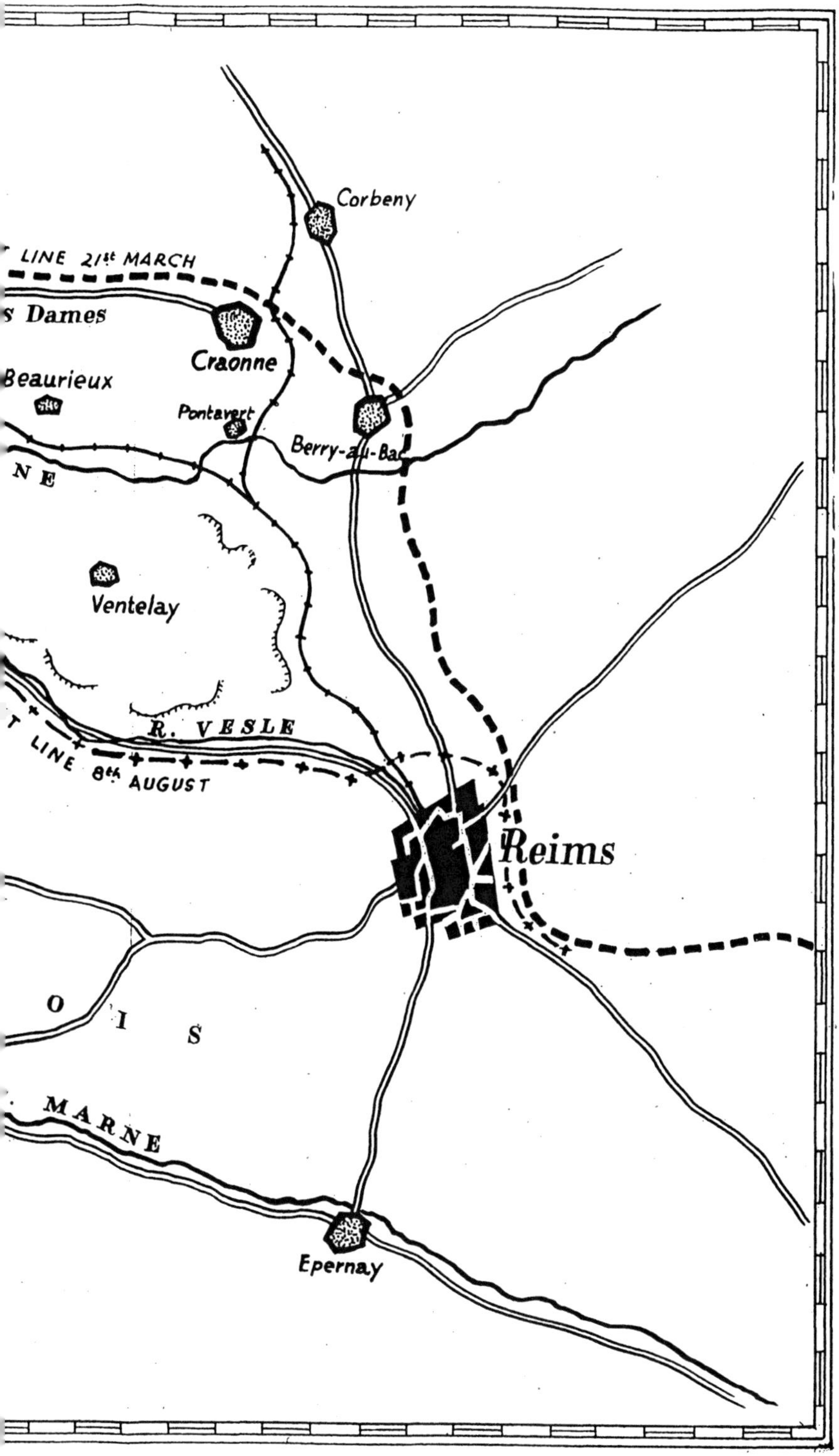
Corbeny
LINE 21st MARCH
s Dames
Craonne
Beaurieux
Pontavert
Berry-au-Bac
NE
Ventelay
R. VESLE
T LINE 8th AUGUST
Reims
O I S
MARNE
Epernay

CHAPTER XIII
THE GERMAN OFFENSIVES IN CHAMPAGNE, 1918

THE BATTLE OF THE AISNE, 27TH MAY–6TH JUNE, 1918

THE Division was in training and reorganising in the Roquetoire area when, towards the end of the month, rumours began to circulate of a move to another part of the line. On the 23rd orders were received to be ready to move on the 25th, and on the 26th the Division began entraining at Pernes, Calonne, Ricquat and Lapugny.

The new area was that of the Sixth French Army on the Aisne front, whither the 50th Division with the 8th, 21st and 25th divisions, subsequently reinforced by the 19th Division, had been sent for rest (this part of the line having been quiet for some time) and to replace certain French divisions concentrated behind Amiens. The British divisions constituted the IX Corps.

The despatches state that: "The British General Staff had always held the opinion that before the resumption of the enemy's main offensive on the Arras–Amiens–Montdidier front, the attack on our northern flank in Flanders would be followed by a similar attack on the southern flank of the Allied Armies."

The 27th and 28th were spent in detraining and 50th Divisional Headquarters were established at Arcis-le-Ponsart—the three infantry brigades in the following areas: 149th—Coulognes; 150th—Courville; 151st—Arcis-le-Ponsart Camp.

The Division had been warned that it would probably go into the front line on or about the 5th of May, and take over, from the 51st French Division, a sector about nine miles north of Rheims and north of the River Aisne. The latter followed a winding course through a wide valley, along which also ran the Aisne Canal, with the villages of Maizy and Concevreux on its southern bank. Over both river and canal there were numerous bridges. South of the canal the hills rose steeply from the canal bank, but north of it, level ground stretched away for a considerable distance through which ran the Aisne itself, the ground rising gradually as it approached the Chronne Plateau, and the Chemins des Dames (which had been captured by the French in 1917). From Chaudardes the front line was approached through the Bois de Beau Marais—a huge wood along the forward edge of which ran the trenches to be taken over by the Division.

The right Divisional boundary ran in a north-easterly direction from Chaudardes to Pontavert, thence La Ville sur Bois to just west of the cross-roads at La Musette (on the famous Route 44) to a few hundred yards north of the latter. From north of La Musette the line ran irregularly west, just north of Chevreux to a plateau named Californie. The left boundary of the Divisional area was Beaurieux–Craonnelle–Californie. Corbeny (in the enemy's territory) lay opposite the sector. Chronne was the left sub-sector. The frontage of the whole sector was about 7,700 yards.

All three infantry brigades were to go into the line, 149th on the right, 151st in the centre, and the 150th on the left. The reliefs were duly carried out, and the troops in the forward area began to take stock of their surroundings. The days which followed were quiet, and work on improving the trenches protected by camouflage screens, was carried out. No Man's Land was very wide and afforded good scope for patrol work, but soon the enemy, who had apparently been "top dog" in No Man's Land, became less active and aggressive, and was forced to keep to his trenches by the Division. On the 25th of May, the 8th Durham Light Infantry raided the enemy, and brought back a wounded prisoner, who provided a much-needed (and valuable) identification.

At about 11 a.m. on the 26th news was received at Divisional Headquarters of a suspected German attack on the morning of the 27th. The enemy's preliminary bombardment was to open at 1 a.m. followed by an infantry assault with tanks at 4.30 a.m. The information had been given by a prisoner captured that morning.

The dispositions of the 50th Division on the 26th were as follows: the 149th Brigade held the right sector with the 4th Northumberland Fusiliers in the front line, the 6th Northumberlands in support, and the 5th Battalion in reserve in Concevreux; the 151st, in the centre, had the 6th Durham Light Infantry on the right, 8th Durham Light Infantry on the left, and 5th Durham Light Infantry in reserve in

Chaudardes; on the left, the 150th Brigade had the 5th Green Howards on the right, 4th East Yorkshires on the left, and the 4th Green Howards at Beaurieux, where Divisional Headquarters were situated.

The 250th and 251st Brigades, R.F.A., had brought their guns into action, some being in the Bois de Beau Marais, others, less sheltered, in the open—but all north, north-west and west of Pontavert.

"The positions were most comfortable, especially 'A' Battery's, with good deep dug-outs for officers and men. The wood was full of violets, lilies of the valley and flowers of all kinds, and it was all very nice and peaceful. Wagon lines were at Glennes and there too everything was *bon*, billets and horse standings being of the best. It was like the old Armentières days of 1915. The O.P.s were under the Chronne Plateau; literally under, for to reach them one went underground through long passages, until one arrived at a door marked with the number of the battery or position to which it belonged. These doors led into rooms from which one looked out across the country through a slit cut in the hill side. They were the most perfect O.P.s we had ever seen, and the walk to them through the wood was delightful. Once more we patted ourselves on the back and said: 'This is where war is waged by perfect gents, the place we have long been seeking.'"*

Alas! for if any unit deserved a rest in a quiet peaceful spot, it was the artillery of the 50th Division; the guns were always first in, and last out of, the line. Theirs was an unenviable existence.

On receipt of information of the impending attack precautionary measures were taken. The artillery was ordered to begin harassing and counter-battery fire at midnight. The 5th Durham Light Infantry of the 151st Brigade were moved to Centre d'Eureux (north-west of Pontavert). The 4th Green Howards were ordered to the dug-outs in Craonnelle and north and north-east of the village; a reserve machine-gun company to the Beaurieux–Craonnelle road, one mile north of Beaurieux. Reserve sections of machine-gun companies were attached to the 149th and 151st Brigades; Battle Stragglers posts were established and additional stretcher-bearers were provided for the advanced dressing stations.

---

*From *The War History of the 1st Northumbrian Brigade, R.F.A. (T.F.).*

The day passed quietly, but in anxiety. The information given by the prisoner—who was a Pole—was detailed and obviously contained at least an element of truth.

At midnight (26th) the Divisional Artillery opened fire, and for an hour blazed away at given targets and on allocated areas. All through this fire there was no reply from the enemy—an ominous sign.

Suddenly, at 1 a.m., there was a fearful and awesome crash. Observers stated that the whole German line leapt into flame; that the enemy's guns must have been placed almost axle to axle so continuous was that first flash. The bombardment which followed was said to have been the most violent the 50th Division had experienced. To the ordinary shells were added gas shells, four kinds being used—lachrymatory, sneezing, lethal and thermits; the gas shelling was principally on battery positions, brigade and battalion headquarters, even Divisional Headquarters being lightly shelled, making the use of masks imperative. Within an hour direct communication between 151st Brigade Headquarters at Evreux and Divisional Headquarters was lost and never regained. The effect of the bombardment was terrific. One Battalion, the 8th Durham Light Infantry, lost telephonic communication with Brigade Headquarters in fifteen minutes, and by 2 a.m. communication forward of Battalion Headquarters to Company Headquarters failed.

At 3.30 a.m. the Durham Light Infantry had reported that the bombardment had levelled out all their trenches, that they had had many casualties both from gas and shell fire, and that only the very forward posts were fightable.

Soon, with the exception of an odd gun or two, both British and French batteries were out of action. About 3 a.m. there was a very slight lull in this terrific hail of shell but no cessation until 4.30 a.m. At that hour twenty-eight German divisions attacked the Sixth French Army on a front of thirty-five miles.

On the 50th Divisional front, however, the German attack developed at 3.30 a.m. on the extreme right from the Ouvrage la Carrière, spreading thence to the left. A slight ground mist, smoke and dust from the bombardment, and the uncertainty of very early morning made visibility bad, and nothing could be seen of the progress of the fighting. The enemy was at first checked on the outpost line, and later on the main line of resistance, by rifle, Lewis and machine-gun fire, and at some points fell back behind a line of tanks. The latter appeared to be of two kinds—renovated captured British tanks and a German pattern, aluminium-coloured and armed with three light guns. It is doubtful whether they attempted to penetrate more than five hundred yards, but they carried the enemy's line forward into the battle zone, the front line of which was broken on the right by about 4 a.m., the remaining posts being shortly afterwards encircled from that direction.

As may be expected, all brigade and battalion narratives of this great attack are brief, and none contain anything but a plain statement of facts as they were known at the time.

To begin with the 149th Brigade: The 4th Northumberland Fusiliers, holding the front line, suffered badly in the preliminary bombardment and had many casualties. But the survivors of the outpost company withdrew to the line of posts where, with rifle and Lewis-gun fire, they broke up the attack and drove the enemy back. But at 4 a.m. the Bosche, led by tanks, came on again and, by sheer weight of numbers, drove the Northumberlands from the posts to the Battle Line. The enemy then broke through the line of posts and advanced so quickly that few men of the left forward company escaped. At 4.15 a.m. the Battle Line was in action, and half-an-hour later had been taken in rear, only a remnant of "D" Company getting away. By this time the Divisional Artillery was practically inactive, having been countered by the enemy's superiority in guns. No support was, therefore, forthcoming for the hard-pressed infantry in the forward areas.

At 5 a.m. (the last message received at Brigade Headquarters from the Battalion) Lieut.-Colonel B. D. Gibson reported that he was holding out in Centre Marceau with forty men. By 5.30 a.m. the line of redoubts had been outflanked from the right: Centre Marceau, attacked from the right front and rear, held out for some time, the survivors finally withdrawing to the Butte de l'Edmond where, with a party of the Divisional Machine-Gun Battalion, a further stand was made. Here Lieut.-Colonel Gibson was killed. He was a Territorial officer of great experience and reputation, a fine soldier and greatly beloved by his Battalion. Only one or two men succeeded in getting back from this position to Concevreux.

"From this time," records the Battalion Diary, "the 4th Northumberland Fusiliers ceased to exist as a fighting unit."

Of the 6th Northumberland Fusiliers (who were supporting the 4th) few escaped. By 4.45 a.m. the Battle Line had been taken in rear from the direction of La Ville au Bois. "No one returned from the centre and right companies of this line. Remainder of left company, under Lieut.-Colonel Gibson (4th Northumberland Fusiliers) withdrew at 5 a.m. This party consisted of forty men."* The Redoubt Line and P.C. Kleber were outflanked at 5.30 a.m. and cut off from Bois de Buttes. At 8 a.m. the remnants of the Battalion joined the Brigade Composite Battalion and withdrew to Chaudardes. All details at the transport lines, billeted in Concevreux, were then organised under Major Robb (4th Northumberland Fusiliers) and Major Rogers.

At 9 a.m. the enemy crossed Pontavert bridges and advanced down both sides of the Canal. The party at Chaudardes then withdrew across the Aisne, for the enemy was on the high ground to the north-west and was advancing down the river bank from Pontavert. This was at 10 a.m.

Details and remainder of the Brigade were then organised on a line running from Concevreux Bridge, along the Canal Bank, to the wood north-west. But again it was but a temporary line from which the troops were driven at about 4 p.m. The Battalion records then state that, for the next four days: "The remnants of the Battalion, now incorporated in composite companies and submerged in other divisions, including 8th, 21st and 25th Divisions, took part in rear-guard actions until the end of the month."

The 5th Northumberland Fusiliers (the reserve battalion of the 149th Brigade) were ordered at 2.40 a.m. to move to Beaurepaire via Chaudardes. They set out along roads heavily shelled and reached their destination just after 4 a.m. The Battalion was then disposed on the open ground south-east of Beaurepaire Wood, as an intense hostile barrage was falling in front of the wood. At 6.10 a.m., under orders, "C" and "D" Companies set out to occupy a line between Butte de l'Edmond and Bois des Buttes. But they ran into an intense barrage and suffered heavy casualties. "C" Company reported they could not reach the line owing to machine-gun fire and the intense barrage. Meanwhile "A" and "B" Companies had also come under an intense barrage, and had serious

---

*Battalion Diary, 6th Northumberland Fusiliers.

losses. The line then fell back to Chaudardes. But the 5th Battalion fared no better than the other battalions for, outflanked again and again, and reduced almost to a skeleton unit, they, with the remnants of all units of the Brigade, took up a line on the heights between Meurival and the Roucy–Ventelay road, which was held until a message was received, at 11 p.m., that the enemy had occupied Ventelay and was advancing on Romain. The party then withdrew to a line running one hundred yards west of Lemoncet Farm, facing north-east.

The Brigade Diary records that, at 10.45 a.m., the 74th Brigade of the 25th Division was arriving: these were the only troops not of the 50th Division who helped the latter in endeavouring to stem the tide which overwhelmed the line throughout the day. The Diary also records another item of importance: "During the fighting since 5 a.m. we had had no artillery support and very few machine-guns. The enemy's artillery advanced very quickly and was continuously in action."

Under such conditions it was an impossible fight! At that period of the War lack of artillery support meant almost certain annihilation.

The 149th Brigade records do not state that the Brigadier (Brig.-General Riddell) was seriously wounded during the 27th. At 7 a.m. he was at 151st Brigade Headquarters with Brig.-General Martin, of the latter Brigade, when the enemy was reported close at hand. As the two Brigadiers hurriedly left the dug-out they found themselves almost surrounded. As they began to fight their way through, the Germans were scattered by a salvo of their own shells, but one, however, unfortunately burst just overhead, and General Martin was instantly killed and General Riddell wounded.

The records of the centre and left brigades of the 50th Division resemble closely those of the 149th Brigade.

It has already been stated that, at 3.30 a.m., the 8th Durham Light Infantry of the 151st Brigade reported that the bombardment had levelled out all "D" Company's trenches, and that there were many casualties from gas and shelling, and that only the very forward posts were fightable. The commander of "B" Company in the Lamoureux Hill defences next reported (at 4.30 a.m.) that his casualties were extremely heavy, but those who were left were in touch with the enemy and managing to hold him up. The company commander then called his officers together and they decided to remain and fight until the last.

"No one of this party escaped," stated the Diary.

Disaster then fell upon another gallant band of the Battalion. The Company Commander of "C" Company got back to Brigade Headquarters and asked for reinforcements. He had lost heavily, his left platoon having been completely annihilated. He collected about forty machine-gunners, a number of men of the 7th Durham Light Infantry, and with this garrison set out to man the big gauge railway near Ouv de Chemin de Fer. The enemy was then seen in very large numbers in the wire in front of their positions, and suffered accordingly from Vickers-gun and Lewis-gun fire. For three-quarters-of-an-hour this position was held. At the end of that period the gallant garrison, much reduced by shell fire, was completely surrounded, and again "no one escaped."

The 151st Brigade Diary tells the story of the 6th Durham Light Infantry (the right Battalion) in the following terse words: "At 4.45 a.m. the company commander of the left company reported to Battalion Headquarters and stated that the Bosche was all over his area. He believed that he was the only one who had escaped." The reserve company was also eventually surrounded.

This tale of disaster in the 151st Brigade ended in the practical annihilation of the reserve battalion—the 5th Durham Light Infantry.

At 6.30 a.m. the 5th Durhams were ordered to send two companies ("C" and "D") to garrison the International Line from Ouv de Toulon to Ouv de Lambert. At 7 a.m. "A" and "B" Companies were ordered to reinforce the previous two. "C" and "D" came into contact with the enemy in Boyeau d'Edmond before reaching their position. But they held up the Bosche for a while until forced to fall back to Boyeau St. Paul. They held this position for half-an-hour, and then discovered that the enemy was behind them in Pontavert; they withdrew to prolong the line near the Dressing Station at Pontavert. The Brigade Headquarters Diary then relates that, "as far as is known the second two companies were surrounded and captured before they could leave their dug-outs. No news of them is to hand."

Three gallant efforts to hold up the enemy—at Beaurieux, at Chaudardes, and at Concevreux—are recorded in the Diary of 151st Brigade Headquarters.

East of Beaurieux Major Gould, of the 8th Durham Light Infantry, and Lieut.-Colonel Birchall, 7th Durham Light Infantry, having collected a number of stragglers at Headquarters of 7th Durham Light Infantry, south-east of Bois Marais, decided to hold a line in an existing trench three hundred yards due east of Cuiry les Chaudardes, running thence north-west to a farm north-east of Beaurieux. This position was established at 8 a.m. and was held until a large enemy force from Beaurieux took it in rear. The party then fought its way through, crossed the river and took up a position on the high ground behind the bridge.

The stand was made by Lieut.-Colonel Kirkup, who had been sick but had left the dressing station to collect men in Chaudardes. He collected thirty men of the 5th Durham Light Infantry, several of the 5th Northumberland Fusiliers, and some machine-gunners—in all about 150. He established a line in front of the village till forced back to the line of the railway immediately behind Chaudardes. The party then withdrew across the bridges—which were "blown" by the Royal Engineers—and took up a line south of the river in touch with some Northumberland Fusiliers on the right and 6th Durhams on the left.

Lieut.-Colonel Walton also collected stragglers and placed them in position to cover Chaudardes from the north-east and the north-west. Another party held the bridgeheads west of Chaudardes. All three parties held on until the bridges had been "blown" by the Royal Engineers.

At Concevreux a battalion of the 25th Division strengthened the line along the river.

The G.S.O.2, 50th Division, then arrived with orders that the whole force was to be placed under one commander and amalgamated as 149th/151st Brigade. Lieut.-Colonel Kirkup took command with Lieut.-Colonel Walton.

About 2.30 p.m. the line was forced to withdraw, being outflanked from right and left. The next position was an existing trench system on the forward slope of the hill south of Concevreux. But it was not long before the enemy's artillery made the position untenable and the force withdrew again, on this occasion to Hill 200, north of Ventelay. At about 6 p.m.

Lieut.-Colonel Robinson arrived and took over from Lieut.-Colonel Walton.

The overwhelming of the 150th Brigade was even more complete. After the terrific bombardment no infantry attack developed against the Brigade front from the north. But, as a result of the enemy's successful advance on the right portion of the Divisional front, and through the 22nd French Division on the left, the Craonne Plateau (or Plateau de Californie) was enveloped from both flanks by about 6.30 a.m. The hostile barrage was maintained on the Plateau to the last and many men were captured in the deep dug-outs before they were able to come out.

Owing to the smoke and dust the O.P.s on the Plateau were unable to report the progress of events.

At about 5.45 a.m. Lieut.-Colonel Thompson reported that his headquarters company was then fighting around his command post and that they appear to be surrounded. No news was received from the 4th East Yorkshires, very few of whose men came back, but it is probable that they were overwhelmed about the same time as the 5th Green Howards.

In view of the general advance made by the enemy along the whole front, the Brigadier (Brig.-General Rees) decided that a counter-attack by the 4th Green Howards could not meet with success. He intended, therefore, to hold the International Line with this Battalion (to which proposal Divisional Headquarters agreed by telephone), moving his Headquarters back to P.C. Terrasse. It was about 7 a.m. when Brigade Headquarters left La Butte to carry out this move, but on arrival at P.C. Terrasse it was discovered that the 4th Green Howards, on the line Mt. Hermel–Tr. Dehart, had also been overwhelmed, and that the enemy was fast approaching P.C. Terrasse from the west. An attempt to organise a defence at this point had to be abandoned.

As a result of heavy hostile shelling Brigade Headquarters had now become dispersed: "the Staff Captain and Intelligence Officer had been wounded earlier in the morning and the Brigade Major was wounded whilst withdrawing towards the Aisne. Brig.-General Rees, it is believed, became too exhausted to continue and was captured. Some few stragglers were collected on the river and placed under the command of such officers as could be found. The Brigade Headquarters ceased to exist temporarily and was not reformed until the arrival of the Division at Vert la Gravelle on the 31st of May."*

The terrible disaster which befell the infantry of the 50th Division on the 27th of May saw the end of all those gallant battalions which, whenever possible, had put up a stout resistance; but the majority were surrounded and forced to surrender before they could come into action.

No less than 227 officers and 4,879 other ranks were killed, wounded or captured during the battle. Practically all these casualties occurred on the 27th, for after that date the 50th Division became intermingled with other divisions which were in a like condition: only a mere handful of the infantry remained.

"No guns were . . . saved." Such is a portion of the Divisional Narrative which tells of the misfortunes of the 250th and 251st Brigades, R.F.A., under the commands respectively of Lieut.-Colonel F. G. O. Johnson and Lieut.-Colonel F. R. Moss-Blundell.

On the right the 250th Brigade kept their guns in action longer than the 251st Brigade, for the latter was quickly enveloped from the left.

The Narrative contained in the Diary of the Former Brigade is interesting as showing the battle from the gunners' point of view: "At 1 a.m. the enemy bombardment commenced. All lines went down within five minutes. Bombardment was very heavy on all forward areas and on battery positions and headquarters. S.O.S. went up about 4 a.m.

"No information was received as to the positions of the infantry or state of batteries; orderlies sent out were almost invariably missing. News received about 4.30 a.m. from C/250 through an infantry officer attached to them. At 3 a.m., when he left, only one gun was in action, remainder having been hit. About 6.30 a.m. Major Shiel and Lieut. Richardson arrived at headquarters and say that A/250 had removed sights and breach mechanism as the creeping barrage has passed them, and the enemy are about eight hundred yards in front of them. Message received from Lieut. Leathart, who had gone over to infantry brigade headquarters, that Yellow Line was being attacked.

"Major Shiel and Capt. Meek (attached from infantry) went out about 7.50 a.m. towards infantry brigade headquarters and Meek brought back report that enemy were close to

---

*Extract from 150th Brigade Narrative.

infantry brigade headquarters, about six hundred yards from Brigade (250th) Headquarters. Second-Lieut. Hopwood had reported from B/250 that they were still fighting with three of the four guns on their main position. A message had also been received that D/250 were continuing to fire. No further news received from C/250. From information received later, personnel from B/250 main position nearly all got away when the enemy arrived on the position. Very few got away from detached section of B, but fair number from detached section of A/250. Very few got away from D/250. Capt. Darling was last seen going towards the enemy with his revolver and Lieut. Earle and remaining gunners were firing the last gun left in action. No one got away from main position of C/250, but most of the detachments got away from detached section where Second-Lieut. Costar was last seen going towards the enemy with his revolver.

"Personnel that got away from batteries when the enemy reached the positions went via Beaurieux to the wagon lines at Glennes. Eleven wagons of D/250, which went up from wagon lines to take ammunition to reserve positions, were fired on at close range by machine-guns; those who were not killed or wounded were captured.

"On arrival at Glennes orders were received to march to St. Gilles, which was reached about mid-day. Batteries unhooked* and remained until 6 p.m. when orders were received to march to Davrégny, which was reached at 9.30 p.m. The night was spent there."

The 251st Brigade, so far as the official account is concerned records: "1 a.m. Division heavily attacked. All guns lost. Casualties of 19 officers and about 250 other ranks (chiefly missing). The whole of the Brigade Headquarters officers and records were lost; 10.30 a.m. Remains of Brigade moved via Fismes and St. Gilles to Cohan."

In *The War History of the 1st Northumbrian Brigade, R.F.A.* (the 250th Brigade, R.F.A.) it is stated that: "Our companion Brigade, 251st, had been even more unlucky than we, for the Bosche walked into the back of their emplacements while they were still firing on their S.O.S. barrage, and captured the whole Brigade from the Colonel down, without them being able to put up a fight."

---

*This refers to limbers and wagons only.

"Over forty officers," states the Divisional Narrative, "and 550 artillery personnel are missing."

Of the Divisional Troops, *i.e.*, Pioneers, Royal Engineers, etc., intended for the occupation of the International (or Yellow) Line as nucleus garrisons, there is little to state. With troops from the reserve battalion they either failed to receive their orders, were unable to reach their positions through the barrage, or met the enemy whilst still moving forward.

The medical units had received the same attention from the enemy, the personnel of the Main Dressing Station at Monacu having to wear their respirators continuously and remain in dug-outs. The Main Dressing Station was withdrawn to Fontaine-du-Vivier as early as 5.50 a.m. All the ambulance cars except one had been destroyed by shell fire, but the evacuation of wounded from the Station by bearers and such transport as could be found, until the farm came under hostile machine-gun fire. Even the hospital at Meurival (about seven miles from the front line) and village were shelled by high-velocity guns (8-in.) which caused gas and shell-wound casualties.

At Beaurieux the Divisional Staff had a narrow escape from being captured *en bloc*. About 9.30 a.m. an officer, who had been sent out towards Craonnelle, returned with the information that the Germans were rapidly approaching Beaurieux. Divisional Headquarters moved at once, but even so the D.A.Q.M.G.,[*] A.D.M.S.,[†] and D.A.D.M.S.[‡] and certain clerks and draughtsmen were captured in the village.

There were many stories of miraculous escapes, of which the following is a curious instance. The last officer to leave 149th Brigade Headquarters (which with other brigade headquarters had been evacuated by 7.30 a.m.) was the Brigade-Major, and as he walked out of the dug-out the enemy was actually establishing a machine-gun on the roof.

On the evening of the 27th (at 6 p.m.) the line held by the remnants of the 50th Division ran from Le Faite Ferme (a mile north of Ventelay), on the right, along the high ground to a point north-north-west of Le Grand Haneau, where French reinforcements were coming into line to connect with the 197th French Division. The 8th Division was on the right

---
[*] Major W. McCracken.
[†] Col. A. Milne-Thompson.
[‡] Major R. M. Handfield-Jones.

of the 50th Division. But the French were unable to reach the high ground in time, and by dusk the enemy had penetrated to Courlandon.

During the night of the 27th–28th the 8th Division had to withdraw south of the line Bouvancourt–Ventelay, the 74th Brigade being ordered to conform. Not only was this movement difficult, but some units did not receive orders, and detachments were captured in the moving. The projected line, north and north-west of Montigny, was never satisfactorily established, and soon after daylight on the 28th the enemy, without much hindrance, made progress towards the River Vesle.

It should be remembered that all throughout the 27th the 50th Division was without artillery support. During the night of the 27th–28th two batteries of the 25th Divisional Artillery were allotted to the 50th Division, but touch could not be obtained with the brigade concerned, nor with the batteries. The morning of the 28th, therefore, still found the 50th Division without artillery support.

About 4 a.m. Divisional Headquarters moved to Brancourt, and at 10 a.m. to Faverolles. At that hour the remnants of the Division and the 74th Brigade (total estimated strength, six hundred rifles) lay along the railway from Jonchery westwards. On the high ground south-west of Jonchery, was a party of four hundred trained reinforcements.

But under continued pressure the line gradually fell back, until by 2 p.m. it was reported as running immediately south of Vandeuil and Hourges to the high ground south-west of Unchair. Shortly afterwards, however, the enemy gained the wood about a mile south-east of Hourges. There were no British troops here to counter-attack and the French were asked to assist, but no effective counter-attack was delivered.

Meanwhile Lieut.-Colonels Walton and Kirkup had organised the defence of Hill 233 near the farm on the Savigny–Jonchery road with troops of the 50th and 8th Divisions. Although repeatedly attacked, the Hill was successfully held for the remainder of the day and the night following.

At about 6.30 p.m. General Jackson was ordered by the Corps Commander to withdraw the Headquarters Staff and the remainder of the Division to the area Jonquery–Cuisles–Baslieux-sous-Chatillon. This move was completed during the early hours of the 29th.

On the 29th stragglers were collected and a composite

battalion was formed under Lieut.-Colonel Stead of the 4th East Yorkshires. This battalion (strength about 950 all ranks) was assembled at Cuisles Château, and on the morning of the 30th of May moved up to join the 74th Brigade. The remainder of the 50th Division was then withdrawn, first to Igny-le-Jard and thence to the area Congy–Courjeonnet–Vert la Gravelle.

On the 2nd of June another composite battalion, consisting of one company drawn from each brigade, under General Marshall, was sent to join the 19th Division. But neither the composite battalion under Lieut.-Colonel Stead, nor that under General Marshall, kept records, and the operations of these two units are, therefore, impossible to follow.

"By the evening of the 30th May, at which date in the centre of his attack the enemy had reached the Marne, the rate of his advance in the British sector had begun to slacken. During the next few days, however, fighting was still intense. On the southern and western portions of the battle front the enemy made daily progress, gaining the northern bank of the Marne from Dormans to Château Thierry, and advancing astride the Aisne to the outskirts of Villers Cotterets Forest, and across the high ground north-east of Attichy. On the eastern flank (where the 50th Division had been fighting) of the salient created by the enemy's advance, the British forces, at this date under the command of the Fifth French Army, withdrew gradually to the line Aubilly–Chambrecy–Boujacourt, where they were able to consolidate."* Although the enemy attacked this line again and again, he was held, and his advance definitely stayed.

The Battle of the Aisne, 1918, was the last operation in the Great War in which the original 50th Division took part. After the Battle of the Somme, 1918, and the Battle of the Lys, its depleted battalions had been made up, but after the disaster of the 27th of May, the casualties were so great† that it was impossible to find troops to refill the ranks of the sorely-stricken battalions. The Division was, therefore, re-constituted, but lost its original identity.

*Extract from the official despatches.

†For instance, when the roll was called at Vert la Gravelle on the 31st of May, there remained only 103 men of the 151st Brigade who were in the line on the 27th of May. By the end of May the Division could only muster 700 fit infantrymen, excluding personnel with the transport and the Quartermaster's Stores.

CHAPTER XIV

THE RE-CONSTITUTION OF THE 50TH DIVISION

ON the 1st of June, Divisional Headquarters were at Vert la Gravelle with the remnants of battalions billeted in the Congy–Toulon area. Every unit was busy reorganising. Late at night, orders were received to form an infantry company of two hundred men out of the 50th Battalion Machine-Gun Company. This was done immediately and at 11 a.m. on the 2nd the company embussed to join the 19th Division.

The disintegration of the Division had begun. On the same day, the Division was ordered to form a composite battalion out of every fit man, the battalion to be ready to move at two hours notice after 8 p.m. A battalion one thousand strong was formed, and sub-divided into two battalions of about five hundred each, one commanded by Lieut.-Colonel F. Walton, 6th Durham Light Infantry, the other by Major A. C. Barnes, of the 4th Green Howards. Both battalions were placed under the command of Brig.-General F. T. Marshall, who had reported his arrival vice Brig.-General H. C. Rees, missing.

On the 3rd the composite battalions, now known as General Marshall's Composite Force, were increased by one more battalion, formed from stragglers and men from Divisional Wing. The three battalions were thus designated: 149th Infantry Battalion under the command of Lieut.-Colonel L. D. Scott, 6th Northumberland Fusiliers; 150th Infantry Battalion, commanded by Major Barnes, 4th Green Howards, and 151st Infantry Battalion under the command of Lieut.-Colonel F. Walton, 6th Durham Light Infantry.

At 5 p.m. two officers and twenty-two other ranks, mounted on officers' chargers, left the Division to report to the 19th Division at Nanteuil as mounted orderlies.

On the 4th General Marshall's Composite Force began training, but was ordered at 8 p.m. to move up to the line on the night of the 5th–6th. On the 5th General Marshall's command (strength 44 officers and 1,400 other ranks) embussed at 8 p.m. at Vert la Gravelle and bivouacked that night in a small wood a quarter of a mile west of Nanteuil. The following night General Marshall's Force went into the line north of Bois d'Eglise, 149th Battalion on the right, 151st in the centre, 150th on the left. During the day the enemy had attacked the 19th Division, but was everywhere repulsed, the IX Corps Commander wiring his congratulations to the 19th Division, and attached troops of the 8th, 25th and 50th Divisions.

Two new Brigadiers reported their arrival on the 7th, *i.e.*, Brig.-General P. M. Robinson (Royal West Kent Regiment) who took over command of the 149th Brigade, and Brig.-General R. E. Sugden (4th West Ridings), who assumed command of the 151st Brigade. On the 8th the composite battalion, under Lieut.-Colonel Stead, which was still in being, was broken up and the personnel joined their Brigade Battalion in General Marshall's Force.

On the 9th of June, the Division (less General Marshall's Force and Machine-Gun Company) moved at 7 a.m. from the Congy–Toulon area to Mondemont–Broyes.

On the 12th General Marshall's Force came out of the front line and moved back into support.

To everyone's regret, the 7th Durham Light Infantry (Pioneers) were ordered to be transferred to the 21st Division. Then on the 18th the Division was ordered to form a composite brigade; the 25th Division received similar orders, their Brigade to be attached to the 50th Division and commanded by Brig.-General Sugden.

The Italians relieved General Marshall's Force in the line on the 19th, the latter rejoining. The Pioneers left the Division on the 20th.

The 50th Composite Brigade was formed under the command of Brig.-General R. M. Robinson from one battalion, 149th Brigade, under Lieut.-Colonel Fitzhugh, and from 150th Brigade, under Lieut.-Colonel Wilkinson, and one from 151st Brigade, under Lieut.-Colonel Kirkup.

On the 24th the 50th Division was ordered to relieve the 8th French Division in the line, and on the 25th the designation of the 50th Composite Division was changed to that of "Jackson's Force"; orders were to go into the line on the night of the 28th–29th. The transport had already moved on the 26th when "Jackson's Force" was ordered to remain in its present areas. The transport returned the following day (27th), and a warning order was received that the 50th Division would shortly move back into the British zone.

Preparatory to entraining for the British zone, troops began to move by stages on the 29th, and on the 30th the Division was still moving.

By this time the edict had gone forth: the Division was to be reduced to cadre strength. The several attempts to keep the original 50th Division in being had failed—failed because sufficient reinforcements to rebuild the strength of the depleted battalions were not forthcoming.

The 50th Division, however, was not allowed to leave the French zone without receiving the thanks of General Maistre (commanding *Groupes des Armées du Nord*). In a letter to the IX Corps Commander he said: "With a tenacity, permit me to say, truly British, you have untiringly reorganised fresh units from the remnants of divisions decimated by the enemy tide. Again and again you have thrown them into the fight, and ultimately they have enabled us to establish a barrier against which the hostile waves have beaten and shattered themselves. This, none of the French who witnessed it, will ever forget."

Huppy was the area to which the Division was moving, and on the 1st of July Troops Staging Orders contained information as to what was to become of the Division on arriving at its destination; units were to be reduced to cadre strength and all surplus personnel transferred to the Base.

On the 5th of July all three infantry brigades of the Division received orders concerning the reduction of battalions to training-cadre strength, the establishment of which was fixed at 10 officers, 51 other ranks and 10 horses; and on the 15th the surplus personnel of all battalions of the 50th Division entrained for the Base. A few days later the three original Trench Mortar Batteries, *i.e.*, 149th, 150th and 151st, were disbanded, and were re-constituted with personnel drawn from the reserve infantry of the Division.

The majority of the reserve infantry were troops withdrawn from Salonika; many of them were suffering from malaria, and were being treated by the medical authorities; only four hours' training a day was allowed them.

On the 15th orders were issued reconstituting the three brigades. The new battalions of the 149th Brigade were the 2nd Royal Dublin Fusiliers, 3rd Royal Fusiliers, 13th Black

Watch. Those who joined the 150th Brigade were the 7th Wilts, 2nd Northumberland Fusiliers and 2nd Royal Munster Fusiliers. The 151st Brigade was formed of the 1st King's Own Yorkshire Light Infantry, 6th Royal Inniskilling Fusiliers, and 4th King's Royal Rifle Corps.

Thus, not one battalion of the old Division remained, though the training cadres were still under the command of General Jackson.*

---

*For Order of Battle of the 50th Division on the 29th of July, 1918, see Appendices.

CHAPTER XV

THE ADVANCE TO VICTORY

THE operations of the new 50th Division in the Advance to Victory may be summarised briefly. After several weeks of training and in the treatment of those officers and men suffering from malaria, the Division joined the Fourth Army, under General Rawlinson, on the Somme. The Battle of Amiens (8th August) had then been fought, and our victorious troops were pressing on. The Drocourt–Quéant Line had fallen, and the breaching of the Hindenburg Line was in progress (2nd August–12th October) when the 50th Division entered into the Battle, taking part in the Battle of Beaurevoir (3rd–5th October).

On the 3rd of October, the Fourth Army attacked between Séquehart and Le Catelet, capturing those villages as well as Ramicourt and the Beaurevoir–Fonsomme line on that front. The 50th Division saw stiff fighting in this battle, but captured Gouy and Le Catelet, beating off a number of counter-attacks. At one period the enemy succeeded in reaching the centre of Gouy, but he was quickly driven out again. The advance was continued, and on the 5th patrols of the 149th Brigade, crossing the Canal at Vendhuile and north of that village, reached Putney and Basket Wood. The 149th and 151st Brigades were withdrawn that night to rest, and the 150th held the Divisional front, some five hundred yards north-east of Vauxhall Quarry.

In the Battle of Cambrai (8th–9th October) the 50th Division again took part and gained its objectives.

The operations which began on the 8th of October were the second and concluding phase of the British offensive, in which the Fourth and Third Armies and the right of the First Army moved forward with their left flank on the Canal line running from Cambrai to Mons, and their right covered by the First French Army.

At 4.30 a.m. and 5.10 a.m. respectively on the 8th, the Third and Fourth Armies attacked on a front of over seventeen miles from Séquehart to south of Cambrai.

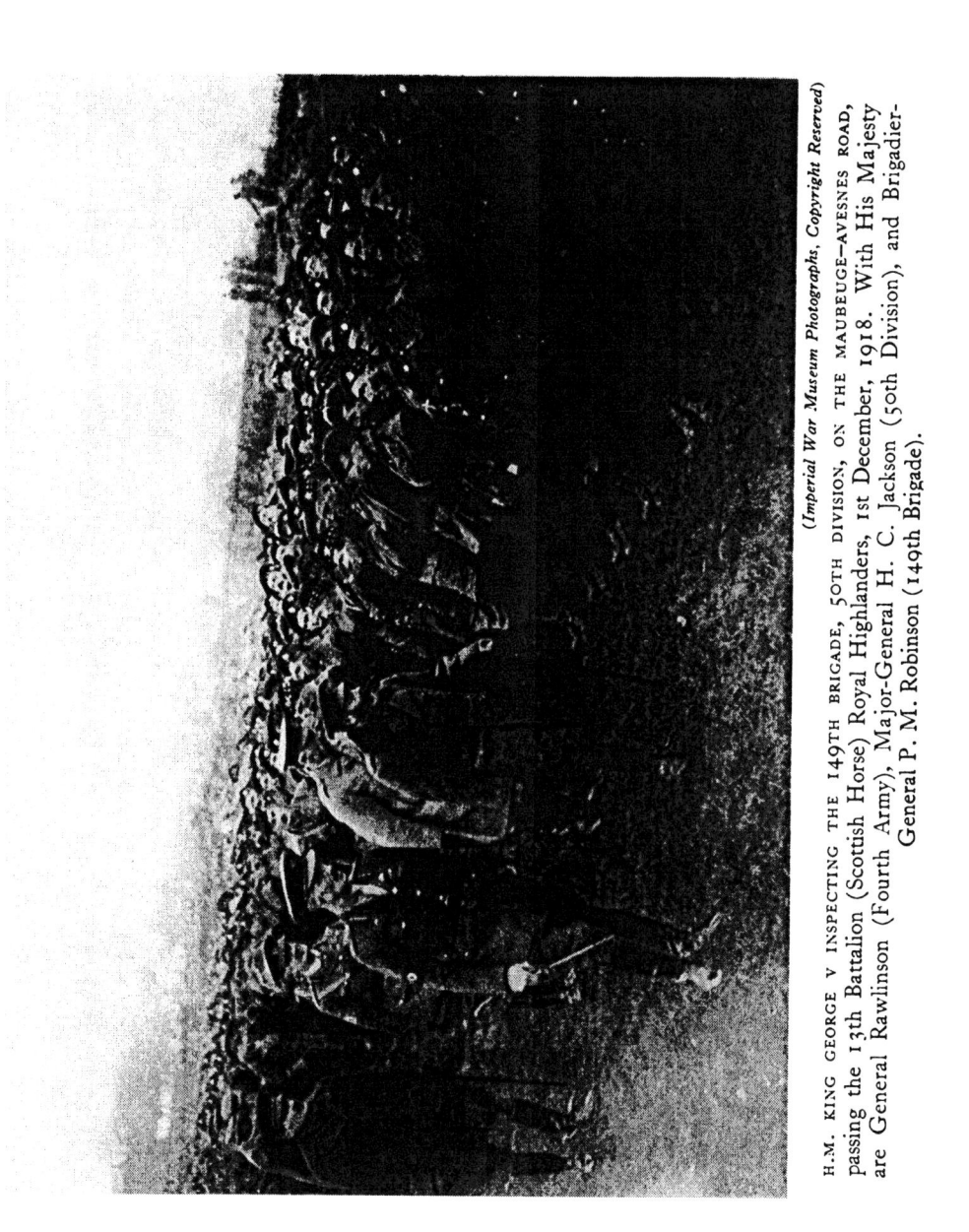

(Imperial War Museum Photographs, Copyright Reserved)

H.M. KING GEORGE V INSPECTING THE 149TH BRIGADE, 50TH DIVISION, ON THE MAUBEUGE–AVESNES ROAD, passing the 13th Battalion (Scottish Horse) Royal Highlanders, 1st December, 1918. With His Majesty are General Rawlinson (Fourth Army), Major-General H. C. Jackson (50th Division), and Brigadier-General P. M. Robinson (149th Brigade).

The 50th Division, with the 66th Division on the right, and the 38th Division on the left, attacked from east of Grouy. Everywhere along the line the operation was a success, and the enemy streamed away from the battlefield in the direction of Le Cateau, all roads converging thereon being reported by our airmen as blocked with German troops and transport. Thousands of prisoners and guns had already fallen into our hands. On the 9th the Fourth and Third Armies again attacked, and by nightfall were within two miles of Le Cateau, had captured Bohain, and were attacking Caudry from the south. Our troops had captured Cambrai and were already three miles east of the town.

The Battle then developed into a pursuit (The Pursuit to the Selle, 9th–12th October) during which our troops, advancing with great determination, drove the enemy from one hastily-prepared position to another, until at last he reached the eastern bank of the Selle River, where he evidently intended making a stand.

But our advance had been so rapid that before forcing the crossings of the River, it was necessary to look to our communications, which had become somewhat disorganised as the result of the quickly-changing line.

It was, therefore, the 17th before the Selle positions were attacked. On that date, at 5.20 a.m., operations began which had as their object the forcing of the Selle positions, and the attainment of the general line of the Sambre et Cise Canal–the western edge of the Forêt de Mormal–Valenciennes. The Fourth Army opened the operations by an attack on a front of about ten miles from Le Cateau southwards, the 50th and 66th Divisions being the attacking troops of the XIII Corps.

The Battle lasted until the 25th of October, by which date our line ran—western outskirts of the Forêt de Mormal–within a mile of Le Quesnoy–Ruesnes–Maing.

By this time the moral and material effect upon the German Armies by the succession of rapid blows dealt the enemy, had cumulated almost in complete collapse. 20,000 prisoners and 475 guns had been captured in the Selle Battle, and the enemy had neither troops nor material to replace them. The German infantry and machine-gunners were no longer reliable, and frequently retired without fighting.

On the 4th of November, the last great battle opened (The Battle of the Sambre) on a front of thirty miles, stretching from the Sambre north of Oisy to Valenciennes. The 50th Division (having been in reserve for a few days) attacked and, with the 25th and 18th Divisions of the XIII Corps, overran the enemy's positions. The 50th Division advanced through the southern portion of the Forêt de Mormal. An advance to a depth of five miles was made on the 4th, and on the 5th a still greater "push" brought the British line well to the east of the Forêt de Mormal.

Thereafter, the enemy was hurrying eastwards in disorder and, although during the succeeding days there were stiff encounters up and down the line, the German troops never really rallied to the attack, so that by the 11th of November, incapable of either fighting or offering further resistance, he was forced to seek an Armistice.

In all these operations the 50th Division had done well. With the exception of the G.O.C., Division (Major-General H. C. Jackson), it is impossible to discover the names of other officers of the original Division. Colonel Anstey's name appears at the outset, but finally disappeared. The Sappers and the Field Ambulances probably contained both officers and men of the old 50th Division, for these units had been posted to the new Division.

Of the Training Cadre there is no trace after the reconstitution of the Division, and when they reached England for demobilisation it is impossible to say. But as the 50th Division did not form part of the Army of Occupation in Germany, the probability is that the remnants of the Northumberland Fusiliers, the Durham Light Infantry, and the Yorkshires reached home a few months after the Armistice.

Appendix A

BATTLE HONOURS

BATTLES OF YPRES 1915
St. Julien.
Frizenberg Ridge.
Bellewaarde Ridge.

BATTLES OF THE SOMME 1916
Flers–Courcelette.
Morval.
Transloy Ridges.
The Ancre.

BATTLES OF ARRAS 1917
First Battle of the Scarpe 1917.
Second Battle of the Scarpe 1917.
Third Battle of the Scarpe 1917.

BATTLES OF YPRES 1917
Second Battle of Passchendaele.

FIRST BATTLES OF THE SOMME 1918
St. Quentin.
Rosières.

BATTLES OF THE LYS
Estaires.
Hazebrouck.

BATTLE OF THE AISNE 1918

Appendix B

50th DIVISION

Landed in France, 15th–20th April, 1915.

G.O.C.

Major-General SIR W. F. L. LINDSAY, till 29/6/1915, replaced by
Major-General EARL OF CAVAN, till 5/8/1915, replaced by
Major-General P. S. WILKINSON, till 24/2/1918
(Brig.-General C. COFFIN, V.C., officiating till 17/3/1918, and
Brig.-General A. U. STOCKLEY, till 24/3/18), replaced by
Major-General H. C. JACKSON.

B.G. R.A.

Brig.-General C. G. HENSHAW, till 24/12/15, replaced by
Brig.-General W. A. ROBINSON, till 21/5/1916, replaced by
Lieut.-Colonel A. U. STOCKLEY (appointed Brig.-General 20/6/1916), till 29/3/1918, replaced by
Brig.-General W. STIRLING.

B.G. 149TH BRIGADE

Brig.-General J. F. RIDDELL, killed 26/4/1915, replaced by
Brig.-General G. FIELDING, till 29/6/1915, replaced by
Brig.-General H. F. H. CLIFFORD, killed 11/9/1916, replaced by
Brig.-General R. M. OVENS, till 6/3/1917, replaced by
Brig.-General H. C. REES, till 2/10/1917, replaced by
Brig.-General E. P. A. RIDDELL, wounded 27/5/1918, replaced on 7/6/1918 by
Brig.-General P. M. ROBINSON.

B.G. 150TH BRIGADE

Brig.-General J. E. BUSH, till 25/1/1916, replaced by
Brig.-General B. G. PRICE, till 25/2/1918, replaced by

Brig.-General H. C. REES, missing 27/5/1918, replaced by
Brig.-General F. J. MARSHALL, till 13/7/1918, replaced by
Brig.-General C. P. HEYWOOD, till 28/9/1918, replaced by
Brig.-General G. ROLLO.

B.G. 151ST BRIGADE

Brig.-General H. MARTIN, till 4/7/1915, replaced by
Brig.-General J. S. M. SHEA, till 17/5/1916, replaced by
Brig.-General P. T. WESTMORLAND, till 6/9/1916, replaced by
Brig.-General N. J. G. CAMERON, till 20/10/1917, replaced by
Brig.-General C. T. MARTIN, killed 27/5/1918, replaced on 7/6/1918, by
Brig.-General R. E. SUGDEN.

DIVISIONAL TROOPS

CAVALRY

"A" Squadron Yorkshire Hussars, to XVII Corps Cavalry Regt., 9/5/1916.

CYCLISTS

50th Cyclist Company, to V Corps Cyclist Battalion, 20/5/1916.

ROYAL ENGINEERS

1st Northumbrian Field Company, numbered 446, 1/2/1917.
2nd Northumbrian Field Company, numbered 447, 1/2/1917.
2/1st Northumbrian Field Company, joined 6/7/1915, transferred to 28th Division, 10/7/1915.
7th Field Company, joined 17/6/1915.
50th Divisional Signal Company.

PIONEERS

7th Durham Light Infantry, became Pioneer Battalion from 151st Brigade, 16/11/1915, transferred to 8th Division 20/6/1918, replaced by
5th Royal Irish Regiment, joined 14/7/1918.

MACHINE-GUN COMPANIES

149th, 150th, 151st Companies, formed 1/2/1916.
245th Company, joined from U.K. 30/7/1917.

50TH BATTALION, M.G. Corps, formed 1/3/1918.

FIELD AMBULANCES.—1/1st, 1/2nd, 1/3rd Northumbrian.

DIVISIONAL TRAIN.—467, 468, 469, 470 Companies, A.S.C.

1/1st (Northern) MOBILE VETERINARY SECTION.

50TH SANITARY SECTION, till June 1917.

TRENCH MORTAR BATTERIES: "X"50 from April 1916, "Y"50 from April 1916, "Z" 50 from April 1916 till February 1918.

HEAVY TRENCH MORTAR BATTERY: "V"50, January 1917 till February 1918.

No. 244 DIVISIONAL EMPLOYMENT COMPANY, from August 1917.

A Composite Brigade, consisting of Three Battalions (one found by each Brigade), and known as 150TH COMPOSITE BRIGADE, was formed on 1st June, 1918, under the Command of BRIG.-GENERAL F. J. MARSHALL.

> 149th Composite Battalion
> 150th   ,,   ,,   } 150th Composite Brigade.
> 151st   ,,   ,,

This Brigade was disbanded on the 30th June, 1918, and the Personnel rejoined their Units.

Appendix C

Headquarters,
28*th* Division.
18th May, 1915.

Dear General Lindsay,

I wish to tell you how much I appreciate the good work done by the Units of your Division which were associated with the 28th Division between the 22nd April and 4th May. The battalions which did especially good service were the 8th Battalion Durham Light Infantry, the 4th Battalion Yorkshire Regiment, and the 4th Battalion East Yorkshire Regiment.

The 8th Battalion Durham Light Infantry were sent up on the 25th April to occupy trenches on the Gravenstafel Ridge. They were heavily shelled and attacked by gas, but held on to their position throughout the day, beating off all attacks made by German infantry. On the 26th they were again heavily attacked by infantry supported by a strong force of artillery, but held on until ordered to fall back to a position further in rear. In the face of a very superior force they carried out this movement steadily and slowly, inflicting severe loss on the enemy, though, unfortunately, at great cost to themselves.

The 4th Yorks. and 4th East Yorks. were associated with the 11th Infantry Brigade on the North front during the severe fighting from the 29th April to the 3rd May. The Brigadier spoke highly of the manner in which they carried out their duties, as did also the Commanding Officers of all battalions in the 11th Infantry Brigade.

I had hoped to be able to see the units and thank them personally for their services, but urgent duties prevented my leaving my Headquarters.

I should be very glad if you would allow the Brigadiers to inform the units mentioned, and especially the 8th Durham Light Infantry, how much I appreciated the good work they did and the gallantry displayed by all ranks.

Believe me yours sincerely,
(*Sd.*) E. S. BULFIN.

Major-General Sir W. F. L. Lindsay, K.C.B., D.S.O.,
Commanding Northumbrian Division.

Appendix D

REORGANISATION OF ARTILLERY, 16th MAY, 1916

1st NORTHUMBRIAN BRIGADE

1st, 2nd and 3rd Batteries.
New Battery formed 10/5/1916 and designated "D". Numbered 250TH BRIGADE, R.F.A. 16/5/1916.
Reorganised 16/5/1916 into three 4-gun 18-pounders and one 4-gun 4.5 in. (Howitzer).
"D" transferred to 253rd Brigade: 4th Durham (Howitzer) Battery joined and was designated "D".
On reorganisation the 1st, 2nd and 3rd Batteries were designated "A", "B", and "C", respectively.

2ND NORTHUMBRIAN BRIGADE

1st, 2nd and 3rd Batteries.
New Battery formed 10/5/1916 and designated "D". Numbered 251ST BRIGADE, R.F.A., 16/5/1916.
Reorganised 16/5/1916 into three 4-gun 18-pounders and one 4-gun 4.5 in. (Howitzer).
"D" transferred to 253rd Brigade: 5th Durham (Howitzer) Battery joined and was designated "D".
On reorganisation the 1st, 2nd and 3rd Batteries were designated "A", "B", and "C", respectively.

3RD NORTHUMBRIAN BRIGADE

1st, 2nd and 3rd Batteries.
New Battery formed 10/5/1916 and designated "D". Numbered 252ND BRIGADE, R.F.A., 16/5/1916.
Reorganised 16/5/1916 into three 4-gun 18-pounders and one 4-gun 4.5 in. (Howitzer).
"D" transferred to 253rd Brigade: D/61 (Howitzer) joined from 253rd Brigade.
On reorganisation the 1st, 2nd and 3rd Batteries were designated "A", "B", and "C", respectively.

4TH NORTHUMBRIAN BRIGADE (HOWITZERS)

4th Durham and 5th Durham Batteries.
D/61 (from Guards Division) joined 21/2/1916. Numbered 253RD BRIGADE, R.F.A., 16/5/1916.
Reorganised 16/5/1916 into three 4-gun 18-pounders.
4th Durham Battery transferred to 250th Brigade.
5th Durham Battery transferred to 251st Brigade.
D/61 transferred to 252nd Brigade.
D/250 joined and was designated "A" 253.
D/251 joined and was designated "B" 253.
D/252 joined and was designated "C" 253.

Appendix E
REORGANISATION OF ARTILLERY, 16th NOVEMBER, 1916

250TH BRIGADE, R.F.A.
Reorganised into three 6-gun 18-pounders and one 4-gun 4.5 in. (Howitzer). "A"253 complete and half of "C"253 joined and were posted, one section to each "A", "B", and "C". "D" remains unchanged.

251ST BRIGADE, R.F.A.
Reorganised into three 6-gun 18-pounders and one 4-gun 4.5 in. (Howitzer). "B"253 complete and half of "C"253 joined, and were posted, one section to each "A", "B", and "C". "D" remains unchanged.

252ND BRIGADE, R.F.A.
Reorganised into two 6-gun 18-pounders and one 4-gun 4.5 in. (Howitzer). "B" Battery was broken up, Right Section transferred to "A" and Left Section to "C". "C" was then redesignated "B".
"D" remains unchanged.

253RD BRIGADE, R.F.A.
On reorganisation this Brigade was broken up, and distributed as under:—
"A" complete and half of "C" to 250th Brigade (*q.v.*).
"B" complete and half of "C" to 251st Brigade (*q.v.*).

1/1ST NORTHUMBRIAN INFANTRY BRIGADE, NUMBERED 149TH INFANTRY BRIGADE, 12/5/15.

4TH	5TH	6TH	7TH
NORTHUMBERLAND FUSILIERS	NORTHUMBERLAND FUSILIERS	NORTHUMBERLAND FUSILIERS	NORTHUMBERLAND FUSILIERS
Reduced to T.C. 4/7/1918	Reduced to T.C. 4/7/1918	Reduced to T.C. 4/7/1918	Transferred to 42nd Division 10/2/1918
Transferred to L. of C. 13/7/1918	Transferred to L. of C. 13/7/1918	Transferred to L. of C. 13/7/1918	

5TH BORDERS joined 5/5/1915, transferred to 151st Brigade 20/12/1915
BRIGADE WAS REORGANISED ON 15TH JULY, 1918.

2ND ROYAL DUBLIN FUSILIERS   3RD ROYAL FUSILIERS   13TH BLACK WATCH

1/1st YORK & DURHAM INFANTRY BRIGADE, NUMBERED 150TH INFANTRY BRIGADE, 12/5/15.

4TH EAST YORKS.	4TH YORKS.	5TH YORKS.	5TH DURHAM L.I.
Reduced to T.C. 4/7/1918	Reduced to T.C. 4/7/1918	Reduced to T.C. 4/7/1918	Transferred to 151st Brigade 11/2/1918
Transferred to L. of C. 13/7/1918	Transferred to L. of C. 13/7/1918	Transferred to L. of C. 13/7/1918	

BRIGADE WAS REORGANISED ON 15TH JULY, 1918

| 2ND NORTHUMBERLAND FUSILIERS | 2ND ROYAL MUNSTER FUSILIERS | 7TH WILTS. |

1/1st DURHAM L.I. BRIGADE, NUMBERED 151ST INFANTRY BRIGADE, 12/5/15.

6TH DURHAM L.I.	7TH DURHAM L.I.	8TH DURHAM L.I.	9TH DURHAM L.I.
Reduced to T.C. 4/7/1918	Became Divisional Pioneers 16/11/1915	Reduced to T.C. 4/7/1918	Transferred to 62nd Division 10/2/1918, replaced by
Transferred to L. of C. 13/7/1918		Transferred to L. of C. 13/7/1918	5TH DURHAM L.I. Red. T.C. 4/7/18 to L. of C. 13/7/1918

5TH LOYAL NORTH LANCS. joined 11/6/1915, transferred 55th Division 20/12/1915, replaced by 5TH BORDERS, transferred to 66th Division 13/2/1918.

BRIGADE WAS REORGANISED ON 15TH JULY, 1918

| 1ST K.O.Y.L.INF. | 6TH ROYAL INNISKILLING FUSILIERS | 4TH K.R.R. CORPS |

Appendix F

ORDER OF BATTLE, 15th JULY, 1918

50TH DIVISION

G.O.C.
Major-General H. C. JACKSON.

G.R.A.
Brig.-General W. STIRLING.

149TH INFANTRY BRIGADE
Brig.-General P. M. ROBINSON.

2nd Royal Dublin Fusiliers.
3rd Royal Fusiliers.
13th Black Watch.
149th Trench Mortar Battery.

150TH INFANTRY BRIGADE
Brig.-General C. P. HEYWOOD.

2nd Northumberland Fusiliers.
7th Wiltshires.
2nd Royal Munster Fusiliers.
150th Trench Mortar Battery.

151ST INFANTRY BRIGADE
Brig.-General R. E. SUGDEN.

6th Royal Inniskilling Fusiliers.
1st King's Own Yorkshire Light Infantry.
4th King's Royal Rifle Corps.
151st Trench Mortar Battery.

DIVISIONAL TROOPS

250th Brigade, R.F.A. ("A", "B", "C" and "D" Batteries)
  (eighteen 18-pounders and six 4.5 in. (Howitzers).
251st Brigade, R.F.A. ("A", "B", "C" and "D" Batteries)
  (eighteen 18-pounders and six 4.5 in. Howitzers).

X/50 Trench Mortar Battery, R.A.
Y/50 Trench Mortar Battery, R.A.
50th Divisional Ammunition Column.
7th Field Company, R.E.
446th and 447th (Northumbrian) Field Companies.
50th Divisional Signal Company.
50th Battalion, Machine Gun Corps.
5th Battalion Royal Irish Regiment (Pioneers).
467th, 468th, 469th and 470th Companies Royal Army Service Corps.
1/1st, 1/3rd and 2/2nd Northumbrian Field Ambulances.
50th Divisional Ambulance Workshop.
1/1st Northumbrian Mobile Veterinary Section.
244th Divisional Employment Company.

INDEX

INDEX TO UNITS

Army Service Corps (Divisional Train), 3, 10, 74, 91, 113, 160, 225

Artillery:—
  1st Northumbrian (250th) Brigade, R.F.A.: 2, 73, 90, 93, 103, 104, 137, 146, 189, 190, 205, 258, 262, 263, 271, 277, 305, 306, 337, 345, 346
  2nd Northumbrian (251st) Brigade, R.F.A.: 2, 56, 74, 90, 103, 137, 146, 190, 205, 258, 262, 271, 272, 277, 305, 337, 345, 346
  3rd Northumbrian (252nd) Brigade, R.F.A.: 2, 72, 74, 76, 90, 103, 137, 146, 190
  4th Northumbrian (253rd) Brigade, R.F.A.: 2, 124, 146, 190
  4th Northumbrian (County of Durham) Howitzer Brigade: 2, 50, 74, 90, 103
  5th Northumbrian (County of Durham) Howitzer Brigade: 3, 50, 90
  1st Northumbrian Ammunition Column: 2
  2nd Northumbrian Ammunition Column 2
  3rd Northumbrian (County of Durham) Ammunition Column 2
  4th Northumbrian (County of Durham) Ammunition Column 3, 50
  5th Durham (Howitzer) Battery, 3, 50
  Royal Garrison Artillery (Heavies) .. 3, 52, 74, 90

Brigades, Infantry:—
  Northumberland Infantry (149th) Brigade: 1, 9, 10, 11, 20, 24, 35, 36, 40, 41, 42, 43, 46, 47, 53, 54, 71, 72, 73, 78, 79, 82, 83, 85, 86, 88, 90, 91, 92, 93, 96, 100, 101, 103, 105, 106, 108,

Northumberland Inf. (149th):—contd.
  109, 115, 116, 117, 125, 129, 133, 134, 138, 139, 141, 143, 144, 148, 149, 151, 158, 161, 162, 164, 169, 172, 173, 175, 181, 183, 184, 189, 193, 194, 195, 196, 198, 200, 206, 212, 213, 216, 224, 227, 228, 229, 233, 236, 237, 240, 241, 242, 244, 247, 248, 249, 250, 252, 253, 254, 258, 260, 262, 263, 266, 275, 276, 278, 279, 287, 288, 289, 290, 292, 299, 300, 301, 302, 303, 304, 309, 310, 314, 320, 321, 322, 323, 327, 329, 333, 334, 335, 336, 337, 339, 340, 341, 343, 350, 351, 352, 354

York and Durham Infantry (150th) Brigade: 1, 9, 10, 13, 15, 16, 23, 40, 41, 42, 43, 53, 54, 58, 71, 73, 79, 85, 86, 96, 100, 101, 103, 105, 106, 108, 115, 116, 117, 120, 125, 129, 133, 134, 138, 139, 143, 144, 149, 150, 153, 154, 157, 161, 162, 164, 170, 172, 173, 175, 181, 182, 184, 189, 198, 200, 206, 207, 212, 216, 221, 222, 227, 228, 229, 230, 231, 233, 234, 236, 237, 248, 249, 250, 252, 254, 260, 262, 263, 268, 269, 270, 275, 276, 279, 280, 283, 288, 290, 291, 293, 297, 300, 301, 303, 304, 309, 310, 311, 312, 317, 318, 320, 322, 323, 327, 330, 332, 333, 334, 335, 336, 337, 344, 350, 351, 353, 354

Durham Light Infantry (151st) Brigade: 1, 9, 10, 11, 20, 24, 27, 41, 46, 52, 53, 54, 58, 71, 73, 78, 82, 83, 86, 90, 91, 92, 96, 100, 101, 103, 105, 106, 108, 115, 116, 117, 124, 129, 133, 134, 139, 143, 151, 152, 153, 156, 157, 158, 161, 164, 169, 170, 172, 174, 175, 181, 182, 189, 193, 195, 198, 200, 206, 208, 211, 213, 216, 217, 221, 223, 224, 227, 228, 229, 230, 233, 236, 237, 249, 250,

INDEX

Durham Light Infantry (151st):—contd.
252, 253, 254, 260, 261, 262, 272, 275, 277, 278, 282, 288, 290, 293, 300, 301, 305, 309, 310, 311, 312, 314, 315, 317, 322, 327, 333, 334, 335, 336, 337, 338, 341, 342, 343, 350, 351, 352, 353, 354

Battalions, Infantry:—

5th Border Regiment: 152, 153, 158, 165, 167, 169, 175, 208, 211, 217, 222, 223, 224, 229, 254, 255

5th Durham Light Infantry: 1, 9, 20, 24, 25, 26, 35, 40, 42, 43, 46, 54, 56, 65, 73, 75, 89, 90, 97, 115, 120, 122, 151, 154, 162, 163, 182, 193, 194, 216, 220, 221, 222, 231, 232, 234, 254, 260, 264, 270, 271, 275, 277, 282, 285, 286, 287, 294, 295, 302, 304, 310, 312, 313, 314, 315, 317, 318, 319, 321, 327, 328, 329, 333, 336, 337, 343

6th Durham Light Infantry: 1, 10, 11, 21, 27, 34, 35, 44, 56, 61, 73, 83, 90, 92, 97, 101, 102, 103, 106, 133, 152, 165, 167, 168, 176, 177, 179, 193, 209, 210, 211, 212, 230, 243, 249, 254, 270, 271, 277, 282, 283, 290, 292, 293, 310, 311, 312, 313, 314, 315, 323, 327, 329, 336, 342, 350

7th Durham Light Infantry: 1, 10, 21, 27, 35, 40, 54, 56, 62, 82, 90, 98, 101, 110, 145, 176, 180, 225, 231, 266, 275, 284, 285, 286, 287, 290, 294, 301, 315, 323, 327, 328, 342, 343, 351

8th Durham Light Infantry: 1, 10, 11, 21, 22, 27, 28, 31, 33, 34, 40, 56, 61, 62, 63, 64, 83, 90, 92, 98, 99, 103, 112, 121, 133, 151, 156, 157, 158, 164, 165, 167, 169, 175, 177, 179, 193, 208, 210, 211, 218, 254, 265, 270, 271, 277, 282, 283, 284, 290, 291, 292, 293, 296, 310, 312, 315, 316, 317, 322, 327, 329, 336, 338, 341, 343

9th Durham Light Infantry: 1, 10, 21, 27, 35, 40, 56, 73, 100, 122, 151, 152, 156, 158, 164, 168, 169, 175, 179, 193, 207, 208, 209, 210, 213, 217, 222, 224, 229, 233, 235, 243, 255

4th East Yorkshires: 1, 9, 16, 17, 18, 19, 24, 35, 40, 42, 43, 46, 60, 75, 77, 90, 103, 115, 126, 128, 139, 148, 151, 154, 157, 162, 163, 182, 183, 184, 188, 191, 194, 216, 217, 218, 220, 232, 249, 254, 260, 263, 264, 268, 269, 276, 279, 280, 281, 282, 302, 303, 305, 311, 317, 318, 323, 325, 330, 332, 337, 344, 349

4th Northumberland Fusiliers: 1, 10, 20, 25, 26, 35, 38, 43, 47, 65, 66, 68, 69, 73, 81, 82, 93, 94, 115, 123, 144, 148, 149, 155, 158, 159, 164, 169, 172, 184, 191, 194, 223, 224, 233, 234, 236, 240, 241, 243, 244, 247, 254, 260, 262, 273, 279, 290, 294, 298, 301, 314, 315, 333, 339, 340

5th Northumberland Fusiliers: 1, 10, 20, 27, 35, 36, 37, 42, 43, 57, 65, 66, 67, 72, 73, 79, 88, 94, 95, 102, 103, 106, 115, 123, 134, 139, 144, 159, 164, 168, 172, 184, 185, 187, 188, 190, 194, 206, 214, 240, 241, 243, 245, 246, 247, 254, 260, 263, 267, 276, 279, 288, 289, 294, 296, 297, 298, 301, 303, 319, 320, 325, 329, 333, 336, 340, 343

6th Northumberland Fusiliers: 1, 10, 27, 35, 37, 38, 43, 65, 69, 73, 79, 80, 82, 88, 95, 96, 101, 102, 103, 107, 115, 119, 120, 144, 159, 169, 172, 181, 191, 194, 213, 214, 234, 240, 241, 254, 260, 263, 266, 276, 279, 289, 290, 294, 296, 301, 302, 303, 304, 319, 321, 322, 328, 329, 333, 336, 340, 350

7th Northumberland Fusiliers: 1, 10, 25, 26, 27, 35, 38, 43, 65, 69, 73, 79, 81, 82, 86, 96, 115, 120, 133, 144, 148, 149, 151, 158, 169, 172, 184, 185, 187, 188, 190, 194, 213, 214, 240, 241, 245, 247, 254, 255

4th Yorkshires (The Green Howards): 1, 9, 13, 16, 17, 19, 24, 35, 40, 42, 43, 46, 47, 54, 56, 59, 61, 73, 75, 77, 82, 103, 106, 115, 116, 126, 127, 128, 148, 151, 157, 162, 163, 173, 182, 184, 194, 216, 217, 218, 220, 221, 231, 232, 234, 248, 254, 260, 268, 269, 270, 279,

THE HISTORY OF THE 50TH DIVISION

4th Yorkshires (The Green Howards):—contd.
280, 281, 282, 291, 293, 303, 311, 317, 318, 323, 324, 325, 330, 331, 337, 344, 350

5th Yorkshires (The Green Howards): 1, 9, 20, 24, 25, 42, 43, 46, 55, 60, 73, 76, 90, 115, 129, 133, 141, 148, 151, 157, 162, 163, 173, 182, 188, 194, 216, 221, 222, 231, 248, 254, 260, 264, 268, 269, 276, 279, 281, 282, 291, 293, 305, 311, 317, 323, 324, 330, 331, 337, 344

Cyclist Company .. 53, 57, 72
Divisional Company (Headquarters) 3, 10, 44, 53, 206
22nd Entrenching Battalion, 301, 302
Northumbrian Divisional Signal Company 3, 44, 45
1st Northumbrian Field Ambulance, 3, 11, 12, 74, 90, 110, 278

2nd Northumbrian Field Ambulance, 3, 6, 74, 90, 110, 226, 278
3rd Northumbrian Field Ambulance .. 3, 74, 90, 110, 112, 278
149th Machine Gun Company, 175, 180, 216, 217, 242, 260, 268, 302
150th Machine Gun Company .. 216
151st Machine Gun Company, 175, 179, 180, 200, 216
Royal Engineers: 1st and 2nd Northumbrian Field Companies, 3, 10, 74, 85, 91, 110, 143, 160, 198, 225, 263, 298, 299
50th Sanitary Section 91
Signal Company 225
31st Trench Howitzer Battery .. 91
149th Trench Mortar Battery, 242, 352
150th Trench Mortar Battery, 216, 311, 352
151st Trench Mortar Battery (Light) 175, 313, 314, 352
Veterinary Corps .. 74, 91, 190, 225

INDEX TO OFFICERS

Alderson, General 23
Anderson, Capt. W., 51, 113, 124, 133
Angus, Major 286
Armstrong, Capt. 297

Bainbridge, Capt. J. S. 263
Baker, Major 299
Barber, Capt. G. C. 26
Barnes, Major A. C. 350
Barr, Capt. 326
Beddoes, Lieut.-Colonel H. R. .. 60
Bell, Lieut.-Colonel M. H. L. .. 17
Bettison, Capt. M. H. 122
Birchall, Lieut.-Colonel 343
Blair, Capt. R. R. 96
Borritt, Lieut.-Colonel .. 92, 97
Boys, Capt. 133
Bradford, Lieut.-Colonel R. B. (V.C.), 152, 165, 168, 207, 254
Bradford, Major 22
Bradford, Capt. 29, 30
Bradford, Capt. T. A. .. 62, 63, 83
Bridgeford, Colonel .. 34, 35
Brown, Capt., 129, 131, 132, 133
Brown, Capt. R. A. 240
Buckley, Capt., 84, 120, 150, 184, 185
Bulfin, General 34, 58
Bush, Brig.-General J. E. 254
Byng, General 292

Callin, Rev. R. W. 307
Cameron, Brig.-General 209

Carey, General 287
Cavan, Major-General the Earl of, 89, 92
Chapman, Lieut.-Colonel. . .. 305
Chapman, Major 138
Charlton, Lieut.-Colonel 263
Charlton, Major B. H. 127
Clark, Capt. A. N. 177
Clifford, Brig.-General H. F. H., 89, 138, 141
Coffin, Brig.-General C. (V.C.) .. 258
Coles, Lieut.-Colonel A. H., 36, 72, 79
Connaught, H.R.H. The Duke of 233
Coulson, Major W. H. 22
Crockett, Capt. N. R. 133

Darling, Capt. 346
Davies, Capt. 297
de Legh, Major H. L. 46
Deverell, Lieut.-Colonel C. J. .. 97
Dodds, Capt. 45

Ensor, Major 121
Eykyn, Capt. and Adjutant G. D. P. 19

Farrell, Capt. Rede 19
Fielding, General .. 72, 82, 89
Fielding, Colonel G. P. T. .. 40
Finlayson, Capt. A. 274
Fitzhugh, Lieut.-Colonel 351
Foster, Lieut.-Colonel A. J., 37, 38

INDEX

Foster, Lieut.-Colonel D. (R.E.) .. 125
French, Sir John, 8, 41, 45, 48, 108

Gibson, Lieut.-Colonel B. D.,
 141, 187, 339, 340
Gill, Capt. 185
Gloag, Capt. 121
Gould, Major 343
Graham, Major 324
Graham, Capt. W. G. 88
Gregory, Capt. T. W. 273
Guy, Major R. F. 133

Haig, Sir Douglas, 108, 135, 136,
 140, 142, 143, 191, 198, 202,
 203, 214, 253, 256, 257
Handfield-Jones, Major R. M. .. 347
Harter, Capt. J. C. 118
Harvey, Capt. 22, 30, 31
Hedley, Lieut.-Colonel J. R. .. 152
Henderson, Lieut.-Colonel A. .. 62
Hesketh, Lieut.-Colonel G. .. 83
Hicks, Capt. 274
Hill, Capt. D. 142
Hirsch, Capt. 220
Hope, Lieut. (Quarter-master) .. 83
Horne, General Sir H. S. 334
Hull, Brig.-General .. 23, 24, 25

Inglis, Capt. M. R. 156
Irwin, Lieut.-Colonel 333

Jackson, General H. C.,
 272, 308, 334, 353, 356
Jackson, Major 326
Jeffreys, Lieut.-Colonel J. W., 107, 152
Joffre, General 135, 136
Johnson, Lieut.-Colonel F. G. O. 345
Johnston, Major 73

Karslake, Lieut.-Colonel H. (R.A.) 125
King, Capt. 274
Kirkup, Lieut.-Colonel, 343, 348, 351

Leathart, Major J. G. 321
Lindsay, General, 10, 23, 58, 72, 89
Ludendorff, General 238

McCracken, Major W. 347
Mackay, Major 45
Maistre, General (French) .. 352
Marley, Capt. 121
Martin, Brig.-General C. F. T. 254, 341
Martin, Lieut.-Colonel H., .. 296
Martin, Major 12
Marshall, General .. 349, 350, 351
Matthews, Major H. C. 19
Meek, Capt. 345
Milburn, Lieut.-Colonel T. A. .. 68
Milne-Thompson, Colonel A. .. 347
Morris, Capt. 186

Mortimer, Lieut.-Colonel J. .. 148
Moss-Blundell, Lieut.-Colonel, F.R. 345

Nancarrow, Capt. J. V. 19
Nicholson, Capt. R. W. 120

Ommanney, Lieut.-Colonel .. 73
Ommanney, Major C. H., 147, 189, 212
Ommanney, Capt. .. 93, 101, 104, 107

Periera, Brig.-General C. E. .. 61
Pierce, Major C. H. 141
Pike, Colonel 332
Pinkney, Lieut.-Colonel E. W. R. 113
Plumer, General 23, 41, 45
Price, Brig.-General B. G. .. 138
Purvis, Capt. 26

Raimes, Major A. L.,
 97, 121, 157, 231, 232
Rawlinson, General 354
Rees, Brig.-General H. C., 254, 344, 350
Riddell, Brig.-General E. P. A.,
 254, 255, 288, 299, 341
Riddell, Brig.-General J. F., 35, 36, 38
Ritson, Major 29
Ritson, Capt. J. A. S.,
 30, 31, 62, 63, 64
Robb, Lieut.-Colonel 268
Robinson, Brig.-General W. A. .. 124
Robinson, Lieut.-Colonel F. .. 297
Robinson, Lieut.-Colonel P. M.,
 344, 351
Rogers, Major 340
Ruthven, Capt. 325

Saltonstall, Capt. 332
Scott, Lieut.-Colonel L. D. .. 350
Scott Jackson, Lieut.-Colonel G.,
 37, 141
Sharp, Capt. B. M. R. (Diary)
 13, 19
Sharp, Capt. B. S. M. 42
Shaw, Lieut.-Colonel G. H., 17, 18
Shea, Brig.-General J. .. 123, 124
Sheil, Colonel, 101, 103, 104, 107
Sheil, Major 345
Shepherd, Capt. R. N. .. 176, 181
Simmons, Major 107
Snow, Lieut.-General T. D'O., 223, 233
Spain, Lieut.-Colonel G. R. B.,
 37, 38, 141
Spence, Lieut.-Colonel G. O., 323, 328
Sproxton, Capt. C. 127
Stead, Lieut.-Colonel .. 349, 351
Stevens, Lieut.-Colonel G. A. .. 22
Stevens, Capt. and Adjutant, 33, 83
Stockley, Brig.-General A. V.,
 124, 254, 258
Stuart, Brevet Lieut.-Colonel A. G.,
 113, 125

372 THE HISTORY OF THE 50TH DIVISION

	Page
Sugden, Brig.-General R. E.	351
Theilmann, Major C. E.	19
Thomson, Lieut.-Colonel, 291, 300, 324, 325, 331, 332	
Thompson, Lieut.-Colonel	344
Thompson, Capt. T. A. L.	268
Thorp, Major H. W. B.	113
Thurston, Colonel H. S.	110, 111
Turnbull, Lieut.-Colonel,	33, 63, 83
Turner, Lieut.-Colonel C.,	139, 142
Veitch, Major E. H.	64, 98, 174
Veitch, Capt.	29, 34

	Page
Walton, Lieut.-Colonel, 343, 344, 348, 350	
Weir, Capt. D. H.	26, 45
Westmoreland, Brig.-General P. F.	124
Wilkinson, Lieut.-Colonel W. T.	139
Williams, Capt.	211
Williamson, Capt. A. R.	181
Wilkinson, Major-General P. S., 92, 100, 113, 116, 117, 118, 125, 134, 143, 153, 159, 170, 172, 183, 212, 223, 227, 229, 233, 254	
Wilkinson, Lieut.-Colonel, 280, 281, 291, 351	
Wilkinson, Major G. E.	141, 165
Wright, Lieut.-Colonel N. I.	187

INDEX TO PLACES

	Page
Achiet-le-Petit	237
Aisne	257, 321, 349
Albert, 137, 139, 192, 193, 194, 195	
Amiens	281, 292, 303, 354
Ancre	183, 202
Arbre Woods and Abeele Area, 71, 74	
Armagh Wood, 48, 58, 72, 75, 104, 125	
Armentières, 90, 96, 97, 100, 101, 107, 310, 337	
Arras	204, 206
Athies-Le Mesnil Line, 265, 266, 268	
Bailleul	117, 123, 134
Baizieux	194, 195
Bapaume	159, 171
Barleux	271, 275, 279, 285
Bazentin-le-Petit and Le Grand, 138, 140, 141, 143, 144, 146, 172	
Beaurepaire	340
Beaurieux	343, 346, 347
Bécourt	139, 194, 195
Bedford House	102, 110
Béhencourt	189, 275
Bellewaarde Lake, 47, 48, 49, 58, 61, 84	
Bellewaarde Ridge	83, 84
Berlin Wood	41, 44, 46, 47
Berny and Belloy in ruins	199
Béthune	308, 310
Blawepoort Farm	102, 104
Boeschepe	11
Boetleer Farm, 22, 23, 27, 31, 32, 33, 34, 45	
Bois Confluent	118
Bois de Beau Marais	337
Boisleux St. Maré	229
Bloke Row	87
Bluff, The, 105, 112, 114, 116, 117	
Brandhoek, 10, 44, 45, 50, 52, 53, 54	
Brie Bridge	257, 260
265, 268, 269, 271, 272, 278, 284	
Brielan Bridge	13
Broodseinde	14

	Page
Bryon Farm	118
Bull Farm	85
Butte de l'Edmond	339, 340
Butte de Warlencourt, 174, 175, 180, 185, 196	
Caix	301
Cambrai	354, 355
Canada Huts	101
Canadian Farm	13, 15
Canal Dug-outs	102, 110
Cayeux	300
Château Thierry	349
Chaudardes	340, 341, 343
Chérisy	207, 208, 212, 218, 230, 235, 236
Clapham Junction	48
Cojeul	207, 208, 209
210, 211, 213, 216, 219, 222, 226	
Concevreux, 335, 336, 339, 340, 343	
Contalmaison	137, 138, 140
Delville Wood	140, 141
Demuin	303
Dickebusch	101, 122
Dranoutre	86
Eaucourt (l'Abbaye), 166, 167, 171, 173, 196	
Estaires, 309, 310, 311, 312, 314, 317, 319, 320, 323, 325, 326, 327, 328, 329	
Estrées	277, 282, 287
Eterpigny Bridge, 257, 265, 270, 271, 272, 284	
Faverolles	348
Flers	161, 169
Flers-Courcelette	143, 145, 146
Flêtre	123
Foch Farm	15
Fontain-les-Croisilles	232

INDEX

Forêt de Mormal	355, 356
Fortuin	18, 23, 35, 41
Foucaucourt, 274, 275, 278, 279,	287, 289
French Farm	103
Frezenberg, 14, 34, 42, 46, 48, 49, 58	
Fusilier Farm	15
Givenchy	327
Glennes	337, 346
Gomiecourt	282
Grand Porte Egal	90, 91
Gravenstafel Ridge	34, 42, 49
Green Line, 260, 261, 263, 264,	265, 266, 267
Gird Trench, 174, 175, 178, 179,	186, 187, 188, 189
Guémappe, 207, 208, 210, 216,	218, 219
Guillaucourt,	259, 260, 297, 298, 301, 302
Haanebeek	18, 33
Halleblaast Farm	104
Hampshire Farm	15, 20
Harbonnières, 294, 298, 299, 300,	301, 302
Hell Fire Corner,	43, 103, 104
High Wood, 141, 144, 148, 149,	151, 153, 174, 182
Hill 23	241
Hill 37	40
Hill 60, 41, 47, 48, 70, 101, 103,	104, 105, 106, 113, 125
Hill 200 (North of Ventelay)	343
Hill 233	348
Hindenburg Line	199, 203, 354
Hohenzollern Redoubt	114
Hooge, 42, 49, 55, 59, 60, 79, 84,	86, 95, 115, 125
Hooggraaf	118
Hooge Woods	55
Hook Sap	183, 186, 187, 189
Hook Trench, 138, 143, 149, 152, 155, 158	
Hospital Farm	68
Houplines	89, 98
Houthulst Forest	240, 241
Jonquery	348
Juliet Farm	24
Keerselare	12
Kemmel	121, 128
Kemmels Hills	118
Kitchener's Wood	23, 24, 37
Kruisstraat, 75, 78, 81, 103, 115	
La Bassée Canal	308, 313
La Belle Alliance Farm	15
La Brique	14
La Crèche	100
La Gorgue	310, 315, 319

La Motte	334
Lamoureux Hill	341
Langemarck	7
Langemarck-Bixschoote	6
Lankhof	103, 117
Laventie	312, 313
Lawe River, 310, 313, 314, 319, 323, 327	
Le Catalet	354
Le Cateau	355
Le Drumez	310, 313
Le Marias Posts	316
L'Epinette	89
Lestrem, 310, 312, 313, 315, 320,	322, 323
Le Temple	44
Licourt, 272, 277, 278, 279, 280,	281, 282, 283, 287
Lille Gate	105, 106
Lindenhoek	87
Lizerne	13
Lock de la Rault	316, 317
Loos Salient	114
Longeau	304
Luce River	257, 303, 304
Lys, River, 257, 308, 311, 312, 313,	314, 317, 318, 319, 320, 323, 327, 334, 349
Mametz Wood, 139, 140, 141, 143,	152, 155, 158, 161, 170, 189, 192, 193
Maple Copse, 75, 78, 80, 102, 106	
Martinpuich, 141, 143, 144, 148,	149, 151, 153, 161, 173, 174
Méharicourt	296
Menin	56
Menin Gate	14, 105
Menin Road, 41, 49, 79, 101, 104,	105, 115
Méricourt	292
Merris	100
Merville, 309, 327, 332, 333, 334	
Méteren	117
Mézières	259, 302, 303
Millencourt	170, 193
Mont des Cats	118
Mont Kemmel	87, 101
Montigny Area	134, 136
Mount Sorrel	75, 103, 104, 125
Mouquet Farm	140
Mouse Trap Farm, 15, 42, 46, 47,	59, 65, 66, 68
Mushroom Trench	90
Neuf Berquin, 328, 329, 331, 333	
Neuve Eglise	86, 87, 101
Neuve Eglise—Lindenhoek— Kemmel	86
Neuve Chapple	107
Nobescourt	260, 263, 264, 271
Oblong Farm	15, 24

374 THE HISTORY OF THE 50TH DIVISION

	Page
Observatory Ridge	104
Oise River	258
Omiecourt	276, 277
Outtersteene	100
Ouv de Chemin de Fer	342
Passchendaele	238, 249, 250
P.C. Terrasse	344
Péronne	198, 275, 285
Pertain	276, 277
Petit Bois	119, 129
Plank Avenue	89
Poelcapelle	12, 13
Polygon Wood	41
Pont Levis, 310, 312, 313, 314, 315, 317, 319, 320, 321, 322	
Poperinghe, 9, 10, 11, 12, 48, 53, 58, 103, 110	
Potijze, 14, 19, 20, 21, 24, 56, 102, 250	
Potijze Château	15, 17, 56, 62
Proyart, 287, 292, 297, 298, 299, 300	
Railway Wood	62, 63
Reigersburg Camp	65
Reninghelst	11, 110
Roquetoire Area	335
Rosières, 287, 288, 289, 290, 291, 292, 293, 295, 297, 298, 299, 301	
Roulers	56, 63, 73, 80, 83, 251
Rudkin House	104, 106
Ryveld	9, 44
St. Christ Bridge, 265, 267, 268, 272, 275, 281, 282, 283, 284	
St. Eloi	114, 117, 121
St. Eloi (Lille) Gate	80
St. Jans ter Biezen	74
St. Jean	14, 20, 42, 69
St. Julien, 12, 14, 15, 18, 19, 23, 24, 25, 32, 35, 36, 37	
St. Quentin	272
Sambre	355, 356
Sanctuary Wood, 48, 54, 55, 56, 60, 72, 77, 79, 80, 82, 83, 102, 105, 106, 113, 125	
Scarpe	202, 205, 212, 258
Selle River	355
Séquehart	354
Shrapnel Corner	56, 106
Somme, 135, 136, 137, 142, 161, 170, 171, 174, 191, 192, 198, 199, 257, 265, 267, 269, 285, 287, 288, 292, 306, 349	
Somme Canal, 267, 268, 269, 271, 274	
South Zwhanhof Farm	13, 15
Spanbroekmolen	118, 126
Stirling Castle	105, 106

	Page
Steenstraat	13, 43
Steenvoorde	5, 10, 41, 52
Terdeghem	44
Thiepval Ridge	142
Tourenne Crossing	240, 245
Trou Bayard, 322, 324, 326, 329, 330	
Turco Farm, 15, 32, 41, 46, 47, 58, 67, 69	
Vandamme Hill	118
Vanheule Farm	38
Vauvillers, 288, 289, 290, 293, 294, 295, 296, 297, 298	
Ventelay	347, 348
Verbrandenmolen	105
Verdun	135, 136, 191, 238
Verlorenhoek, 14, 21, 27, 33, 34, 35, 40, 44, 46, 49, 58, 63, 64, 73	
Vert la Gravelle	345, 350
Vierhoek	331
Vierstraat	87, 122, 125
Vieux Berquin	331, 332, 333
Vlamertinghe, 8, 9, 10, 11, 12, 45, 46, 54, 65, 68, 78, 83	
Vimy Ridge	114, 202, 203
Vis-en-Artois	207, 216, 218
Wancourt, 207, 209, 212, 213, 216	
Warloy	193, 195
Watou	10, 53
Welch Farm	12
Westoutre	118
Wieltje, 14, 16, 20, 24, 27, 35, 36, 40, 42, 47, 56, 57, 67, 101, 102	
Winezeele	9, 44
Wippenhoek	74, 113
Wittepoort Farm	56
Wytschaete, 104, 118, 122, 123, 124, 125, 134	
Yellow Line	345
Ypres, 7, 9, 11, 12, 16, 20, 41, 42, 45, 47, 53, 54, 55, 57, 59, 74, 75, 80, 95, 104, 105, 110, 239	
Ypres Salient, 7, 13, 14, 41, 45, 47, 48, 49, 57, 87, 90, 100, 106, 114, 118, 123, 204, 233, 239, 242	
Yser Canal, 8, 13, 14, 15, 16, 57, 90, 239	
Zillebeke, 44, 53, 54, 56, 75, 104, 106, 115, 118	
Zillebeke Lake	16, 74, 103, 106
Zonnebeke	14, 21, 35, 41, 43, 49
Zouave Wood	61, 79, 82
Zwarteleen	105

INDEX GENERAL

	Page
Acts of Bravery	273, 274
A.D.M.S. Diary	225
Aisne, Battle of the (27th May–6th June, 1918)	335, 349
Allied Line (27th–28th March)	300
Ammunition replenished under heavy fire	51
Anecdote: Well-known General and gas-mask	98
Area of interest to 50th Division	257
Artillery barrage "particularly good"	223
Artillery in action	50
Artillery, Officers Commanding	2, 3
Asphyxiating gas at Ypres	12
Attack, The final	300
Battalion Medical Officers	44, 45
Battle of St. Julien ends	48
Bellewaarde, The action of (16th June)	83
Bellewaarde, The battle of (24th–25th May)	57
Butte de Warlencourt, The (1916)	171
Butte de Warlencourt: Good work by machine-gunners	180
"Camp A"	9, 10, 13
Cambrai, Battle of	354
Christmas Day, 1915, all try to be "cheery"	107
Commander-in-Chief (Sir John French) inspects and congratulates	48
Commanding Officers and Units at out-break of war	1, 2, 3
Conspicuous bravery: C.S.M. Allan and 2107 Private J. Scott	67
Conspicuous gallantry and devotion to duty: Lieut. R. P. Bluett recommended for Military Cross; No. 1523 Corporal Cheery, No. 1606 Lance-Corporal Filer, and No. 1541 Private Scott recommended for D.C.M.	112
Conspicuous conduct: Lieut. Palmer and Private Bell bring in wounded man	100
Conspicuous conduct: Sergeant Coppick and stretcher-bearers	95
Conspicuous conduct: Two gallant N.C.O.s, Corporal J. A. Cook and Corporal H. Smirthwaite	273
Co-operation with Lahore Division	36
Counter-attack on St. Julien	23
D.C.M., Corporal Smith wins	40
Despatches by Sir John French	8

	Page
Diary of A.D.M.S.	11, 12, 44
Difficulties of Mobilisation	4
Divisional Artillery, attacked by mustard gas	248
Divisional Artillery and Officers Commanding	3, 4
Division left England, 16th April, 1915	5
Division mentioned in Official Despatches	212
Durhams' night march *via* Zonnebeke	21
Enemy notice boards	88
Estaires, The Battle of (9th–11th April, 1918)	310, 327
Flers–Courcelette, The Battle of (15th–22nd September, 1916)	143
Final Attack, The	300
Fine physique of Battalion	1
First casualties	15
Food by pack animals	243
Frezenberg Ridge, The Battle of (8th–13th May)	48
Garton, Lieut., cuts the wire under heavy fire	39
Gas attack on 150th Brigade	126
Germans dressed in khaki	33
Gravenstafel, The Battle of (22nd–23rd April)	6
Gird Trench and Hook Sap (The Somme)	183
Hazebrouck, The Battle of (12th–15th April, 1918)	332
Hooge: Whit-Monday gas attack, conspicuous conduct	60
Hook Sap and Gird Trench (The Somme)	183
Jesmond Jesters Concert Party	95
Lahore Division make counter-attacks	41
Last of the 15-pounders	93
Le Transloy, The Battle of (1st–18th October, 1916)	164
Livens gas projectors installed	230
Location of Units, April 1915	44
Mobilisation	3, 4
Morval, The Battle of (25th–28th September, 1916)	161
Mud from head to foot	199
Nature study in trenches	81
Nissen Huts	258
Nissen Huts, not issued yet	193

	Page		Page
Northumbrian Division at disposal of Second Army (General Plumer)	9	St. Julien, Attack through Fortuin,	17, 18
Northumbrian Division, now 50th Division	54	Scarpe, First Battle of the (9th–14th April, 1917)	205
New Battalion joins the Brigades,	352, 353	Schools of Instruction	77
		Somme Crossings, Actions at the (24th–25th March, 1918)	274
Officers Commanding Artillery,	2, 3	Steenvoede area allotted to Division	5
Operations of the 50th Division (11th April, 1918)	327	System of Redoubts	310
Operations on the Arras-Neuve Chapelle Front	45	The Salient Again	100
Orders to attack through Fortuin,	17, 18	Three German Armies select areas of attack	257
Overseas to Boulogne	5	Training of bomb-throwers	53
Overseas to Havre	5	Training in North Wales	4
		Trench Weapons: "Jam-pot," "Battye bomb," and "Hairbrush"	76
"Passchendaele, No Bloody", if?	203		
Pigeons fly over lines	95		
Pill Boxes	241	Units and Commanding Officers at out-break of war	1, 2, 3
"Plumer's Force"	41, 50, 52		
Raiding Party	129 et seq.	Victoria Cross won by Lieut.-Colonel Roland Boys Bradford	168
Re-constitution of the 50th Division	350	Virgin Mary toppled over from her upright position at Albert	194
Rosières, The Battle of (26th–27th March, 1918)	288		
Ruined by holocaust: Farms, quarries, windmills, villages, woods	172	We were *not* retiring	30
		Winter of 1916–1917	192
Sambre, Battle of the	355	Ypres, The Battles of (1915)	6
St. Julien, The Battle of (24th April–4th May)	12	Ypres Salient, Principal roads and villages	14, 15
		Ypres Salient, The first time	14

Lightning Source UK Ltd.
Milton Keynes UK
UKOW042016191212

203910UK00001B/49/A

9 781843 422068